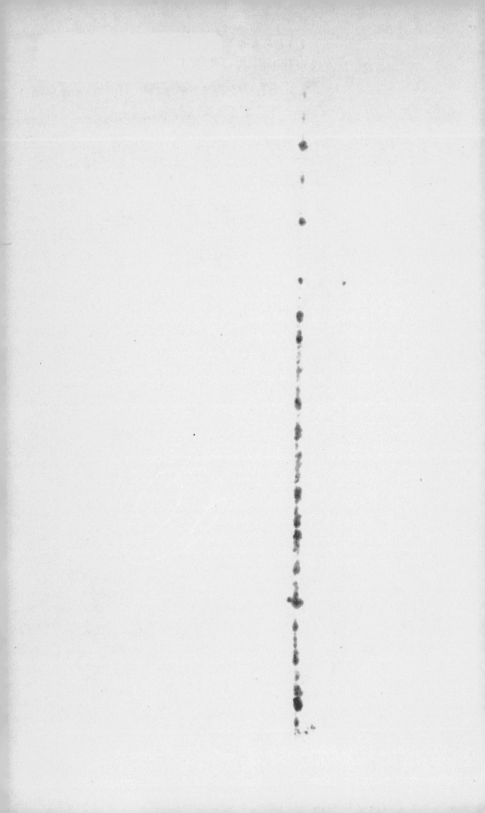

# Modern Experiments in Telepathy

Basil Shackleton

# MODERN EXPERIMENTS

## IN

# TELEPATHY

*by*

## S. G. SOAL, M.A., D.Sc. (Lond.),

Senior Lecturer in Pure Mathematics, Queen Mary College, University
of London; Past President of the Society for Psychical Research;
Perrott Student in Psychical Research, Trinity College, Cambridge
(1948); and Fulbright Research Scholar in Parapsychology (1951)

*and*

## F. BATEMAN, M.Sc. (Lond.)

*with an introductory note by*

## G. E. HUTCHINSON

*Sterling Professor of Zoology at Yale University*

## SECOND EDITION

## NEW HAVEN
## YALE UNIVERSITY PRESS

*Printed in Great Britain*

TO OUR WIVES

# Contents

# Illustrations

# Introductory Note

A good book ordinarily needs no introduction. It will be evident to anyone who examines this book carefully that the authors have indeed written a most excellent work on telepathy. It is sober, factual and detailed, three virtues that are essential in any writing on a difficult and controversial aspect of experimental science. They have incorporated into their account a great deal of fascinating new material. It is, in fact, the sort of book to which no outsider should, in normal circumstances, contribute an introduction. The circumstances are, however, not normal.

The whole literature of parapsychology is disfigured by books and articles which are supposed to be critical evaluations, but which on examination turn out to be violent attacks by people who either have not read the works they are attacking or have wilfully misunderstood them. Soal and Bateman give some examples in Chapters IV and XX of the present work, but there are plenty of other like documents. The purpose of this introduction is simply to ask reviewers and critics not to add to the volume of such unscientific literature. Genuine criticism is, of course, to be welcomed, though this introduction may well be attacked as a plea for an uncritical attitude. What are obviously to be avoided are attacks based on work that has been discredited or superseded, rather than what is reported, or on preconceptions about what was done when something quite different has in fact been done, or on *a priori* rather than on empirical considerations. It should be quite unnecessary to ask for such consideration to be given to a serious work; anyone who knows the writings, even of able and eminent men, that have appeared from time to time on the matter will realize that unhappily a plea for fairness and sanity is still necessary and may in part be in vain.

Bertrand Russell has said that in approaching the work of a philosopher it is necessary first to read him from his own point of view so that one comes to understand him, and then to read him again making every possible criticism that can be made against his position. Such an attitude is surely also the correct one to take about the matters discussed in this book. The present writer has tried it and is convinced that Soal and Bateman withstand honest attack extremely well. Other more ingenious critics may, of course, discover loopholes; but until they do, there would seem no alternative to acceptance save a blind agnosticism which would make the development of any empirical knowledge totally impossible.

G. E. HUTCHINSON

*27 November 1953*

# Preface

In this book we have attempted to give a fairly detailed account of the better class of experiments in extra-sensory perception which have been carried out during the past thirty-five years. The authors' own experiments with Mrs. Gloria Stewart and those of S.G.S. and Mrs. K. M. Goldney with Basil Shackleton have been given special emphasis for several reasons. In the first place, the Soal-Goldney report on the Shackleton experiments which appeared in the *Proceedings* of the Society for Psychical Research (December 1943), is now not easily accessible and of recent years there have been many requests for an authoritative account of these experiments. Only the expense involved has prevented the Society from reprinting the original report. Moreover, this book contains the first complete account of the work with Mrs. Stewart that has yet appeared. The present book, therefore, will constitute the only authoritative source of information for those who wish to study the paranormal powers of this remarkable subject in any considerable detail.

In a book intended not only for the educated reader but also for the scientific student it was felt to be essential that exact figures by means of which the results of the numerous experiments are assessed should be given wherever these are available. Nowadays, most of us, whether we are scientists or not, have acquired some notions of probability, perhaps from discussion of football pools and racing. That rather irritating phrase 'the odds against chance are so-and-so', which may ring in the ears of the reader like a clipped and debased coin, is an abbreviation for 'the odds against the deviation in the score of this experiment from the expected value arising in the absence of any cause tending to produce such a deviation (or, as we say, 'by chance') are so-and-so'. We have throughout used the term 'odds' instead of 'probability' because of its significance being more immediately apprehended by the non-mathematical reader.

The experiments described in this book are concerned mainly with the guessing of figures on cards or of pictures. A poser which has often been put to one of the authors runs as follows: 'You say that Shackleton or Mrs. Stewart can guess which of five symbols another person is looking at or thinking about. But I should be much more impressed if they were able to read something which I have written in my pocket-book. Why only cards?' We think the answer is that people like Shackleton, rare as they appear to be in the community, exhibit, after all, only a very rudimentary form of telepathy or extra-sensory perception. They are quite unable to tell you *what* you are thinking about, but only *which* of a limited number of objects. And even this feat they can only achieve on the average about two or three times perhaps in twenty-five trials. It may be objected that certain mediums like Mrs. Piper or Mrs. Blanche Cooper showed a very intricate knowledge of the affairs of their sitters which they could not have obtained through normal means. That is true, but seldom did they produce such knowledge to order or in reply to questions asked by the sitter; it came to them spontaneously. Such mediums nearly always fail when they are asked to guess cards or pictures or to do simple experiments in telepathy. Despite their greater intrinsic paranormal capacity they are not suited generally for experimental work of a statistical kind and this is the only kind of work which, at present, is likely to influence orthodox scientists.

This book deals only with extra-sensory perception, and no account has been given of the apparently successful experiments in psycho-kinesis which have been carried out on the other side of the Atlantic. The authors have had no practical experience in this field, and further, like many others in this country, they feel that the evidence obtained from dice-throwing has not yet been sufficiently substantiated, or properly interpreted.

The experimental work in telepathy arose out of a vast hinterland of spontaneous paranormal happenings reported through the centuries. Except for a very few outstanding cases like those of D. D. Home, Eusapia Palladino or of St. Joseph of Copertino, the evidence for so-called telekinesis and other 'physical' phenomena has no such reassuring background and most of the records of physical mediums are tainted with fraud.

The authors are deeply indebted to Dr. G. D. Wassermann of Durham University who has brought his detailed knowledge of many branches of science and his energetic and perspicacious criticism to bear on almost every chapter of this book.

To Dr. Donald West, experimental investigation officer of the Society for Psychical Research, we express our gratitude for his interest in the book and for allowing us to describe some of the recent work carried out by Mr. G. W. Fisk and himself.

We tender our thanks to Dr. Rhine and his fellow workers at Duke University for permission to discuss their numerous experiments, to Professor Gardner Murphy, Dr. Gertrude Schmeidler and others whose work we have cited at some length.

We wish to thank certain members of the staff of Queen Mary College, more especially Dr. F. C. L. Brendel, Mr. L. A. Rozelaar, and Dr. H. S. Allen, for most valuable assistance in the actual conduct of the experiments with Mrs. Stewart. Mrs. K. M. Goldney, M.B.E., is, of course, well-known for the leading part she played in the Shackleton experiments.

Nor must we forget to pay tribute to Mrs. Stewart and Mr. Shackleton, the two gifted sensitives without whose continued co-operation this book would never have been written and to the memory of another, more gifted perhaps than they, Mrs. Blanche Cooper, who, alas, is no longer with us.

Finally, we would express our great appreciation of the expert and excellent typing by a member of the staff of H. W. Walden and Co.

S. G. S.
F. B.

*15 June 1953*

### Note on References

The references at the end of this book are grouped under the headings Chaps. I—XX, and the items for each chapter are serially numbered from one onwards.

A reference in the text of, say, Chap. XV which is to be found in the *same* chapter in the reference list is indicated thus: *McMahan*[8] which means that it is item No. 8 in Chap. XV.

But a reference to, say, *Elkisch* in the text of Chap. XV which is to be found in, say, Chap. V of the list is given as a footnote to Elkisch*, say *V, 8.

# CHAPTER I
# Historical—Spontaneous Cases— Early Experiments

Cases of apparent thought-transference, of the seeing of future events in dreams and the awareness of what is happening to friends or relatives at a distance without the use of normal means of communication have been reported in ancient as well as in modern times, among both primitive and civilized peoples. Classical and Hebrew literature contain many such records. Joseph dreaming by the Nile foresaw the coming of the seven fat and seven lean years. St. Augustine relates that one of his pupils asked the Carthaginian diviner Albicerius to say what he, the pupil, was thinking about. Albicerius answered correctly that the pupil was thinking of a line of Vergil, and actually recited the passage, though he was a man of little education. If the story is authentic, Albicerius was a step ahead of our modern adepts, who are able to tell us only which of five symbols an experimenter is looking at.

Then there is the case of Sosipatra,[1] a lady don, who interrupted a philosophical lecture she was giving to describe in detail an accident that was happening to her kinsman Philometor who was riding in his carriage many miles away. She saw the carriage overturned, the occupant's legs in danger of being crushed, and his extraction by servants unharmed except for cuts on the elbows and hands. This description appears to have tallied with the actual facts, and Sosipatra won thereby a reputation for omniscience.

If it is impossible to check these ancient tales, it is far from easy to arrive at the truth concerning the numerous modern instances of which they are the prototypes. Quite recently a London newspaper* invited its readers to submit their 'sixth sense' stories, offering a prize of a guinea for each one published. Letters containing accounts of uncanny experiences or prophetic dreams appeared day after day for many

* Cf. *The Star* on various dates in June and July 1951.

B 1

weeks. Taken at their face value many of these accounts were of extraordinary interest, and the whole collection of several hundred would suggest that psychical experiences are relatively common in our twentieth century. But one wonders what proportion of the tales were sheer inventions, and in how many cases a real experience of the narrator was embellished and falsified, perhaps almost out of recognition. Such cases, of course, are little more than *prima facie* material for investigation by the competent psychical researcher. Quite apart from the possibility of deliberate invention or hoax, there are the more subtle falsifications which arise out of distortions of memory to which we are all subject to a greater or lesser degree.

For instance, a man dreams that he sees a cat run over by a motorcar. Next day he actually witnesses an accident in which a tabby cat is killed by a blue car. Probably he failed to record his dream in writing immediately after waking but told it to his wife at the breakfast table. But when he sees the actual accident, he is quite likely to believe that his dream-cat was a tabby and that his dream-car was a blue one. And stranger still, when he tells his wife about the incident on his return home, she is likely to believe that he spoke of a *tabby* cat and a *blue* car in recounting his dream at breakfast. The moral of course is that when one has a vivid dream which appears to relate to the future, one should write down the details precisely as one remembers them immediately after waking and post the record to the Society for Psychical Research.

Some prophecies of disaster whether by dreams or given through mediums may bring about their own fulfilment by preying on the mind of the victim. In such cases a paranormal explanation is often superfluous. George Borrow in his book *The Bible in Spain* relates how, one morning on the outward voyage, a sailor told him of a dream he had had during the night. The man had seen himself falling from the mast. A little later in the day he was ordered aloft, was struck by a flying jib in a squall, hurled into the sea, and was swept away before a boat could reach him.

Borrow's habit of colouring his narratives is well known, but even if we grant his veracity in this instance, it is not certain whether the poor fellow might have escaped disaster had his mind not been disturbed by apprehension and worry induced by the dream.

But if we consider only those cases in which the reporting is strictly accurate, there still remains the question as to how far the correspondences observed between the dream and its fulfilment, the statements by the seer and the actual events to which these statements appear to refer, may not have been the result of the blind and meaningless juxtaposition of circumstances which we call chance. In a world where myriads of events from the simplest to the most complex are being endlesslo shuffled and reshuffled, might we not, at times, expect to emerge sets ly circumstances which show a deceptive appearance of being causalyf related? It is certain that in everyday life we encounter curious coincidences which our reason suggests can only be the result of accident. The surname of one of the writers is an uncommon one, and when he took over his present flat near Wandsworth Common, he did not know the names of the other occupants of the house. Judge, then, of his surprise when he learned that the people downstairs were of the same name as himself though the spelling was slightly different. By consulting telephone directories and statistics of houses and flats in London, we could without much difficulty form a rough estimate of the probability of there being a dwelling house in London which contained two unrelated persons named Soal, Soul or Sole.

But if we attempted to apply statistics to a case like that of Sosipatra, we should be setting ourselves an impossible task, for we should require numerical data which it would have been impossible for us to obtain, even if we had been her contemporaries. We should, for instance, have had to ask how many people there were in Greece, who, like Sosipatra, were guessing at the doings of distant relatives, and how often these people were wrong. We might indeed be able to form an estimate of the percentage of accidents which overtake the drivers of coaches, but if it turned out that Philometor's coachman was a reckless fellow who upset the coach on an average once a fortnight, our carefully compiled estimates would be of no use, and our probabilities would require revision.

Let us now glance at a modern case taken from *Phantasms of the Living*,[2] the famous classic by Gurney, Myers and Podmore. A girl of about ten years of age was walking along a country lane, reading a book on geometry. Quite suddenly her surroundings seemed to fada away, and she saw her mother lying apparently dead on the floor of e little used room at home, known as the 'white' room. Near her on the floor was a lace handkerchief. The child was so upset by this vision that instead of going straight home she rushed to the doctor's house and persuaded him to go home with her. They found the woman lying on the floor of the 'white' room suffering from a severe heart attack. Beside her was the lace handkerchief. The doctor arrived in time to save her life. The case is a good one. The story is not one that a child of ten would be expected to invent in a crisis. Moreover, it was verified that she did visit the doctor before going home. Quite possibly, however, the tale was 'helped' by the addition of details after the event. The mention of the lace handkerchief may have been an embellishment of the vision added to make the story sound more impressive, or it may even have been a distortion of memory. The cardinal fact is that the child acted on her vision and went straight to the doctor.

Quite recently in the *New York Times Magazine*[3] a physician tried to discredit the case by suggesting that the child's mother may have been an hysteric who frequently imagined she was having heart attacks, and hence there would be nothing very remarkable in the child's conjuring up a vision of her parent suffering from such a seizure. The suggestion does not seem very plausible. Had the woman been subject to such attacks, genuine or imagined, the doctor would surely have mentioned the fact to the investigators. Moreover, in after life the girl frequently spoke about the incident as something unique in her experience, which she would scarcely have done had the vision been a mere exercise of the imagination and not a vivid hallucination.

It would, of course, be quite impracticable to form any reliable estimate of the probability that such a set of coincidences was the result of chance; there are in the case too many subsidiary probabilities whose empirical values are beyond our reach.

The physicist or physiologist might reject the case on two counts. First he would urge that we have no precise figures giving the probability that the whole thing was not a mere coincidence. Our intuition based upon everyday experience assures us that it would be absurd to suppose that such a concatenation of circumstances could be the work of accident, but the scientist would not be satisfied of the soundness of mere intuition. Further he might insist that since on one occasion the child had shown that she was aware in some mysterious manner of what was going on out of sight and hearing, she ought to be able to repeat the performance again and again. She ought to be able to say for instance what the scientist was doing at a specified time. Actually such demands might be very unreasonable since the urgency of a life and death crisis might have been a vital factor in the passing of the barrier which such messages from outside normally encounter before they emerge into consciousness. In fact, the scientist would put the ability to receive a telepathic impression on the same level as the ability to do a sum, or write from dictation, or play tennis. Such comparisons may not apply. Moreover, there are many psychological experiments which are not strictly repeatable.

But we must remember that the average biologist or psychologist has no burning desire to establish extra-sensory perception. He would, indeed, rather see it discredited because it queers his pitch. He is trying to show that the brain is nothing but an immensely complicated electronic machine governed by the laws of physics, and that mental processes are isomorphically related to the working of the machine.

Now the phenomena of telepathy and clairvoyance indicate strongly that there are aspects of mental behaviour which are not completely subject to the laws of present-day physics. These phenomena seem to be incompatible with the fundamental set of assumptions on which the physiologist and the psychologist are working.

Since its foundation in the year 1882 the Society for Psychical Research has investigated many hundreds of spontaneous cases, some as good or better than the one we have just discussed, and others of slighter interest. Needless to say, such investigation is a highly skilled task requiring tact in dealing with witnesses, knowledge of the right questions to ask, ability in cross-examination, and so on. Many of the people who devoted a great deal of time to this work in the earlier years of the Society's existence were persons of high academic standing such as Frederick W. H. Myers, Mrs. Henry Sidgwick, Sir William Barrett, Miss Alice Johnson, Edmund Gurney, and Frank Podmore. No labour was spared by these devoted investigators in making long journeys to interview witnesses, and, in his Obituary of Edmund Gurney, Myers states: 'Almost every witness of importance in *Phantasms of the Living*[2] (and many whose names do not appear in that book) had, before the book was published, been personally visited by one of ourselves.'

With certain reservations we can accept the bulk of the cases published in *Phantasms of the Living* and in the *Proceedings* and *Journal* of the Society as being factually accurate. The role played by chance coincidence in the production of veridical correspondences is strictly undetermined, though it appears inconceivable in the light of everyday experience that the most detailed of the cases reported could be accounted for by mere chance. Moreover, it is to be noted that spontaneous paranormal experiences gathered from widely different historical periods and regions of the world exhibit a conformity to type. Tyrrell has pointed out that even the most diverse cases possess certain common features.

The story of Sosipatra, for example, might have been mistaken for one of those published in *Phantasms of the Living*[2] had English names been substituted.

But though we have been collecting spontaneous cases for sixty years, we seem to have learned little concerning their true nature or of the obscure mental processes which produce them. Though roughly they conform to certain types, every new case presents a distinct problem of its own. We do not know which features of a case are important and which are trivial for an understanding of the underlying mechanisms. We obviously cannot vary the physical or psychological conditions one by one and see what happens; we have to accept what Nature provides

5

without being able to do anything about it. In fact, the spontaneous case of telepathy contains too many diverse elements; it is complex beyond our understanding, and at all costs we must concentrate on some simpler type of paranormal happening. This does not mean that we should cease to investigate cases of apparitions, telepathic hallucinations, prophetic dreams, and mediumistic utterances, for these may provide valuable suggestions and clues for experimental work. There is still scope for a vast amount of what might be called 'Natural History' work in psychical research. Should opportunity offer, there is room for quasi-experimental studies of mediums of the calibre of Mrs. Leonard or Mrs. Piper. We think we can now say that emphasis has definitely shifted from such complex phenomena as the observation of trance mediums and spontaneous cases to simple experiments in the guessing of cards or pictures. Experiments in telepathy are, of course, no new thing. As far back as 1883 Mr. Malcolm Guthrie[4, 5], assisted by Dr. (later Sir) Oliver Lodge[6], was carrying out experiments in thought-transference, using as percipients two young ladies from a drapery emporium in Liverpool. On 6 November 1884, for example, the experimenter sat behind a screen and gazed at a piece of silver paper cut in the form of a teapot. The young lady, acting as receiver and sitting on the far side of the screen, with her chair-back against it, replied: 'Is it bright silver, something like a kettle? . . . A teapot?' The girls were also very successful in registering tastes, colours, and in imitating diagrams. Some of the drawings produced in these and similar experiments of the period showed very remarkable resemblances in shape to the originals, and even today the accounts published in the early volumes of the *Proceedings* of the S.P.R. make fascinating reading. The chief drawback of these early experiments with objects and drawings was that it was difficult to assign precise figures for the odds against the resemblances noted being due to chance. At that period statistical methods were in their infancy, and there were few text-books giving even an elementary treatment of the subject.

In the year 1881–2 Sir William Barrett and others conducted thought-transference experiments with the young daughters of Mr. Creery,[7] an English clergyman, using playing cards. Although no systematic use was made of statistical formulae, it is clear that the results obtained were high above chance expectation. Later on, unfortunately, two of the girls were caught cheating by Professor and Mrs. Sidgwick. One sister was found to be conveying information to the other by means of a code consisting of head movements, slight coughs, etc. This discovery of course throws grave doubt upon the genuineness of the earlier series.

## CHAPTER II

# Early Statistical Experiments
# (1916-34)

The earliest controlled experiments permitting of statistical investigation on any considerable scale were carried out during the first world war by Dr. John E. Coover,[1] a sceptical psychologist, at Stanford University, California.

Coover investigated a variety of alleged 'supernormal' powers, and published his findings in 1917 in a bulky volume[1] which was, in part, a dissertation on elementary probability theory. He was, we believe, the first man to test by the theory of probability whether a person can be made to turn round by another person staring at the back of his head, and came to a negative conclusion. But his chief claim to our attention is the 10,000 guesses at the figures on playing cards made by about 100 students in an experiment to test telepathy.

## Telepathy and Clairvoyance

At this point it is advisable to distinguish between a *telepathy* experiment and an experiment in *clairvoyance*.

The word *telepathy* was coined in the year 1882 by F. W. H. Myers, a famous classical scholar and an inspector of schools. He defined it to mean the apparent transference of ideas, sensations, images and feelings from one mind to another without the aid of the five senses. There are certain objections to such a definition. The word 'transference' for example suggests a spatial exchange as of eggs from one box to another which is unjustified by the observed facts. Then there is the use of the word 'mind' which has no very clear meaning. And nowadays we know that Man has many more than five senses; he has, for instance, receptor organs for the appreciation of heat and cold, etc.

But on these counts only trifling emendations would be needed to modernize Myers's definition.

7

The real difficulty in formulating a definition of telepathy arises from the fact that during the past twenty years considerable evidence has been amassed which seems to establish the reality of another extra-sensory faculty which had the misfortune to be labelled *clairvoyance*. Now experimentally it has proved extremely difficult to discriminate between telepathy and clairvoyance.

We shall first give a tentative definition of clairvoyance: If a person A experiences a present mental pattern which corresponds wholly or in part with the sensory aspects of a past, present or future physical object or event, in such a way that the observed correspondence cannot be accounted for by sense perception or inference based on sense perception or by chance coincidence, we say that *clairvoyance* has taken place provided that the physical object or event is never at any time normally perceived by anyone.

At first sight it might seem that the addition of the final phrase would make it impossible to verify any supposed case of clairvoyance and this is generally true except in experimental cases in which a very special technique is employed which will be described in Chap. XV, p. 251.

Our definition of *telepathy* is as follows:

If a present mental pattern of A wholly or in part corresponds to a past, present, or future mental pattern of a person B (who may be living or dead) and the correspondence cannot be accounted for by sense-perception or inference based on sense-perception or by chance coincidence we shall say that *telepathy* has occurred, provided that the possibility of clairvoyance has been eliminated.

Here again in the great majority of spontaneous and in many experimental cases of extra-sensory perception it is impossible to say whether telepathy or clairvoyance has taken place.

Let us consider one or two examples.

(*a*) If a person A opens a new pack of playing-cards in a dark room, puts them through a mechanical shuffler, and then selects various cards with a gloved hand, and a second person B, in the dark, guesses a sufficient number of the cards correctly, should we be justified in saying that *clairvoyance* has taken place? The answer is, according to our definition, clearly in the negative; for whoever checks B's guesses against the order of the actual cards will perceive these cards normally and the alleged clairvoyance cannot be distinguished from telepathy of a precognitive kind existing between B and the person who did the checking.

(*b*) If a person A thinks of the names of various playing-cards without having any actual cards or physical representations of them before him and a second person B in a distant room writes down his guesses and after he has done so A writes down the names of the cards he thought of

8

in their proper order and if it is then found that B has made sufficient correct guesses to make chance-coincidence very improbable, can we say that *telepathy* has occurred? The answer is 'no' because there may have been *precognitive* clairvoyance by B of the future physical record made by A.

(*c*) Suppose that in (*b*), the other conditions remaining the same, A does not at any time write down the cards he thought of but checks B's record of his guesses from memory. In this case clairvoyance is eliminated and we can say that telepathy has taken place.

(*d*) In a great many experiments one person (the agent) looks at a card which another person (the percipient) in another room tries to guess. In this case it is impossible to discriminate between telepathy and clairvoyance. Such experiments are known as experiments in 'general', or 'undifferentiated' extra-sensory perception.

## Methods of Evaluation

Suppose that an experimenter thoroughly shuffles a pack of 52 playing-cards, cuts it, and looks at the top card. As he does so he presses an electric key which gives a signal to a person in a distant room to write down his guess at the *suit* of the card. Having looked at the card the experimenter replaces it in the pack, which is then reshuffled. The experimenter cuts the pack again and draws a second card. Suppose that in this way 1,200 guesses are made. It will be clear from Appendix B, p. 370, that the probability $p$ of the suit being guessed correctly at each trial is given by $p = 1/4$.

The expected number of correct guesses in 1,200 trials, if nothing but chance is operating, is therefore $1,200 \times 1/4$, i.e. 300. This does not mean that the guesser would get exactly 300 successes. If he did a large number of batches of 1,200 trials he would get sometimes more and sometimes fewer than 300 successes (or hits). But if he continued indefinitely, the average of his various totals would approximate very closely to 300. This we shall call his 'mean score'. The difference between his actual score and the mean score is known as his 'deviation'. Thus if his actual score in the experiment is 345 the deviation is + 45 and if he obtains, say, only 255 hits the deviation is − 45. Now if there is only random guessing large deviations from 300 will be infrequent and the larger the deviation the less frequently will it occur. To discover just how likely it is that a given deviation is due to chance alone, we compare it with a theoretical number known as the 'standard deviation'. This number is found as follows. If $p$ is the probability of success at each trial and $N$ is the total number of trials (or guesses) the standard

9

deviation is known to be $\sqrt{[Np(1-p)]}$. Thus in our case with $N = 1,200$, $p = 1/4$, the standard deviation is $\sqrt{(1,200 \times \frac{1}{4} \times \frac{3}{4})}$, i.e. 15.

We wish to know how our deviation compares with the standard deviation. We therefore form the quotient actual deviation/standard deviation and this is called the critical ratio (for short CR).

Thus the larger our deviation the larger the CR will be. In card-guessing we are often as interested in negative as in positive deviations. Hence, as a rule, we are concerned only with the numerical magnitude of a CR and not with whether it is positive or negative.

Now with large values of $N$, the binomial distribution approximates (except at the extreme tails) to the 'normal' distribution, and we can read off from the normal probability tables the probability that random guessing will give a CR equal to or exceeding the CR obtained in our experiment. Thus, a CR of 2 implies that our actual deviation is of such a magnitude that a positive *or* negative deviation of equal or greater magnitude would be expected to occur only once in about 22 similar sets of guesses if pure chance only were at work.

We express this briefly by saying that CR $= \pm 2$ implies a probability $P = 1/22$, i.e. 0·045. Similarly CR $= \pm 3$ corresponds to $P = 1/370$ and this means that a positive or negative deviation *numerically* equal to or exceeding our observed deviation would be likely to occur by chance alone on the average once in 370 experiments with the same number of guesses.

Most psychologists consider that an effect is sufficiently pronounced to warrant serious consideration if, in an experiment, they obtain a positive or negative deviation equal to or exceeding 2·8 standard deviations, and the chance of the occurrence of such a deviation from mean expectation (positive *or* negative) is given by $P = 0·005$, i.e. odds of 200 to 1 against chance. Throughout this book we shall accept this level of significance as indicating that some factor other than chance is at work, though most experiments have yielded much higher deviations.

Some workers in biology have considered that odds of 20 to 1 against a result being due to chance, though far from being conclusive, are yet sufficiently interesting to require the repetition of an experiment to see if a similar result is obtained again. It does not much matter whether we draw the line at 20 to 1, 50 to 1, or 100 to 1, so long as we realize that such odds are no conclusive proof of the existence of an extra-chance factor, but merely an indication that the experiment is worth repeating perhaps several times or on a larger scale.

What odds are to be regarded as furnishing conclusive proof in a paranormal experiment will depend upon circumstances. If, for instance, we suspect that the design of the experiment is faulty, or that there is a possible leakage of information through normal sensory channels of communication, or that our statistical formulae are inapplicable to the case under consideration, then clearly odds against chance of even a million to one would be of no value. Or again, if the effect we are investigating is inherently very improbable, we certainly should not be satisfied with odds of 1,000 to 1. Telepathy, clairvoyance, and precognition are of course inherently improbable from the viewpoint of orthodox scientific doctrine, but telepathy at least is becoming much less improbable as the number of successful experiments (already very considerable) goes on increasing, provided of course that the experiments are well controlled. But in a precognition experiment we might reasonably demand a higher critical ratio than in an ordinary telepathy test.

In order to assist readers who desire to do card-guessing experiments of their own, we have given in Appendix C, p. 379, the values of the odds against a result being due to chance which correspond to various critical ratios (CR). In using this table, the reader must carefully bear in mind that $n$ gives for any CR the odds against a deviation *positive or negative* equal to or exceeding the observed deviation being the result of pure chance. Thus in our example with $N = 1,200$, $p = 1/4$, suppose that the person guessing at the suit of a playing-card made 345 correct hits instead of the 300 to be expected by chance-coincidence. His deviation is +45 and his CR is 45/15, i.e. +3. We infer from Table 11 that the odds against his score lying outside the limits $300 - 3 \times 15$ and $300 + 3 \times 15$, i.e. outside the limits 255 and 345 are nearly 369 to 1.

If we were interested only in *positive* deviations, that is scores *above* the mean score, the value of $P$ would have to be halved. Thus the odds against the score being in excess of 345 would be about $2 \times 370 - 1$ to one, i.e. 739 to one.

It is, however, a fact that many card-guessers do sometimes produce scores which are for a time persistently below the 'mean score', and such negative deviations are as much evidence for extra-sensory perception (ESP) as the corresponding positive deviations. It might be, for instance, that the guesser possesses some unconscious motivation which causes him to suppress the correct card-image, and permits an incorrect image to become conscious. If a person is getting the cards wrong more often than he ought to on the theory of chance, this surely suggests that at some level of awareness he knows the *correct* card, though for some perverse reason its image never emerges into normal consciousness, but is replaced by the image of a wrong card. Many examples of this will be noted when we discuss the Shackleton and Stewart experiments.

For this reason, that investigators have often as much interest in

11

negative as in positive deviations, the value of $n$ represents the odds against the occurrence of a positive *or* negative deviation of a given magnitude.

## Coover's Results[1]

In a telepathy experiment two persons are essential—the 'sender' or 'agent' who looks at the cards one by one, and the 'receiver' or 'percipient' who records his guesses. The sender and cards are usually in one room and the guesser in another. The purpose of this is (i) to ensure that it is absolutely impossible for the guesser to catch any glimpse of the cards, and (ii) to prevent him from receiving any signal intentional or unintentional from the sender or from anyone else that would enable him to identify the card by normal means.

Coover[1] used altogether 105 guessers and 97 senders. He sat with his sender in one room while the student being tested sat in an adjoining room. Each student who acted as guesser was made to do about 100 guesses, and altogether 10,000 guesses were recorded. Having shuffled and cut the pack of 40 cards, Coover threw a die for 'odds' or 'evens' in order to decide whether or not the sender should look at the face of the card drawn. He then turned up the card, and the sender concentrated on it or simply put it aside without looking at the face, according to whether the die had registered an even or an odd number. After having exposed the card or laid it aside face downwards, Coover tapped with his pencil on the table as a signal for the guesser in the next room to write down his guess. After replacing the card, Coover reshuffled and cut his pack, and threw the die again.

Of the 10,000 guesses recorded by the 105 students just 5,135 corresponded to trials in which the agent had looked at the cards,  while the remainder corresponded to trials in which the cards had not been looked at but whose order had been preserved. The guesser did not know whether or not the agent looked at the card. To-day we should think of the trials in which no one saw the cards until the checking as *clairvoyance* tests, but Coover merely intended them to serve as an empirical 'control' on the trials in which the agent concentrated on the cards.

Coover reported that neither the 5,000 odd telepathy trials nor the 'control' series showed any significant deviations, when considered separately, from mean chance expectation. He concluded that there was no evidence for telepathy, and this finding was greeted with a chorus of satisfaction from American psychologists who were hostile to the paranormal.

12

Later, however, it was pointed out by both Professor Cyril Burt and Dr. R. H. Thouless[2] that in the grand total of 10,000 guesses no fewer than 294 were correct as compared with an expectation of 250.

Now Coover had used packs of playing-cards from which the twelve picture cards had been removed, so that each pack contained 40 cards, i.e. the cards 1–10 of the four suits.

The reader can verify that with $N = 10,000$, $p = 1/40$, the standard deviation is 15·61 and the critical ratio 44/15·61, i.e. 2·8 which, according to the normal probability tables, gives odds against the result being due to chance of about 200 to 1. It is known, however, that the normal distribution is a good approximation to the binomial distribution only when $(q - p) D^3/6d^4$ is small, where $D$ is the observed deviation from the mean score, $d$ is the standard deviation, and $q = 1 - p$.

In our example $D = 44$, $d = 15·61$ and owing to the small value of ($p = 1/40$) the above expression is equal to 0·227 which is not small. It follows from this that the above odds of 200 to 1 are somewhat exaggerated and 160 to 1 would be a closer approximation to the true odds.

A possibility, of course, is that *clairvoyance* may have been operating during the 'control' series, and as the deviations in the 'telepathy' and 'control' series are of about the same order, it is also possible that clairvoyance was at work throughout the 10,000 trials.

On the other hand, it is possible that Coover's method of obtaining a series that was approximately random by hand-shuffling a solitary pack of cards was inefficient. A pack of cards tends to cut at certain places more easily than at others, and if the card situated in such a place happened to be a popular symbol such as the Ace of Spades, this card would turn up more frequently than the other cards and also be guessed more often. This would tend to increase the number of correct guesses.

So far as we are aware, however, no one has produced any evidence from Coover's original lists of cards and guesses that factors of this sort were present. It is hard to believe that he overlooked the significant excess of correct hits on the 10,000 trials, and if he was aware of it, why did he not continue with the experiments or try to discover what was responsible for the abnormal deviation?

At the outset of the investigation Coover declared that nothing less than odds of 50,000 to one against the operation of chance would convince him of the reality of telepathy. Had he gone on scoring positively at the same rate for another 18,000 trials, he would more than have achieved his self-imposed odds. Coover's 10,000 trials with playing-cards constitute only a small fraction of the successful experiments that have been carried out since his day, and even had they given completely negative results, all they would have demonstrated is that, if one works with about a hundred guessers chosen at random, one cannot be sure of discovering a good telepathic percipient. S.G.S. did thirteen times as many trials as Coover before he found two good percipients. We have dwelt at some length on Coover's unimportant experiments because even today they are cited by psychologists who are ignorant of the extensive literature of card-guessing as furnishing a disproof of telepathy. Thus, writing in the autumn (1950) number of the *Modern Quarterly*, John McLeish,[3] who is Staff Tutor in Psychology at Leeds University writes: 'Coover, the Stanford University investigator, came to a negative conclusion after a long investigation under laboratory conditions (1917) and until his death resisted all attempts by others to "cook" his results.' But he carefully omits all mention of the odds of 160 to 1 against the hypothesis that Coover's results were due to chance. If there was any 'cooking', it was done by Coover, who suppressed the fact, and not by those who pointed it out.

Another psychologist, Professor Chester E. Kellogg,[4] writing in *The Scientific Monthly* (October 1937), eulogizes Coover's work as 'a notable example of painstaking, thorough research and exact treatment of numerical data'. But a man who disregards odds of 160 to 1 can hardly be considered either 'painstaking' or 'thorough'. And Coover's method of obtaining a random sequence of cards by shuffling and cutting a single pack would scarcely pass muster nowadays.

Professor L. T. Troland[5] of Harvard University was probably the first man to invent a machine for testing telepathy. The experimenter gazed into a darkened box, and in the centre of his field of vision he saw a single spot of light. By means of an electrical contrivance an illuminated square was caused to appear, sometimes to the left and sometimes to the right of the centre spot, by the pressing of a switch which operated in a random or haphazard fashion. The guesser or percipient had to say whether the square was on the left or on the right, and he recorded his guess automatically by pressing another switch. The assumption was that when Troland pressed his button it was as likely for the square to appear on the left as on the right, and therefore the chance of the guesser's being correct would be $\frac{1}{2}$ at every trial.

Strange to say only 603 trials were made, and 284 correct guesses were registered as compared with an expectation of $\frac{1}{2} \times 603$, i.e. 301·5.

This gave a negative deviation of 17·5, and, since $p = \frac{1}{2}$, $N = 603$, our formula on p. 10 gives the standard deviation as $\sqrt{(\frac{1}{2} \times \frac{1}{2} \times 603)}$, i.e. 12·28. The critical ratio is only about $-1·4$, and no significance can be attached to the result. But later experiments suggest that, if one works on an even chance (which implies a relatively large standard deviation compared with what one would have with, say, 5 possibilities) one would

14

generally have to do a very much larger number of trials than 603 to get a significant result. Troland would doubtless have realized this if he had had any experience with, say, Dr. Rhine's cards or playing-cards. Moreover, guessing at only two alternatives becomes very boring, and this in itself would probably tend to inhibit the telepathic faculty. Troland's work seems to have been done round about the year 1917.

Of much greater importance were the experiments carried out at Groningen, Holland, in the year 1920 by Heymans, Brugmans, and Wynberg[6].

In the best of these the subject, i.e. the guesser, a young man called van Dam, sat blindfolded by himself in a room in front of a sort of large chess-board which contained 48 squares instead of the usual 64, there being 6 rows numbered along the edge 1 to 6 and 8 columns lettered A to H, so that any one of the 48 squares was fixed by a letter and a number, e.g. C4. The experimenters were in a room immediately above van Dam's room, and they watched him through a thick pane of glass let into the floor. The watching psychologists selected one of the 48 squares by drawing a card from each of two shuffled packs, one containing numbers 1–6 and the other letters A–H. They then willed van Dam to point to the chess square on his board, and observed him make his choice through the glass pane. In 187 trials he was right 60 times, whereas by chance alone his expectation would be about 4 successes. There is therefore no doubt whatever that some factor other than chance was operating. About a half of the 187 trials were carried out, however, with van Dam and the psychologists in the same room. The subject succeeded better under the more rigorous conditions in which the experimenters were in the room above.

As Whately Carington[15] points out, the experimenters had to record the subject's choice from a distance of several feet and through a thick pane of glass, and they may have made mistakes. This possible source of error could have been obviated if a separate recorder had sat beside van Dam. It was altogether unfortunate that the experimenters who knew the chosen square watched him while he was groping over the board. Quite possibly they became excited when his hand was in the region of the right square, and they may have made some slight movement which afforded an auditory cue. Whately Carington did not think this possible, but we cannot share his optimism, even though he had visited the scene while we have not. It is well established that vaudeville 'telepathists' such as Fred Marion[7] can succeed in finding hidden objects by observing small movements or changes in breathing on the part of the audience when the searcher approaches or recedes from the hiding place. It has been shown that 'telepathic' horses which tap out answers to sums with their hooves often obey a signal given, perhaps unconsciously, by their trainer, and cease tapping at the correct number.

Nor are we impressed by the argument that van Dam did significantly better when he had been dosed with alcohol or bromide, for the effect of the drug might be to sharpen his sensitivity to small sounds for a time.

One might suggest that this subject may have been a sensitive of Marion's type, and that telepathy may have played no part in the performance. It is only fair, however, to point out that the experimenters were highly competent psychologists, and would naturally be on their guard against the possibility of auditory cues.

Miss Ina Jephson, [9,10] a member of the Council of the Society for Psychical Research, did pioneer work in the investigation of clairvoyance as distinct from telepathy. In 1924 Dr. R. A. (now Sir Ronald) Fisher[8], the statistician, devised an elaborate scoring system for paranormal experiments with playing-cards. If a person guesses at a card drawn from a well-shuffled pack of 52 playing-cards, his chance of getting the card absolutely correct is 1/52, and his chances of getting colour and suit right are 1/2 and 1/4 respectively. And as there are 13 values for each suit his chance of getting the value correct is 4/52, i.e. 1/13. But it often happens that the guesser scores only a partial success. For instance, if the actual card were the King of Hearts, the guess King of Diamonds would be correct in everything except suit, and is a better shot than King of Spades which has only the value correct. But even the guess Jack of Clubs would be worth something, since the guesser has recognized that the card is a 'picture' and not a 'plain' card.

Dr. Fisher[8] assigned a numerical score to each degree of correctness, ranging from absolute correctness to nothing correct, in accordance with the mathematical probabilities of the various grades of success.

Instructions[9] were sent by post to some 240 persons of untested psychical ability, and each person was asked to complete 25 trials, but not to attempt more than 5 guesses on the same day. The percipient was asked to take an ordinary pack of 52 playing-cards, shuffle it thoroughly, and draw out a card face downwards. He was then to guess the denomination of the card, record his guess, and write against it the true value and suit of the card (e.g. KD or 2S). After replacing the card in the pack, he was to reshuffle and repeat the operation until five trials had been recorded. In this way Miss Jephson collected 1,200 sets of 5 guesses.

Of these 6,000 guesses no fewer than 245 were completely correct, as compared with an expectation of 6,000/52, i.e. 115. Further, 3,307 were correct as regards colour compared with an expectation of 3,000, and 1,832 correct in suit as against the 1,500 chance would predict. These

16

results, we need hardly say, correspond to odds against chance which run into astronomical figures.

Moreover, the 1,200 sets of 5 guesses, when scored by Fisher's system, showed a sharp drop in score from the first guess of the set to the second. The score then remained almost stationary till the fourth trial of the set, and rose at the fifth or final trial to nearly its original value.

'Decline' effects of this sort have been confirmed by much of the card-guessing of recent years. Miss Jephson regarded the decline as a fatigue effect, but it is connected more probably with changes in psychological tension.

The real weakness underlying Miss Jephson's work arose from the fact that the great majority of her subjects performed the experiments in their own homes, using their own cards and under no supervision by the experimenter.

It is easy to imagine possibilities which might operate in favour of successful results.

(1) A considerable percentage probably used a single pack of playing-cards whose backs were more or less worn or soiled. Through constant handling of the cards the guesser would learn to recognize, perhaps sub-consciously, certain of them from slight markings or cracks on the backs.

(2) Careless manipulation might permit the guesser to glimpse the colour or suit of a card, or its reflection may have been seen in the surface of a polished table.

(3) Some of the percipients may have done several sets of five guesses on the same day and sent in the best set. There are many persons who understand so little of statistical practice that they would see nothing at all reprehensible in this.

(4) The 'decline' effect observed might be accounted for if certain of the participants did not record their guesses until they could start off their five with a correct hit—begin with a bang as it were; others may have wanted to end up with a bang.

It was therefore important to repeat the investigation under approximately error-proof conditions. This work[11] was carried out in the spring and summer of 1929 by Miss Jephson, Mr. Theodore Besterman and S.G.S. The novel feature of this undertaking was that it was designed not only to make fraud or error difficult on the part of the guessers but also to prevent any individual experimenter from faking the results.

A large number of shuffled playing-cards with plain backs were placed in blue envelopes which just fitted the cards. The envelopes were of such material that they could not be rendered transparent by strong light, X-rays, alcohol, or the like. They could not be opened without there being moisture traces left and they bore on both sides the impress of the Society for Psychical Research's stamp. The envelopes were sealed and dispatched to 559 percipients in weekly batches of five in five successive weeks. The smallest detail of the preparation and dispatch of the envelopes and of the checking of results was supervised by an umpire, Col. Dick.

A total of 9,496 guesses was recorded, and analysed by Fisher's method, but the results showed no signs of any extra-chance factor. Nor was there any definite evidence of a 'decline' effect.

It seems probable that the phenomenal success of Miss Jephson's earlier experiment could be attributed to the sources of error we have enumerated above.

We shall see later that overwhelming evidence for the faculty of apparent clairvoyance was obtained by Dr. Rhine and his disciples, but Miss Jephson will rank as a pioneer in the exploration of this territory.

## Dr. Estabrooks's[12] Experiments

In 1926, Dr. G. H. Estabrooks, a psychologist of Harvard University, carried out three short series of telepathy experiments with a number of college students, using an ordinary full pack of playing-cards. Dr. Estabrooks himself acted as agent or sender, assisted by one or two other persons. In the main series the agent and guesser were in the two halves of a relatively sound-proof room separated by a partition in which were double doors, closed during the experiments. An electric device clicked every 20 seconds as a signal for the subject to record his guess, and each card was exposed to the agent's gaze for 20 seconds. Each time a 'red' playing-card was turned up, Estabrooks switched on a red light to enhance the effect. About 80 guessers were individually tested, and, with a few exceptions, each was allowed to do about 20 guesses. Dr. Estabrooks rejected the trials of subjects who were of a critical or analytic turn of mind—the rejection taking place, of course, *before* the subject's guesses were checked with the 'target' cards. He declared that the best subjects he found were those who regarded both the experiment and the experimenter as a nuisance to be got rid of as soon as possible, and not those who took a minute interest in the details.

Estabrooks[12] analysed his results for colour and suit only. Out of a total of 1,660 trials in the three main series the guess was right for colour 938 times, as compared with an expectation of 830. The reader will easily verify that, with $p = \frac{1}{2}$, the critical ratio is 5·3, and the corresponding odds over eight millions to one. The suit was right 473 times, whereas chance would predict only 415 hits. The odds against chance here exceed 900 to 1.

18

Estabrooks also noted that the first half of a set of 20 trials gave a significantly higher score than the remaining half. This sort of decline characterizes much of the later work including that of Mrs. Stewart and of David Kahn.

On one occasion after a batch of subjects had completed their guesses, they were removed to a room 60 feet distant from the agent's room and retested individually with another 20 guesses. Of the 640 trials recorded, 307 were right as regards *colour* and 130 as regards *suit*, as compared with chance expectations of 320 and 160 respectively. Both these results are somewhat below the chance values, and the odds against the negative deviation of 30 for suit amount to more than 150 to 1. This tendency for subjects who have been scoring high above the chance level to change suddenly to scoring below chance has been frequently noticed. Here it may have been due to the guessers losing their confidence in being able to cognize the cards at an increased distance. They may have felt isolated and cut off from the agent. In the light of later work it seems improbable that the increased distance had any physical effect on the results, and it is possible that the subjects could have been conditioned to work effectively from the more remote room.

Dr. Estabrooks, however, seems to have become discouraged, for he did not continue the experiments. Possibly he felt that the critics would attribute the original high scores to unconscious whispering or some other form of auditory leakage of information.

## Early Distance Experiments

The earliest records we can find of attempts to transmit thought over considerable distances are the experiments of Usher and Burt[13],[14] in 1907. An agent in Bristol attempted to transmit drawings and playing-cards telepathically to a receiver in London at pre-arranged times. In a second series by the same authors, the agent was in Prague and the receiver in London. So far as the drawings are concerned, Usher and Burt claimed resemblances between those made by the receiver and agent but they did not attempt any numerical evaluation.

Later on Whately Carington[15] applied to this series what is known as a matching method. Code numbers were affixed to the drawings and originals. Pairs of originals (i.e. the agent's drawings) were selected in haphazard fashion, and to each pair were added the two drawings of the receiver or percipient which were supposed to correspond to the two originals. The four sketches were then submitted to a judge, who knew nothing of Usher and Burt's work, and he was asked to indicate which 'reproduction' he thought most resembled each original. This would often be something in the nature of a Hobson's choice, but he was asked to do his best. Eleven judges tried their hand at the job. If there existed only fortuitous resemblances between the originals and the drawings intended for them, we should expect about 50 per cent of the pairs to be correctly matched. Actually out of a total of 249 pairs, 144 were correctly matched, i.e. 57·8 per cent, and this gives odds of more than 60 to 1 in favour of the resemblances being genuine. The result is suggestive though, of course, far from conclusive.

Thirty attempts[14] were made to transmit the image of a playing-card. These led to only 2 complete hits but there were some partial successes such as 6D for 6S, etc. In some cases two guesses were recorded for a single card, and so S.G.S. was able to score only the first 25 trials by Fisher's method. The observed mean score was 16·11 as compared with the theoretical mean of 11·18. This gives a critical ratio of 2·46 and corresponding odds of more than 70 to 1—a result which is again suggestive, especially as certain guesses could not be scored.

## *The 1927–9 experiments of S.G.S.*

In February 1927, Dr. V. J. Woolley[16] carried out a mass experiment for the Society for Psychical Research in co-operation with the B.B.C. Dr. Woolley and the agents (of whom S.G.S. was one) were locked for the night in the Society's séance room, all telephone communication being cut off. Sir Oliver Lodge in a B.B.C. studio announced the nature of each experiment, and gave the signal for the listeners to record their impressions. Various interesting objects such as a spray of white lilac, a Japanese print of a bird standing beside a human skull, etc., were presented to the agents' gaze, and in two tests a playing-card chosen at random from a full pack. In all, 24,659 listeners sent in their results to the Society on postcards. The experiment was quite inconclusive as regards evidence for telepathy, since it was impossible to organize any control tests for the study of mass preferences for such objects as playing-cards, flowers, etc. It does not help us much to know that, when the agents concentrated on the two of clubs, 190 of the 24,659 listeners thought of this card, unless we also know how many would have said 'two of clubs' even if the agents had thought of no card at all.

About 127 of the listeners who had obtained some apparent success in the B.B.C. test consented to take part in a new experiment to be held on Wednesday evenings, and in response to a radio appeal by Professor Julian Huxley this number was increased later to 579.

The participants[17] were informed that a small group of agents would meet at an address in London at the same time every week, and that in general, these senders would concentrate successively for ten minutes on each of three objects chosen by S.G.S. Each guesser was furnished with a photo of the group of agents. The objects chosen during the first few months consisted of things calculated to create a lively emotional interest, such as mechanical toys, etc., and the subjects were given no hint of their nature. However,[17] for the session 1928-9 the subject matter was more restricted, and the percipients were sent notices telling them that No. 2, for instance, would be a geometrical figure, a letter of the alphabet, a playing-card, or a three-digit number, as the case might be.

This kind of restricted test was statistically evaluated by means of 'controls'. For instance, on a certain number of evenings, the percipients would be notified that a letter of the alphabet was to be shown the agents whereas in reality no such experiment was carried out. The control experiment would tell us how many times each letter would be likely to be chosen without any help from telepathy. It was then only necessary to pool the controls and compare, by means of a chi-squared test, the proportions in which the different letters of the alphabet were guessed in the control experiment with the proportions obtained when the agents concentrated, say, on the letter H.

In all the tests we found no significant difference in these proportions and no evidence that the agents' efforts to transmit a particular letter, number, or figure had any effect on the distribution of the various symbols guessed.

The free material was more difficult to evaluate. A scoring system was eventually elaborated, based on the empirical proportions in which the whole group tended to guess the various objects such as red flowers, dogs, hats, etc.—something after the same principle as Fisher's system for playing-cards. No significant evidence of telepathy was obtained. It was noted that occasionally a person would score a spectacular success, but seldom or never was this same person able to repeat his performance.

For example,[17] on 5th October, 1927, S.G.S. came to the meeting-place ready to create an exciting conflagration by dropping concentrated sulphuric acid on a mixture of sugar and chlorate of potash. At the last moment, however, he decided that he could not risk blackening the ceiling and filling the room with fumes of chlorine peroxide. He therefore made the agents concentrate on a toy rabbit instead. Surprisingly, percipient No. 28 from the Midlands sent in his impression as follows: 'October 5th (8.50-9 p.m.). Something crackling or spluttering as water dropped on acid. Irritating fumes. Idea of ammonia.' This man afterwards wrote to say that he had no interest in chemistry either professionally or as a hobby. He continued with the tests for eleven weeks, but recorded nothing else of interest.

The 579 percipients were living in all parts of the British Isles, and a few sent in impressions from France, Holland, the Channel Isles, India, and New Zealand. On many occasions S.G.S. arranged for additional agents to co-operate with the London group. Their number varied from 20 to 68. They were chosen from widely separated localities, and were either professional men and women or in positions of trust. But this innovation appeared to have no effect on the success of the experiments.

The failure of this large-scale investigation[17] was all the more disappointing from the fact that the bulk of the persons taking part claimed to have had spontaneous psychical experiences of various kinds. They included dowsers, crystal-gazers, spirit mediums, automatic writers, astral travellers, and blind persons.

The reasons they gave in their letters for believing in the possession of telepathic powers show considerable variety as the following extracts testify:[17]

(a) 'During my army service, when I have been asleep, I could always rely on being awakened by a voice calling my name, whenever any officer or N.C.O. was visiting my post.'

(b) 'I find people can't lie to me. I read their thoughts and they bungle the lie.'

(c) 'Sir, having proved telepathy to be positive in a small room and having found that my dog can read my thoughts, I would be favoured, etc.'

(d) 'Between my husband and me there was an intense communication without words. During the last months of his life I was afraid to think when near him.'

(e) 'I never dream silly dreams or have nightmares, but I dream whole histories at long intervals.'

(f) 'I possess psychic powers and a pair of eyes that flash fire when they please.'

Another early experiment making use of the radio was carried out by Professor Gardner Murphy of Columbia University. On 3rd March, 1924, a group of 40 agents operated from Chicago, and tried to transmit names of animals, etc. The experiment again seems to have been somewhat inconclusive, owing perhaps to the absence of control tests and adequate statistical standards of comparison.

## Appraisal

Our own feeling is that, with the exception of Estabrooks's work and perhaps the Groningen experiments, the use of statistical methods up to about the year 1932 yielded results which were either wholly negative or at best suggestive rather than conclusive regarding the operation of a paranormal faculty. What is chiefly noticeable is a curious lack of persistence on the part of some experimenters. One psychologist after another would make a few half-hearted attempts to demonstrate telepathy, and then abandon the task. One reason was that, during the first three decades of the present century, the subject was considered hardly respectable in most academic circles.

A psychologist who received a special grant for the purpose might perform a limited number of experiments with impunity so long as the investigation appeared to prove that telepathy did not happen. But if an academic man showed any enthusiasm and a tendency to go on in the face of discouragement, he would soon be frowned upon and accused of wasting his time. His sanity might even be doubted. The general scientific opinion of the day insisted that telepathy was merely an exploded superstition, a thing decently buried, which it would be unwise to resurrect. The subject of parapsychology was associated in the academic mind with fortune-telling and fraudulent mediums, with astrology, phrenology, numeralogy, and similar nonsense.

How were these circumspect and cautious professors to know that, before the half-century had turned, the mental climate would have so far changed that the Universities of Oxford, Cambridge, and London, would be conferring doctorates for theses on the paranormal? How could they guess that in a few years the Rockefeller Foundation, the Royal Institution, and the Fulbright Commission, would be taking an active interest in promoting parapsychological studies or in acquainting the public with advances in this field? The important Waynflete lectures at Oxford University (Eccles, 1953) and Dr. Thouless's Friday evening lecture at the Royal Institution have only given expression at higher academic levels to the increasing attention which parapsychology has received from academic bodies. Parapsychology is no longer a field in which a professor of 'English' or 'French' at a university can give opinions without being thoroughly read in the literature of the subject. There is, of course, no shortage of people who feel that, because they are qualified in psychiatry or psychology, they are competent to pass judgment on the work of the parapsychologist. The 'expert' knowledge of such persons is usually based on some quite elementary books on the subject which omit the essential experimental details without which a proper evaluation of the work is not possible. It would be interesting to meet the psychiatrist or psychologist who has perused every page of the 49 volumes of the *Proceedings* of the Society for Psychical Research, and who remains a complete spcetic. It is no coincidence that those most sceptical of ESP research are almost invariably those who are least acquainted with the facts.

For instance, at a recent committee meeting at a British university which had to decide on a grant towards ESP research one professor maintained that the 'experiments simply could not be true'. To prove it he was prepared to pit his skill against any random selector and guess every number correctly which the machine would produce. This, he maintained, could always be done by suitable trickery. The grant was, nevertheless, awarded and this suggests that the university had greater faith in carefully planned experiments than in the pronouncements of some professor who had probably just heard of parapsychology for the first time.

The Society for Psychical Research during this period (1916-34) followed its old tradition of studying spontaneous cases but it is only fair to add that it spent many hundreds of pounds on printing, with the fullest detail, long statistical investigations of telepathy and clairvoyance which led only to negative conclusions, and which, but for the Society's aid, would never have seen the light.

# CHAPTER III

# The Early Work at Duke University

A quarter of a century has passed since two young botanists of Chicago University resigned their teaching appointments and arrived one day on Professor William McDougall's doorstep at Cambridge, Massachusetts, just as he was leaving for a world tour. They were Dr. Joseph Banks Rhine and his wife, Dr. Louisa E. Rhine, who, without influence or financial assets, were anxious to devote their lives to the scientific study of what became known later as Extra-Sensory Perception or briefly ESP. They spent a year studying psychology and philosophy at Harvard, and in 1927 migrated to Duke University, North Carolina, where McDougall had recently been appointed professor of psychology. Here Rhine worked in the psychological laboratory, and began ESP experiments in his spare time. By 1931 card-guessing tests were in full swing.

Dr. Rhine possessed two human qualities which were to stand him in good stead—unquenchable enthusiasm allied to a dogged pertinacity. His fibre was tough as that of the farming stock from which he sprang, and adverse criticism did not deter him. He just went on—answering his critics and devising new experiments to obviate their objections.

He was blessed by circumstances, for William McDougall, F.R.S., was a past-president of the Society for Psychical Research who was vitally alive to the potential importance of a scientific study of telepathy, and the president of Duke University watched the progress of the new experiments with interest.

Perhaps Rhine's greatest innovation in technique was his substitution for playing-cards and numbers, which had hitherto constituted the stock material for such experiments, cards known as Zener cards on which were inscribed five symbols—the plus sign, circle, square, the five-pointed star and the wavy lines. The cards were made up into packs of 25, and each pack contained exactly five cards of each symbol.

25

Playing-cards were used by the early experimenters mainly because they were easily obtained, but they have their disadvantages. There are too many symbols for the guesser to bear them all in mind. Further, many of the configurations are too much alike, so that the five of hearts, for example, might easily be mistaken for the five of spades.

But the chief objection is that certain cards have strong associations in the minds of almost everyone. In the B.B.C. experiment* of 1927 (p. 20), when some 24,000 persons were asked to guess a playing-card, about one in every eight wrote down an ace and one in every 24 chose the Ace of Spades, which was the most popular card, the next in order of preference to the aces being the nine of diamonds, commonly known as 'the curse of Scotland'.

Now the fact that most people tend to evoke images of their favourite cards or of their 'lucky' suits must militate against the emergence of telepathic images. The delicate and fleeting telepathic image will be ousted by the habitual mechanical image. Undoubtedly there are preferences associated even with Rhine's symbols, but these are not so marked as with playing-cards.

One of the most remarkable features of Rhine's investigation was the large number of high-scoring subjects discovered during the first three years' work. There were no fewer than eight major subjects most of whom produced results with odds against chance-coincidence of millions to one, and in addition there were a number of lesser lights. Never has such a galaxy of extra-sensory talent been gathered by a single experimenter or in so short a period. Dr. Rhine's first important monograph[1] Extra-Sensory Perception appeared in 1934, and it evoked a storm of hostile criticism from psychologists throughout the length and breadth of America.

Rhine, we think, was the first experimenter who tried to isolate telepathy from clairvoyance. Hitherto the majority of successful experiments in thought-transference could be equally well interpreted as being due to some unknown power of the human mind which extracted information from the material objects themselves. That is, when an agent looked at a playing-card, the guesser in the other room might be getting either the mental image in the agent's mind or information derived from the card itself. The experiment did not allow us to discriminate between the two alternatives. But Rhine arranged tests in telepathy which apparently excluded clairvoyance, and vice versa.

In many of the early 'pure clairvoyance' experiments, Dr. Rhine and the guesser would sit on opposite sides of a small table. Rhine would shuffle and cut a pack of 25 Zener cards inscribed with five types of sym-

* II, 16.

bols. He would lay the pack on the table face downwards, and the subject would lift off the cards one by one, and, holding each card face downwards, guess the symbol on its face. Rhine recorded the guess on a scoring sheet, and the guesser without seeing the face value placed the card face downwards in a separate pile. When all 25 cards had been guessed, the experimenter would compare the subject's guesses with the actual cards in the new pile, and the guesser watched the checking.

Sometimes, however, the guesses were checked against the 'targets' after every five trials, and in this case it would be possible, since the pack contained equal numbers (five) of each symbol, for the guesser to be guided in his guessing by noting the numbers of circles, stars, etc., which had already turned up. If, for instance, four of the first five happened to be circles, the guesser would be well advised to cease calling circles for the rest of the pack. His total score would then on an average be about 6 instead of 5.

There was also obviously the possibility that, in the case where the subject saw the backs of the cards as he guessed them, he might notice (perhaps subconsciously) small specks and irregularities on the backs of certain of them, and, through watching the checking, associate these specks with the designs on the faces. When the same pack was run through several times, the knowledge so obtained might enable him to recognize consciously or subconsciously the marked cards. Even if only one or two cards could be thus identified, the guesser's average would soon rise significantly above chance expectation.

At this time of day, however, we need not unduly emphasize such defects. To do so, indeed, would be to misunderstand Rhine's plan of attack. His general practice was to begin with fairly loose conditions of control, and only after his subjects had gained confidence would he tighten them up. As he expressed it in a letter he wrote to S.G.S. in 1936: 'We work here on the principle that you must first catch your butterfly before you can pin it down.'

Our view is that the above-mentioned sources of error probably did produce a spurious increase in the scores of even the major subjects *while these were working under the less rigid conditions*, and it is possible that the smaller extra-chance scores of some of the minor subjects may have been wholly due to the presence of sensory cues.

Nevertheless, there are quite enough experiments described in *Extra-Sensory Perception* in which guessers and cards were separated by opaque screens, or in which the experimenter and the guesser were in different buildings, to justify Dr. Rhine's claims to have demonstrated clairvoyance (as then understood).

## The Work of Hubert Pearce[1,2]

Even if Rhine's claim to have demonstrated pure clairvoyance rested only on the work of one gifted subject, Hubert Pearce, it would be irrefutable unless we assume that Pearce, a student for the ministry, was in collusion not only with Dr. Rhine but also with Dr. J. G. Pratt, who has been for twenty years one of the most responsible workers in parapsychology at Duke University.

Pearce, whose parents appear to have possessed clairvoyant gifts, began by shuffling a pack of Zener cards which was then cut by Dr. Rhine. Pearce lifted off the cards one by one, holding each card face downwards, and looking away from the pack as he made his guess. The unsatisfactory features here are that the guesser not only shuffled the cards himself but lifted them and held them one by one. A competent conjuror would, one feels, succeed without difficulty under these conditions in scoring above chance expectation. In 650 trials he scored 279 hits, which is an average of 10·7 hits per 25 instead of the expected 5.

There is of course the possibility that Pearce did catch a glimpse of the underside of the card and such experimental conditions are unsatisfactory. He next ran through 475 trials with the variation that he made his guess *before* lifting off the card. In this series he scored 236 hits which gave an even higher average of 12·4 per 25.

An experiment was now done with 25 packs of freshly printed cards which the subject had never seen before. Each pack was run through only two or three times, and the results were not checked until the end of each set of 25 guesses. There was thus little opportunity for Pearce to learn the cards from their backs. We shall be on the safe side if we consider only the *first* runs through the 25 different packs. On these 625 trials 235 hits were scored, which shows an average of 9·4 hits per 25, with astronomical odds against chance. Everything depends here, of course, on whether Pearce had any opportunity to mark or study these newly printed cards before the experiment started. Dr. Rhine assures us that Pearce had no such opportunity. We are told that the cards used were opaque to light from a 100-watt light-bulb, and were cut from heavy white cardboard.

Pearce then did 300 trials with the cards concealed behind a screen, and scored 99 successes—an average of 8·3 per 25. Here the sceptic might ask: 'Did Pearce himself shuffle the pack and if so did Dr. Rhine give it a cut behind the screen? He mentions cutting the pack in the previous test.'

28

## The Down-Through (DT) Technique[1]

Pearce himself at this stage suggested an innovation. He thoroughly shuffled the pack, watched by Dr. Rhine. This shuffling, Rhine notes, was prolonged and thorough, and Pearce habitually turned away his eyes from the cards. Moreover, after the shuffling, the pack was always cut by Rhine himself. Under these conditions it does not seem possible that Pearce could have arranged the cards in a special order to any useful purpose. The pack was left lying face downwards on the table, and the subject guessed the cards through the pack from top to bottom without disturbing the pile. Twelve different packs were used in this experiment, and 1,625 trials recorded. These gave a total score of 482, with odds of the order of $10^{20}$ to 1 against chance.

It was noted that Pearce scored best on the last five cards at the bottom of the pack, and next best on the top five, while the central fifteen showed a lower average. This is a typical decline effect.

It might be suggested by the critic that, since the total scoring rate was only 7·4 hits per 25, as against an expectation of 5, Pearce achieved his results normally by catching a glimpse of the bottom card as the pack was being cut, and frequently identifying the top card by means of specks on its back. But it would be absurd to imagine that Rhine should have overlooked such an obvious possibility. If the significance were due entirely to successes on the top and bottom cards, he would surely have discovered this during the counting which he mentions.

Unless we assume that throughout the experimenter was *incurably negligent* it is difficult to believe that Pearce could have made high scores under such varied conditions by fraud alone.

But later on clairvoyance was fully confirmed by the experiments of Martin and Stribic,[4,5] who caused their best subject, Mr. C.J., to run through 91,475 trials by this DT method, with the additional precaution that the pack of cards was always placed behind a screen.

This subject maintained an average of nearly seven hits per 25, with astronomical odds against chance.

The undoubted success of the DT method makes it almost impossible to suppose that clairvoyance can be explained in terms of any form of radiation or waves emanating from the surfaces of the cards and impinging on the brain of the guesser. For the waves or radiations coming from each of 25 cards would result in a confused blotch, and not a single image of any particular card. It is inconceivable that the subject's brain would be able to utilize such radiation to enable him to say that the 14th card was a circle and the 18th a cross. Moreover, in Rhine's

DT experiments with Pearce there were sometimes a dozen other packs of Zener cards lying on the table, and radiation from all these together would make confusion inextricably worse confounded.

## The Pearce-Pratt Series[2]

We have watched Dr. Rhine tightening up his conditions one by one with Hubert Pearce, and we now reach the crucial experiments in which Pearce and the cards were in different buildings of Duke University, 100 yards apart, and in one case 250 yards apart.

In this series Dr. J. G. Pratt[2] was the experimenter. Pearce and Pratt synchronized their watches. Pearce went to a cubicle in the library, and Pratt to the physics building, 100 yards away. Between the two buildings there was no telephonic communication. According to a previous arrangement made with Pearce, Dr. Pratt, having shuffled his pack of Zener cards, lifted off the top card at a specified time and laid it face downwards on the centre of the table. Thirty seconds later Pearce wrote down his guess. A minute after removing the first card Pratt lifted off the next card, and Pearce made his guess half a minute later. Pratt continued to lift off the cards at the rate of one a minute. When the pack had been run through, Pratt reshuffled and cut it, and it was run through again. Thus 50 guesses were done at each sitting. At the close of the day's work Pratt and Pearce sealed up their record sheets, and delivered them independently to Dr. Rhine. The results were then checked.

Here there appears to be a lacuna in the report which does not inform the reader if the checking was done immediately after the handing in of the records by Pearce and Pratt to Dr. Rhine. If, for instance, the sheets had been laid aside or put away in a drawer to be checked at leisure, there is just the possibility that Pearce might have gained access to them. Nor is it stated whether Rhine and Pratt were both present at the checking. However, in correspondence, Dr. Pratt has assured us that before leaving their respective buildings both Pearce and he made duplicates of their respective records of calls and targets. They met a few minutes after the finish of each experiment and each furnished the other with a copy of his own record.

There would seem, therefore, to be no point in Pearce's tampering with the record he had deposited in Rhine's office since Pratt retained copies of both targets and calls.

A total of 750 trials was made with Pearce 100 yards from the cards, and 261 hits were counted, compared with a chance expectation of $\frac{1}{5} \times 750$, i.e. 150. This gives a critical ratio of 10·1, with odds against chance amounting to $10^{20}$ to 1. The average is 8·7 hits per 25. At one group of experiments in the above series Dr. Rhine himself was present in the physics building, and watched Pratt handle the cards and check the results. The scores on these occasions were:

12, 3, 10, 11, 10, 10.

This is a small group of only 150 guesses, but the scores are of the same order as in the rest of the work.

If, therefore, Pearce and Pratt were in a conspiracy, we must assume that Dr. Rhine had now joined it!

In a longer series of 1,075 trials, Pratt removed himself and the cards to the medical building, while Pearce remained in the library, the distance between them being now about 250 yards. This series gave 288 hits, which is an excess of 73 over chance expectation, and corresponds to odds of the order of $10^7$ to 1 against chance, with an average score of 6·7 hits per 25. There were apparently spells during which extra-sensory perception was not working or was producing negative deviations, for there were three packs of 25 for which the score was 0. There were, however, five runs with 12 hits and one with 13.

On the whole 1,825 trials the total score was 549 compared with the 365 which chance would predict, the odds against chance being about $10^{20}$ to 1.

It will be realized that in these 'distance' series all normal cues from cards are definitely ruled out. The abundant confirmation of Rhine's work by others makes it unnecessary to consider the theory of collusion. Nor is it plausible in view of Pratt's statement above to suppose that there was a 'chronic' delay in checking the records.

## Pure Telepathy

In a telepathy experiment designed to exclude the possibility of clairvoyance it is essential that no actual cards or written representations of the symbols to be transmitted should be employed. The subject matter must consist only of mental images. Now here we encounter a difficulty. A person who thinks of the five Zener symbols is apt to produce certain habitual patterns or arrangements. For instance, if he images a long series of such symbols, he may unwittingly think of crosses more frequently than squares, and, if the guesser has similar unconscious preferences, this may spuriously augment the number of successes. If on the other hand he selects mentally sets of five in advance, and tries to permute the sets in various ways in his head, the tendency will be for him to avoid repeats of the same symbol, and in the long run he will have far fewer repeats than would occur with, say, well-shuffled packs of cards. This error , however, will be far less serious than that of the too frequent choice of a particular symbol, but there is still the danger that the sender may fall into some habit which happens to coincide with a habit of the guesser—such as, for instance, the choice of a star for the middle symbol of successive groups of five. It would be more satisfactory if the sender were to write down a long series of the digits 1 to 5 selected from a table of random or haphazard numbers, or from a telephone directory, and then associate *mentally* (without making a written record) each digit with a Zener symbol, e.g. 1 = square; 2 = plus sign; 3 = star; 4 = wavy lines; 5 = circle.

The sender would merely run down his list of numbers, and image the corresponding symbols.

It would, however, still be possible for the percipient or receiver to read the numbers from the list by *clairvoyance*, and by a lucky guess hit on the sender's code. But this could be largely obviated by the sender's changing his mental code at intervals.

In his early work described in *Extra-Sensory Perception*[1] Rhine did not employ a code, but relied on his agents to permute sets of five symbols (possibly with repeats) in their heads.

In this case it was of course necessary for the transmitter to postpone the recording of the five symbols on paper until the receiver had written down his five guesses. The method could not give a random list of symbols for transmission, but so long as the sets of five were sufficiently varied, and there was approximate equality in the numbers of each symbol, the expectation of hits and the standard deviation would differ very little from their theoretical values.

One method by which we discover whether or not the sender's sets of five show any preference habits is to make what is known as a 'cross-check' by scoring for hits the first set of five against the second, the second against the third and so on. If the average per 25 thus obtained were close to 5, this would show that there were no habitual preferences running through the different permutations.

Hubert Pearce[1] made pure telepathy (PT) tests with four different agents. There was usually a 'transition' period when Pearce changed from one technique to another, and he did not score well on the first 175 PT trials. Pearce and the agent were in the same room, and the former sat with closed eyes waiting for the regular tap of a telegraph key by which he was informed that the agent was visualizing a Zener symbol but had no actual card in front of him. Pearce called out his guess, and then the sender recorded both the guess and the imagined symbol.

In 1,225 PT trials Pearce achieved an average of 7·2 per 25, with odds against chance of more than $10^{12}$ to one.

It is interesting to note that during the same period in which these PT trials took place, Pearce also carried out 1,775 pure clairvoyance trials with an average of 7·1 hits per 25.

It is not clear whether the clairvoyance and telepathy tests were rigidly alternated with each other, or randomly interspersed in equal batches, but, so far as can be gathered, Pearce scored about equally well with pure telepathy and pure clairvoyance.

On the occasions when a stranger was introduced to watch Pearce at work, his scoring, which had been quite high before the entry of the fresh observer, invariably declined for a few runs to about chance level, and then rose again to its original level, or even above it, as the subject became adjusted to the presence of the newcomer. Among the witnesses was Wallace Lee, the magician, who confessed himself baffled by Pearce's performance, which he was quite unable to imitate. Pearce, however, was ill on this occasion, and his actual score (37/125) was not very remarkable.

## Effect of Drugs

Not the least important of Rhine's early findings was his demonstration that ESP processes are affected by certain drugs. There has long been a tradition among certain tribes in South America that clairvoyance can be induced by the imbibing of a concoction made from the peyotl plant, which contains the alkaloid mescal, but the evidence is inconclusive. Experiments with Europeans have been singularly unsuccessful, and at present we know of no drug which renders people clairvoyant or telepathic who are not ordinarily so in the normal state. It had, however, been noticed by Warcollier, the French experimenter, that his subjects appeared to be more successful as percipients after a moderate libation of alchohol, but this was a judgment formed from clinical experience.

Rhine, however, showed that the scoring levels for both pure clairvoyance and pure telepathy were influenced by two drugs, sodium amytal and caffeine citrate, in the cases of certain gifted percipients.

Pearce[1] was given 6 grains of the sleep-producing drug, sodium amytal. Just before taking the dose he had scored 29 hits in 50 trials under the clairvoyance condition. Half an hour after swallowing the drug he became very drowsy, and Rhine then set him to guess cards still by using clairvoyance. He started off badly, his first three scores being 5, 4, 3. He then tried to pull himself together in spite of increasing sleepiness, and scored a 10. After that his score slumped until the eleventh run of 25, when he scored another 10. He had to give up after the thirteenth run. His average for the 'drug' period was only 6·1 hits per 25.

D                                            33

This result is suggestive only; to make it conclusive the drop in score would have to be observed on a great many occasions. However, a similar effect was noted in the case of another high-scoring subject, A. L. Linzmayer, who was given 15 grains of the same drug at a time when he was scoring an average of 6·8 per 25 at clairvoyance.

During the time he was under the influence of the drug Linzmayer obtained only 86 hits in 425 trials, which is just one above chance expectation. More information is required here; we should have to know how many of the 960 trials which gave a pre-drug score average of 6·8 per 25 were done immediately before the drug was taken, before we could draw any safe conclusions about its effect. That is, we ought to have the score on *equal numbers of trials made on the same day* just before and during the drug period.

The effect of caffeine citrate on Pearce's clairvoyant scoring is more persuasively shown, though even here it is not certain that the higher scores were not due to *suggestion* rather than to the effect of the drug. On five occasions when Pearce's scoring was below its best, he was given 5-grain doses of caffeine, and, after a short interval, put through several runs with the cards. On each occasion there was a marked rise in the score average.

Just before the caffeine was taken, 450 trials gave an average score of only 7·2 hits per 25, whereas after the ingestion of the drug 750 trials gave an average of 10 per 25. The increase appears highly significant, though we could estimate it more accurately if we knew the actual scores for each run of 25.

Caffeine would appear to have an effect on the ESP faculty similar to its effect on the intellectual powers. The taking of a cup of coffee does not make a man a better mathematician; it only makes him for a time better able to concentrate his powers when he has become tired or distracted. There is no evidence whatever that caffeine caused Pearce to exceed by much his normal scoring rate, which was about 9·7 hits per 25. All it appeared to do was to restore him to this level when he had fallen below it. We doubt whether we are ever likely to discover a drug which will make normal people clairvoyant any more than we are able to turn a person with an insensitive ear into a gifted musician by dosing him with drugs.

## Effects on Pure Telepathy

Dr. Rhine's best subject for telepathy experiments was George Zirkle, a graduate assistant in the psychology department of Duke University. Like Shackleton and Mrs. Stewart, Zirkle apparently did not succeed in clairvoyance tests—i.e. when no one thought of the cards to be guessed (see Chaps. X and XII). During the period when his health was good, he scored an average of 14·8 hits per 25 for 1,300 pure telepathy trials.

From Rhine's account[1,2] it would appear that the conditions of the experiments were somewhat more stringent than those which prevailed with Pearce. The guesser, Zirkle, and the sender, Miss Sarah Ownbey, were in different rooms, sitting where they could not see each other, but with the communicating door open. Miss Ownbey, without any actual cards, made up permutations of the Zener symbols in her head, five in advance, and tapped with a telegraph key to let Zirkle know that she was thinking of a specific symbol. The subject called aloud his guess, and the sender then recorded both Zirkle's call and the symbol in her mind.

The sender and receiver were about 10 feet apart, and in order to drown any possible sub-vocal whispering by the former while she concentrated on her symbol, an electric fan was kept going throughout the experiment. The average score for 750 trials under these conditions was 14·6 per 25.

In another series the distance between sender and receiver was increased to about 30 feet, and 250 trials gave the even higher average of 16 hits per 25. In one run of 25, Zirkle obtained 23 hits. This is, of course, phenomenal scoring, and obviously we are entirely dependent on the accuracy of Miss Ownbey. She had to record both her own image and Zirkle's call and her memory may have failed her sometimes. There was apparently no third person present to record Zirkle's guess in writing, and to ensure that the sender was kept in ignorance of it till the end of the experiment. In any case there was no need for Zirkle to call his guess aloud. He could, if it distracted him to write, have pointed to one of five symbols on five cards, and a recorder could have written it down.

If, of course, we feel we cannot accept these results, it would be useless to lay stress on the drug experiments made in connection with them, and we shall allude to these only briefly.

After two runs averaging 13·5 hits per 25, a 5-grain capsule of sodium amytal was given Zirkle by Miss Ownbey. An hour later, when he was becoming very sleepy, he was put through 300 pure telepathy trials under the somewhat unsatisfactory conditions mentioned above with Miss Ownbey as sender. His average score fell from 13·5 to 7·8 per 25. Three hours after the ingestion of the drug, by which time Zirkle was seeing double and suffering slightly from hallucinations, though still able with effort to walk straight and to read without difficulty, he was made to do another 300 trials in telepathy. But this time his score had fallen to an average of 6·2 hits per 25. Four hours had now elapsed since the taking of the drug, and Zirkle was given a 5-grain capsule of caffeine citrate, without being told the nature of the drug. During the next hour, he was put through a final 300 trials, and on these his average rose to 9·5 hits per 25.

An interesting feature of this experiment is that Zirkle was not told the nature of the drug which was administered by capsule, and, if he had no knowledge of what to expect, the effects could hardly be explained by suggestion. It is by no means certain, however, that he would not identify the drugs from his initial symptoms.

For those who feel they can accept the conditions of the experiments, the work with Zirkle on the effects of drugs on the level of the ESP scores is in general agreement with Rhine's own findings with Linzmayer and Pearce.

## Appraisal

To sum up, we feel that we must reluctantly reject those experiments described in this chapter in which the percipient had any opportunity, either to handle the cards, or to see their backs while he made his guesses. Even DT tests are somewhat unsatisfactory unless the experimenter himself thoroughly shuffles and cuts the pack behind a screen. But after this rejection is made, there still remains a very considerable residuum of results including the Pearce-Pratt series, for which, if the reporting is accurate, it is difficult to imagine any normal explanation.

# CHAPTER IV

# Reactions of the Psychologists

That there were undoubted weaknesses in those early experiments with Zener cards would, we have no doubt, be freely admitted by Dr. Rhine himself. In certain of the clairvoyance tests there was the possibility of the subject's 'learning' the cards from specks and irregularities on their backs, more especially in the cases when the guesser witnessed the checking, or himself lifted off the cards. And, unfortunately, some of the cards intended for commercial use became warped in storage, so that, when certain of them were held at a special angle to the light, the designs became plainly visible through the backs. Other cards* appeared to show irregularities in the design near the edges. However, when Rhine discovered these defects, he issued a warning in the *Journal of Parapsychology* with instructions that the cards should be screened from the guesser. In any case we have seen that such defects could not possibly account for, say, the high scores obtained in the Pearce-Pratt clairvoyance series described on p. 30.

The main criticism from American psychologists did not, however, focus on the possibility of the guesser's getting cues from the backs or edges of the cards, though this was probably a real source of error in some experiments.

The critics were mostly concerned with the accuracy of the formula employed by Rhine in working out his standard deviation.

It will be recalled that Rhine made up his packs of 25 cards so that each pack contained exactly five cards of each Zener symbol, i.e. 5 circles, 5 plus signs, 5 squares, 5 stars and 5 wavy lines. Nobody seriously disputed that, on an average, a person who guessed through a well-shuffled pack would expect to get 5 guesses right. But the formula $\sqrt{(N \times \frac{1}{5} \times \frac{4}{5})}$, i.e. $0.4\sqrt{N}$, which he used for his standard deviation, was based on the assumption that the chance of a correct guess at any trial was always the same and equal to 1/5. The formula, known as the 'bi-

* III, 3.

nomial' formula, assumes that the chance of success does not vary from one guess to another.

If a guesser takes a pack of Rhine's cards and calls 'plus' for the top card, the reader will agree that, since this top card is just as likely to be any one of the five symbols as any other, the chance of the call's being correct is clearly 1/5.

But suppose it happens that the first five cards in the pack all bear the symbol 'plus'. The guesser does not know this because we are not checking until we have run through the whole pack. At his sixth guess, however, if he calls 'plus' his chance of being right is nil since there are no more 'plus' signs in the pack. And if he calls, say, 'circle', his chance is no longer 1/5, but 1/4, since now there are only four possibilities to consider. From this extreme example, it will be clear that if we guess through the pack, the chance of success fluctuates as we proceed from the first trial to the last. If Rhine had made up his packs by selecting random digits 1 to 5 by means of a machine or from mathematical tables, the dispute would not have arisen, but in that case his packs would have contained varying numbers of the different symbols. Subsequent mathematical investigations of the problem by Greenwood, [1,2] Sterne,[3] Greville,[4] and others, demonstrated that the standard deviation with Rhine's pack depends actually on the number of times each symbol is guessed, but that it could not exceed $0.408\sqrt{N}$, as compared with the value of $0.4\sqrt{N}$ employed by Rhine. The difference in the two formulae is quite trifling, and the small discrepancy could not possibly have accounted for the high critical ratios which he obtained with his best subjects.

It is important, however, for the reader who wishes to do some card-guessing to understand that the odds against the results being due to chance given in Table 11, p. 379, imply that $N$, the total number of guesses made, is sufficiently large for the distribution to approximate to a 'normal distribution'. The tables should not be used for fewer than about 200 guesses ($N = 200$), or the odds obtained may be exaggerated, especially when the deviations from the mean are large.

For example, if we scored 11 hits on a single run of 25 guesses, the *true* odds against our getting 11 or more correct hits by chance as worked out directly from the binomial expansion of $(\frac{4}{5} + \frac{1}{5})^{25}$ are nearly 180 to 1,* whereas, if we put $N = 25$ in the formula $0.4\sqrt{N}$, we should have a standard deviation of 2 and a critical ratio of $\dfrac{11-5}{2}$, i.e. 3. The corresponding odds read off from the table would be 369 to 1, but, since here we are considering only *above*-chance deviations, the odds would

* About 150 to 1 with Rhine's packs.

work out at $2 \times 369$ to 1 approximately, i.e. 738 to 1, a value which is wildly wrong.

All doubts as to the essential validity of the mathematical methods of evaluation employed were dispelled when Sir Ronald Fisher, the English authority on statistics, announced in 1935 that if the records reported were correctly observed, and published without selection, the departure from expectation could not be ascribed to chance. He went on to suggest that criticisms should be directed towards the conduct of the experiments rather than to the handling of the data.

## Inadequate Shuffling

Another criticism[5] often made by the psychologists was based on facts well-known to bridge players. When a pack of cards is shuffled in the ordinary way and cut, the new arrangement of the cards is not completely independent of the old. If, for instance, there are originally three circles which came together, it is not an uncommon experience to find them still together even after one thinks one has given the pack a good shuffle. Cards tend to cling together, and there may be several little sequences that remain undisturbed, unless indeed the shuffling is exceptionally thorough. If, then, the habits of the guesser happen to fit in with the first arrangement of the cards so as to produce a high score, it may be argued that, since the new arrangement has features in common with the original this also may be favourable for high scoring, provided that the guesser has sequence habits which remain more or less constant. This reasoning, however, is vague, and the argument is unconfirmed by experiment.

It may, however, be granted that the successive arrangements obtained by repeated shuffling of a pack of Rhine's cards are not perfectly haphazard or random selections drawn from the 623, 360, 743, 125, 120 possible arrangements of the 25 cards. The shuffling of a single pack of cards cannot produce a distribution that is random in all respects. But the real question at issue is: Do the types of non-randomness that shuffling introduces cause the chance expectation and standard deviation of the scores to differ seriously from their theoretical values? Can the high average scores made by good subjects be even partially accounted for by such differences? This is a question which can be and has been settled by experiment. The method consists in the choice of a high scoring series and then in the checking of each column of 25 guesses against an arrangement of 25 cards for which it was not intended.

Thus we might compare the first guess run with the second card run, and the second guess run with the first card run, the third guess run with the fourth card run, the fourth guess run with the third card run and so on through the series. By counting the numbers of hits we could find the average score and the average standard deviation for 25 trials in this 'cross-check', and compare these empirical values with the theoretical values, i.e. 5 and 2 respectively.

Many of the highly successful series carried out at Duke University and at other American universities in which shuffled packs of cards were used have been cross-checked in this way, and in no case were the empirical values found to differ significantly from the theoretical values.

When several packs of cards are used in an experiment instead of a single pack, the effect of linkage among card-patterns is so small that it need scarcely be considered.

The ghost was laid, we hope finally, by the labours of Dr. J. A. Greenwood,[7] a statistician, who matched two hundred different arrangements obtained by the repeated shuffling of thirty packs of Zener cards against each of a hundred guess runs taken from the records of five of Rhine's high-scoring subjects.

Thus half a million separate matchings of card-pairs were made, and these gave a mean score of 4·9743 per 25 with empirical standard deviation 2·0058. The distribution was found to be in excellent agreement with the binomial distribution.

During the past ten years several investigators have prepared their card sequences from lists of random digits 1–5, thus dispensing with the task of shuffling packs of cards. The two subjects, Basil Shackleton and Gloria Stewart, found no difficulty in maintaining high scores for long periods while guessing against card orders based on such lists selected from the last digits of seven-figure logarithms. If there is any reason to suppose that such sequences of digits possess non-random properties, a cross-check of cards against calls can always be applied.*

## Optional Stopping

If a person who has no extra-sensory powers whatever makes a long series of trials at guessing Zener cards screened from his sight, he will find that, if he works out the critical ratio for his grand total at intervals of, say, five hundred guesses, this ratio does not remain constant, but has its ups and downs. The same thing would be observed if two shuffled packs of Zener cards were paired off against each other a large number of times.

Now it has been shown mathematically that, if one is prepared to go

---

* The whole of the Shackleton series of 11,000 trials was subjected to such a cross-check with results that were in excellent agreement with probability theory.

on guessing indefinitely, one would ultimately reach any assigned critical ratio however large. It was therefore suggested by the psychologist Clarence Leuba,[8] in 1938 that an experimenter might keep a subject guessing cards until he had obtained a critical ratio, positive or negative of, say, 2·8 or 3, and then stop the series. He might proceed in the same way with a number of subjects stopping each at a favourable point. This would not necessarily result, when the scores of the different subjects were totalled, in a significant extra-chance score for the whole, because the experimenter might be aiming at high negative critical ratios with certain of his subjects so that positive and negative deviations might cancel out. But it would look as if a number of people had produced abnormal scores, some below and some above chance expectation. The investigator would have to meet the charge that he had obtained his high critical ratios by stopping subjects when they had reached favourable critical ratios.

The situation, however, is not so serious as might appear at first sight. In the first place, the fact that theoretically we can get any critical ratio if we go on long enough clearly applies not only to card-guessing but to thousands of other statistical experiments in many branches of science.

But biologists, psychologists, and engineers are not accused of pursuing their experiments until they reach a point where the odds against chance are satisfactory. Moreover, most good subjects who guess cards begin to score above chance expectation from the very start, and the critical ratio goes on steadily increasing, and soon attains a value too high to be attributed to the cause we are discussing. Further, experiments are stopped as a rule for quite other reasons than that the critical ratio has reached a certain magnitude. By assigning an upper limit to the total of trials we intend to carry out *before starting the experiment*, it is possible to apply a correction to the value found for the critical ratio so as to allow for the effects of 'optional stopping' anywhere within the predetermined range. Appropriate formulae have been suggested by both Dr. Greenwood* and Dr. Greville.[9]

If anyone imagines that it is really practicable to obtain a critical ratio of, say, 4 or 5 by dint of doing enough trials, we are afraid he will be sorely disillusioned. As he goes on he will discover that the upward trends of positive deviations which seem so promising are inevitably followed by devastating negative deviations which undo all the good work, and after about a hundred thousand trials the guesser will begin to realize that apparently he will be on the job for the rest of his life.

So far as high critical ratios are concerned, the question is of academic rather than of practical interest. But since it is not outside the

* XVI, 1.

bounds of ordinary patience for experimenters to reach three standard deviations by going on long enough with an ESP investigation, it is, we consider, unsafe to accept such a low standard of significance. For, if the trend of scoring is consistently upwards, the experimenter should obviously continue until he reaches a critical ratio which is significant beyond all question. If, however, there has been no very consistent upward trend, but a series of ups and downs, there is little reason for the experimenter to stop at 3 standard deviations and to cite this temporary peak in the score as evidence of extra-sensory perception.

This may seem to the reader inconsistent with the criterion of 2·8 standard deviations for significance suggested on p. 10. We should, however, employ such a low grade of significance (odds of 200 to 1) only when making comparisons involving small blocks of data taken from a much larger whole whose consistent significance is beyond all dispute.

For example, the Shackleton series of some 11,000 precognitive trials gave an over-all positive deviation of more than thirteen standard deviations, with odds exceeding $10^{35}$ to 1 against the operation of chance. And under certain fixed experimental conditions, the scoring was *consistently* above chance expectation. But in deciding whether, say, the score obtained in a particular evening's work of 300 trials showed evidence of ESP we should be justified in using a much lower standard— e.g., 2·8 standard deviations.

It has sometimes been said that, by experimenting with a number of persons, stopping each one when he has made a score a little above chance expectation, and totalling all the separate scores, an experimenter could get a high CR. In theory this would be true if the experimenter were able to continue indefinitely with the series, but with only limited time at his disposal, the method might not prove a practical proposition. It would be as if a gambler at Monte Carlo tried to make a regular income by playing every night, and stopping as soon as he was a little in pocket. The handicap, we need hardly point out, is that on some nights the luck would be against him from the first throw and the bad luck could last so long that he would be out of pocket for those nights. In the same way some of the subjects would score below chance expectation at the beginning, and to transform these negative deviations into positive ones, the experimenter would sometimes have to continue for such a large number of trials that, even though he ended up with a positive deviation in his grand total, this would not usually be significant, owing to the increase in the standard deviation with the number of guesses.

## Unconscious Whispering

One of the hardy perennials among the stock objections which psychologists urge against experiments in telepathy is the suggestion that, when a sender concentrates on an object or mental image, he may whisper its name, or some associated word, under his breath. Though the sounds emitted by the agent might be far too faint for the guesser in the next room to be consciously aware of them, yet they might, it is said, be of sufficient intensity to register at a subconscious level. That is, some part of his mind might register them, and so the receiver might get a clue to the sender's thoughts.

As far back as 1895 two Danish psychologists, F. C. C. Hansen and Alfred Lehmann[10], tried to show that some telepathy experiments carried out by Professor and Mrs. Henry Sidgwick, in which a hypnotized subject guessed two-digit numbers drawn from a bag and looked at by the hypnotist, could be explained away by involuntary whispering of the numbers by the agent. It was supposed that a person under hypnosis possessed more acute hearing than in the normal state, though for this there is no very conclusive evidence. To test the theory, the two psychologists sat with their heads close to the foci of two concave mirrors, and one of them thought hard of a number, keeping his lips closed. It was claimed that the other was frequently successful in picking up the number through involuntary whispers which proceeded from the agent. The question arises whether a person without moving his lips can produce either voluntary or involuntary whispers, or anything beyond inarticulate sounds in the nose and throat.

However, a few simple tests carried out by S.G.S. recently show that it is quite possible for a person to keep his lips firmly closed, and consciously articulate such words as LION or PELICAN sufficiently clearly for them to be identified by a listener who places his ear an inch or two from the whisperer's mouth and who has been told that the choice lies among the names of five given animals. The vowel sounds, indeed, can be produced by forcible breathing or by nasal snorting and certain consonantal sounds such as the L-sound do not require the use of the lips.

But a considerable number of the Sidgwick experiments had been successful with the agent and guesser in distant rooms, and the theory could scarcely apply to these. And it was conclusively shown by Professor Sidgwick[11] and Professor William James that the kind of errors made by their guessing subject were not such as would arise from mishearing faint whispers. That is, he showed no undue tendency to mistake 'nine' for 'five', 'seven' for 'eleven', etc.

At a later date Hansen and Lehmann admitted the cogency of the

Sidgwicks' experiments and arguments, and agreed that involuntary whispering was improbable as an explanation of the results.

Nevertheless, the theory was resurrected by Dr. J. L. Kennedy,[12] an American psychologist, in 1938. Kennedy showed bitter hostility to the subject.

After having failed to get any significant results in his own experiments, he concentrated on attacking the work of others. Kennedy placed two blindfolded persons at the foci of parabolic mirrors and found that when one of them concentrated on a mental task, whispers relating to this task could be picked up by the other. Whether these whispers are really 'unconscious', and whether they could be of any assistance to someone in the next room guessing cards at the rate of 25 a minute (as in the Stewart experiments), are questions which Kennedy does not answer.

So far as we are aware, there is no conclusive evidence that a class of persons exists whose acuteness of hearing is far outside the limits of the normal range, though isolated cases suggest such a possibility.

There was, for instance, the Latvian peasant child, Ilga K., studied by Professor von Neureiter,[13] Dr. Hans Bender,[14] and others. It was reported that this child, a mentally retarded girl of ten, could read any text, even one in a language foreign to her, when her teacher stood behind her 'silently' reading the text. A German commission which made dictaphone records of its experiments with Ilga K. came to the conclusion that her apparent thought-reading powers could be explained in terms of a very acute auditory capacity. The investigations proved beyond all doubt that the majority of Ilga's performances were due to slight auditory aids which she received from the agent standing a few feet away from her. Dr. Bender, however, maintained that in certain cases genuine thought-transference was strongly suggested.

The case was in the hands of ingenious experimenters who were also competent psychologists and physiologists, and it shows that we cannot rule out entirely the possibility that a supposed telepathic subject may be succeeding by means of an extremely acute hearing, until we have demonstrated that he still succeeds when placed at a considerable distance from the sender. At least two highly successful long-distance tests have now been reported, one by Dr. Rhine and one by ourselves; these are described in Chap. XVI.

## Errors in Recording and Checking

Certain of Rhine's critics suggested that his significant results might, in part, be accounted for by the supposition that the experimenters made numerous errors in recording the lists of guesses or card-symbols, or in ticking off correct hits, or in counting the numbers of such hits.

Now in a modern experiment no such errors should occur. The guesser in one room writes down his or her own guesses in ink in the guess column of an empty scoring sheet, and this list, signed by the subject, must from its very nature be accepted as final. Again, the experimenter prepares the lists of card-symbols *before* the experiment is held —perhaps from tables of random figures. These target lists are entered in the card-columns of empty scoring sheets, so that we have independent records of guesses and card-targets on separate sheets. Once recorded, these lists must be accepted as final. We must assume that the experimenter shows the correct number to the agent, and that the latter looks at the correct card corresponding to the number. Any subsequent mistakes would arise either during the comparison of the two lists or in the counting of the hits ticked off as correct. Moreover, a re-check can be made, and is made after the experiment.

But in some of the earlier methods used at Duke University and elsewhere there was a possibility of undetected error in the recording of either the subject's guesses or the order of the cards in the pack. We have seen how, in certain of the pure telepathy tests, the guesser called out aloud his guesses which were recorded by the experimenter who was also the agent. Similarly in some of the early clairvoyance tests the experimenter recorded the subject's guesses, and afterwards the order of the cards in the pack. A re-check of the guess lists was not possible in such cases, and the target-list could not be re-examined once the pack had been re-arranged.

Dr. Kennedy of Stanford University made a study of experimenters' errors by comparing their lists of targets and calls with independent records compiled by a second person. At a psychological congress he claimed that no fewer than 400 mistakes were found in 79,100 trials. He had, however, included among his recorders an old lady who was either hoaxing Kennedy or not very clear about what she was supposed to do, for she made mistakes by the dozen. Apparently her work helped to produce a goodly record of errors.

Fortunately, Professor Gardner Murphy[15] had become informed of Kennedy's activities, and came to the meeting primed with the details of similar experimental studies in one of which 175,000 voice calls were recorded with only 175 mistakes—an average of only one error in a thousand trials. Dr. Gardner Murphy's elaborate analysis, replete with graphs, impressed everyone that such errors were like angels' visits, few and far between, and incapable of accounting for the high scores. Kennedy, we understand, left the meeting a very discomfited man,

Many long series of experiments have been re-examined for errors in the checking of coincidences between target-cards and guesses. Such re-checks have shown that, almost invariably, the correct guesses are underestimated rather than overestimated. Checkers tend to overlook coincidences between target-card and guess and very seldom tick off guesses as correct when they are incorrect. Such errors are usually on the safe side. Thus Dr. Greenwood,[7] in a re-check of his 500,000 card matchings, found 90 mistakes, and of these 76 were hits which had passed unnoticed.

It is quite clear from these re-checks of successful or unsuccessful groups of data that in no case was the net error in checking and counting sufficient to affect seriously the significance or lack of significance of the series.

## Improper Selection of Data

It was suggested by several psychologists[16] that perhaps Dr. Rhine had repressed batches of data which gave only chance results. To take a purely imaginary example, an experimenter might test a large number of persons with the Zener cards. He might decide on the basis of the first 100 trials that some individuals were performing so badly that it was not worth his while to go on with them. The investigator might then abandon these low scorers, and continue only with those whose work showed a positive deviation on the first 100 guesses.

This would be perfectly legitimate if he started afresh with them, and discarded the high scores on the first 100 trials. But if he retained these initial scores, and added them to the subsequent data, he would be guilty of one of the worst statistical crimes—unsound selection of material. By discarding only the low or chance scores of the first 100 trials, he would have biassed his grand total improperly in favour of positive deviations.

There is no evidence that Rhine fell into this error in his early work, but it is perhaps a pity that he did not discuss this possibility in *Extra-Sensory Perception*, and so disarm criticism.

There is another point which may have occurred to the reader. We read in the newspapers and scientific journals of people who have obtained high scores in ESP experiments. But may not there be large numbers who amuse themselves with Zener cards, and who obtain only chance results which never see the light of publication? And may there not be serious young men all over the country who are doing thousands of trials and getting nothing out of it at all, and who do not even think it worth while to report their negative findings? If the results of all

46

experiments were pooled, might it not turn out that the grand total of hits did not deviate significantly from chance expectation?

The answer is, we think, that the real evidence for extra-sensory perception is contained in a limited number of well-controlled investigations by different people which have each registered such tremendous odds against the chance-coincidence theory that on no reasonable estimate of the existing numbers of experiments with negative results would their effect be nullified.

The Pearce-Pratt* series (p. 30) gave odds of the order of $10^{20}$ to 1 against chance on 1,825 trials with Zener cards. Now nobody in his senses could believe that $10^{10}$ or ten thousand million sets of 1,825 trials have been done in the whole world since the year 1931. But if we posit this absurd estimate as an upper limit, that would still give us odds of $10^{10}$, i.e. ten thousand millions to one against the supposition that the Pearce-Pratt results were a run of pure luck.

But, it may be objected, we are putting too much faith in the honesty of the three people concerned. Perhaps after all they may have been in collusion to fake the experiment.

There are, however, other careful series of experiments for which the odds against chance-coincidence are far greater. For instance, Dorothy R. Martin and Frances P. Stribic† of the University of California, carried out an excellently reported series of experiments using the DT clairvoyance technique with the packs of cards behind a screen. Their best subject, Mr. C. Jencks, obtained in 91,475 trials an average of nearly 7 hits per 25 with odds against chance of a truly astronomical order. A committee of American psychologists, asked to comment on the report, pronounced it adequate. Possibly the only weak point was that the 'card' records were written on the same sheet as the subject's guesses and adjacent to them, a procedure which might lead to undetectable errors in recording. A partial check, however, was made on the principle that an accurate card run must contain exactly five cards of each symbol, and this check, so far as it went, was satisfactory.

Another very good series was the Pratt-Woodruff[18] clairvoyance experiment consisting of 60,000 trials, which gave odds of more than a million to one against chance (see p. 56 for details).

Up to the year 1940 there were fewer than a dozen card-calling series reported by American workers which excluded most of the sources of error discussed in this chapter, and which at the same time produced odds against chance of more than a million to one. Of these satisfactory high-scoring series some were open to the objection (that of Riess[19,20] for instance) that the results were dependent on the good faith of a single

* III, 2.                          † III, 4, 5.

experimenter, or that the guesser might have gained access to the records (left lying in a drawer) before they were checked by the investigator. But even though the number of these impressive series is strictly limited, it is difficult to suppose that all of them were elaborate hoaxes engineered for personal notoriety, or to mystify the public. For nearly all the experimenters were persons in responsible academic positions, and one or two were known to be sceptics before they began their investigations.

But in addition to the small number of experimenters who obtained high scores there was a greater number of apparently trustworthy people who reported positive results with odds against chance varying between 100 to 1 and 1,000 to 1.

It would, however, be difficult to make out a case for extra-sensory perception on these minor results alone, since we have no means of estimating the number of unpublished series which gave purely chance deviations. We know that a good many psychologists in America including Professor E. T. Adams,[21] J. C. Crumbaugh,[22] Dr. J. L. Kennedy, Dr. Raymond Willoughby,[24] C. P. and J. H. Heinlein,[23] either published or recorded in manuscript form long series of negative investigations with Zener cards, running sometimes into tens of thousands of trials. And there must have been larger numbers of ordinary people who purchased packs of cards, and experimented with them privately without getting any results of interest.

The situation in ESP with regard to experiments with small odds against chance is, to some extent, paralleled in the biological sciences. Professor Evelyn Hutchinson[25] of Yale University has pointed out that many hundreds of papers are published every year in various branches of psychology and biology, describing experiments which support hypotheses with odds of no more than a hundred to one, and that the authors and editors seem well pleased with them. He remarks drily that, when this collection is considered as a whole, on the theory of probability alone, some of these papers are likely to contain erroneous conclusions, though just which papers it is impossible to say. Hutchinson adds: 'It would seem that in the ordinary orthodox sciences the position relative to chance is by no means so satisfactory as it is in the best parapsychological studies.'

The evidence for ESP, then, rests mainly on the high-scoring series, and, as the number of well-controlled and witnessed experiments with odds of millions to one against chance increases, it becomes less and less easy for ordinary scientific men to ignore it or brush it aside.

Unfortunately, high-scoring subjects who can maintain their average over a long period appear to be rather rare. So far as we know, none has been found in America since 1938, but in England Miss G. M. Johnson, tested with Mr. Tyrrell's* electrical machine, Mr. Basil Shackleton,† and Mrs. Gloria Stewart, investigated by the authors, have all three produced scores with astronomical odds against chance over periods varying from two to five years.

## General Criticisms

In 1938 the American Psychological Association arranged a symposium for the discussion of the adequacy of the experimental methods. Most of the sources of error we have discussed in this chapter were threshed out at the meeting and it was generally agreed that the methods at that time in use at Duke University were satisfactory. Indeed, Professor Chester Kellogg, hitherto one of the bitterest critics of extra-sensory perception, said in effect to Rhine: 'Go on with the methods you are now using, and you will find that you get no more extra-sensory perception.' This prophecy, we need hardly say, has been belied by the events of the past ten years.

Kellogg's†† animosity towards the whole subject may be judged from a paragraph he wrote in *The Scientific Monthly* for October 1937.

He said (p. 332):

'Since Dr. Rhine's reports have led to investigations in many other institutions, it might seem unnecessary to prick the bubble, as the truth eventually will out and the craze subside. But meanwhile the public is being misled, the energies of young men and women in their most vital years of professional training are being diverted into a side-issue and funds expended that might instead support research into problems of real importance for human welfare. This has gone so far that a new *Journal of Parapsychology* has been founded.'

This same critic said of the Pearce-Pratt experiment for which the odds work out at $10^{20}$ to 1 against the chance coincidence theory:

'Taking all the groups together, the results are positive and *somewhat significant, perhaps sufficiently so to warrant further study of the problem*' (italics ours). One wonders what odds Professor Kellogg would require to merit the appellation 'highly significant' as opposed to 'somewhat significant'.

It is interesting to contrast Professor Kellogg's cavalier dismissal of extra-sensory perception as a 'craze' and a 'side-issue' with the words of another distinguished psychologist, Mrs. Margaret Knight,[26] who writes as follows in *Science News* No. 18, November 1950:

* VI, 13.          † VII, 1; IX, 1.          †† II, 4.

'But as Thouless convincingly argues, it is a waste of time to conduct further laborious experiments merely to demonstrate the occurrence of ESP. This has now been established beyond reasonable doubt. The aim of future experiments should be to *elucidate the conditions* of its occurrence, for in this way alone can we hope to explain its nature. It will no doubt be many years—perhaps generations—before we can determine whether the phenomena fit into the accepted framework of knowledge, or whether they necessitate a revision of the whole system of postulates and presuppositions on which the modern scientific conception of the universe depends.'

Here we have two diametrically opposed views of the importance of ESP research.

A few critics took the position that, however great the odds are that the results of a card-guessing experiment are not due to chance, yet chance may have been responsible, since theoretically it is capable of producing *any* deviation from the average however great. It is, of course, *theoretically* possible for a monkey playing with the keys of a typewriter to tap out *by chance* a Shakespearian sonnet. But would anyone in his senses who came across such a feat believe that 'chance' was responsible? He would believe that he was hallucinated, or that the monkey had been marvellously trained, or he would accept almost any explanation rather than believe that the whole thing was a piece of pure luck. The answer to the assertion that chance, like certain *pères de famille, est capable de tout* is that it applies equally to all other fields of activity in which statistical methods are used. If statistics proved to be unreliable and of no practical value in biological work, experimenters would cease to make use of them, but this is not the case.

One or two extremists even suggested that the laws of probability need to be re-stated when applied to the large numbers of trials we meet with in card-guessing. But Dr. Greenwood's[7] monumental check of half a million guesses matched against cards for which they were not intended gave results which were in perfect accord with the laws of probability (see p. 40).

After 1938 the wave of criticism by American psychologists subsided. Criticism became more moderate in tone, or confined itself to points of minor importance and was sometimes helpful rather than destructive. The chief objections then urged against the research were the difficulty experienced in the finding of any subjects showing ESP ability, and the vagaries of the faculty, which apparently did not manifest itself in the presence of certain observers, especially those of a sceptical turn of mind. In the opinion of many psychologists these obstacles put ESP outside the range of scientific experiment. These are real difficulties, but not insuperable ones. Without question, the Linzmayers, the Pearces, the Shackletons, and the Stewarts are hard to discover, but this is no argument against the organization of an intensive search for them. One will certainly not find them by sitting in a psychology laboratory, twiddling one's thumbs and waiting for them to turn up. One must make contact with people interested in psychical research, and so get to hear of persons who believe themselves to be the possessors of psychical gifts. The experimenter in telepathy must have drive and energy, and be forever making enquiries after promising subjects and carrying out tests with them. And when a good subject is found, the psychologist should be prepared to conduct the experiments in the percipient's own home. If a couple of rooms are available, the experimental conditions can, with a little care, be made as watertight as can be desired. These gifted persons cannot be expected to make tedious journeys to and from a psychological laboratory, when the work can be done under more favourable conditions in their own homes.

As regards the presence of outside observers, the case of Shackleton showed conclusively that open-minded visitors do not necessarily prevent a good telepathic percipient from scoring at his usual high rate. By 'open-minded' we mean persons who have no strong bias in favour of ESP and no strong prejudice against it, but who are willing to accept evidence of a reasonably high standard.

But if being a telepathic percipient implies a susceptibility to unconscious influence by other minds, it is highly probable that the presence of a hostile observer will have an inhibiting effect on the guesser. Moreover, it is not easy to maintain scepticism about such a subject as ESP at a purely intellectual level; it easily degenerates into dislike, suspicion, and even hatred. It is idle and misleading to compare ESP with the better known mental processes, and argue that, because a man can do a piece of arithmetic correctly while he is being watched even by someone who dislikes him, or play a winning game of tennis in the presence of one who wants to see him lose, therefore a card-guesser ought to be unaffected by sceptical or antagonistic observers. For ESP is an unconscious faculty not under the control of the will of the possessor, who is not guided by any feelings of success or failure. Musical and poetical composition are, in part, processes which are matured in the unconscious regions of the personality, but ESP is wholly unconscious. The man who guesses an average of nine cards correctly out of 25 has not a glimmer of a notion how he does it. Unlike the tennis player, he cannot profit from his mistakes. But one would not expect even a poet to produce a good poem if he were surrounded by people who, he felt, viewed his activities with half-concealed scorn or humorous contempt.

The best he could do would be to churn out a few passable verses from which the informing spirit of poetry would be absent.

It is, however, surely sufficient that telepathy has been demonstrated over and over again by Basil Shackleton* and Mrs. Gloria Stewart† in the presence of academic visitors whose emotional scales were not heavily weighted on the side of either belief or disbelief.

It has often been urged against experiments in ESP that the findings—unlike those of physics and chemistry—cannot be repeated by other workers. If the statement means that Mr. Jones, agricultural chemist, or Dr. Brown, industrial psychologist, cannot, by running through a few packs of Zener cards after supper, be certain of getting extra-chance scores, we shall not dispute it.

At present the thing is not so easy as all that. The truth is that experiments in telepathy are difficult to repeat, but not impossible. One obvious reason is that the investigator is in the position of a chemist who wishes to experiment with some extremely rare substance that is hard to procure. In our case a human subject with high-grade extra-sensory powers corresponds to the rare substance. We feel convinced, however, that almost anyone whose mind is not completely closed to the possibility of ESP, or who is not animated by a desire to disprove it, can, with sufficient patience and hard work, obtain satisfactory evidence of its occurrence, after perhaps some initial disappointment.

Actually, many of the specific findings of ESP such as displacement of hits on to adjacent card-targets, decline of scoring down the run, and significant below-chance guessing, have been noted again and again by independent investigators.

Professor Hutchinson[25] has some interesting remarks on the question of whether ESP experiments can be repeated. No scientific experiment can be repeated unless the relevant conditions remain the same. In a telepathy experiment two such conditions are the presence of a good subject, such as Pearce or Shackleton, and the presence of a suitable agent. It is absurd to insist, as some scientists have done, that the same effects ought to be obtained when anyone else is substituted for Pearce or Shackleton. If a chemist observed some curious results while working with a rare element like europium, it would be silly for his critics to maintain that if the supply of europium was exhausted, no credit could be given to his discoveries unless he could obtain the same results with the use of, say, cerium or lanthanum.

The early criticism of ESP was concerned almost entirely with methods of experiment and evaluation; it was only rarely that ideological issues were raised. One man, however, H. Rogosin,[27] a psychologist of

* IX, 1.     † XV 10.

New York University, attacked Rhine on the ground that his interpretations of the Duke University experiments struck at the fundamentals of scientific thinking.

Rogosin[27] seems to have been particularly incensed by the attack of Waldemar Kaempffert, Science Editor of the *New York Times*, on psychology, which he called a 'sorry pseudo-science—in no position to give itself airs', and the contention of John J. O'Neill, Science Editor of the *New York Herald-Tribune*, that, if Rhine is upheld, all of traditional psychology might be 'thrown out of the window'. Above all, the conclusion of the psychologist Lucien Warner, that controls to allow for the effects of telepathy and clairvoyance should be employed as a matter of laboratory routine in all psychological experiments, seems to have touched Rogosin on the raw.

After a few ineffective attempts,[27] that will not bear examination, to discredit Rhine's methods, Rogosin appeals to Aristotle, Hobbes, and Locke in support of his contention that nothing can enter the mind except through the gateway of the senses, or by rational inference from data of sense perception.

It appears that men like Jeans, Eddington, and Millikan are to be held responsible for the 'present lamentable idealistic trend of modern culture'. It seems that the speculations of these physicists are being used to support Rhine's theories, and the susceptible American public is 'again being heavily propagandized in favour of a dualistic arrangement of psychological data.'

For centuries, we are told, science has been combating 'magic' and animistic theories, and now, *under the guise of science itself*, age-old misconceptions are being fostered. Rogosin believes that it is the duty of psychologists and scientists to 'combat "magic" wherever and whenever it appears', and that 'superstition should not be encouraged in our society.'

'Psychical ideas', says Rogosin, 'are anti-social in the fullest sense; they prevent people from thinking about how to reconstruct our society so that the people in it may get the maximum benefit possible.' As to this, he might have argued that the study of the remote nebulae, of dead languages, or of the mathematical theory of prime numbers are equally 'anti-social' employments. Rogosin thinks ESP is essentially 'a reaction against the materialistic trend of our times.' It is 'a flight from reality', 'a retreat from reason', 'a return to mysticism'. The wide publicity which Rhine's work has received indicates, according to Rogosin, that 'our organs of information are predominantly favourable to the theory of idealism.' But surely our better newspapers and broadcast programmes are merely a reflection of what the most intelligent people in the community are thinking.

Rogosin concludes his article with this parting shaft of prophecy:
'If, as Professor Gardner Murphy claims, Dr. J. B. Rhine's work will be remembered in the twenty-fifth century, I am inclined to believe it will be regarded as the twentieth century counterpart of astrology and phrenology.'

Although the above was written as late as 1939, Rogosin's trite arguments today have a faded, familiar, almost Victorian flavour. He still clings to the mechanistic conceptions of the last century. And how reminiscent of the days of Thomas Huxley is Rogosin's diatribe about the duty of science to combat superstition and magic! Then there is the complacent assumption that nothing can exist in the universe which does not obey the laws of present-day physics—a physics whose theories are in the melting pot! How should man, whose limited sensory apparatus was evolved in the first place to enable him to survive in a hostile world, and not to comprehend the mysteries of the universe—how should such a creature have the presumption to imagine that he can know more than a tiny fraction of what is happening in space and time? The nature of time and space themselves may be forever beyond the grasp of his intellect.

# CHAPTER V

# Confirmatory Series and Group Studies

The validity of any piece of scientific research depends ultimately upon its confirmation by other investigators working under improved conditions of control. But after we have fairly established the existence of the faculty of ESP, the next step is to carry out experiments designed to answer certain questions as to the conditions under which it operates, the classes of people who exhibit it in a marked degree, and so on. For instance, are children more successful at card-guessing than adults? Is ESP common among the inmates of mental hospitals? Is the faculty correlated with intelligence in any way? The only way in which we can answer such questions is by comparing the ESP performances of groups of individuals selected at random from distinct populations having the different characteristics we wish to investigate. We could, for example, select 100 children at random all belonging to the same age group, and 100 adults, and make each person run through 500 ESP trials. We could then find the average pooled score per 25 trials of the 200 persons and count how many children and how many adults made scores which were above and below this average. By means of a four-fold contingency table we could then estimate whether, on the whole, the children had done better than the adults.* It would, of course, be essential that the children and the adults were tested with the same procedure and under similar conditions. It would not do, for instance, if the adults were all Frenchmen and the children English. In fact, the individuals tested in the two groups would have to be selected randomly from the respective populations.

* It is not strictly correct merely to apply a test of significance to the difference in the mean scores of the two groups and it is perhaps unfortunate that Dr. Humphrey and Dr. Schmeidler whose work is described in this chapter have frequently used this method, but we do not think that their conclusions are seriously invalidated.

## Confirmatory Series

### (i) THE PRATT-WOODRUFF SERIES (1939)*

So far we have considered experiments in which the subject indicates his response by calling aloud the card-symbol, or writing down his guess. But in the present series of experiments carried out by Pratt and Woodruff in 1939, a cognitive response is replaced by a motor response. The guesser and the experimenter, Woodruff, sat on opposite sides of an opaque vertical screen 18 inches high by 24 inches wide with a horizontal slit between the bottom of the screen and the table. Beneath this slit was a row of five blank cards, and above these, pinned to the screen on the guesser's side, were cards bearing the five Zener symbols. The order of these symbols was not known to Woodruff, the experimenter handling the cards, but was known to the guesser and could be seen by the second experimenter Pratt while the test was in progress. One of the experimenters shuffled a pack of Zener cards very thoroughly and cut it with a paper-knife.

If the guesser thought the top card of the pack was, say, a plus sign, he would touch with a pointer the blank card which was directly underneath the plus sign on the screen. On seeing the pointer through the slit at the bottom of the screen, the experimenter would place the top card face downwards opposite the blank card chosen. The guesser would then point to the blank card which he thought corresponded to the new top card, and the experimenter would lift off this card, and place it opposite the appropriate blank card.

The second experimenter, Pratt, was sitting on the guesser's side of the screen and made an independent record of the guesser's choices. The guesser's pointer flew rapidly from one blank card to another, and the first experimenter, Woodruff, followed its rapid motion with his eyes, quickly placing each card on its proper pile. Pratt was sitting at a table a few feet behind the guesser but somewhat to her right so that he could watch her pointer. The placing of the 25 cards occupied only about 20 seconds, and a check was then made. The number of correct cards under each symbol was counted by both experimenters, and the score recorded on separate sheets independently by Pratt and Woodruff. A third record was also kept for filing. At the end of 25 trials, the guesser would change the order of the five Zener symbols pinned on the face of the screen, so that this order was always unknown to the first experimenter who handled the cards while guessing was in progress.

As the experiment was a clairvoyance test, the first experimenter did not look at the faces of the cards when he lifted them off, and, at the

* IV, I8.

rapid rate maintained, we can be certain that auditory cues were ruled out, especially since the card-dealer had his eyes constantly fixed on the fast-moving pointer, and not on the backs of the cards. To prevent the possible loss of any of the data, serially numbered identifiable sheets were used. In all, 60,000 trials were recorded and the positive deviation above chance expectation was equivalent to 4·99 standard deviations, with odds against chance-coincidence of at least a million to one. This experiment is of special interest, since a number of unselected persons were used as guessers, and group tests seldom yield a very significant score.

## (ii) A 'BLIND MATCHING' TEST[1]

In the experiment described above it is stated that the pointing by the guesser was always a little ahead of the placing of the card by Woodruff. But if this was not the case, it might be deemed possible for the guesser to get a glimpse of the card as it was being placed by peering through the slit. This was obviated however by a small vertical screen 3 inches high which was placed 3½ inches behind the aperture on the experimenters side of the screen. This possibility was, again, ruled out in the following experiment done by Pratt in 1936 at Columbia University, New York.[1] The screen with a slit at the bottom was used, as in the preceding description. But, instead of the guesser having the five Zener symbols pinned on his side of the screen in a row, he was asked to point to any one of five blank cards, each of which had a Zener card concealed beneath it. These blank cards were in a row under the slit, and adequate precautions had been taken to ensure that neither Pratt nor the guesser knew the order of the five symbols under the blanks. As the subject pointed to a blank card, Pratt would lift off the top card of his shuffled pack, and place it face downwards in one of five boxes which had been put opposite the five blank cards. In this manner the guesser was making Pratt match the cards of his pack against five *unknown* cards.

At first sight it would seem that, for the guesser to make a correct matching, two separate acts of clairvoyant perception would be necessary. He would have to divine the card on top of Pratt's pack as well as the order of the symbols under the five blank cards. But it may well be that the subject was able to distinguish between likeness and unlikeness in a single act of clairvoyance, without its being first necessary for him to identify the actual symbols.

When the 25 cards were distributed in the five boxes according to the guesser's directions, the screen was removed, the five key-cards under the blanks were turned up, and the number of correct hits under each symbol was counted by both Pratt and the guesser. For the next run of

25 a fresh set of five key-symbols was concealed under the blank cards with the same elaborate precautions.

The guesser, a Mrs. M., who had previously been successful with a less rigorous technique, was, on 30th October, 1936, set to work with the 'blind matching' procedure, and between this date and November 9th she ran through 7,800 trials. These gave a positive deviation from chance expectation of 188 hits, which corresponds to a critical ratio of 5·2 and odds of almost five millions to one against chance.

Towards the end of this period her scoring had begun to wane, and on November 10th she was put back on the less careful procedure, in the hope that she would recover her former high level. There was no improvement, and she was returned to the 'blind matching' technique, and put through another 13,700 trials with only chance results. The effect of this dilution with chance data was to reduce the critical ratio of 5·2 for the first 7,800 trials to a critical ratio of only 3·2 on the total of 21,500 guesses done by the blind matching technique. Thus the final odds against chance were only about 720 to 1.

It is, of course, open for the sceptic to argue that had Pratt continued with Mrs. M. for a few more thousand guesses, the total score would probably have fallen to chance level, but, even so, the block of 7,800 consecutive trials which gave odds of two millions to one against chance could scarcely be a mere run of luck, even if selected anywhere from a group of 21,500.

### (iii) THE MARTIN-STRIBIC SERIES*

During the years 1937–9 an extensive series of clairvoyance tests was carried out by Dorothy R. Martin and Frances P. Stribic of the University of Colorado. In all, 311,750 trials were made by 322 guessers, but we need concern ourselves only with those experiments in which the safeguards appear to have been fairly adequate. Thirteen subjects were tested individually by means of a DT (down through) procedure which we shall describe.

The guesser was seated at a table, and was separated from the experimenter by a 15 inch by 18 inch opaque, wooden screen without any apertures. The experimenter shuffled and cut the pack of Zener cards, and placed it face downwards in front of her, taking care not to see the bottom card. The guesser on the other side of the screen then wrote down a list of 25 guesses intended for the 'down through' order of the pack. He then brought his list of symbols to the experimenter, and seated himself on her left.

The experimenter turned the top card of the pack face upwards, and

* III, 4, 5.

called out its value which was recorded by the guesser on his sheet opposite the corresponding guess. After the card was recorded, the experimenter checked the accuracy of the record, and then lifted off the card. This process was repeated for each card in the pack. At the occurrence of a 'hit', a line was drawn on the list through card and call, and the 'hit' was checked by both experimenter and subject from the card lying on top of the pack.

After September 1938, however, the recording of card values was done by the experimenter, the subject's guess-list being shielded during the process. At the end of a run of 25, the experimenter verified that the list of card-targets contained exactly five cards of each symbol.

Sometimes a trained student was employed in place of the principal experimenter, but there was no evidence that the rate of scoring varied with the person who acted as experimenter, and this negatives any suggestion that high scores were due to the incompetence or dishonesty of any particular experimenter.

The best of the thirteen subjects, Mr. C. Jencks, who did 25,000 guesses, obtained an excess of 1,893 hits above chance expectation, which corresponds to a critical ratio of 29. The next best, Mr. R. Simmons, obtained results which gave a critical ratio of 11 in 12,500 trials, while the results of three others gave critical ratios of 6 or more. No one can question the tremendous significance of these results.

The best subject, Mr. C. Jencks, was put through another 25,000 trials with the variation that now he was asked to guess up through the pack from bottom to top, and in this series he did even better.

In another series with Mr. Jencks ten packs of Zener cards were shuffled, and placed in a row behind the screen by the experimenter. One of the packs was then isolated from the rest, and pushed close to the centre of the bottom edge of the screen. Mr. Jencks, who had not seen any of the packs, was then asked to guess 'down through' this chosen pack. For the next run the pack previously used would be returned to the row, and another pack pushed out to the front, and the subject would be asked to concentrate on this pack. It was found that with 110 packs selected in this way Mr. Jencks obtained a positive deviation of 349 hits from chance expectation, and this corresponds to a critical ratio of 16. When his guesses for the isolated pack were scored against the orders of the cards in each of the nine packs which remained in the row, the average number of hits per 25 was only 5·02, as compared with 8·17 per 25 on the chosen packs.

This demonstrates a strange selective action in the ESP process which apparently is under the control of the guesser's own volition. It also renders the hypothesis that clairvoyance has its basis in some kind of physical radiation emanating from the cards themselves extremely improbable.*

Another interesting feature of the 'up through the pack' guessing of Mr. Jencks was a progessive decline in the scoring rate as he worked through the pack from the first five cards guessed to the last five.

Perhaps the chief weakness in this series was the use of undergraduates as experimenters.

## Group Experiments

We have seen that the really compelling evidence for ESP, or *psi*, as it is sometimes called, rests on the performances of a small number of persons who have scored consistently above chance expectation over considerable periods. But such individuals are hard to discover, and many experimenters try to obtain results of lesser significance by pooling the scores of a large number of quite ordinary persons chosen more or less at random.

The assumption underlying such tests is that out of, say, a hundred persons a small percentage may possess some slight *psi* capacity, which may show up in the pooled results as a slightly significant positive deviation. The method is not very promising. In the first place we know that individuals do not always display the same type of ESP. One will tend to get positive deviations on the 'target'-card, another below-chance deviations, and others may displace their hits on to the preceding or following cards. Positive and negative deviations—if we assume that some of these are due to ESP and not to chance—may tend to cancel each other, and so the whole group may show a score which is near to chance expectation. Further, unless we decide before we start that each person is to make the same number of guesses, say, 500, and that, say, just 100 persons are to be tested, there is the possibility that by watching the critical ratio of the total score as we proceed, we may go on till we reach a CR of, say, 2·8 (odds 200 to 1), and then stop at this favourable point. We are quite convinced that a great many group demonstrations of ESP are spurious, being due to optional stopping. Very often it turns out that in a group of 50 persons with a total score corresponding to 2·8 standard deviations there is not a single individual whose score is in any way remarkable, or who shows the least promise. If we were to test each of these persons separately over any length of time, probably not one would exhibit any signs of real ESP capacity. To claim that a *group* shows evidence of ESP, while the individuals composing it do not, is, to

* This is a challenging result to those who, like Mr. Spencer Brown, maintain that ESP is a mere statistical artifact due to non-randomness.

say the least, disturbing. It is, of course, perfectly legitimate to test, say, 300 persons for ESP, pick out the best scorers, and subject each of them separately to a further extended investigation.

Perhaps one or two illustrations will make this clear.

In the year 1940–1 A. A. Foster[2] deputed Miss Doyle to carry out ESP tests with Red Indian children living a primitive life on the western Canadian plains. Fifty children were put through 125 guesses each with Zener cards; the screened matching method described on p. 56 was used. On the total of 6,250 trials 1,347 hits were obtained, compared with an expectation of 1,250. The deviation is +97, and the critical ratio 3·07, with corresponding odds against the result's being due to chance of a little over 400 to 1.

A further experiment based on a 'Yes' or 'No' response ($p = \frac{1}{2}$) led only to chance deviations.

At the end of his paper the author remarks:

'Finally it may be said that at least one group of American Indian children have given scores in ESP card tests that are ascribable only to the ability known as extra-sensory perception.'

Surely the conclusion is unjustified. There is no mention whatever of the individual scores. Nor is there any attempt to submit the children who made high scores—if any such existed—to further careful tests. Here we have merely a suggestive result, the *beginning* of an investigation which is never completed. We cannot even be reasonably sure that the experimenter, who had had only a brief experience of this sort of work, was really competent.

Next let us consider an investigation carried out by Robert Shulman[3] with 141 mental patients at the Hudson River State Hospital, New York, in 1937. The patients were classified by the resident physician into 14 groups according to the nature of the mental illnesses from which they suffered. Thus there were the involutional melancholics, the manic-depressive-manics, the alcoholic psychotics, and so on, the numbers in the different groups ranging from 5 to 25. The method used was the screened matching procedure, which has the advantage that the guessers need not learn the symbols, but only have to point to them with a stick.

A total of 79,500 trials (clairvoyance) was given to the 141 subjects, but there were variations in the numbers of trials done by each subject. On the grand total there was a small deviation of +55, which is quite insignificant. Widely different numbers of trials were done by the 14 groups, and in only one group—that of the manic-depressive-depressed patients—was there a significant deviation from the expected number of hits. This group of 12 persons did 12,250 trials, and achieved a critical ratio +3·388. If this is considered *in isolation*, the corresponding odds against the result being due to chance amount to about 1,400 to 1, but, since the result was chosen as the best out of 14 results, the true odds would be only about 100 to 1 against chance. When, however, we come to examine the separate performances of the twelve persons who constitute the manic-depressive-depressed group, we find that not one of these is in the least impressive. It is true that ten of the twelve achieve small positive deviations, and that one patient's score just reaches two standard deviations, but neither of these facts has much mathematical significance. Moreover, there is no attempt whatever to continue experiments with individual members of the manic-depressive-depressed group. The investigation must be considered to be quite inconclusive, and similar objections apply to a great many of the group experiments done in America.

Some experimenters, having worked with a large number of unselected persons and obtained no significant deviation, either positive or negative, rather than admit failure, resort to what they call 'finer tests' of ESP. They look for significant 'decline' effects in the run of 25, and, if these are absent, they search for more obscure abnormalities in the distribution of hits. Some of these 'second order' effects are so recondite that it is easier to regard them as statistical artifacts than as evidence of ESP. And even when these methods fail, the over-enthusiastic investigator can still perform dichotomies on his material to his heart's content. He will attempt to show, for example, that the women have scored above chance, and the men below chance, and that the difference between the average scores is significant. Or, if this does not succeed, he will divide his group into those who like outdoor sports and those who prefer indoor amusements, and see whether this arrangement separates the positively-scoring 'sheep' from the negatively-scoring 'goats'. It is pretty certain that, if he tries hard enough, he will hit on a classification that gives odds of about a hundred to one against chance. The fact that there is no very significant deviation in his grand total of hits from what chance might be expected to produce is quite a minor consideration with this kind of experimenter, because he is determined to discover evidence of ESP at all costs, and he usually does discover it—to his own satisfaction at least. These remarks, however, do not apply to the very significant dichotomies discovered by Humphrey and Schmeidler in the sections which follow.

## ESP and Personality

There is no really conclusive evidence that persons who rate high in intelligence tests are good ESP guessers. Dr. Betty M. Humphrey[4] of Duke University correlated ESP scores of persons who took part in five group experiments with their intelligence ratings as determined by various scales such as the Stanford-Binet test, the Henmon-Nelson test, and the psychological examination for American college students. Only in two cases out of seven were significant positive correlations obtained, and these two gave odds of only 100 to 1 in favour of an association between ESP scoring and some type of intelligence. Miss E. M. Bond[5] of Duke University made a study of a group of 22 fourth and fifth grade retarded school children, but found no correlation between their ESP performance and their intelligence ratings.

In the experiments by S.G.S. at University College, London, he* tested large numbers of very intelligent students, but did not find a single person who was able to guess consistently above chance expectation.

One high-scoring subject discovered by Raleigh M. Drake[6] in America was a boy of sub-normal intelligence. The case, however, is a somewhat dubious one and might possibly be accounted for by auditory promptings by the boy's mother. On the other hand, one or two of Rhine's gifted ESP guessers, such as Pearce and Linzmayer, appear to have been college students of some intellectual ability. The two subjects, Basil Shackleton and Mrs. Stewart were, we should say, both of normal intelligence.

Nor does there appear to be any very convincing evidence that mental patients are good at card-guessing. It is true that a few psychiatrists, such as Dr. Ehrenwald,[7] have reported instances of telepathy between themselves and their patients. But these were clinical observations, and not experimental tests. Moreover, even the best of these cases will hardly bear critical examination; the incidents described seldom seem to be outside the range of chance-coincidence or other normal explanations. And to make matters worse, psycho-analysts interested in telepathy often show a misplaced ingenuity in finding symbolic interpretations of the weak cases which they present as evidence of thought-transference.

But there are no satisfactory experimental findings to justify the conclusion that psychotics of any class are better card-guessers than normal people.

## The Work of Dr. Betty M. Humphrey [13,14,15,16,19,20,26]

Attempts have been made by Dr. Humphrey of Duke University to establish a correlation between certain personality traits and ability at ESP guessing. A group of ordinary persons is divided into two classes,

A and B, according to the way in which they respond to some personality test, T. The members of the group, who are kept ignorant of their gradings, are then asked to do the same number of guesses at ESP cards, or to make drawings in response to pictures concealed in envelopes. The tests may be of the clairvoyance type, or may allow the operation of telepathy from an agent. Numerical scores are allotted to each person's performance, and the total scores for classes A and B are found. The problem is to discover a test T which separates the guessers into a class A, say, which has a total score significantly above chance expectation, and a class B whose total score is at or below chance expectation. It may happen, however, that the positive deviation of class A and the negative deviation of class B are neither of them separately significant, but that the algebraic difference of the two deviations is very significant.

The underlying assumption is that, when a large group of people is set to work at guessing cards, a certain small percentage will possess the kind of ESP ability which tends to make them score above the level of chance, and another small percentage the kind of ESP ability which tends to produce scores below chance expectation by the systematic avoidance of the target. If positive and negative ESP are both operating, the total score on the whole group may not differ much from chance expectation, since the positive and negative ESP deviations will tend to cancel each other. In other words, these two sorts of ESP would yield scores both above and below the average, but the total effect might well be negligible. Thus a group experiment, which at first sight was a failure, might in reality be highly successful, because some people possessed ESP of a positive kind and others the ability to score below the chance level.

But does this sort of thing happen frequently in actual practice? We think we can assure the reader that *in general* it does not. There is a very simple test for the detection of this kind of effect. We have only to apply what is known as a chi-squared test to each person's score, and add the various values of chi-squared. We then have recourse to a well-known table first compiled by Karl Pearson. We have applied the test to a large number of group experiments with over-all scores at chance level, and never did we find evidence of this mixed sort of scoring. But possibly a few groups do exhibit it.

## Two Types of Personality

Dr. Humphrey's 1946 experiments were based upon some observations made by Miss P. Elkisch[8] on children's drawings. Miss Elkisch found that a child or an unsophisticated adult, when asked to draw something 'out of his own head', will reveal by the way in which he executes his drawing certain facts about his inner personality.

Generally Miss Elkisch[8] was able to distinguish between what she called 'expansive' sketches and 'compressive' sketches. The 'expansive' type of drawing showed imagination, vitality, freedom of expression, and a sense of background in relation to the object drawn. The 'compressive' type showed timidity, inhibition, lack of imagination, and a failure to make the best use of the space available. We are all familiar with the 'expansive' type of person in ordinary life. He or she talks incessantly, expresses his or her views freely on every subject; indeed, the less his knowledge of the subject, the more he will talk about it. He is the person who likes 'to hear himself talk', though his intelligence is sometimes of a very mediocre quality. Usually he is a 'good mixer' when he is not a bore. His general habit of mind may be inaccurate.

The inhibited or 'compressive' type, on the other hand, talks but little, and hates to talk about subjects of which he has not made any careful study. His intelligence is often of good quality. Being often sensitive to the mental quality of the people he meets, he does not readily unburden himself to those with whom he feels he has little in common. Hence he is not 'hail fellow, well met'. He is often meticulous in the formulation and expression of his thought and so does not talk freely. He often detests flights of fancy and vague conjectures.

## The First Experiments

It occurred to Dr. Humphrey[18] that, if in a clairvoyance experiment a person were asked to make a sketch aimed at a drawing contained in an opaque sealed envelope, there might be found to exist some relation between the expansive-compressive quality of the sketch and the paranormal ability of the person to respond to the drawing in the envelope. Fortunately, Dr. C. E. Stuart[9, 10, 11, 12] of Duke University had perfected a preferential matching method, based on statistical principles, which enabled an experimenter to estimate the degree of resemblance or association between the drawings in four sealed envelopes and four sketches made by a guesser and intended to resemble the drawings in some way. Stuart's theory was that a person's paranormal response to a concealed drawing need not take the form of a more or less accurate reproduction of either the form or the precise meaning of the drawing. For instance, if the drawing was a ship, the subject might respond by sketching a flag-staff, or even a fish. A numerical score was allotted to each person's performance with the four sealed envelopes. This score

F                                    65

was based upon matchings made independently by two judges, and, on the assumption that there was no more than a chance resemblance between the four originals and the four sketches intended for them, the average score worked out at 40.

The next thing was to decide which sketches showed 'expansive' and which 'compressive' characteristics. A judge, who knew nothing as to which sketches were successful and which failures, examined each sketch, and assigned to it a score of 1 if it showed obvious 'expansive' qualities, 0 if it was clearly a 'compressive' sketch, and $\frac{1}{2}$ if the issue was doubtful. Thus, as there were four sketches, each guesser would be given a score lying between 0 and 4, and those with total scores of 2 or more were ranked as 'expansive', while those with scores less than 2 were labelled 'compressive'. Actually the rating was done independently by two judges, and the average score for each drawing was taken as the true score. It was found, as a rule, that the judgments were in close agreement.

It then remained to total the picture guessing scores of the 'expansives' and those of the 'compressives', and find out whether there was any significant statistical difference between them.

Dr. Humphrey's initial discovery[13] was based on the picture-guessing performances of 96 subjects, 41 of whom were rated as 'expansive' and 55 as 'compressive'. Subsequently she applied[26] the method to five other series of clairvoyance experiments with drawings. It was found that the 'expansives' scored on the average above chance expectation, and the 'compressives' below the chance level. When the results of all six series were pooled, it was noted that the difference between the scores of the 'expansives' and 'compressives' was highly significant, with odds against its being due to chance amounting to about 300,000 to 1.

Further, the total score of the 'expansives' showed a positive deviation above the chance level with odds of 1,000 to 1 against its being due to chance, while the total 'compressive' score was below the chance score, the negative deviation corresponding to odds of 2,500 to 1.

Yet the grand total of 'compressives' plus 'expansives' showed a score that was not significantly above or below the score that chance might be expected to produce. In fact the *total* result showed no evidence of ESP.

It would seem, then, that the 'expansives' on the whole produced sketches which had points of resemblance with the originals in the envelopes, but the 'compressives' apparently on the whole tended to *avoid* in their drawings the characteristics of the original, and so achieved a smaller degree of resemblance than even chance guessing might be expected to produce. This systematic avoidance of resemblances and ideas associated with the drawing inside the envelope must

66

surely imply that at some level of his mind the 'compressive' subject was aware of this drawing, but from some perverse motives drew a sketch which differed from it.

But even more curious findings are to follow. So far we have dealt only with the case of drawings concealed in envelopes and not looked at by an agent. The 'expansive-compressive' technique was now applied[14] to six series of tests in which a 'sender' in a distant room looked at pictures. In these experiments the guessers who drew sketches were trying to respond to the thoughts of the agent who concentrated on the pictures. The drawings made by the 239 subjects were scored for success or failure exactly as in the previous clairvoyance tests, and the subjects rated as 'expansive' or 'compressive' from their sketches.

But now it was found that the 'compressives' and not the 'expansives' scored on the whole above chance level, while the 'expansives' scored below chance expectation. In other words, as soon as telepathy was introduced, the findings[14] were reversed completely. This was fairly consistent over the six series of tests. The difference between the average scores of 'compressives' and 'expansives' was quite significant, with odds against chance of 312 to 1. When the same subject was given ESP tests at different times, it was found that his 'expansive' or 'compressive' rating did not always remain unchanged. A person who drew an 'expansive' sketch on one occasion would perhaps draw a 'compressive' one at another time. This change appeared to be due to a change of mood. It was usually accompanied by a change from above-chance scores to below-chance scores. Thus the 'expansive-compressive' rating did not necessarily correspond to any permanent trait in a person's mentality.

In conformity with the above discoveries, Miss McMahan* found that 'expansive' subjects, who had been selected because they had produced high scores in clairvoyance tests, scored well below chance expectation when they were made to do tests in 'pure' telepathy. On the other hand, 'compressive' subjects who had scored below chance expectation in clairvoyance tests obtained large above-chance scores with 'pure' telepathy (cf. Chap. XV, p. 255).

## Later Experiments

It was hoped that the 'expansive-compressive' technique would also serve to separate the 'high scorers' from the 'low scorers' in experiments with Zener cards. Promising results were reported at first,[16] but later series showed that the test was unreliable with this class of material.

A man's personality is revealed to some extent by his likes and dis-

* XV, 8.

likes, and the late Dr. Charles Stuart[17] studied the relation between guessing ability and personality along these lines. He compiled a list of sixty items likely to be of interest to the ordinary college man or woman. Each item was inserted in a question such as: 'Do you like dramatics?' or 'Do you like geography?', etc. If the student had a moderate liking for the item he wrote L against it, and if he liked it very much he wrote LL. If he was indifferent he wrote I, and if he rather disliked it, he wrote D, while DD denoted intense dislike. The sixty items were then scored by the experimenter who awarded +1 for L, +2 for LL, 0 for I, −1 for D, and −2 for DD. The algebraic sum of the sixty scores gave the 'interests score' of the individual. Each member of the group was allotted a score before taking part in a clairvoyance experiment with Zener cards.

Now Stuart divided his group into two sections on the basis of their interest scores. He made a 'histogram', or graph of the distribution of scores, found the 'median' score, i.e. the score which was attained or exceeded by half the members of the group, and marked on each side of it points known as the 'quartiles', the upper and lower quartiles being the scores which were attained or exceeded by three quarters and one quarter respectively of the members of the group. All scores lying between the quartiles belonged to the 'mid-range'. The extremely high or extremely low scores were those which lay beyond the two quartiles, i.e. outside the mid-range. A large negative score meant that the person possessed a large number of dislikes and few likes, and *vice versa* for a high positive score. These two classes together constituted the 'extreme' scores. A moderate score lying inside the 'mid-range' implied a person who had a normal number of both likes and dislikes, The 'extreme' group consisted of students with either a very wide or a very narrow range of college interests.

In sixteen series of clairvoyance experiments with Zener cards there were 258 guessers rated as 'mid-range', and 259 as 'extreme range'. The 'mid-range' group produced a positive deviation of 108 on 17,775 trials, and the 'extreme' section a negative deviation of 133 on 17,900 trials. These results in themselves are of borderline significance, but the odds against there being such a marked difference in the two series are about 700 to 1.

## A Combination of Tests

Miss Humphrey[19] next applied the 'expansive-compressive' technique to the scores of 515 of the above 517 subjects. This separated the group into high and low scorers, but the difference in the scores of the two sections was not significant.

When, however, she picked out the smaller group that was both 'mid-range' and 'expansive', and compared its average score with that of the group which was both 'compressive' and 'extreme', she found she had achieved a much more significant dichotomy.

The 'mid-range'-expansives produced a positive deviation of 82 (CR = +2·40), while the 'extreme'-compressives gave a negative deviation of 111 (CR = −2·58).

The odds against chance for such a score difference work out at nearly 2,000 to 1.

## A New Set of Questions

Dr. Humphrey[19] studied the replies to the sixty questions made by the persons who took part in three of the sixteen above-mentioned clairvoyance series. She noticed that there were fourteen questions to which the high-scorers and the low-scorers responded very differently, and from these she constructed a new scoring scale which proved more satisfactory than the one based on the original 60 questions. When this scale was applied to the remaining thirteen series, it divided the group into two sections with significantly different mean scores. Further, in the 'high-scoring' section the majority of students showed positive deviations, while in the 'low' section the majority showed negative deviations.

It is of interest to learn that 'high-scorers' like history, dramatics, bridge, formal occasions and salemanship, are indifferent to cowboys, stamps, birds and dislike nature study.

'Low-scorers' like military drill, boxing, animal zoos, geography, and dislike algebra.

All this may sound fantastic, but it does look as if the method has succeeded when applied to certain groups of unselected persons by experimenters at Duke University. On the face of it these experiments ought to be repeatable with other groups in other universities. We ought to be able to obtain similar results in England. Dr. West,[18] in London, has applied the 'expansive-compressive' treatment to fifty British subjects, using both pictures and ESP cards, but with no success. Would all the other experiments fail when tried out in this country? If so, why? We should not, of course, expect to get a significant dichotomy if the group tested did not contain any persons possessing even a rudimentary gift for ESP. But why are the Americans so consistently successful when they work with quite ordinary people as subjects? It is to be hoped that investigators in other countries will lose no time in repeating these fascinating and important experiments.

There is, of course, the further question whether the significant positive deviations produced by the 'expansives' or 'mid-range' persons in the 'interests' scale are flashes in the pan which would not appear again if we continued to apply ESP tests to the 'high-scorers'. If it were found that the 'high-scoring' section went on scoring above chance expectation for a considerable period, these methods would have immense practical value.

## Dr. Schmeidler's Experiments[21, 22, 23 24, 25]

Dr. Gertrude Schmeidler of the City College, New York, has been working on rather different lines. Since 1943 she has been trying to discover whether belief or disbelief in the possibility of paranormal cognition on the part of the guessers has any effect on the score in an experiment with ordinary Zener cards. She noticed early that people who laughed at ESP tended to score below the chance level, while the believers tended to score a little above expectation. Then she commenced experiments on a very large scale. She divided her guessers[21] into two groups, which she nicknamed 'sheep' and 'goats'. A 'goat' was a person who, before making his guesses, had expressed a conviction that ESP was impossible under the conditions of the experiment; a 'sheep' was a person who, if not optimistic, thought that it might occur. The 'goats' in short were the unbelievers. In one of the early tests Dr. Schmeidler, in order to make things as unpleasant as possible for the 'goats', provided them with blunt stubs of pencil and dirty scraps of paper on which to record their guesses. The 'sheep' on the other hand were accorded all the amenities. She found that the average score of the 'sheep' was a little above 5, and that of the 'goats' a little below. This was encouraging, and she persevered.

Dr. Schmeidler[22] had collected up to the year 1948 the huge aggregate of 185,725 guesses, using a clairvoyance technique. Of these 97,725 were made by the 'sheep' and 88,000 by the 'goats'. A permanent record of the card-targets was made from tables of random numbers before the experiment began. The card-lists were concealed from both the experimenter and the guessers.

It was found that the average score per 25 of the 'sheep' was 5·15 and that of the 'goats' was 4·92. These averages appear at first sight to be very close to 5, the chance score. But owing to the enormous number of trials, the score of the 'sheep' is so far above the chance level that it would be expected to occur only once in 400,000 such colossal experiments! The 'goat' score on the other hand is very little below chance expectation with odds of about 50 to 1.

The difference between the scores of the 'sheep' and 'goats' is so marked that it could be expected to happen only once in a million and a half such experiments.

The 'goat' may be perfectly friendly and imagine he is trying his best, but at some unconscious level of his mind he disapproves of what he is doing, and this, thinks Dr. Schmeidler, prevents ESP from operating in the positive sense, and the 'goat' produces a negative deviation in conformity with his negative attitude.

Dr. Schmeidler[23] next made use of a technique that had been perfected by Dr. Ruth Monroe, who employed the Rorschach ink-blot test to estimate the degree of social adjustment in college students.

In this method the subject is handed a series of ten cards on each of which is printed an irregular ink-blot. Certain of the cards are in colour and the rest without colour. The subject is asked to describe what he sees in each blot in much the same fashion as a person sees pictures in the fire. According to the type of response he makes he reveals to the psychologist characteristic clues as to the nature of his personality. Those who do not concentrate on small details but respond to the figure as a whole are generally fond of abstract thinking. Persons who see figures in motion—climbing monkeys for instance—are as a rule endowed with a rich emotional life, while those who are influenced mainly by the coloured cards are more responsive to their external environment than to the inner working of their minds. By means of a scoring system applied to the Rorschach indications the psychologist Dr. Monroe was able to discover how well a student was adjusted to the social group in which he lived and worked. It was found that those who were badly adjusted to their environment could not make the best use of their intellectual abilities. Acting on this hint, Dr. Schmeidler gave Rorschach tests to 650 of her card-guessers. She thus divided the group into four sections—the well-adjusted 'sheep' and the poorly-adjusted 'sheep', the well-adjusted 'goats' and the poorly-adjusted 'goats'. Her surmise was that the 'sheep' who were well-adjusted would get higher scores than the mal-adjusted 'sheep', and the well-adjusted 'goats' would produce larger *negative* deviations than the poorly-adjusted 'goats'. That is to say, poor adjustment tended to inhibit both 'positive' scoring and 'negative' scoring. Dr. Schmeidler was careful to complete her scoring of the Rorschach test before she saw the students' clairvoyance results. She found that experiment confirmed her conjectures. The group of 'sheep' who had been given the Rorschach test had an average score of 5·12 hits per 25 but the well-adjusted 'sheep' scored 5·18 hits per 25.

All the 'goats' who had taken the Rorschach test had an average score of 4·96 per 25 but the well-adjusted 'goats' scored an average of only 4·87.

The difference between the average scores of the well-adjusted 'sheep' and the well-adjusted 'goats' was very significant,* and the odds against its being due to chance work out at about 25,000 to 1.[22]

On the other hand, there was a quite negligible difference between the average scores of poorly-adjusted 'sheep' and poorly-adjusted 'goats', which were each at about chance level.

From an examination of the Rorschach record Dr. Schmeidler[23, 24, 25] isolated several factors which appear to inhibit good ESP guessing. She found that her guessers did badly if (i) they were strongly inhibited, and unable to respond freely to a situation, or (ii) they worked too hard intellectually, or (iii) they were over-emotional.

She also expressed the view that it was important for the experimenter to create a mental atmosphere in which the subjects would feel at home. She found that in a group where the atmosphere was felt to be cold and intellectual, only those members who were themselves cold and intellectual would make good scores. Dr. Schmeidler thinks that the personality traits which correlate with ESP scoring are not fixed, but vary from one group to another, and are different in different experimental situations.

If this is true, it is going to make confirmation of the work of Humphrey and Schmeidler exasperatingly difficult.

(The figures quoted in this section are taken from a report made by Dr. Schmeidler at the 1948 Symposium of the Society for Parapsychology and published in the *J. of Parapsychol.*, Vol. 13 (March 1949), pp. 23–31. The work is still in progress and more recent totals are to be found in *Jour. of S. P. R.*, Vol. XXXV, November-December 1950.)

* The significance is, in all probability, somewhat exaggerated, since throughout her work Dr. Schmeidler falls into the error of taking the individual guess as her unit for a basis of estimation instead of the individual subject. The correct method is indicated on p. 55.

# CHAPTER VI

# Early Experiments in Prediction

In everyday life we are constantly making successful predictions of future events in the material world and of a person's behaviour. For example: (i) 'He will fail in his examination next year.' (ii) 'Soal will go to North Wales next Easter.' (iii) 'It will be high tide at Southend at 5 p.m. next Monday.' Such predictions are really statements of probability based on observations made in the past. The first two, however, cannot be regarded as practical certainties. However unpromising the student's past record may have been, there is the possibility that he may make a tremendous effort between now and next June, and so falsify the prediction. And although Soal has, with a few exceptions, visited Wales each Easter for the past twenty-eight years, and prefers Snowdonia to any other district in the British Isles, he may be prevented by illness or death from going there next spring.

The third case is an example of scientific prediction. Scientists have investigated certain regularities in the order of Nature, and they are able to predict with great accuracy such phenomena as eclipses of the sun and moon, the state of the tides, etc. Such predictions are essentially statements about the probable average behaviour of enormous numbers of atoms of which the earth, the sun and the moon are composed. Physicists can predict the statistical behaviour of even complex molecular systems with astonishing accuracy. On the other hand questions which the classical physicist might have asked such as the *precise* position of a specific electron at any time can no longer be asked in modern physics. The quantum mechanist can only ascertain the *probability* that a given electron is to be found at a specific locality within some molecule. The behaviour of an individual atomic system cannot be accurately predicted because prediction implies some measurement. But any measurement of an individual atomic system requires a measuring instrument that is of the same order of magnitude or of energy as the system measured. Hence the act of measurement will appreciably disturb

73

the system and so exact prediction becomes impossible. On the other hand when a large system such as the sun is observed the process of observation causes only minute interference and exact prediction is possible.

An important feature of all such prophecies, whether ordinary or scientific, is that we know how and why we make them, and the facts on which they are based. They are probable inferences from facts known at the time when the prediction is made. But what distinguishes them from so-called 'psychic' predictions is that the person who makes a psychic prediction has no notion of how he does it. He is unaware of any facts that guide him in his prophecy. In the majority of such predictions it is extremely difficult to imagine how the seer could be guided by any present knowledge he may possess. For instance, a psychical subject predicts the order of a pack of 25 Zener cards as it will be in an hour's time when it has emerged from a mechanical shuffler and then been cut by another person. Anyone, of course, can predict, on an average, the correct positions of five cards on the theory of chance-coincidence, but what of the person who predicts an average of seven over a large number of runs? We cannot conceive that even a Newton or an Einstein could consciously perform such a feat by rational inference. In the last resort we might suppose that the guesser had had an extraordinary run of luck, but the hypothesis is not a very satisfactory one if the odds against it are of the order of a hundred thousand or a million to one.

If there is a kind of prediction by human beings which cannot be based on inferences drawn by them from a consideration of the present state of the universe, it seems probable that our conceptions of time will have to be revised. It might well be due to some peculiarity of our inherited brain structure that mental patterns arise which appear to be serially ordered in time. Possibly in an unconscious state mental patterns co-exist without being arranged in a temporal order. But as we do all our conscious thinking in time, we are quite unable to understand how this can be. Psychic prediction may remain for ever outside the grasp of our intellects, which were evolved primarily for dealing only with the physical world.

Many well-attested cases have been recorded in which a dreamer apparently foresees a future event in his own life in vivid detail, as though he were present as an actor or a spectator. We need only refer the reader to the admirable collection of cases of prevision made by the late Mr. H. F. Saltmarsh[1] from records published in the *Proceedings* and *Journal* of the Society for Psychical Research over a period of fifty years. There are also numerous cases described by Charles Richet, E. Osty,[2] J. W. Dunne,[3] and others.

A typical example is the following taken from Dunne's well-known book *An Experiment with Time.*

Mr. Dunne[3] dreamed one night in the autumn of 1913 that he was looking from a high railway embankment at a scene which he recognized as being situated a little to the north of the Firth of Forth Bridge. Below him was the open grassland with groups of people walking thereon. The scene came and went several times, but, the last time, he noticed that a train going north had fallen over the embankment. He saw several carriages lying near the bottom of the slope down which large blocks of stone were rolling. Realizing that he was dreaming, and that this was possibly one of his prophetic dreams, Mr. Dunne tried to get the date of the accident, but was only able to form an impression that it would happen sometime in the following spring.

Next morning he told the dream to his sister who recalls that he mentioned March. Jokingly they agreed to warn their friends against travelling north during the succeeding spring.

On 14th April, 1914, the 'Flying Scotsman' jumped the parapet near Burntisland Station, about fifteen miles north of the Forth Bridge, and fell on to the golf links twenty feet below.

The usual argument against dream-prevision is based on the fact that millions of people have been dreaming every night for hundreds of years, and of these a large proportion remember their dreams. It is only to be expected, therefore, that a certain number of these dreams will to a greater or lesser degree resemble some future experience of the dreamer. We have then no means of knowing whether or not even the most remarkable cases are anything more than the high lights of chance-coincidence.

The argument, with regard to dreams, may be irrefutable, but it has much less force when applied to certain mediumistic cases of precognition.

At a sitting with the medium Mrs. Blanche Cooper[4] in January 1922, a communicator gave the name of Gordon Davis and claimed to have known S.G.S. the sitter as a boy at school. S.G.S. had indeed known a boy of that name who lived at Rochford near Southend. He had been in the same class as S.G.S. for geography and he sometimes brought poisoned spears and other savage weapons in order to illustrate the lessons. S.G.S. lost sight of Davis after he left school and did not meet him again until the summer of 1916. One Sunday when S.G.S. was returning from leave Davis recognized him on the platform of Shenfield railway station. Davis and S.G.S., who were both cadets at that time, travelled together to Liverpool Street and Davis told S.G.S. that next day he had to give a lecture to his fellow cadets on the ceremony of mounting guard. He did not even mention that he was married. Shortly afterwards both went to France and one day in 1920 S.G.S. heard from a man at Rochford that Davis had been killed. The 'spirit' of Davis who spoke through Mrs. Cooper mentioned a wife and child and also volunteered correctly several names of persons connected with Rochford and known to S.G.S. He recalled bringing 'harpoons and things' to school and said he 'was for brighter geography'. S.G.S. asked him where they had last met and 'Davis' answered at once: 'It was on the train. We talked about guards but not train guards.'

At a second sitting 'Davis' did not speak in person but 'Nada', Mrs. Cooper's 'control', gave a detailed description of Davis's house, which S.G.S. noted down. Three years later in April 1925 S.G.S. found that Davis was still alive and practising as an estate agent in Southend. The description of the house given through Mrs. Cooper tallied exactly with the house in which Davis was actually living in 1925. But at the time of the sittings he and his family were living in London in a flat and their furniture was in storage. They did not move into the Southend house till several months after the date of the sittings, though between the first and second sittings Davis had visited the house for the first time with a view to taking it over.

All the following statements made by the medium about the 'future' house were correct:

(1) A dark tunnel ran through the house (into the back garden).
(2) There was a 'verandah' opposite it (actually a seaside shelter).
(3) It was in a street whose name began with two E's (Eastern Esplanade).
(4) The pictures on the walls were all of mountains and the sea and one picture showed a road between two hills.
(5) There was a black bird on the piano (an ornamental kingfisher).
(6) Two funny 'saucers' on the walls, and some curious vases.
(7) There were two brass candlesticks downstairs.
(8) There were a woman and child in the house (Mrs. Davis and small son).

Moreover not a single statement by the medium was false. It was possible to find empirical probabilities for the various statements and combine them by multiplication. It was found that the odds against the description as a whole fitting a house chosen at random in a town worked out at several million to one. It is very probable that precognition played a part in this case. Though at the time of the sittings Davis possessed most of the articles of furniture he could hardly have known in January 1922 that the bird would stand on the piano or the candlesticks be relegated to the basement of the future house.

76

## Dr. Rhine's Experiments

Rhine began his experiments in prediction by asking Hubert Pearce to write down a list of 25 Zener card symbols. Pearce was then asked to shuffle a pack of Zener cards for (in one series) 15 seconds in the presence of Dr. Rhine. The order of the cards in the pack was then checked against Pearce's list of guesses. In 16 runs of 25 he obtained an average of 7·7 hits per run, with corresponding odds against chance of about ten million to one.

Of course, the obvious objection to this sort of experiment is that the guesser himself shuffled the cards. But these were only preliminary explorations.

Rhine[5] next carried out a series of 113,075 prediction trials with 49 guessers and 11 experimenters taking part. In these tests the guesser wrote down or dictated a list of 25 Zener symbols. An experimenter then shuffled and cut a pack of cards, holding them face downwards all the time. The experimenter himself—who had up to this stage not seen the list of guesses—checked off the order of the cards in the shuffled pack from top to bottom against the subject's list. The guesser witnessed the checking and counting of hits.

Of the total of 113,075 guesses there was an excess over chance expectation of 614 hits, which corresponds to nearly 4·5 standard deviations, with odds of over 100,000 to 1 against chance. The rate of scoring (5·14 hits per 25) is very low indeed, and the bulk of the successful guessing was done by George Zirkle, one of Rhine's best subjects, and a group of 32 school children who had been selected on account of their good performances in previous ESP tests.

## ESP Shuffle Experiments

It occurred to Dr. Rhine that the significant scoring in the previous experiments might be explained otherwise than by the supposition that the guessers were anticipating the future order of a shuffled pack. It might be that the experimenter had become subconsciously aware by clairvoyance or telepathy both of the subject's list of guesses and of the order of the cards in the pack which he was holding. His fingers might then be guided by ESP to place a card here and there in a position so as to agree with the symbol in the corresponding place in the guess-list. If this happened, the crucial point in the proceedings would be the last cut, which determines the final order. He would only have to manoeuvre a card into the right position once in five or six runs to obtain the observed rate of scoring.

The alternative hypothesis to prediction by the guesser, then, was that the experimenter used ESP to match his pack with the subject's list.

In order to test this theory, Dr. Rhine[6] and his assistants carried out one of the biggest card-guessing projects ever undertaken. In all, 211,525 card matchings were made by 203 guessers. We shall here, however, confine ourselves to 51,525 trials in which the conditions appear to have been satisfactory.

The experimenter shuffled a pack of Zener cards behind a screen, and laid it on the table out of sight of the guesser. The subject then shuffled a second pack, holding it face downwards with the intent of making it agree with the concealed pack. He was allowed to make as many shuffles as he desired. A second experimenter was present, who watched all operations, and witnessed the checking of the order of the cards in the guesser's pack against that in the concealed pack. These 51,525 trials with concealed target packs and double witnessing yielded an excess of 424 hits over chance expectation. This corresponds to a critical ratio of 4·57, with odds of about 180,000 to 1 against chance. The average number of hits per 25 trials, however, was only 5·2.

In 41,775 of these trials the checking was done independently by two persons, and this batch gave a positive deviation of 348, with corresponding odds of about 30,000 to 1.

If the experimenter made no methodological errors in this work (such as letting a number of persons match simultaneously the *same* pack of Zener cards)—in which case the ordinary formulae for expectation and standard deviation would not strictly apply—it would appear that the guessers possessed a significant, though slight, ability to use ESP in shuffling a pack of cards so as to make it match a given concealed pack.

Since the success obtained in the contemporaneous shuffling experiments at least equalled that of the prediction tests, it would seem that hand-shuffling is inadequate for the demonstration of precognition.

## Mechanical Methods

Dr. Rhine[7] next decided to fix the future order of the cards in the pack by mechanical means. Two methods were adopted. The subject and experimenters were in different rooms. In the first method the subject, having recorded his list of 25 predictions, pressed a buzzer. This was a signal for an experimenter in the next room to stop turning the handle of a shuffling machine which contained 50 Zener cards. The shuffled pack was removed from the machine and laid face downward on the table.

The experimenter then compared the order of the first 25 cards, counting from top to bottom, with the subject's list of guesses intended for them. A second experimenter watched the checking.

This was known as the PDT (prediction-down-through the pack) technique, and up to 1st October 1940, various experimenters had carried out 235,875 trials by means of this method or a slight modification of it. These yielded an excess of 425 over expectation, and the not very significant critical ratio of 2·14 (odds of about 30 to 1 against chance). In his report Dr. Rhine seems to have included 2,250 trials done by Mr. G. N. M. Tyrrell* in England using his electrical machine. As Mr. Tyrrell's work involves a totally different technique we have not included these trials in the PDT group.

In the second method the subject sat before a row of five blank cards on which were to be placed later five key-cards bearing the five Zener symbols in some order. The subject was asked to match a pack of shuffled Zener cards against what he imagined would be the five future key cards. In the meantime an electrically driven cage containing six ordinary dice was being rotated in another room.

When the subject had laid down his 25 cards in five piles opposite the imagined key cards, he pressed a buzzer, which was a signal for one of the experimenters in the next room to stop the dice cage. A large number of envelopes had been prepared, each containing five key-cards in random order. The envelopes were numbered serially, and the sum of the digits turned up by the six dice indicated the particular envelope to be opened. The five key-cards were removed and placed in their proper order, one on each blank card, in the subject's room. The number of correct hits was then counted and checked by the two experimenters present, each keeping an independent record. This, in essence, was one procedure.

In a variation the order of the key-cards was determined by the stopping of the card-shuffling machine immediately the subject had finished his matching against the imaginary key-cards. The order of the first five different symbols in the shuffled pack was taken as the order of the key-symbols.

Seven series[7] totalling in all 154,675 trials were carried out by various experimenters, using one or other of these matching methods up to 1st October 1940. In two series by Rhine and Gibson 27,700 guesses were made by a group of adults, and another 12,500 by a group of children. It is reported that the adults yielded a *negative* (below chance) deviation of 239 hits, which corresponds to a critical ratio of −3·5 while the child group produced a *positive* (above chance) deviation of 123 and a critical ratio of +2·7.

* Cf. Chapter VI, p. 87.

Now Dr. Rhine says that a few preliminary experiments of a less rigorous kind with the group of adults had resulted in a negative deviation and that therefore he was expecting the main experiment to produce a below-chance score with the adults, but not with the children.

In his grand total for the seven series he has treated his negative deviation of 239 as if it were a positive deviation, and so obtains for his grand total of 154,675 trials a positive deviation of 509 hits above expectation. This seems to us a very dubious procedure. One feels that, if the adults had yielded a *positive* deviation of 239, he could easily have found reasons for *not* changing it to a negative deviation, in working out his total deviation.

If, indeed, we retain the −239 deviation for the adults in the Rhine-Gibson series, the total deviation on the seven series is reduced to only +31, compared with a standard deviation of 160·5, and is without any significance.

On the other hand, if we sum the values of chi-squared, i.e. the squares of the critical ratios, for the seven series, we get a total chi-squared of nearly 27, and with seven degrees of freedom we should expect a larger value only about once in 3,000 times.

This demonstrates that something other than chance has been at work, and an examination of the seven series shows that the abnormal value of chi-squared is almost all due to the two large deviations, one positive and one negative, in the Rhine-Gibson experiments with children and adults. There is nothing at all remarkable about the other five series. It does seem that in these two series prediction has been working positively with the children and negatively with the adults. The cancelling out of positive and negative deviations accounts for the small total deviation of +31.

## The Elimination of Psycho-kinesis

By the year 1941 Rhine had already found some evidence which tended to show that certain persons can influence by their volition the fall of an ordinary die. That is, by concentrating on, say, 'threes', they can cause the corresponding face of the die to turn up more often than would be expected on the theory of probability. We are not concerned here with the evidence for psycho-kinesis (PK) as it is called. Some people consider the experiments to be inconclusive, but PK is at any rate a possibility to be taken into account.

Dr. Rhine asked whether it might not be possible for the guesser, by using some combination of ESP and PK, to influence slightly the motions of one or two cards inside the mechanical shuffler so that they occupied final positions which agreed with his previously recorded predictions. Or again, in the matching experiment might he not learn by ESP that envelope No. 21 contained the five key-symbols in a certain order, and then, having matched his pack of 25 cards to this order, influence by PK the falls of the six dice so that they registered 6, 6, 6, 1, 1, 1, or any other numbers which totalled 21. However far-fetched and fantastic this may sound it is at any rate a logical possibility if psycho-kinesis is a reality, and if it can work in co-operation with extra-sensory perception. If this is the correct explanation, it means that the subject was not predicting a future event before it happened but was merely changing the present so that it tallied with a past event.

In order to meet this contingency, Dr. Rhine[10] planned a very ingenious experiment. The PDT method was employed in an experiment in which 51 persons wrote down predictions of the 'down-through' order of packs of Zener cards as they would emerge from a mechanical shuffler operating two days, and in some cases ten days, later. It was decided that, after it was taken from the shuffler, each pack was to be given a cut at a definite number of cards from the top. The novelty lay in the rules which determined (a) how many turns should be given to the handle of the shuffler, and (b) at which card the cut should be made. Dr. Rhine instructed his secretary that, when the two-day or ten-day interval had expired, she was to consult a morning paper, the *Durham Herald*, and obtain from it the temperature extremes for the preceding day. The smallest digit other than 0 was to decide the number of revolutions of the mechanical shuffler, and the sum of all the digits of the temperature extremes (less 25 if necessary) was to decide the number of cards from the top at which the cut in the pack was to be made. Rhine argued that, even supposing the guessers used ESP and PK to interfere with the shuffling, all their efforts to manoeuvre certain cards into certain positions in the pack would be thwarted by the final cut, which was decided by a physical event over which they would have no control.

In all, 51 persons made out prediction lists for a total of 2,302 runs of 25 cards. Of these, 1,169 runs of 25 were intended for packs which would be shuffled and cut in two days' time, while the remaining 1,133 runs were intended for packs to be formed in ten days' time.

Actually neither of the series yielded significant deviations from expectation. In fact, on the total of 57,550 trials the deviation was only +11 hits, which is quite negligible.

Having failed to discover any direct evidence of psychic prediction, Rhine went on to discuss what are called 'salience effects' within the run of 25 trials. For instance, he asked: 'Was the average rate of scoring higher on the first five guesses and the last five guesses than on the fifteen in the middle of the run?' In this case, there was no significant difference. Again, if the run was split up into five consecutive segments of five trials each, we might compare the rate of scoring on the first and last guesses of a segment with that on the three central trials. But here again on the grand total there was no significant difference. Of course, if one makes all kinds of sub-divisions in the data, one will find significant effects here and there.

Dr. Rhine, however, relied mainly on a very recondite relation between the salience effects of the 'run' and the 'segment', which he calls the 'covariance ratio'. For this he finds odds of about 625 to 1. But it would be quite possible to argue that such a *recherché* effect might well be a mere statistical artifact; and especially so when we find that only 70 shuffled packs of cards were used as targets for the 2,302 guess-runs.

Thus numbers of subjects were guessing at the same pack of cards, and this would give rise to statistical complications. Though Dr. Rhine seems to think that the effect he describes could not have been due to this, we are not so certain.

But even had he obtained a straightforward positive deviation in favour of psychic prediction, it might be questioned whether his method of taking temperature readings logically excludes the possibility of the guessers' making use of psycho-kinesis (perhaps guided by ESP) to ensure that the pack was cut in a favourable place. For if we are to assume that PK can influence the fall of dice even at a considerable distance, then might it not also affect the mercury threads* of the thermometers used to take the official temperatures?

Most investigators up to the present have omitted psycho-kinesis as a theoretical possibility in precognition experiments.

The results obtained in this series would seem to be suggestive rather than conclusive.

## Mr. Tyrrell's Experiments

The late G. N. M. Tyrrell held a place of high distinction among English psychical researchers. His Pelican book,[11] *The Personality of Man*, is already a popular classic, and probably the best book of its kind in the language. He was the author of an extremely original and fascinating theory of the genesis of ghosts and apparitions. His main interest was in the philosophy of psychical research, and on this aspect of the subject he has written many books and articles. But Mr. Tyrrell

* It might, however, be urged that a mercury thread is essentially a static system and that PK can operate only on moving systems (e.g. falling dice).

was also an electrical engineer, and some fifteen years ago he invented and experimented with an ingenious machine which he used to demonstrate not only clairvoyance and undifferentiated ESP, but also psychic prediction.

Mr. Tyrrell had noticed that Miss G. Johnson, an inmate of his house, apparently had a hunch for finding lost objects, and he decided to make use of this gift in ESP experiments. He first constructed[12] a very simple piece of apparatus consisting of a wooden screen to which were attached five boxes in a row, closed with sloping ends on one side of the screen and open on the other. An experimenter sitting on one side of the screen would thrust a pointer horizontally into one of the boxes, and Miss Johnson on the other side would lift the lid of the box which she thought contained the pointer. The five boxes were padded to make them sound proof.

Miss Johnson was very successful with this apparatus, but the chief objection was that the guesser, by oberving the sequence habits and preferences of the person who inserted the pointer rapidly in one box after another might soon learn what to expect.

However, Miss Johnson still succeeded even when a list of the numbers 1–5 arranged in random order was used to decide the sequence of pointer insertions. Mr. Tyrrell was therefore encouraged to devise a more elaborate machine on similar principles.

This consisted[13] essentially of a row of five boxes each of which contained a small electric lamp. The lamps were connected by wires to five keys which were operated by the experimenter from a table situated several feet away. Each box was fitted with a sloping lid which could be lifted by Miss Johnson, who sat behind a large screen. When a key was pressed by the experimenter, the corresponding lamp was lighted, and the subject, at a signal from an electric buzzer, lifted the lid of the box which she thought contained the lighted lamp. The opening of any box automatically drew a line upon a paper tape, and a success was recorded by a double line.

By means of a commutator in the circuit the connections between lamps and keys were interchanged, so that, with the commutator in operation, the experimenter did not know which lamp he was lighting when he pressed a given key. Thus the apparatus could be used for tests of clairvoyance alone as well as for tests of telepathy with possible clairvoyance, i.e. undifferentiated ESP. The five keys could be dispensed with and a rotating switch with a single arm, known as a mechanical selector brought into play. This arm was driven by an electro-magnet and ratchet device and when it came to rest in a random position it made a contact which lighted one of the five lamps.

83

A most ingenious device incorporated into the apparatus was a delay-action relay.

By this means one of the five circuits was selected by the experimenter pressing a key, but the lamp inside the corresponding box did not light until Miss Johnson closed the circuit by lifting the lid. The use of this gadget absolutely prevented her from getting any clue to the correct box through the escape of light or heat.

When both the commutator and the delay-action were in operation, the only thing that differentiated the five circuits was the contact made by the experimenter's keys, and, in order to know by clairvoyance which box to open, Miss Johnson would have to be aware of the connections inside the commutator. Thus, for the guesser to succeed under these conditions, quite a complicated act of clairvoyance would be required.

Miss Johnson could not succeed by becoming aware by clairvoyance that one lamp was charged to a higher potential than the others, because there was a common wire connecting all the lamps, and when the key was pressed, all were simultaneously charged.

Since the machine recorded only success or failure, and not the lamp number selected by the experimenter, it would be impossible for Miss Johnson's mind to go forward in time to the moment when the tape was being examined by Mr. Tyrrell, and obtain from his mind precognitively the number of the lamp. In other words, when the commutator or the mechanical selector was in action, Miss Johnson could apparently succeed only by using clairvoyance.

The apparatus was proof against hitches of all kinds. For instance, if the guesser opened two boxes simultaneously, the success-recorder was thereby put out of action, and only a single line appeared on the tape, thus registering a failure. Nor could she peep into a box before opening it, for as soon as the lid was raised even a fraction of an inch, a trial was recorded.

The work was done at the rate of about 60–70 trials a minute, and it would have been impossible for Miss Johnson to leave her table and look over the screen towards the experimenter's table without causing an obvious hitch.

The use of the commutator would break up any of the experimenter's sequence habits which happened to coincide with those of Miss Johnson.

The keys were rendered silent by means of mercury contacts.

Mr. Tyrrell had to exercise incredible patience in getting his subject psychologically adapted to working with the new machine. It was a long time before she could score above chance level, even with the keys directly connected with the lamps—that is, without the commutator.

Again and again he had to revert to the old 'pointer' apparatus. But when success came with the lamps it came with a vengeance. In 1,271 consecutive trials with the lamps, the subject chose the correct box 373 times, which gives a positive deviation of 118·8 hits above chance expectation, and corresponding odds of $10^{15}$ to 1 against chance. In these tests telepathy from Mr. Tyrrell, the experimenter, was a possibility.[13]

Next, the commutator was introduced, and the scores immediately dropped to chance level once more. Mr. Tyrrell now began to mix experiments in which the commutator was in action in batches of 50 or 100 with others in which there was direct connection between keys and lamps. It almost seemed as though Miss Johnson could read from Tyrrell's mind which kind of experiment he was doing. For in 500 trials with the commutator in action she obtained 101 hits, which is just 1 above chance expectation, whereas in 576 trials where there was direct connection between keys and lamps she got 225 hits, as compared with the expected number 115·2. Here the odds against chance are of the order $10^{25}$ to 1.

But when Miss Johnson returned from a holiday in September 1935, Tyrrell found that she had adapted herself to the experiments with the commutator, in which the experimenter did not know which lamp he lighted when he pressed a key. In 4,200 trials under these conditions she obtained a positive deviation of 178 hits with corresponding odds against chance of $10^{11}$ to 1.

Strange to say, Miss Johnson offered no unconscious resistance to the introduction of the delay-action mechanism. Ostensibly this would seem to be the most difficult condition of all, since, with no lamp alight, the target for clairvoyance has apparently disappeared. To succeed, she would have to trace clairvoyantly the connection from the key chosen through the commutator to the lamp which she lights herself by raising the lid of the correct box. This appears to be a most complicated feat of ESP.

Nevertheless, a series of trials without the delay-action alternated in batches of 50 with another series in which the delay-action operated showed that there was no real difference in rates of scoring under the 'easy' and the 'hard' conditions. Approximately equal numbers of guesses gave a difference of only 4 in the numbers of hits. The odds against chance for each condition were of the order $10^9$ to 1.

Miss Johnson did not take kindly to the use of the mechanical selector, as she complained that its noise disturbed her. She did, however, succeed brilliantly for a long spell of 7,809 trials in which a list of random digits 1–5 (compiled previously by means of the selector) was used to decide the order in which the experimenter pressed the keys. During this series the commutator was in action, and so telepathy from Tyrrell was excluded. The 7,809 guesses yielded a positive deviation of 279·2 hits, the corresponding odds being of the order $10^{14}$ to 1 against chance.

We think this unequivocal success with lists of numbers prepared beforehand puts out of court any suggestion that Miss Johnson had in the past achieved extra-chance scores by following a trick method discovered by Mr. G. W. Fisk.[13]

In October 1935, Mr. Fisk found that in the case where a human operator selects the five keys according to his own whim, anyone entirely destitute of any ESP faculty can do as well as Miss Johnson if he uses a very simple system. The guesser selects any box, say, No. 1 and keeps on opening it at every trial until he sees the lamp alight in this box. He then changes to, say, No. 2, and continues to open this till he scores a success. He then changes to, say, No. 3, and when the lamp lights goes on to No. 4, and so on. The system does not work, however, when random numbers are used to determine the order in which the keys are to be pressed by the experimenter. The reason is that, when the operator chooses the keys 'out' of his head, so to speak, he tends to select each key at more regular intervals than would be the case with a mathematically random method of choice. In a random list of digits 1–5 any particular number, say 4, turns up at very irregular intervals. We might find three 4's in succession, and after that, not another 4 in the next twelve digits. But a man who makes up such a list from his head will, as a rule, space the digits at approximately regular intervals. As a consequence, the guesser who keeps on repeating the same digit has not to wait so long for a success on the average as he would were the order of the digits perfectly haphazard and irregular. He therefore scores more hits in the same number of trials with the human operator.

The same method can be used in connection with Dr. Rhine's packs of Zener cards in which each symbol occurs exactly five times, but, it should be noted, only when the guesser is told, whether he is right after every trial.

It would not work with randomly distributed packs containing different numbers of each symbol.

As Miss Johnson was unwitnessed while she was opening the boxes, it cannot be proved that she did not employ Fisk's method, but the fact that she scored equally well when the order of the five keys was randomly selected is sufficient to establish her faculty of clairvoyance. Moreover, several persons did watch her when she was working with the 'pointer' apparatus, and not one of the witnesses reported that she was guessing by any system. And repeated opening of the same box would have been glaringly obvious. The probability is that she never employed Fisk's method. But the shock of the discovery that others could duplicate much of her work by merely employing a system appears to have affected her scoring very adversely. For many months her results remained at the chance level, although later she made a partial recovery.

## Precognitive Clairvoyance

Between October and February, 1935–6, Tyrrell[13] tried an interesting variation. In certain blocks of trials with the commutator in action Miss Johnson opened a box about half a second *before* the experimenter pressed a key. In 2,255 such trials there were 539 hits, which is an excess of 88 above chance expectation. The odds against chance are here about 270,000 to 1.

An inspection of the tape showed that in the case of every hit the box was really opened before the key was pressed by a fraction of a second corresponding to the amount of overlap of the 'trial' and 'success' lines. Telepathy from Tyrrell was ruled out, since the use of the commutator prevented him from knowing which of the lamps he was lighting.

The simplest explanation is that Miss Johnson used clairvoyant prediction to guess the lamp which was to be lighted in about half a second's time. Tyrrell himself has suggested a far less plausible hypothesis. The alternative to prediction is to assume that Tyrrell had clairvoyant and telepathic gifts of which, up to then, he had never shown the slightest sign. When Miss Johnson opened the box, we might suppose that Tyrrell used telepathy to learn subconsciously the box she had chosen. He could then, by clairvoyance, trace the connection through the commutator from the lamp to the key which would have to be pressed in order to light that particular lamp. He would then press the key, and the lamp would light. The explanation is improbable for if Tyrrell possessed such remarkable powers rivalling those of Miss Johnson herself, why did he consistently fail to score above chance level when he took her place at guessing which box contained the lighted lamp?

We cannot assume that Miss Johnson employed precognitive telepathy, because, if her mind ran ahead to the moment when the tape was inspected, this would not have helped her, since there is no record of which lamp was lighted at each trial, but only of the fact of success or failure.

## The Experiments of Whately Carington

S.G.S. can still see Whately Carington sitting at Cambridge in front of his electric calculating machine, perfectly oblivious of his material surroundings and the rather drab outlook from his window. So did he appear to rare visitors a year later, sitting in the study of his tiny cottage at Sennen Cove, Cornwall, whither he had removed with his wife, owing to straitened means, talking tirelessly about human survival and his theories of telepathy, and never seeming to notice the great seas that were breaking off Land's End.

For Carington, the eccentric recluse whose originality would have made a name for him in more orthodox branches of science, the unusual and the psychic seem to have held an irresistible fascination. As a young man at Cambridge he engineered fake séances in which an undergraduate disguised to play the part of an eminent medium and a telescopic fishing rod complete with hooks and line, used to whisk objects around in the dark, played prominent parts.

Carington, who had been an airman in the First World War, was later engaged in research for the Air Ministry, and it was during this period that he investigated the famous 'Abram's Magic Box',[14] by means of which it was claimed diseases could be diagnosed. He was also one of the earliest experimenters with the psycho-galvanic reflex, and these researches were described in his book *The Measurement of Emotion*,[15] published in 1922. Twelve years later he used the method of the reflex and of reaction times to Jung's word association test to investigate the psychological nature of the so-called 'spirit controls' of mediums. Carington[16, 17] employed a statistical method to demonstrate that such trance personalities as Mrs. Leonard's 'Feda' and Mrs. Eileen Garrett's 'Uvani' are, in reality, repressed aspects of the mediums' own personalities, and not the spirits of the dead Indians or Arabians which they claim to be. The question whether the personalities who communicate through mediums, and purport to be the sitter's surviving relatives or friends, have any existence independent of the medium remained unanswered. Carington had thought at first that a person's mental reactions to stimulus words, either vocal or as registered by the psycho-galvanic reflex, would provide an infallible system of mental measurements, uniquely characteristic of the given person, which could be used to identify him after death, much in the same way as his finger-prints serve to identify him in his lifetime. But extensive experiment proved that the method was not so reliable as was at first hoped, and eventually Carington abandoned this line of investigation. But his work will be remembered as a courageous and brilliant attempt to answer the most vital question that confronts mankind: If a man die, shall he live again?

## Experiments with Drawings

By the year 1938 Whately Carington had reached a dead end with his work on the nature of the trance-personalities of mediums. He next decided to devote his energies to experiments in ESP.

In this field, he had already made one small excursion. He had induced some forty persons in the year 1935 to take part in a dice prediction experiment. The subjects were instructed to guess beforehand the face which would turn up when an ordinary cubical die was shaken in a cup. Nowadays, the interpretation of such an experiment would be ambiguous, as it might be regarded either as an experiment in prediction, or as a test of psycho-kinesis. But in 1935 the word psycho-kinesis, or PK in brief, had not yet been launched upon the world.

Carington[18] collected 51,210 single-die throws, and by a strange fluke the number of correct predictions was 8,535 which is the exact number (one-sixth) that chance would be expected to produce. With his usual ingenuity, Carington, having failed to obtain direct evidence of prediction, tried to show that the distribution of hits was abnormal in other respects, but we think he was mistaken in his conclusions.[19]

When he took up ESP work again in 1939, he intended at first to carry out rigorous experiments with packs of ordinary Zener cards, but his wife dissuaded him from this course.

He decided to use free-hand drawings of common objects as his target material. Cambridge was to be the centre for transmission, and most of his guessers were people living in Great Britain, Holland, and the United States. In all, 741 persons took part, many of them connected with the psychology departments of British and American universities.

Carington[22, 23, 24, 25, 26, 27] was assisted in his task by a little group of Cambridge men, namely Professor C. D. Broad, Dr. R. H. Thouless, the psychologist, Dr. Irving, a statistician, and Mr. Oliver Gatty.

Very briefly, Carington's procedure, after it had become standardized, was as follows. Each experiment comprised 10 drawings exposed one on each of 10 consecutive nights.

On the day of each test Carington selected at random a three- or four-figure number from some mathematical table. This decided the page at which Webster's dictionary was to be opened. Carington then took from the given page the first concrete object that could be reasonably drawn. Mrs. Carington then made a careful sketch of the object, and this sketch was pinned up in Carington's study, where it remained from 7 p.m. till 9.30 a.m. the following morning. The window of the room was heavily curtained, and the door locked, so that no one save the two Caringtons could have any knowledge of the sketch. At 9.30 a.m. the sketch was removed and locked in a box.

Each of the several hundred guessers taking part had been provided with a sketch-book containing ten pages, one to be used on each of the ten nights of the experiment. The subjects had been instructed to make a sketch of what they thought the drawing in Carington's study represented, and to label it. At the end of the ten days' experiment the sketch-books were returned to Carington, who passed them on to Dr. Thouless. The percipients' drawings, which bore no dates, were given code numbers by Thouless for the purpose of future identification.

After an interval of a few days, a similar ten days' test was carried out, and altogether there were five ten-day experiments with a few days' interval between experiments.

The hundreds of drawings were then detached from the books, and thoroughly randomized. They were then posted, together with the 50 original sketches randomly mixed to an independent judge, Mr. M. T. Hindson.

Mr. Hindson, who had no normal means of discovering on which evening or in which of the five experiments any particular sketch was made, was asked to match every drawing against every original.

If he decided that a given drawing clearly resembled an original, he was to assign to the drawing a score of one, if there was a doubtful resemblance, a score of one-half, and if he judged that there was no resemblance at all, a score of nought was awarded.

In order to evaluate the results of his large-scale matching, Carington made use of a statistical formula due to Mr. W. L. Stevens.* The underlying principle is, however, very simple. Let us suppose that 'ship' is an original in one of the five experiments. Suppose also that in all the four remaining experiments taken together Mr. Hindson judged that there were 2,000 hits and that of these, 30 were hits on 'ship'. Let us also assume that in the 10-day experiment for which 'ship' was one of the originals there were 400 hits of one kind or another. By simple proportion we should expect $\frac{30}{2,000} \times 400$, i.e. 6 hits on 'ship' in this experiment if nothing more than chance was at work. If, however, we actually found a great many more than 6, and this happened also for the other originals, we should have reason to suppose that the fact that a 'ship' had been exposed as an original on one of the ten days had somehow caused the guessers to draw an unusual number of 'ships' during these ten days.

What Carington realized very early in his investigation was that when, say, a 'ship' was chosen for a particular night, the number of 'ships'

* IX, 2.

drawn on that night was seldom significantly above expectation, but that the proportion of 'ships' during the ten days of the experiment in which 'ship' was one of the ten originals greatly exceeded the proportion obtained in any one of the other four experiments. In other words, if 'ship', say, was the original for Wednesday evening, the percipients would be producing 'ships' not only on this evening but also on one or two evenings before and after Wednesday. Indeed, the farther we receded from Wednesday in the before and after sense, the less pronounced was the tendency to draw ships. The fact that there was a definite tendency to draw 'ships' on, say, Tuesday evening at which time Carington had not even chosen his object from the dictionary, seemed to show that his subjects possessed the faculty of psychic prediction. The statistical findings confirmed Carington's observations. The final odds against the results being due merely to chance worked out at about a thousand to one for the first five experiments.

The main result of Carington's investigation was the conclusion that telepathy was in no sense a 'now or never' process. It was not focused very sharply with regard to time. The subjects did not appear to receive their impressions always during the period when the original was exposed in Carington's study.

Since Carington had selected his guessers more or less at random, he felt confident that he had discovered a repeatable technique that would yield successful results to any experimenter who was willing to take the necessary trouble. Repetitions of the method by others have, however, given uncertain results. In 1944–5 four series of experiments with drawings on the general lines of Carington's investigations were carried out by the American Society for Psychical Research,[28] but, except in the case of the first evening, the results were without significance. One feels, however, that Carington was justified in his objection that the experimenters had not followed his original technique at all closely, and the reasons he gave for the failure sound plausible.

In 1946, Dr. Gertrude Schmeidler and Mrs. Lydia Allison[29] of New York carried out another four experiments in which 99 persons in all made about 10 drawings each. The experimenters used Carington's 'catalogue' method of scoring based on formulae due to Dr. R. A. Fisher (see p. 93). Two of the four experiments were of the 10-day type favoured by Carington, and these gave insignificant results. In the other two experiments groups of college students took part, and each person made his or her ten drawings in response to the ten originals on the same day. The one done at Bard College was highly successful, giving odds of 10,000 to 3 against chance. The other, in which only seven persons participated, yielded chance results.

91

The whole series[29] gave odds of about 50 to 1 against chance, but this degree of success is rather better than Carington's own prediction for a group of only 99 persons doing about ten drawings each. With a hundred participants doing ten drawings each, one would anticipate on the basis of Carington's larger scale experiments odds of only 33 to 1.

It cannot be said, therefore, that the results obtained in this series as a whole contradict Carington's own findings. But it is clear that there is a considerable element of variability in the results of such tests; some groups seem to be very successful, and others to be devoid of any paranormal ability.

## The Catalogue System

One serious drawback to Carington's first method of scoring by the matching of every drawing against every original is that it takes no account of the relative frequencies with which people tend to guess various objects. Suppose, for instance, that two of the originals selected by the experimenter were TREE and ICE-AXE. The first is a very common object, and likely to be thought of by a considerable number of persons, whereas the second would be only rarely chosen. Yet a hit on ICE-AXE would be awarded the same score of 1 as a hit on TREE. The odds against the correct guessing of 'ice-axe' are far greater than those against the correct guessing of 'tree', and a system which ignores this is insensitive, and fails to make the best use of the material.

Another disadvantage is the immense labour involved in the matching of the drawings. Mr. Hindson was an excellent judge, but an incompetent one might miss many real points of resemblance between drawings and originals. In any case, the final odds against chance will vary considerably according to the ideas of the different judges who do the matching, and this is not a very satisfactory state of affairs. This does not mean that a judge, by varying his methods, could produce significant results out of chance material, so long as he was kept in ignorance of the dates on which the different drawings and originals were made.

It implies only that some degree of significance might be lost by bad matching.

Carington therefore set out to devise a simpler and more sensitive method of scoring. Essentially he wanted to know the frequencies with which the members of a large group of people of approximately the same cultural level, could be expected to draw various objects when no ESP was involved.

His first step[27] was to count the number of times each object such as 'elephant' was drawn or mentioned by his guessers in all the experiments in which this object was not used as an original, and also to find the total number of persons who took part in such experiments. Thus, in the experiments where 'elephant' was not a 'target', 6 elephants were drawn or mentioned, and the number of persons who took part was 496. Hence the frequency for the object 'elephant' is 6/496, i.e. 0·012. Similar counts were made for the other objects guessed in the experiments, and the number of times each object was guessed was tabulated in a catalogue, which also gave the number of experiments in which the object was used as a target.

Now let us suppose that 'elephant' was used as a 'target' or 'original' in a fresh experiment. Consider any individual participant in this new experiment. If he draws 'elephant', the true frequency for 'elephant' is now $(6 + 1) / (496 + 1)$, i.e. 7/497, and not 6/496. But if he does *not* draw 'elephant', the frequency will be $6 / (496 + 1)$, i.e. 6/497. If, of these two values, the appropriate one is called $p$, we give the guess a score equal to $(1 - p) \log_{10}(1/p)$ if it is a hit on 'elephant', and a score of $-p \log_{10}(1/p)$ if it is a miss.

The variance, (i.e. the square of the standard deviation) can be shown to be $p(1 - p)[\log_{10}(1/p)]^2$.

The values of these three expressions can be worked out for values of $p$ at suitable intervals, and tables have been compiled from which they can be read off. We then have to sum the algebraic scores for all the different guesses to get the *total* score, and the sum of the variances gives the total variance.

In $n$ trials with probability equal to $p$ in each case, the expected number of hits is $np$, and the expected number of misses $n(1 - p)$.

Hence the expected mean score will be

$$np (1 - p) \log_{10}(1/p) + n(1 - p)[-p \log_{10}(1/p)],$$

i.e. zero, if we assume that only chance is in operation.

It follows, therefore, that the deviation of the total score from the expected score is the same as the total score itself.

Hence to obtain the critical ratio we have only to divide the total observed score by the square root of the variance. The odds against chance can then be found from Table 11, Appendix C.

It is, of course, essential that anyone making use of Carington's catalogue[26] should issue precisely the same instructions to his group of guessers as those laid down by Carington himself in the experiments from the data of which the catalogue was compiled. It is also advisable that each person should make just ten drawings, as was the case with Carington's percipients. Further, a new group of subjects should be used for each ten-day experiment.

When Carington's[27] eleven sets of drawings were scored by means of his catalogue, he found that all eleven scores were positive, i.e. above chance expectation, and that the final odds against chance were of the order 100,000 to 1 for the grand total score.

The use of the catalogue has its own peculiar drawbacks. One is that the guesser's drawing must agree accurately with the experimenter's original drawing in order to score a success. Thus, when the original is 'horse' a drawing of a donkey or a mule or a clothes-horse will count as a failure, and only a horse will be considered a hit. On one occasion when Carington had selected a 'bow-tie' as his original, he noted that several people sent in 'hour-glass', which, of course, suggests that they had got the shape correct. Scored by the catalogue, such interesting efforts had to be dismissed as failures.

By this time the reader has probably asked himself how much reliance can be placed on the figures which give the frequencies with which people are likely to think of different objects. If so, he has found the weak spot, the Achilles' heel of Carington's procedure. In the first place, it would appear that 741 persons making about ten drawings each (actually an average of 11·4 per person) is much too small a number on which to base a sound estimate of the smaller frequencies. For it is fairly certain that we may expect, not only considerable secular variations in these frequencies, but also variations when we pass from one group of persons to another, For instance, 496 persons between them drew 6 elephants. Is it not easily possible that another group of the same size might produce only 1 or 2, and that a third group might draw as many as 10?

A story about an elephant in an evening newspaper during the period when the last group was making its drawings might easily account for the extra number of elephants. Our point is that, unless one made a most prolonged and elaborate investigation, one could not hope to obtain even a reasonable approximation to the true frequency.

It will, of course, be obvious to everyone that the high scores obtained on certain originals are not due to telepathy, but can be attributed to some seasonal or topical influence which happens to operate at about the time when the original is selected. If an experimenter chose a daffodil from the dictionary at the end of April, he might expect quite a crop of daffodils from his guessers. This, of course, is a glaring example, but the same kind of influences must be active all the time on a smaller scale.

Carington's argument was that topical or seasonal influences cut both ways. If they raise the scores on some originals, they must lower them on others. That is to say, if on certain occasions some originals yield high positive scores because they happen to be popular at the time of the experiment, there will be other originals (e.g. holly in summer-time) so unpopular that they will be guessed scarcely at all, and these will yield large negative scores.

The argument would be a valid one if the experimenter could go on selecting hundreds or thousands of originals in a random fashion. *In the long run* topical tendencies would even themselves out. But in Carington's method only ten originals were used in an experiment, and with such a small number there is a very serious danger that mere topical effects may be mistaken for telepathy. It is true, of course, that very marked instances of topical influence (e.g. mention of turkeys at Christmas time) would be easily detected by a careful examination of items which gave unusual positive scores, and their effects discounted, but less obvious cases might easily be passed over. The main criticism is that we can have no certainty that in a small number of tests the effects under discussion even approximately cancel themselves out.

It is remarkable that positive total scores were obtained on every one of the eleven sets of originals used by Carington. On the assumption that it is just as likely that a score will be positive as negative, the odds against the production by chance of eleven positive *or* eleven negative scores is 1,024 to 1 (i.e. $2^{10}$ to 1), but here again is this basic assumption justified?

Since the smaller frequencies with which the various objects tabulated in the catalogue are guessed are probably underestimated, and the secular variations of such frequencies unknown, it seems very possible that Carington's final figure of 100,000 to 1 for the odds against chance is far too large. What is required is an intensive investigation of the mass-preferences of different cross-sections of the population for common objects, and until this has been carried out, considerable doubt must exist as to the reliability of the results obtained by the use of such catalogues.

# CHAPTER VII

# Card-Guessing Experiments 1934-9
# by S. G. Soal

## (1) *Experiments with Marion**

When S.G.S. first read Dr. Rhine's† monograph *Extra-Sensory Perception* in the autumn of 1934 he was sceptical. During the six months which preceded its publication, S.G.S. had been carrying out an extensive series of experiments with the vaudeville telepathist, Frederick Marion (Josef Kraus), whose remarkable displays of pseudo-telepathy were exciting great interest in scientific circles. One of Marion's spectacular gifts was his ability to recognize a new playing-card that he had previously handled when it had been mixed with several other cards of identical make and design. The following is a record* of one of the earlier experiments:

'*17th January*, 1934. At 3.30 p.m. I handed Marion from a perfectly new pack the Queen of Diamonds which he held in his hands for a few seconds. He then handed me back the card and left the room, the door being closed. I chose five other cards at random from the pack, added to them the card touched by Marion and, holding the six cards under the table, shuffled them and then slid them one by one on to the table, backs upward, so that the six cards were laid out separately on the table. Marion was recalled to the room and seated himself on my left so that I could overlook his every movement. The other persons present were also watching carefully. Marion tapped the back of each card in turn with his first and second fingers, sometimes pushing a card aside. He then turned up a card and it was the Queen of Diamonds. The whole experiment took a minute from the instant when Marion was handed the card to the instant when he turned up the correct card.'

We soon discovered by means of certain tests that what Marion recognized was the actual piece of pasteboard which he had previously touched, and not the value on the face of the card.

† III, 1.          * II, 7.

There were indications that Marion used tactual discrimination in picking out the card he had previously touched, and his constant tapping of the backs of the cards as they lay on the table suggested that he was examining the contact which the different parts of the card made with the wooden surface.

A type of experiment which puzzled S.G.S. for a considerable time is exemplified in the following record:

'*7th February*, 3.51 *p.m.* The light-proof shutter was drawn over the window and the lights switched off. In total darkness I handed Marion a new card, the Ace of Hearts, whose back he had not previously seen. He held it for few seconds face downwards, and, having received it back, I placed it on top of a small pile of five cards of black suit which I was holding face downwards in one hand. I shuffled the six cards under the table still holding them face downwards. I then held the pack horizontally and at the level of the edge of the table. Immediately the light had been switched on I slid the cards one by one face downwards on to the table. Marion had not previously seen the backs of any of the six cards which were from the same new pack. He was not allowed to touch any of the cards as they lay on the table but he waved his fingers in the air over each card in turn thus indicating whether we were to slide the card to the right or the left. He was presently left with five cards on the right and one on the left. This one he said was the correct card. It was turned up and found to be the Ace of Hearts.' We carried out 21 tests under these conditions and Marion was successful in picking out the right card, first try, 11 times. The odds against getting 11 or more successes in 21 trials are about 5,340 to 1 ($p = 1/6$). Throughout, Marion never touched a card from the moment he handed back the card in the dark.

The probable explanation, we discovered later, was that while holding the card in the dark he slightly flexed it, so that, when it lay on the table with the other five cards which he had not handled, it presented a slightly convex surface which caused it to stand out from the rest. Thus he was able to identify it.

When in a subsequent series S.G.S. thoroughly flexed all six cards in the dark after Marion had returned the card he held, the experiment failed consistently.

We carried out similar experiments* with stiff millboard which could not be flexed by ordinary handling. These cards were about 4 millimetres thick, and bore on their faces either a black triangle or a red spot. In total darkness S.G.S. would hand Marion a card with a red spot. He would feel it for a few seconds and hand it back. S.G.S. would then add it to a pile of similar cards with black triangles on them. After shuffling

* II, 7.

the cards, S.G.S. held the pile face downwards at the level of the table. When the light was switched on he slid the cards one by one on to the table, face downwards. Marion was then allowed to stroke and feel the cards, but not to lift them. In seventeen tests of this sort he was successful in picking out the card with the red spot nine times. The odds against this are 1,510 to 1.

In these tests the recognition must have been by touch. Slight irregularities on the edges probably gave him his cues.

When, however, the millboard cards, cut with smoother edges were placed in envelopes, and the experiment arranged so that all sensory cues were ruled out, Marion failed. Although he appears to have an unusually sensitive touch, Marion did not succeed in emulating the alleged feats of the blind osteopath, Captain Lowry, of whom it was said that he was able to distinguish the pips on a playing card by touch alone.

This work with Marion, carried out at the office of the University of London Council for Psychical Investigation and published under the title *Preliminary Studies of a Vaudeville Telepathist,** London, 1937, demonstrates how essential it is to prevent guessers from handling the cards or seeing their backs in telepathy and clairvoyance experiments.

THE HIDE AND SEEK GAME

Another series of experiments with Marion* had important implications for the study of telepathy. By means of a statistical method, we investigated his power of rapidly locating small objects that had been concealed in a room by an audience of about half a dozen persons who knew the hiding place and whose bodily movements he was able to observe. Briefly the method adopted was as follows:

Six tin boxes provided with lids were placed around the room in six chosen positions, e.g. one on the floor, one on a small table, one on the ledge of a book-case, etc. These positions were numbered 1–6 in clockwise order. The object to be hidden was a small unscented white handkerchief. This handkerchief was given to Marion to hold for a few seconds, and he then handed it back to S.G.S. Meanwhile the sitters had seated themselves round a large table in the centre of the room. Marion then left the room accompanied by one of the audience, and the door, which had no keyhole, was carefully closed. S.G.S. then took from his pocket a die, and shook it in one of the tin boxes. He did not speak aloud the number which turned up, but showed it to Miss Beenham, the recorder, who entered it in her note-book. The fall of the die decided in which of the six boxes the handkerchief was to be hidden. S.G.S. then walked

* II, 7.

round the room with the handkerchief in his hand, now and then stopping at a tin, taking off the lid, and putting it on again. When he came to the tin in which the handkerchief was to be placed he carried it to the middle of the floor, put in the handkerchief and closed the lid carefully; he then carried the tin back, and put it down gently in its position. He then gave every tin a random push, and put the die in his waistcoat pocket.

All took their seats, and S.G.S. shouted to Marion to come in. It was understood that the audience were to follow Marion with their eyes in all his movements round the room, willing him to go to the right tin, but that they were not to give him any obvious indications such as a nod of the head or other sign. Complete silence was preserved while Marion was in the room.

As regards Marion himself, he was told that he was not to touch any tin unless he meant to lift it and open it. If the tin which he opened contained the handkerchief, the experiment was, of course, finished, but if the tin did not contain the handkerchief, he was to open one of the remaining five tins. After he had opened the second tin, the experiment was finished, whether this tin contained the handkerchief or not. As soon as Marion entered the room, or usually before his entry, Miss Beenham, the note-taker, laid her stop-watch on the number shown in her note-book, or else turned the page. The lids of the tins that had been opened by Marion were not replaced until Marion had left the room again for the next experiment. The tins were always replaced in their original positions. The tins whose lids had been removed as well as the tin in which the handkerchief was to be hidden afresh were carried to the centre of the room, and the lids then replaced. When the handkerchief had been concealed, and the tins replaced in their original positions, each tin was given a random push of a few inches.

When Marion entered the room, his eyes would seem half-closed, his left hand would usually be on his forehead and his right hand extended at the level of his head. He would then begin to walk rapidly round the room usually in a counter-clockwise direction. As he came to each tin, he would pause slightly, and wave his right hand once or twice above the tin, bringing it as a rule to within two inches of the lid, but without touching the tin. He would pass on, doing the same thing at each tin. When he had completed the circuit of the tins, he would stride across to one particular part of the room, say towards the book-case, hesitate a moment, and then cross to the tin on the gramophone. Then suddenly he would return to the book-case, and, without any hesitation, open the tin on its ledge, and pull out the handkerchief.

The chance of his opening the correct tin at first try is, of course, given by $p = 1/6$, and in 91 trials of this kind we should expect him to find the handkerchief first try 15 times. He actually scored 38 successes, and the odds against this result being due to chance are nearly 71 millions to 1.

There was, then, no question that Marion could locate the handkerchief under these conditions.

We next did experiments which showed that Marion* could not find the handkerchief more times than chance would predict when no person present knew in which tin it was hidden. During these tests Marion would say after opening a wrong tin: 'I was only guessing. I got no real feeling at all.'

We also showed that Marion's holding or 'sensing' the handkerchief before he left the room had nothing to do with his success or failure. He also succeeded, when no actual object was hidden, in discovering the imaginary hiding place concentrated upon by the audience.

We next investigated the part played by the audience in Marion's success.

In the first series* S.G.S. would accompany Marion outside the room, and lead him into the outer office. During their absence, after the die had been thrown and the handkerchief concealed, all the sitters would completely cover their heads, shoulders, arms, chests, and trunks with thick blankets and press their fingers into their ears. Marion and S.G.S. were then recalled to the room and S.G.S. remained uncovered, moving about the room in such a way that he could watch all Marion's movements, and placing himself so that Marion could never get his back between him and a tin box. Under these conditions Marion did not succeed in locating the handkerchief more times than chance would predict.

The next plan was to have an opaque white curtain rigged up across the window end of the room. When the light-proof shutter was drawn over the window, the movements of legs, arms, etc., of a person standing behind the curtain were invisible to anyone inside the room. At intervals in the curtain, at the level of a man's eyes, were tiny peepholes a quarter of an inch in diameter, so that the people behind the curtain could watch Marion's movements inside the room without Marion's being able to see any part of their own bodies.

In these experiments Marion and S.G.S. left the room together, and the other sitters threw the die and concealed the handkerchief. They then went behind the curtains and Marion and S.G.S. were recalled. The people behind the curtain watched Marion through the chink holes, and willed him to go to the correct tin, being very careful not to disturb

* II, 7.

the curtain in any way. S.G.S. acted as umpire. As he did not know where the object was hidden, he could give nothing away.

In a total of 64 tests of this kind, Marion found the handkerchief only 13 times at first try, which is just a chance result.

These tests showed that, for Marion to succeed, it was vitally necessary that he should be able to see some part of the body of a person who knew in which tin the handkerchief was hidden.

In another series* of experiments Marion succeeded brilliantly when followed round the room at a distance of about a yard by a single person who knew the hiding place. In these tests S.G.S. went outside the room with Marion, and acted as umpire on his return. The other members of the group, excepting the person who followed Marion, were watching him from behind the curtain.

In some tests the follower was asked to put over his head a tea-cosy of thin coarse linen, and over this was a black, stockinette hood which covered his face, neck and shoulders. He was able to see Marion through the mesh, but his features were quite invisible to Marion. Under these conditions Marion was right first try five times out of five (odds 7,775 to 1 against chance). This experiment showed that Marion did not rely necessarily upon changes of facial expression for his cues.

We next had constructed* a light, rigid, plywood box 50 inches high. The box was open at one end, and in the bottom a circular hole was cut. This box was put over the follower's head, so that his neck passed through the circular hole, and the very light weight of the box was supported by his shoulders. The arms, trunk, and legs, down to the ankles, were enclosed in the body of the box. The follower's head was then covered by a rectangular, cardboard hood which rested on top of the box, and an oval hole in a vertical face of the hood was covered with stockinette through which objects in the room could be seen. As the man who wore this contraption followed Marion in his circuit of the room, only his feet and $1\frac{1}{2}$ inches of his legs were visible. The man's head made no contact with the interior of the hood, and movements of his head *relative* to the trunk, i.e. noddings or rotatory movements, were absolutely invisible to the onlooker. Trunk movements from the hips could be observed by the rotation of the box and hood. The man gave the impression of a weird sort of walking robot, and we nicknamed this contrivance the 'robot-box'. S.G.S. left the room with Marion, taking him, as usual, away into the office. The robot-box and hood were placed upon Mr. H. S. Collins, and he stood near the door ready to follow as soon as Marion entered. The die was thrown and

* II, 7.

101

a small fur toy cat put into the corresponding tin. The die-throw was recorded by Miss Beenham, and the die concealed.

The tins were manipulated as usual, and the sitters, including Miss Beenham, all went behind the curtain, and watched through the chink holes. Marion and S.G.S. were then recalled, and S.G.S. acted as umpire, watching Marion and the tins. Mr. Collins followed Marion round the room, stopping when he stopped, and willed him to open the correct tin.

We did six experiments under these precise conditions. The first was a complete failure, but the remaining five were all successful at first try. (The odds against five or more successes in six trials are 1,504 to 1.)

Marion's performance must therefore be considered a brilliant success. This makes it more than ever probable that, when Marion is followed, he gains his principal clues from the movements of walking, e.g. hesitation in footsteps, sudden stoppings, turnings, startings, accelerations, and retardations on the part of the follower. When we remember that the constantly swaying box is not altogether under the control of the wearer, it does not appear likely that much reliable information could be gained about slight movements of the trunk.

We next had constructed* a kind of sentry box on wheels. This box was 6 feet 7 inches high, and closed on three of its vertical sides and at the top and bottom. The front of the box was left open, so that a man could enter and stand comfortably in it. The open front of the box could be covered by five rectangular panels of plywood, each about 14½ inches high, so that by the removal of a panel any part of the occupant's body could be exposed to Marion's gaze. For instance, if the four lower panels were in position, and the uppermost panel were removed, his head and neck alone would be visible. When all five panels were in position, the man was completely invisible. He himself, however, was able to watch Marion through the tiny crevice that separated the top panel from the one immediately below it.

This wheeled box was provided with a pair of handles fixed to its base, so that the box could be pushed round the room from behind in such a way that the panelled front of the box was always facing Marion. The small wheels under the box were so arranged as to allow the box to be rapidly turned to face in any direction, and to allow free movement both backwards and forwards. In order to gain space for these evolutions, we removed the central table from the room.

By wheeling the man round in the box we hoped to eliminate all cues that Marion might obtain from the movements of walking. Needless to say, the person who pushed the box round went outside the room with

* II, 7.

Marion and S.G.S., while the others retired behind the curtain. Thus the only persons who knew where the object was hidden were the man in the box and those behind the curtain.

In the first series with the sentry box Mr. Collins was wheeled round behind Marion with all the panels removed, so that his whole body was exposed to Marion's gaze. Marion was very successful under these conditions.

A number of tests was then made* with all the panels closed, so that no part of Mr. Collins was visible. Under these conditions Marion failed to find the object more often than chance would predict.

In a final series all the panels were in position, except the top one, so that Mr. Collins's stockinette-covered head alone was visible. It was during this series that we observed on several occasions how Marion would glance repeatedly at the hooded head while he was hesitating with his hand over a tin, apparently waiting for a tell-tale movement that would inform him whether or not he was at the right tin. Marion succeeded in these tests, the odds against chance being 2,408 to 1 for 25 trials. It is certain that involuntary head-movements on the part of Mr. Collins furnished the cues by which Marion located the hidden object.

It is probably persons of the emotional type who, in their anxiety to see Marion succeed, unconsciously give away hints. Apparently he does not succeed with those who are on their guard, and who keep their muscles well under control. But persons of the 'motor' type are to be found in any considerable audience and they serve as living signposts to warn him when he is approaching his objective or receding from it.

These experiments* have an important lesson in connection with the testing of telepathy. They show that no experiments can be considered satisfactory if the guesser is able to see any part of the agent's body. When the subject has only a small number (five or six) symbols from which to make his choice, the possibility of visual codes *elaborated unconsciously* when the same agent and guesser work together over any considerable period of time is too patent to be overlooked.

The question arises: Is Marion aware of the methods he employs in finding hidden objects, or does he really believe that he succeeds by means of telepathy? The answer probably is that, after years of practice, the reading of *indicia* has become a subconscious mental process which Marion is entirely unable to analyse. He certainly claims to possess powers of telepathy and clairvoyance, but S.G.S. personally discovered no evidence of such powers. He does not score above chance expectation when an agent behind a screen looks at Zener cards or

* II, 7.

playing cards. Nor does he succeed with numbers or drawings enclosed in opaque envelopes. When, however, numbers or drawings are inscribed on cards which Marion is able to manipulate in view of his audience, he may succeed by watching the reactions of the audience as he runs through the cards one by one.

Marion employs no confederates, and is in a class apart from the stage 'telepathists' whose entertaining, though empty, performances have been a feature of radio and music-hall programmes for many years. The latter work in pairs, use elaborate visual or auditory codes, clever mis-direction of attention, pre-arrangement, or midget radio sets. Marion, on the other hand, has a flair for interpreting slight movements on the part of his audience, changes of posture and breathing, etc. He possesses also a highly developed tactual sense. Marion has also submitted his powers to the fullest scientific examination, and this the numerous pairs who make use of codes and tricks are never willing to do. Certain performers of the latter type, while very careful not to claim that they use genuine telepathy in their stage performances, nevertheless have done their best by indirect means to inveigle the public into the illusion that they really possess paranormal powers. These people would like to be credited with extraordinary telepathic gifts, but know quite well that their performance could not stand up to any scientific investigation. Instead of admitting that they are entertainers and disclaiming extra-sensory powers, they take refuge in non-committal phrases.

Fortunately, the *majority* of stage 'telepathists' today adopt a more straightforward attitude, and freely admit that they do not employ extra-sensory means.

## (2) *The Repetition of Dr. Rhine's Work by S.G.S.*[1]

### 1. THE CARDS

The Zener cards used throughout this investigation were made by a firm of playing-card manufacturers, and the backs were similar to those of the firm's ordinary playing cards. It will not be necessary to describe the backs of the cards in detail, since they were never exposed to the gaze of the subjects while the latter were making their guesses.

The card to be guessed was either covered by a rectangle of white cardboard or completely hidden by a screen, or, in a very few cases, sealed in an opaque envelope.

On the faces of the cards the five symbols Plus, Circle, Star, Rectangle and Wavy Lines were printed in thin red lines. From the outset S.G.S. made it impossible for the guessers to 'learn' the cards from specks, etc., on their backs, or from any impressions that might be showing faintly through the backs. He did this (i) by never allowing the subjects when they were guessing, to see the backs of the cards, and (ii) by never using the same pack twice, for the same guesser, in an afternoon's work.

S.G.S. now decided to compile, by the use of mathematical tables, a *random* sequence of 1,000 card-symbols. This series was then split up into 40 consecutive blocks of 25. The 40 corresponding sets of 25 cards were put into 40 envelopes, which were numbered 1–40 and kept in two cardboard boxes, each containing 20 envelopes. Originally the 40 blocks were in the order of the random series, and the envelopes stood in their numerical order in the boxes. The first time after such a new random series had been compiled, the percipients worked through the envelopes in the order in which they stood in the boxes. But when the thousand cards had been guessed, the envelopes were shuffled in the boxes, and, before each pack was used, the cards were themselves shuffled out of the guesser's sight. The greatest care was taken in clairvoyance experiments to prevent the subject from catching a glimpse of the bottom card of the pack.

At the beginning of each week's work the packs were taken out of the envelopes, the envelopes were shuffled among themselves, and the packs were replaced so that the pack which was, say, in envelope 19 was now to be found in, say, envelope 12. This was to prevent subjects who came week after week from learning the composition of the packs in any of the envelopes.

A fresh random distribution of 1,000 cards was compiled *on an average* after each 4,000 guesses, and 31 such distributions were compiled from the tables during the five years' investigation. To be strictly accurate, the first random distribution by means of tables was made in January 1935, after about 1,700 guesses had been recorded.

When the cards first arrived in November 1934, they were spread faces downward on a large table and thoroughly mixed by three persons; they were then picked up into packs of 25 by the three persons, consecutive cards being chosen at random from different parts of the pile.

One advantage of the use of packs containing cards randomly distributed as compared with packs containing exactly five cards of each symbol is that the binomial formulae can be applied to any large group of cards and guesses, even if this is not composed of exact multiples of 25. This was of importance when we came to the study of displacement, in which it is convenient to consider groups of 23 or 24 card-symbols (see Chap. VIII, p. 125).

We shall now give a brief description of how the random sequences were compiled. S.G.S. had at his disposal 1,200 cards, there being 240 of each symbol. He first associated with each of the symbols, Plus, Circle, Star, Rectangle, Wavy Lines the respective numbers 1, 2, 3, 4, 5. He then read off from Chambers's *Seven-Figure Mathematical Tables* the *last* digits of the logarithms of the following numbers:

$$10078, 10178, 10278, \ldots 99978.$$

The numbers chosen were thus taken at intervals of 100, so as to ensure that the last digits in the logarithms should be independent. If the digit happened to be one of the numbers 1 to 5, it was entered on the list, or, more precisely, the corresponding card-symbol was written. If the digit happened to be 6, 7, 8, 9, or 0, it was not entered but ignored. From this sequence a random series of about 450 cards was obtained. The process was then repeated with, say, the following numbers:

$$10043, 10143, 10243, \ldots 99943,$$

and so on, until a list of 1,000 cards had been compiled. The actual cards were then chosen one by one according to the above list from the 1,200 cards.

## 2. THE GUESSERS

In the summer of 1934 more than a hundred persons living in or around London who had taken part in the 1928–9 long-distance experiments* of S.G.S. were circularized (see Chap. II, p. 20). Between 40 and 50 people responded, and ultimately some 23 of these came to 13d, Roland Gardens, S.W.7. to take part in the new experiments. Several of these persons claimed to have had psychic experiences of various kinds.

As the weeks went by, other subjects were obtained, some through the kindness of Professor Burt of University College, London.

In November 1935, in the hope of providing a stimulus, we offered valuable money prizes to persons who were able to score 12 or more hits in 25 guesses under controlled conditions. Though we gave publicity to these offers, the response was disappointing.

In the autumn of 1936, S.G.S. approached about fifty spiritualist mediums. As a result, one well-known automatic writer, one fairly well-known trance medium, and four lesser known clairvoyants came to be tested at Roland Gardens or elsewhere. None of the mediums obtained any positive results.

In November 1936, in the hope of finding fresh and younger subjects, S.G.S. removed the experiment to the Psychological Laboratory at University College, London. Here, through the interest of Professors Burt and Flugel, his colleagues on the University of London Council

* II, 17.

for Psychical Investigation, S.G.S. was accommodated in a cubicle, and the work was continued with young students taking courses in psychology, while several of the post-graduate students rendered material assistance by acting as witnesses or as agents. Here S.G.S. was able to test students of various nationalities, including over a dozen Indians, two Chinese, two Egyptians, one American, one Greek and several from the nearer parts of Europe. In the summer vacation of 1936, four members of a Welsh family were tested in their home in North Wales for pure clairvoyance, the PCB technique being used (see p. 109). One of these, a young man of 21, was a good hypnotic subject in whom S.G.S. was able to induce sensory anaesthesia to pain caused by deep pricking with a needle. He was unsuccessful, however, when tested in the hypnotic state with 500 clairvoyance trials, obtaining a deviation of only 5 above expectation.

Another professional hypnotic subject was tested for both undifferentiated ESP and clairvoyance at University College. This subject, a man of about 45, showed very marked ability to recognize a playing-card by minute specks on the back when the card was mixed with five others. He was not allowed to touch any of the cards, and the recognition was shown to be purely visual. He succeeded in this feat only when in the hypnotic state, and was then right ten times out of ten. When, however, he was tested for telepathy and clairvoyance by means of the UT and PCB techniques, he failed completely to show any capacity for extra-chance scoring. One blind Indian was tested for clairvoyance at University College. As S.G.S. lifted off each card from the pack, the blind man was allowed to lay his finger on the *edge* only. However, in 500 trials he obtained a quite insignificant deviation of −6.

In the summer term of 1938, Mrs. Eileen Garrett, the well-known trance medium, came to University College to be tested with Zener cards. Three years earlier, she had obtained remarkable results both in telepathy and clairvoyance experiments while working with Dr. Rhine[2] in America.

In one such series of 3,525 clairvoyance trials carried out in her normal state, she obtained 888 correct hits. This is a deviation from chance expectation of +183, i.e. over 7 standard deviations, with corresponding odds of more than $10^{11}$ to 1 against chance. Of this series Dr. Rhine remarks: 'Out of 3,525 trials for clairvoyance done in three days, 1,550 were made with a distance of at least 15 feet and with at least one wall between the cards and the sensitive, and these yielded a *higher average* score than did the remaining 1,975 trials made with the cards on the table with the sensitive.'

In another series of 625 trials[2] at pure telepathy she scored 336 correct hits, this being equivalent to an average of 13·4 correct hits per 25 guesses sustained over 25 packs of cards. There is no question about the phenomenal significance of these results. It is interesting to note that Mrs. Garrett succeeded much better at telepathy than at clairvoyance, her averages over a period of twelve days being 10·1 hits per 25 and 5·7 hits per 25 under the two conditions while guessing in the normal state. In the trance state, as the spirit guide 'Uvani', her corresponding averages were slightly less—namely, 9·1 and 5·6. Apparently, going into trance did not assist her card-guessing faculty in the least.

In 1935, Mrs. Garrett was again at Duke University doing her preshuffle (prediction) card tests, but this time her average on 23,700 trials was very slightly below chance expectation, though not significantly so. She expressed herself as being 'fed up' with card-guessing, and she was probably feeling the same, when, two years later, she came to London. At any rate she did not show a glimmer of any paranormal faculty,[3] either with S.G.S. acting as experimenter, or when other persons took charge. We tried her at pure clairvoyance and with agents looking at the cards, in the waking state and in trance as the spirit-control 'Uvani', but it made no difference. She scored consistently at the chance level under all conditions.[3] On a grand total of 12,425 trials, she scored just 2,515 hits, which is only 30 above chance expectation, the deviation being less even than the standard deviation (44).

Why so many good card-guessers should peter out, and seemingly lose their ability in a short time, is one of the major puzzles of psychical research. Time and again it has happened that someone, who, over a period of two or three years, has been guessing above chance to the tune of astronomical odds, has suddenly, within a few weeks, lost every vestige of paranormal faculty. Sooner or later this has happened to every subject who has been investigated in England and America. It is all the more strange, because good trance mediums like Mrs. Piper and Mrs. Leonard have retained their telepathic powers for twenty or thirty years. If parapsychology is to make any real progress, it will be essential for us to discover why significant positive scoring suddenly disappears or is replaced by negative scoring, and to find out the conditions under which a good subject can maintain extra-chance results over a considerable period. But it is not necessary for the establishing of telepathy that the same subject should go on producing extra-chance scores indefinitely. For telepathy is a biological and not a physical phenomenon. Even a psychologist cannot go on using the same rats and monkeys indefinitely. Nor do all psychological experiments produce the same results when repeated.

## 3. CLAIRVOYANCE EXPERIMENTS 1934–9

In all, 108 persons took part as guessers in the pure clairvoyance tests. Five distinct techniques were used which will be denoted by PCA, PCB, PCS, PCM, and PCD.

(i) *PCA and PCB.* The only difference between the PCA and PCB methods is that, with the former, the checking up was done after every five trials with the guesser looking on, while, with the latter, the checking was not done until the 25 guesses were completed, and the guesser was not allowed to watch the checking.

Our chief object in checking after every five trials was to inform the guesser as quickly as possible whether he had succeeded or failed, in the hope that it might be possible for him to learn by his mistakes. There was the possibility that success might be accompanied by some peculiar introspective feeling. Since random packs of cards were used, there was not the same objection to our checking after every five trials as there was in the case of Rhine's packs, which contain exactly five cards of each symbol.

It was planned originally for each subject to do 500 guesses with the PCA method, and then another 500 with the PCB method. But it soon became obvious that, with the first method, there was no sign of improvement through practice, and after 1936 all subjects were started with the PCB method.

As a general rule three persons were present at the experiments. They were the guesser or subject (S), the experimenter (E) (S.G.S. with few exceptions), and the witness (W). They were seated as shown in the figure, the experimenter and guesser facing one another on opposite

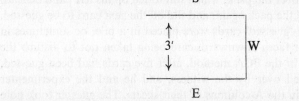

sides of a table and about three feet apart. The witness sat at the end of the table. The experimenter was the person who dealt out the cards and generally supervised the procedure. The witness, who had to be an intelligent and observant person, was present to keep a duplicate record of guesses and card-targets, and to watch every detail of the recording and procedure. The experimenter and witness were each provided with a scoring-sheet, foolscap size, and designed to accommodate two sets of 25 guesses. For each set of 25 there were two columns, the one on the left headed G (guesses) and the one of the right headed A (actual cards). The two columns were divided into 25 rectangular cells. There were also spaces on the record sheet for the name of the guesser, the date, the number of the pack, the times of the first and last guesses, totals correct, remarks, and there was a statement at the bottom of each sheet which read: '*This independent record has been checked with the duplicate and found to agree. Signed* ———.' (For an example of a record sheet, see p. 138.)

The experimenter was also provided with a clean, white rectangle of cardboard, just a little larger than a Zener card and cut from a postcard. As has been described (p. 105), the random series of 1,000 cards was ready for use in 40 envelopes, each containing 25 cards, the envelopes being in a determined order in two cardboard boxes on the table.

The experimenter took the proper envelope from the box, and, and holding it below the level of the table, removed the pack of 25 cards, which he shuffled (unless a new random distribution had just been made) beneath the table. He next rested the pack face downwards on the palm of his left hand, and covered it with the rectangle of white card. He then raised the palm of his left hand, until the white card on top just reached the level of the table. With the thumb and forefinger of his right hand he slid off the top card on to the table, covered by the rectangle of white card. He then *immediately* lowered the pack again below the level of the table.

The guesser or subject (S) now called aloud his guess for the covered card lying on the table. Both experimenter (E) and witness (W) recorded the guess in the appropriate cells of their scoring-sheets in the G (guesses) column. The experimenter then removed with his right hand the covering card, put it over the pack, which still rested on his left palm beneath the table, raised the pack again, and slid off the next card to be guessed, and so on. The 'guessed' cards were placed in a pile, or sometimes in rows, with their faces downward, care being taken not to disturb the original order. In the PCA method, after five cards had been guessed, they were turned over by the witness, and he and the experimenter recorded them in the A-columns of their sheets. The guesser took note of his successes, watching the checking. When the column of 25 cards was complete—after 5 checkings had taken place—the experimenter and witness ticked off the correct hits, and entered the totals, the time of the last guess, etc. at the foot of the column. (E) and (W) then compared scoring sheets, card by card and guess by guess, to see that they tallied. In point of fact, errors were very rarely found, but they could usually be rectified by a reference to the pack, whose cards still retained their original order. Both witness and experimenter then signed the statement referred to above when the two sets of 25 in the sheet were complete, each person signing on both sheets. The next envelope was then taken from the box, and the work proceeded as before.

With the PCB technique, the cards were not checked until the set of 25 guesses was complete. The guesser (S) then walked away to a remote part of the room, or went behind a screen, and, in his absence, (E) and (W) checked the results, and filled in the blank A-columns of their sheets. The average time for the subject to guess 25 cards was nearly 4 minutes, but in later experiments with Shackleton and Mrs. Stewart during or after the War it was speeded up to about a minute or less. In the present series, however, the guessers were allowed to choose their own tempo at guessing. Usually a subject guessed from 200–250 cards in an afternoon, but certain more rapid workers did 500 or more guesses in an afternoon. After March 1935, S.G.S. did not, except in special circumstances, allow any person other than (E), (W) and (S), to be in the room during the guessing, but as a rule two or three subjects were tested consecutively in the same afternoon, appointments having been made for them to come at specified times.

At the end of each afternoon's work, the last witness placed the duplicate scoring sheets in an envelope, sealed it in the presence of S.G.S. and posted it as soon as possible to Dr. C. E. M. Joad. The other copies were retained by S.G.S.

It is interesting to note that both the PCA and PCB techniques gave results which showed a slight tendency to score negatively, that is *below* chance expectation.

On the total of 50,075 trials for PCA and PCB taken together there was a negative deviation of 201 hits, which gave a critical ratio of −2·24, with corresponding odds of about 40 to 1 against chance.

By another method of scoring, which takes into account the variations in the numbers of target-symbols and guess-symbols in the different packs—a method due to W. L. Stevens, which is perhaps slightly more accurate though very laborious—a critical ratio of −2·44 was obtained, with corresponding odds of about 68 to 1.

This negative effect may quite well be genuine. It is supported by the fact that on the 299 different occasions on which PCA or PCB experiments were carried out, above-chance scores were obtained on 111 occasions, below-chance scores on 151 occasions, and scores which agreed exactly with theoretical expectation on 37 occasions. Ignoring the last group we find that the odds against our getting as many as 151 negative deviations on 262 occasions work out at about 74 to 1.

We have described the PCA and PCB methods at length, because these were the only techniques which led to a slightly significant deviation.

(ii) *PCS* (1938–9)[1]. This method in which 26 guessers took part differed only from the preceding method in that the subject was screened from the cards by an opaque screen, about 3 feet broad and 2 feet 6 inches high, which was placed across the centre of the table. The experimenter laid the pack to be guessed face downwards on the table close to the centre of the screen. He enquired whether the guesser was

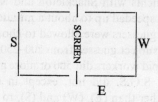

ready, lifted off the top card, and laid it face downwards on the table without looking at it. At the same time he called out 'First guess' or 'Next', as the case might be. The guesser called aloud his guess, which was independently recorded by both (E) and (W). The subject did not move from his seat behind the screen during the checking at the end of 25 trials. He was told, however, how many hits he had made at the end of each 25.

(iii) *PCM*.[2] This was the 'screen and pointer' method described on p. 56, Chap. V. It was used only by Mrs. Garrett and one other subject. The guesser sat behind a black metal screen, 2 feet broad by 1 foot 6 inches high, which stood on the table. Between the bottom edge of the screen and table was a gap half an inch high, through which the subject could push a light, metal pointer. The screen stood over the centre line of a row of five 'target' cards which were fixed faces upward to the table by means of drawing pins; they bore in order the symbols Plus, Circle, Star, Rectangle, and Wavy Lines. The experimenter sat facing the screen, and, with his left elbow resting on the table, held the pack of cards in his left hand close to the centre of the screen, the backs of all the cards being towards him. At the signal 'First guess' or 'Next', the subject had to guess the bottom card of the pack (i.e. the card nearest the screen), and to indicate his guess by pointing with the rod at the corresponding 'target'-card. The experimenter then lifted off the bottom card, and, without looking at its face, placed it carefully opposite the 'target'-card chosen by the subject. At the end of 25 guesses the 25 cards thus found themselves arranged in five piles, all the cards being face downwards. A count was then made of the successes under each symbol, and these were recorded on a scoring sheet thus:

112

$$
\text{Total 5} \left\{ \begin{array}{ll} + & 1 \\ O & 0 \\ S & 2 \\ R & 1 \\ W & 1 \end{array} \right.
$$

The count was carefully checked by the witness.

(iv) *PCD*. This is the DT (down through the pack) method often used by Dr. Rhine. It was employed with only three subjects, one of whom was 'Marion' (Josef Kraus) the well-known vaudeville telepathist.[1] In the case of Marion, the experimenter (S.G.S.), the witness, and the guesser sat at a table, Marion being provided with a scoring sheet. S.G.S. took one of the envelopes out of the box, and, holding it under the table, shuffled the cards, and replaced them in the envelope. He then placed the envelope on the table, with the flap closed and a rubber band round the envelope to keep it closed. *Before* the cards were shuffled, and while they were under the table, Marion was allowed to touch them once, since he claimed that this was essential if he was to succeed. The envelope containing the cards was placed in front of Marion on the table, flap downwards. He then wrote down in the G-column of his scoring sheet with extreme rapidity a series of 25 card-symbols. When he had finished, S.G.S. ran through the list, asking him to say definitely what any carelessly drawn symbol was intended to represent. This was essential, because Marion sometimes made his rectangles very like his circles. S.G.S. was also particularly careful to see that Marion did not get a glimpse of the last card in the pack, since some records which he had produced of experiments he had conducted when alone proved that he had been scoring significantly by unwittingly getting a glimpse of the last card as he laid the envelope on the table, no rubber band having been used. After we were satisfied about the entries in the guess-column, we took the cards out of the envelope, and checked the results with Marion watching. Under these conditions he obtained only 910 hits in 4450 trials, which is just a chance result. He still continued, however, to produce for our inspection highly significant scores which he claimed to have obtained while experimenting by himself. These amounted to tens of thousands of trials, and the high scores were to be partly accounted for by the fact that Marion managed to glimpse the bottom card.

The grand total of experiments in pure clairvoyance with all techniques was 70,900 trials and these yielded a *negative* deviation of 160 hits, which, however, is not significant (CR = −1·50).

## 4. EXPERIMENTS IN UNDIFFERENTIATED ESP[1] (1935–7)

We made no experiments in pure telepathy in which the possibility of clairvoyance was excluded, and the tests now to be described allow for either clairvoyance or both to operate. Two techniques were employed; they will be referred to as UT (undifferentiated telepathy) and UTM (undifferentiated telepathy by a screened matching method).

(i) *UT*. The room at 13d Roland Gardens, S.W.7, was first systematically examined to find out whether there were any reflecting surfaces which might enable the guesser to see the exposed card, even while sitting behind a screen. As a result of a great many experiments, it was found that the only source of reflection that might give any assistance to a guesser was the sliding glass lid of a bookcase. At the commencement of each afternoon's work this was adjusted by being slid up. In the cubicle at University College S.G.S. satisfied himself that, when the screen was in use, there were no reflecting surfaces that could give the guesser any assistance. At Roland Gardens the guesser and agent (or sender), who also acted as a witness, were seated about 5 feet apart at each end of a table, and on the centre of the table rested a plywood screen, measuring 8 feet by 3 feet, suspended by cords from the ceiling. There was no crevice between the bottom of the screen and the table. The experimenter (S.G.S.) sat on the same side of the screen as the agent, but at the side of the table and close to the screen. The experimenter and guesser (unless the latter was in trance) were each provided with a scoring sheet identical with that used in the PC experiments. Beneath the table there was fixed a vertical board which prevented the guesser from seeing the agent's feet or legs. Thus every part of the agent's body was screened from the guesser's view.

The experimenter was also provided with five rubber stamps of similar make and weight, together with a red or green ink-pad. The stamps bore the five Zener symbols and the impressions they produced on the scoring sheet measured about $\frac{1}{2}$ inch by $\frac{3}{8}$ inch.

To have used a pen or pencil for the recording of the 'target' symbols would have been fatal, since a number of tests showed that if the experimenter recorded his card *before* the subject had made his guess, the latter was able to recognize the plus symbol by the lifting of the pencil, the rectangle by the time taken to draw it, and so on, and indeed most of the symbols could be identified by the sound of the pencil strokes. It might, of course, be suggested that as the *rubber* parts of the five stamps were slightly different in size and shape, this might lead to auditory discrimination of the symbols. But this rather far-fetched hypothesis is refuted by the fact that 84 people did the experiment, and all failed at such delicate discrimination, both individually and in the mass.

At University College the same screen was used; it was fixed in a vertical position by wooden guides attached to the wall, but the distance between the guesser (S) and the agent (W) was only about four feet. Similar rubber stamps were used; S.G.S. had three sets of these.

The pack rested on the table near the centre of the screen, face downwards. The experimenter closed his eyes, lifted off the top card, and held it close to the screen, its face towards the agent. With closed eyes the experimenter called out 'First guess' or 'Next', as the case might be. This was the signal to the guesser that the agent had begun to look at the card. The experimenter then quickly opened his eyes, and recorded the card-symbol in the appropriate cell of the A-column of his scoring sheet by means of the proper rubber stamp. Meanwhile the guesser behind the screen recorded his guess in pencil in the G-column of his sheet, *without* calling it aloud. As a signal that he had made his guess, the subject tapped twice on the table with his pencil. By adopting this procedure, the experimenter, who did not know which card he had lifted from the pack until he had opened his eyes, could give nothing away by the inflections of his voice. No words were spoken during the guessing except the words of the signal. The guessed cards were placed faces downward on the table in a pile, care being taken not to disturb the order. When the column of 25 guesses was complete, the guesser, *without leaving his seat behind the screen*, handed his scoring sheet with the G (guess) column filled in to the experimenter. The latter, with the agent watching closely, copied the subject's list of guesses on to his own scoring sheet, and filled in the subject's empty A (target) column from the record on his own scoring sheet. The agents were all specially instructed to watch every step of the checking, and a comparison was made of the two sheets guess by guess. The agent and experimenter each signed both records, the successful guesses having ticks placed opposite them, and the total for each 25 being entered at the bottom of the appropriate column. The guesser remained behind the screen during the checking. He was informed of his score after each 25 guesses, and praised when he made seven or more correct hits.

Before starting work with a fresh subject or agent, the experimenter and agent usually held a preliminary consultation as to the nature of the imagery to be employed by the agent. For instance, if the sender claimed to be a good visualizer, it would be agreed that he should glance at the exposed card, shut his eyes, and imagine the symbol drawn in red paint on a white canvas or with chalk on a blackboard. In other cases it was decided that the agent should represent to himself wavy lines by an image of waves breaking on a beach, the plus by a cluster of wooden crosses in a war cemetery, etc. In a few cases the sender employed either visual or auditory *verbal* imagery. But in every case it was firmly impressed on the agent that *during the guessing he must keep his lips tightly* closed. In certain cases it was agreed that the agent should glance once at the card, shut his eyes, and dismiss it from his mind by thinking of something quite different.

## Involuntary Whispering[1]

No special precautions were taken to obviate the possibility of so-called involuntary whispering by the agent, or normal leakage through changes in breathing. Had S.G.S. discovered any subjects who scored positive results over any considerable period, he would have tried the effect of distance on the scoring. But the very fact that some 82 persons who tried the telepathy experiments obtained no apparent success of any kind strongly indicates that, if involuntary whispering ever helps people to score above chance expectation, this effect must be an excessively rare one.

A certain guesser, Mr. Hu,[1] a Chinese student at University College, had been credited by an investigator (who was testing the ability of students to interpret correctly subliminal auditory impressions) with the power of detecting faintly-whispered words that were below his normal threshold of recognition. He made 800 UTM guesses but obtained only 171 correct hits as against the 160 expected by chance. After completing this series, he did another 200 trials one day when he was fresh, Miss Elliott acting as agent. S.G.S. asked Miss Elliott to whisper very faintly the name of each card while she looked at it. Mr. Hu, who was sitting 4 feet—the normal distance—away from the agent, scored only 36 correct guesses, which is below expectation (40). He was then allowed to do another 200 guesses with Miss Elliott now whispering repeatedly the name of each card far more loudly than before. This time he scored 47 hits, a result which is again without significance.

## The Use of Codes

At 13d Roland Gardens, S.W.7, the agent and guesser who worked together were, as a rule, almost strangers to each other, and generally met at the office of the University of London Council for Psychical Investigation for the first time. But in one case a mother and daughter played the parts of guesser and agent, in another a father and daughter, in a third two brothers, and in two other cases pairs of close friends. At University College the agent and guesser were often friends or at least acquainted. The question arises, therefore, whether it would not have been possible in such cases for information to have been transmitted from agent to receiver by means of a simple code employed with an intent to deceive the experimenter.

116

If any code were used when sender and receiver were separated by an opaque screen, as in the present series, it would have to be either (i) a 'timing' code, or (ii) an auditory code consisting of such sounds as coughs, scraping or tapping of feet, sounds of hand-movements or of pencil on the table, blowing, and so on. The possibility of (i) is ruled out by the fact that S.G.S., the experimenter, dealt out the cards in his own time, and gave the signal 'Next' at his own pleasure. The agent, who was not permitted to speak during the guessing, sat close to S.G.S. and a vertical board fixed beneath the table prevented the guesser from seeing the agent's feet or legs or from making contact with them. As a result of special tests, it was found that, if this precaution is omitted, it is easily possible for the agent to use a code consisting of such movements as the opening and closing of the heels, the crossing of the toe of one boot over the other boot, all of which motions are so slight that they would escape detection unless the experimenter were looking under the table.

As regards the possibility of auditory codes, whenever S.G.S. heard the agent make any unusual noise, he made a secret mark opposite the guess on his scoring sheet, and waited to see if the noise were repeated when the same card symbol was turned up again. S.G.S. never succeeded in detecting any such auditory code.

## The Results of the UT Technique[1]

In all, 76 persons were tested by this method, and, of these, 28 did a thousand guesses each. The grand total of 44,100 trials gave a positive deviation of only 18 above expectation, which is less than a quarter of the standard deviation (84). The result provides a strong argument against the involuntary whispering theory so light-heartedly espoused by certain psychologists in their attempts to explain away telepathy. Nor does it appear that subjects are able to discriminate between the sounds made by the five rubber stamps, the rubber parts of which measure $\frac{1}{2}$ inch by $\frac{3}{8}$ inch. Indeed, such theories as we have discussed seem to be nonsensical when put to a practical test.

(ii) *UTM* (*Screened Matching Technique*).[1] Thirteen guessers, including Mrs. Garrett, the trance medium, were tested by this method in the summer and autumn of 1937. The apparatus consisted of the metal screen described in the PCM experiments with the $\frac{1}{2}$-inch gap between the bottom edge and the table. The agent and guesser now faced each other on opposite sides of the screen, while the experimenter sat at the side of the table close to the screen, and on the same side as the agent. As in the UT experiments, the experimenter closed his eyes and lifted off the top card for the agent to visualize, holding it close to the centre of the screen. With closed eyes the experimenter called out 'First guess' or 'Next'. Not until the guesser's pointer had come quite definitely to rest on one of the five 'target' cards, did the experimenter (who had opened his eyes immediately after giving the signal) place the exposed card face downwards opposite the 'target' card indicated by the subject. The other details are the same as in the PCM technique. The chief danger of this method lies in the possibility that the agent or experimenter, watching the motion of the pointer along the row of cards, may make some involuntary audible movement that will cause the guesser to stop the pointer opposite the correct card, which, of course, is known to both agent and experimenter.

Another serious objection is that the method does not readily permit of the experimenter's obtaining an exact record of each card-symbol opposite its corresponding guess.

With the matching method the total number of trials was 13,350, and of these, 2,703 were hits. This gives a small positive deviation of 33, which is even less than the standard deviation (46).

The grand total for all telepathy experiments UT and UTM is 57,450 trials on which there was a positive deviation of 51, a number much less than the standard deviation (96).

In the five years which these experiments occupied a total of 128,350 guesses were collected by S.G.S., all done under his direct supervision, and 160 persons were tested for telepathy or clairvoyance. The total deviation is a negative one of 109 hits, which is less than the standard deviation (143).

An examination of the 50,075 UT trials shows that the most popular symbol was the *circle* (guessed 10,526 times), and the most unpopular was the *rectangle*, which was guessed only 9,440 times; the actual order of preference was circle, wavy lines, plus sign, star, rectangle.

## Some Exceptional Scores[1]

The highest positive score in clairvoyance was made by a young student at University College, London, who, in a set of 500 PCB guesses, obtained 128 correct hits—equivalent to +3·13 standard deviations estimated by Stevens's method. But when this young man was tested again with another set of 500, he scored only 102 hits, and S.G.S. was unable to get into touch with him for further work.

The lowest score was a PCA set of 500 trials with only 77 correct hits, the equivalent of −2·67 standard deviations, but here again, when the guesser did another 500 trials under similar conditions, she obtained the quite normal score of 103 hits.

The only positive score in the telepathy-cum-clairvoyance work of the slightest interest is that of Mrs. G. Stewart, whose work is described in the next chapter. The lowest UT score was made by Mr. E. Fisher, a young psychology student, who had suffered from nervous breakdown. On his first thousand guesses he made only 168 hits (equivalent to $-2 \cdot 53$ standard deviations), and two of his forty scores for 25 guesses were zeros. However, on a second thousand, his score rose to 193, a result which, though still slightly below chance (200), has no significance.

# CHAPTER VIII

# The Discovery of Basil Shackleton
# and Mrs. Stewart*

One gloomy February afternoon in 1936 S. G. S. was sitting in the office at 13d, Roland Gardens, London, S.W.7, carrying out routine experiments in card-guessing. He had then been working for fifteen months without a gleam of success. Suddenly the door opened and a tallish, well-groomed man of about thirty-six entered. He was Basil Shackleton, the well-known photographer, whose studio was then in Frith Street off Shaftesbury Avenue, W.1. Though he had telephoned to say he would call one day that week, he was not actually expected on this particular afternoon. Shackleton explained that he had read an article in the Sunday press dealing with the experiments. He was not, he said, interested in the prizes offered for sensational scoring. 'I have come', he declared, 'not to be tested, but to demonstrate telepathy.' He went on to say that often of an evening he had amazed his friends by 'guessing through a pack of playing cards from top to bottom', and getting 'most of them right'. That afternoon there happened to be present in the room Mr. J. Aldred, an old friend whom S.G.S. had known since 1922, and a lady, Mrs. Crane, who took part in the 1928–32 long-distance tests. Mrs. Crane had come by appointment to do some guessing but she kindly consented to wait till Shackleton had finished, since he had to leave early. No one in the room had met Shackleton before. After S.G.S. had introduced him to the Zener symbols and explained the procedure, he was seated behind the 3 feet by 3 feet plywood screen which was usually in position above the table. Mrs. Crane was placed on the same side of the screen as Shackleton and directly behind him, so that she might watch him. Mr. Aldred acted as agent, or sender, with S.G.S. as experimenter. S.G.S. and J.A. sat together on the opposite side of the screen in the usual positions described under UT in the preceding chapter. S.G.S. was especially on his mettle as he stood to lose a not inconsiderable sum of money should Shackleton score a

* VII, 1.

120

twelve, since he had offered a prize for a score of this magnitude. The agent, therefore, was earnestly exhorted to keep his lips firmly closed during the periods of guessing. Shackleton recorded his guesses on a scoring sheet. On the first pack of 25 he scored a 10 and on the second a 7. Everyone thought this an excellent start, but Shackleton seemed disappointed, and said the scores were 'very poor'. He asked if 'this lady', meaning Mrs. Crane, could take J.A.'s place as agent. Whereupon J.A. rose and sat beside Shackleton on the other side of the screen, while Mrs. Crane took his place. Shackleton now scored a 7, a 6, a 6, and a 3. After the last set of 25, he declared it was useless for him to continue. He was best at this kind of thing in the evening especially after he had had a drink or two.

Shacketon promised to visit us again in a fortnight's time when he would be less busy, but actually we did not see him again until the afternoon of 27th March, 1936, when Mrs. Dwyer acted as agent and witness for eight runs of 25. The score this time (37/200) was slightly below chance expectation. A third visit on April 3rd again produced disappointing results (48/200). Shackleton now said that he would like to try the experiment in his studio at Frith Street and J. Aldred and S.G.S. called there on June 25th.

At Shackleton's suggestion he and the two experimenters adjourned to a local public house for a drink.* They then returned to the studio, and rigged up an efficient screen out of large sheets of stiff cardboard, one sheet of which was fastened beneath the table. S.G.S. had brought with him rubber stamps, scoring sheets, and one of the two boxes of Zener cards. J. A. acted as agent and witness. But once more the result was a fiasco, for Shackleton made only 41 hits in 250 trials. This time he blamed the noise of the traffic outside, which was certainly disturbing. In all, Shackleton had done 800 UT trials, and had made 165 hits, which is quite a chance result. No one at that time dreamed of the hidden significance which lay beneath this commonplace scoring. Yet, despite the lack of success, S.G.S. felt that Shackleton was no ordinary guesser. He seemed so confident, so certain of his powers, that one felt it was only a matter of time before he produced something surprising. S.G.S. and Shackleton were not to meet again till December 1940, when the blitz was over London.

In that year, 1936, S.G.S.† had made the acquaintance of another very promising subject who, like Shackleton, was later to make history.

---

* The two experimenters, however, were careful to drink only a single glass of beer each.

† VII, 1.

Mr. D. A. Stewart, a young consulting engineer, was introduced to S.G.S. by Harry Price in the month of May. This man acted as subject in 1,000 UT trials with either Mrs. Johnstone or her daughter as agent. Mr. Stewart, who met the Johnstones for the first time at 13d, Roland Gardens, S.W.7, scored only chance results. He told us, however, that his wife believed herself to be the possessor of psychical gifts. She was, unfortunately, occupied during the afternoons and unable to come to Roland Gardens. Mr. Stewart then suggested that Mrs. and Miss Johnstone and S.G.S. should visit his home at 18, Marchmont Road, Richmond, Surrey, one evening, and try some experiments. The first visit took place on June 5th. A very efficient screen was rigged up by the suspension of a thick doubled blanket from a line stretched across the room so that the free ends of the blanket rested over the centre of a small table. Mr. Stewart fixed a drawing-board in a vertical position beneath the table to prevent any contact of feet. It was arranged that Mr. Stewart should sit in a line at right angles to the screen through its centre and about 12 feet away on the side of the screen opposite to that on which the agent would sit with the cards. Miss Johnstone and S.G.S. sat at the table on one side of the screen with Mrs. Stewart on the other side. Mrs. Johnstone sat close behind her daughter. These dispositions made, the room was examined for the possibility of reflections, but no adjustments were found necessary. The procedure then followed strictly that described under UT (p. 114), with Miss Johnstone acting as agent and witness. Owing to a late start, only four sets of 25 were guessed, and the scores for these were 7, 8, 7, 8, the average time for Mrs. Stewart to guess 25 cards being about four minutes. No speaking was allowed while the guessing was in progress. The result was encouraging, and the same group arranged to meet again on the evening of June 17th. This time Miss Johnstone was again the agent, except for one run of 25 during which her mother took her place. The scores on this occasion were not so promising. In all, 1,000 trials were done in six sittings with either Miss Johnstone or her mother as agent. None of the scores was sensational, but on the 1,000 guesses Mrs. Stewart made 238 correct hits. This is 38 above chance expectation, and corresponds to odds of about 370 to 1 when considered as an isolated set. However, at this stage some 18 other persons had completed sets of 1,000 UT guesses, and in addition about 25,000 PC guesses had also been recorded. When estimated against this background, Mrs. Stewart's performance has little or no significance. We are not, however, on that account justified in ascribing it to chance, and subsequent developments suggest that the chance explanation is a very improbable one. Mrs. Stewart now began her second thousand

UT guesses, but unfortunately, the work was interrupted by the summer vacation, and was not resumed till November. It soon became clear that only chance scores were being produced, and S.G.S. felt he could not afford the time spent on the journeys to Richmond. From now onwards only occasional sittings were held, and the second thousand was not completed till June 4th, 1937. The same agents, Miss and Mrs. Johnstone, were employed throughout, until the final 100 guesses, for which Miss Rita Elliot was agent. On her second thousand Mrs. Stewart scored only 209 hits, a purely chance result. Now and then hope flickered for an instant, as for example when on 28th May 1937 the subject started off a run of 25 with six hits in succession.

In the summer of 1938 she did 925 UTM trials, using the pointer and the screen with the half-inch gap mentioned on p. 117. But she made only 191 hits, which is only six above chance expectation. After this, S.G.S. felt it was useless to continue with the experiments.

Until the autumn of 1939, S.G.S. still believed that it was practically impossible—at any rate in England—to find persons who could demonstrate ESP by guessing at the figures on Zener cards. He drew attention to this record of persistent failure by articles in the Press, and by lectures given to the British Psychological Society in London and in Glasgow, and to the Society for Psychical Research.

In November 1939, this growing scepticism received a shock. Whately Carington had brought to the notice of S.G.S. the striking results obtained in his picture-guessing tests discussed at length in Chapter VI. With remarkable pertinacity Carington insisted that S.G.S. should re-examine his experimental data. Carington suggested that S.G.S. should compare each guess, not with the card for which it was originally intended, but with the immediately preceding card and the immediately following card, and count up the hits. For, according to Carington, the faculty of extra-sensory cognition might not function in such a way that the subject always hit the target at which he was aiming. Just as a rifleman may show a personal bias which causes him persistently to strike the target at a point to the left or right of the bull's eye, so it might happen that the guesser at Zener cards, all unwittingly, was guessing correctly not the card the experimenter was looking at, but a card which was one or two places earlier or later in the sequence. Carington even suggested that this dispersed type of ESP might prove eventually to be more widespread than the exact type of cognition which so many experimenters had searched for in vain. Carington himself had found that his subjects did not always get the impression of a picture on the night when it was pinned up, but sometimes a correct sketch was made a night or two earlier or later in the week. There is, moreover, a vast amount of experience drawn from sittings with mediums which goes to suggest that these subjects can seldom divine those thoughts which are in the focus of the sitter's attention. The medium will refer to some trifling event known to the sitter, which happened last week or yesterday or a year ago, and make no mention at all of what is occupying her client's mind at the moment.

It was in no very hopeful spirit that S.G.S. began the task of searching his records for this 'displacement' effect.

As Mrs. Stewart was the only 'telepathy' subject who had shown any promise at all, S.G.S. decided to re-examine her 2,000 UT guesses. He began by counting hits obtained by comparing each guess (i) with the card immediately preceding the actual card for which the guess was intended, and (ii) with the card immediately following the card for which the guess was intended. This will be clear from the examples given below:

| (i) | Actual card | Guess |
|-----|-------------|-------|
|     | +           | S     |
|     | W           | +     |

| (ii) | Actual card | Guess |
|------|-------------|-------|
|      | +           | S     |
|      | S           | W     |

Example (i) shows a *post*-cognitive hit. The guess S is wrong for the card + for which it was intended, but the *next* guess + is correct for this card, though wrong for the card W at which it was aimed.

Example (ii) shows a *pre*cognitive hit. The guess S is wrong for the card + for which it was intended, but correct for the card S which was the next card to be looked at by the agent.

The term 'precognitive' is, perhaps, not a very happy one, for there is no evidence that the guesser *knows* beforehand what the next card turned up is going to be. He merely makes a guess which turns out to be right. He has seldom any inner conviction that he is right, nor can he produce any reason on which his guess is based. But as the word is now in general use, it is not easy to change it, nor indeed would it be worthwhile, and so long as we understand clearly what it means, no harm is done by the use of this rather inexact term.

Nowadays it has become the custom to call a hit on the next card a (+1) hit, and a hit on the immediately preceding card a (−1) hit, while a hit on the 'target' or 'actual' card is a (0) hit. Similarly a hit on the next card but one, i.e. the card *two* places ahead in the sequence, is known as a (+2) hit, while a hit on the card two places behind that which is being actually looked at by the agent is a (−2) hit.

It is obvious that, in a set of 25 guesses, the maximum number of possible (+1) hits is 24, since the *last* guess cannot give rise to a *pre*-cognitive or (+1) hit, and the maximum possible number of (−1) hits is also 24, since the *first* guess cannot give a *post*-cognitive or (−1) hit.

Hence in 25N guesses the *expected* number of *precognitive* (+1) hits will not be 5N but $\frac{1}{5} \times 24N$, i.e. 4·8N, and the expectation of *post*-cognitive (−1) hits in N sets of 25 will also be 4·8N.

Similarly, since there are only 23 possibilities of *precognitive* (+2) hits in a closed set of 25 guesses, it follows that in N sets of 25 the chance expectation of (+2) hits is one-fifth of 23N, i.e. 4·6N; the expectation of (−2) *post*-cognitive hits will also be 4·6N.

Before S.G.S. had finished scoring the first thousand guesses of Mrs. Stewart for (+1) and (−1) effects, he saw that he had made a remarkable discovery. He found there were 221 post-cognitive (−1) successes as compared with an expectation of 40 × 4·8, i.e. 192, and 225 pre-cognitive (+1) successes as against the same expectation of 192. These correspond to positive deviations equivalent respectively to 2·34 and 2·72 times the standard deviation. But S.G.S. asked himself: Would these post-cognitive and precognitive effects disappear in the *second* thousand trials, just as the success on the 'target' or 'actual' card had petered out?

To the amazement of the experimenter the (−1) and (+1) effects on the second thousand continued unabated. There were in fact 232 pre-cognitive and 221 post-cognitive successes. These correspond to positive deviations which are equivalent respectively to 3·23 and 2·34 times the standard deviation.

So that, on the whole of Mrs. Stewart's 2,000 UT trials, we have the following results:

TABLE 1

|  | Hits | Deviation | Standard deviation | Critical ratio |
|---|---|---|---|---|
| On 'target' (0) card | 447 | +47 | 17·89 | +2·63 |
| Post-cognitive (−1) | 442 | +58 | 17·53 | +3·31 |
| Precognitive (+1) | 457 | +73 | 17·53 | +4·16 |

Thus, on the three 'central' counts, (+1), (0), (−1) taken together, we have 1,346 hits with a positive deviation of 178 from chance expectation. We cannot, however, work out the standard deviation in the usual way by the binomial formula, which would give $0.4\sqrt{(2,000 + 1,920 + 1,920)}$, i.e. 30·57. The reason is that the three scores on (+1), (0), and (−1), would not vary independently of each other. If, for instance, the guesser had the tendency to repeat the same card-symbol, say +, several times in succession, then if he happened to be scoring well on the 'actual' (0) card, he would automatically score well on the (+1) and (−1) cards. But if, on the other hand, he were scoring below chance expectation on the 'actual' card he would tend to make low scores on both the (+1) and the (−1) cards.

Thus we might have the following patterns:

| (a) | Guess | Card | or (b) | Guess | Card |
|-----|-------|------|--------|-------|------|
|     | +     | W    |        | +     | S    |
|     | +     | +    |        | +     | O    |
|     | +     | S    |        | +     | W    |

In case (a) a hit on the middle card produces automatically a hit also on the (+1) and (−1) cards, while in (b) a miss on the middle card causes a miss on both the (+1) and (−1) cards.

This means that, although the chance expectation is still equal to one-fifth of the combined total of (+1), (0), and (−1) guesses, yet the variance from the expected number of hits may differ considerably from that given by the usual formula.

However, Professor M. S. Bartlett,[1] of Manchester University a few years ago worked out a systematic method by which the theoretical standard deviation can be calculated from the guessing patterns actually

used by the subject. Thus the pattern $\begin{matrix} + \\ + \\ + \end{matrix}$ is accorded a much higher

theoretical variance than the pattern $\begin{matrix} O \\ W \end{matrix}$.

When S.G.S.[2] applied this method to Mrs. Stewart's 2,000 trials, he found that the true value of the theoretical standard deviation for the combined total of (+1), (0), and (−1) hits was 29·5, which is just slightly less than that found above (30·57) by the ordinary method. This makes the results slightly *more* significant than we had at first thought them to be. In fact, the correct value of the critical ratio is now 178/29·5, i.e. 6·0, which gives odds against chance exceeding $10^8$ to 1. But since in the 1934–9 card-guessing experiments there were, in all, 128,350 trials (i.e. 64 batches of 2,000), to get the true odds we must divide our figure $10^8$ by 64. This still gives odds of more than a million to one against the possibility that Mrs. Stewart's performance was the result of chance.

Mrs. Stewart's scores themselves are not in any way sensational. To give the reader an idea of the sort of result she was producing, we shall quote the number of hits she obtained in the 40 successive runs of 25 guesses which constitute her second thousand. These are the *precog-nitive* (+1) scores, and it will be borne in mind that the chance average is 4·8 hits per 25.

## Second Thousand

(+1) *Precognitive Scores*: 2, 8, 9, 5, 1, 1, 8, 5, 11, 7, 6, 6, 10, 3, 4, 7, 6, 6, 6, 5, 6, 5, 9, 2, 4, 6, 7, 5, 8, 8, 5, 2, 2, 4, 10, 8, 7, 4, 7, 7.

It will be noticed that only eleven of the forty scores are below the chance average (4·8).

The reason why there is so little difference between the binomial standard deviation and that given by Bartlett's method is that Mrs. Stewart, like most other guessers, tends to change her guess from one symbol to another. Very seldom does she repeat the same symbol three or four times in succession. Had she done so, we should undoubtedly have found a considerable difference between the estimates of standard deviation given by the two methods.

## The Results of Basil Shackleton

After making this discovery of (+1) and (−1) displacement in Mrs. Stewart's results, S.G.S. went on to examine a good many more of his UT records without at first finding anything abnormal. It was not till after Christmas 1939 that he decided to look up Shackleton's 800 trials. At once he found the same effects as were present in Mrs. Stewart's work. On the 'target' (0) card the deviation (+5) was not in the least significant, but on the precognitive (+1) card there were 194 hits and on the post-cognitive (−1) card 195 hits, as compared in each case with an expectation of 153·6. These give positive deviations which are equivalent to 3·6 and 3·7 standard deviations respectively.

On the total of 2,336 combined (+1), (0), and (−1) guesses there are 554 hits, as compared with the expected number 467·2. This gives a positive deviation of 86·8, and the standard deviation worked out by Bartlett's method is 18·3 (by the binomial formula it is 19·3). The critical ratio is 86·8/18·3, i.e. 4·74.

The odds against chance are about $4 \times 10^5$ to 1 for an isolated set of 800 guesses, but as there are about 160 blocks of 800 in the whole 128,350 trials, we must divide the above odds by 160. Thus the final odds against the possibility that Shackleton's results were due to chance are still more than 2,500 to 1.

Shackleton had worked with four different agents: Mr. J. Aldred, Mrs. Crane, Mrs. Dwyer and Mr. Hechle. On (+1) and (−1) guesses combined he obtained positive deviations with the first three, all exceeding 2·3 standard deviations, but with the last-mentioned agent his deviation was negative, though not quite significantly so.

Ultimately S.G.S. examined all his UT records for (+1) or (−1) effects but Shackleton and Mrs. Stewart were the only two subjects whose work showed any evidence of displacement. Nor was there any significant displacement on the UT trials taken as a whole.

In the cases of Mrs. Stewart and Shackleton, hits were counted on the second, third, fourth cards, and so on as far as the eighth cards in either direction, but the only interesting feature revealed was significantly low scoring on the (+2) precognitive card; the deviation amounted to about −3 standard deviations for each subject.

So far there was no reason to suppose that either Shackleton or Mrs. Stewart was predicting events in future time. For, at the instant when the subject made his or her guess, the *next* card to be looked at by the agent was lying face downwards on top of the pack. By exercising the faculty of *clairvoyance* in the present the guesser might have known what the following card was going to be, without probing into the future in any way.

If, however, it were ultimately proved that the guesser's source of information is the mind of the person who looks at the cards, then the guesser would be predicting a future mental state of this person, which did not exist at the moment of guessing. At this stage of the investigation it was therefore an open question whether or not time displacement entered into these anticipatory effects. However, we may use the word 'precognitive' in referring to (+1) or (+2) displacements, if we abstract from the term its purely temporal implications.

## Multiple Determination and Reinforcement

It will have been noticed that with Mrs. Stewart the (+1) precognitive effect was rather more marked than the (−1) post-cognitive effect, while with Shackleton the rates of scoring on (+1) and (−1) were almost the same. It would be reasonable to suppose that both the (+1) image and the (−1) image were subconsciously present in the guesser's mind, though only one of them successfully emerged into his normal consciousness. When the two images were of different card-symbols, obviously only one of them could be chosen. But the following question arose: Would the guesser be more frequently successful when the (+1) and (−1) symbols happened to be the same than when they were different? In other words, when the two symbols were the same (say both circles) would they tend to reinforce each other?

A preliminary inspection of the 1936 records seemed to suggest that this was the case. A guess is said to be 'multiply determined' when the target-card which precedes it and the target-card which follows it are of the same denomination. This is illustrated by the actual card-patterns of type (i):

Type (i)     *Actual card sequence for* MD guesses

```
         O                          O
  ───→   +        or        ───→    O
         O                          O
```

We shall call a guess 'non-multiply determined' (NMD) if the target-cards which immediately precede and follow it are of different denominations. This is shown by the examples of type (ii):

Type (ii)     *Actual card sequence for* NMD guesses

```
         O              O              +
  ───→   +   or  ───→   +   or  ───→   +
         S              +              O
```

The arrow denotes the point in the sequence at which the subject is making his guess.

We can now formulate the problem more precisely. In type (i), in which the target-card is sandwiched between two cards of the *same* denomination, will Shackleton or Mrs. Stewart score at a significantly higher rate on, say, (+1) cards than he or she will score on (+1) cards in type (ii) in which the 'target' card is sandwiched between cards of *different* denomination? And, of course, the same question arises for their scoring on (−1) cards in the two types of pattern. This is probably the simplest statement of the problem, and it was suggested in this form by Professor Herbert Robbins, a statistician at the State University of North Carolina, to Dr. J. G. Pratt and to S.G.S. when on a visit in the year 1951.

In any investigation of the reinforcement effect we are concerned essentially with an even-numbered guess and the odd-numbered cards which immediately precede and follow the guess or with an odd-numbered guess and the even-numbered cards which precede and follow it. It was pointed out by Professor Bartlett that, when we choose such patterns for analysis, there must be no overlapping of the cards. That is to say, no card in any pattern must also belong to any other pattern. Otherwise the effects will not be statistically independent.

It would not do, for example, to select, for our first pattern, cards $(1_↑3)$, and for our second, cards $(3_↑5)$, and for our third, cards $(5_↑7)$, etc. To secure independence we must choose for our odd-card patterns $(1_↑3)$, $(5_↑7)$, $(9_↑11)$, and so on, up to $(21_↑23)$.

Similarly for the even-card patterns we select $(2_\uparrow 4)$, $(6_\uparrow 8)$, $(10_\uparrow 12)$, and so on up to $(22_\uparrow 24)$.

The arrows denote the position in the sequence at which the subject makes his guess.

Thus, in a series of 25 guesses, only 12 (6 even and 6 odd) patterns will be available, and this means that about 50 per cent of the material has to be discarded in the interests of statistical safety. Having chosen our patterns in this way, we have only to count the number of MD patterns, the number of NMD patterns, and the numbers of $(+1)$ hits on each type. To discover whether there is a significantly larger proportion of $(+1)$ hits on MD patterns than on NMD patterns, we construct a simple $2 \times 2$ contingency table, and evaluate chi-squared.

When this method* was applied to the 1936 work, it was found that Mrs. Stewart's 2,000 guesses showed no evidence of reinforcement, and that Shackleton's 800 trials were suggestive only, the odds in favour of reinforcement in his case being about 25 to 1†. However, the later experiments with Shackleton (1941–3), when evaluated by the above method, gave highly significant evidence for the reinforcement hypothesis (see Chap. XI, p. 181). When Mrs. Stewart was investigated again in 1945 it was found that her significant scoring had now shifted on to the target or (0) card, and that the positive scoring on the $(+1)$ and $(-1)$ cards had disappeared. It has not been possible, therefore, in her case to obtain any additional data on the question of reinforcement and multiple determination. We shall see later that her rate of scoring was influenced by target-patterns of a different kind.

The earliest observation on record of $(+1)$ and $(-1)$ displacement in card-guessing was made in 1938 prior to the publication of the work of Carington and S.G.S. Dr. C. G. Abbott,[3] an astro-physicist, who was at one time Secretary to the Smithsonian Institution at Washington, carried out a successful repetition of Rhine's clairvoyance tests with Zener cards, using himself as the subject. Dr. Abbott noticed that, when he was feeling tired or run-down, he failed to guess correctly the card at which he was aiming, but that his guess was often right for the immediately preceding or following card. In 1949 this scientist[4] tested himself again with the cards, and reported quite significant $(+1)$ and $(-1)$ displacements, the deviations being about equal in magnitude and each approximating to 2·8 standard deviations.

It is worthy of note that neither Mrs. Stewart nor Basil Shackleton was discovered by the blind application of routine tests to a large number of persons in the hope that a genuine telepathic percipient would soon appear. To experiment at random is not very hopeful. It is far better to seek out those persons who are reputed among their friends to possess paranormal powers.

Nor does it seem—in spite of Rhine's experience to the contrary with his own students—that the English university student is promising material for psychical investigation. Of the eighty-odd students tested by S.G.S.* at University College, London, there was not one who provided even tolerable evidence that he or she possessed any gift for extra-sensory perception, and Dr. Thouless's experience with Glasgow students would appear to be in agreement. It is among those who cultivate intuition and feeling rather than intellect that we should prosecute our enquiries. We offer these observations because it appears to be the rule that, whenever an academic psychologist takes up psychical research, he almost always experiments with students. But the mental processes of the average British student being of a logical and fact-assimilating nature differ radically from those of the intuitive sensitive. And we might add that many psychological laboratories are ill-adapted to the study of extra-sensory cognition. Too often they are noisy places with students scurrying along the corridors to their class-rooms at the clanging of a bell. To function well, the sensitive needs freedom from distraction, the presence of friendly people who are prepared to adapt themselves to his mental idiosyncrasies, and, above all, the absence of formality and fuss. Neglect of these conditions, which experience has shown to be essential, will lead inevitably to frustration, to the accumulation of chance scores, and in the end, to the psychologist's abandoning the study of a delicate faculty, the laws of whose emergence are not yet properly understood.

* VII, 1.

131

# CHAPTER IX

# The New Experiments with Basil Shackleton[1]

## *Details of the Experiments*

In December 1940, having published the aforesaid discoveries of displacement, S.G.S. sought out Basil Shackleton with a view to further experiments. He was now in London again, after having been discharged from the Army owing to ill-health. He had moved from the Studio in Frith Street, and now occupied premises in the basement of 59, Shaftesbury Avenue, London, where he lived and carried on his business as a photographer. S.G.S. thought it advisable to tell Shackleton something about the interesting effects that had been discovered, but did not enter into much detail as Shackleton was quite willing to try some fresh experiments. He suggested that, as he was a busy man, the tests should take place in his studio. With the precautions S.G.S. intended to adopt there could be no objection to this suggestion, especially as the earlier 1936 experiments had yielded positive results when carried out at Roland Gardens, S.W.7.

The question S.G.S. had next to decide was whether the new experiments were to make use of Zener cards bearing the five geometrical symbols, or whether to substitute a different sort of material. The Zener cards had the obvious advantage of a clear-cut one in five chance of success, but on the other hand, S.G.S., after using them for five years, had grown very sick of the sight of these somewhat arid diagrams. Eventually, S.G.S. decided to effect a compromise by substituting for the Zener cards others bearing five pictures of different animals. The great advantage of a one in five chance was thus retained. In wartime, however, it was not easy to obtain large quantities of cards with identical backs, such as had been previously used, and S.G.S. therefore modified his technique so that five cards only would be required instead of the 40 packs employed in the earlier experiments.

After one or two preliminary trials, S.G.S. decided to ask Mrs. K. M.

Goldney (K.M.G.), a fellow member of the Society for Psychical Research, to assist him with the investigation. Mrs. Goldney had previously worked with S.G.S. in the investigation of Marion*, the vaudeville telepathist (see Chap. VII, p. 96). She has been a member of the S.P.R. for some 26 years, and a member of its Council for several years. She has travelled widely, has had great practical experience in many branches of psychical research, and is an expert in the detection of fraud. Owing to her medical experience, she has been specially selected to take a leading part in the investigation of physical mediums. During the War she held the important post of Assistant Regional Administrator at W.V.S. Headquarters in London, covering Region 10 with its four counties of Lancashire, Cheshire, Cumberland and Westmorland. At the conclusion of hostilities she was awarded the M.B.E. for her services.

No one who knows K.M.G. will question either her great ability or her integrity or the meticulous accuracy of all her work. Not only did she play a leading part in the present experiments with Shackleton, but she also rendered valuable assistance with the Report on them which appeared in the *Proceedings*[1] *of the S.P.R.* for December 1943 (Part 167, Vol. XLVII).

Basil Shackleton, our sensitive, was a photographer, an artist in his profession, with an arresting style and original conception of treatment, well-known for his striking protrait studies. He passed the early part of his life in South Africa, with which country his family has connections. Not until he was 23 years of age did he become aware that he possessed unusual psychical gifts. So far as could be ascertained, he had no particular interest in Spiritualism; nor did he practise automatic writing. He told S.G.S. and K.M.G. that he had on various occasions applied his faculty of intuition to the forecasting of winners in horse races with much profit to himself. None of his relatives appears to have possessed similar paranormal powers.

Shackleton claimed to be able to sum up a person's character by a flash of intuition, and his thumb-nail sketches of strangers to whom he was introduced were often very amusing and accurate.

Shackleton, unfortunately, did not at the time of the experiments enjoy good health, and suffered from duodenal trouble and the loss of one kidney.

Some five years ago he emigrated to South Africa and engaged in fruit-farming. There, with his wife and family, he still prospers, and occasionally writes to S.G.S. and K.M.G. His health has improved, and, though at times he feels a nostalgia for 'that odd place London', he does not wish to return.

## Types of Experiment

There were two main types of experiment. In the first, the card to be looked at by the agent was determined by means of a list of random numbers (1 to 5) prepared beforehand by S.G.S., or in a few cases by some other person. This type of experiment will be referred to as a PRN (Prepared Random Numbers) experiment. In the second type of experiment, the card to be looked at was determined by a counter selected by touch by one of the experimenters from a bag or bowl which contained equal numbers of counters in five different colours. This type of test will be called a COUNTERS experiment.

We shall begin with a description of the PRN experiments. The technique which we shall describe was for all practical purposes standardized by 7th March, 1941, in the seventh sitting of the series. A screen was in use on the card table from Sitting No. 1 on 24th January 1941, but the additional precaution of the enclosing and screening of the five cards inside a box was adopted on and after 7th March 1941. The introduction of a second experimenter whose function was to control Shackleton first took place on 7th February 1941, at Sitting No. 3.

## Personnel

In general, four persons took part in the experiments. They were
(1) the guesser or percipient Basil Shackleton referred to as (P);
(2) the sender or agent referred to as (A);
(3) the experimenter controlling the agent referred to as (EA);
(4) the experimenter controlling the percipient referred to as (EP).

In addition, on most occasions a fifth person was present, who acted as an observer; he is referred to as (O).

From January 1941, till June 1941, the role of (EA) was assumed by S.G.S., and that of (EP) by K.M.G. and various other persons. On and after 14th August 1941, K.M.G. usually played the part of (EA), while S.G.S. acted as (EP). This change-over gave to each experimenter experience of the different roles.

## The Studio and Ante-Room

The experiments were conducted in Shackleton's studio. This is below the level of the street, and none of the rooms has any windows. The rooms consist in the main of a large studio and an ante-room. There are, in addition, some small private apartments, which are reached from the ante-room through a curtained archway and from the studio through the door $D_3$. (See p. 136.) The ordinary entrance to the studio from the

134

ante-room is by the door $D_2$. The folding entrance doors, $D_1$, lead to a short passage from which stairs ascend to the outer door of the building, which opens on the street. The shaded area in the plan between ante-room and studio is intra-mural and hollow, and the walls are not solid but built-up with plywood, plaster-covered, as are also the doors. The screened-off portion shown in the right hand corner of the studio is a temporary plywood platform used for photographic purposes.

## The Card Table and Cards

The card table (size 24 inches square and 25 inches high) was situated in the studio at a distance of about 9 feet from the dividing wall between studio and ante-room. It was lighted by a powerful photographer's lamp, L. Standing on this card table was a plywood screen (size 31 inches wide by 26 inches high) with an aperture (3 inches square) in its centre. The plane of the screen was about parallel to that of the dividing wall. The agent was seated on that side of the screen remote from the ante-room, and the experimenter (EA) sat or stood on the side nearer to the ante-room. Resting on the table on the agent's side of the screen was a rectangular box with its open face towards the agent. (See Plates 1, 2.) Inside this, on the floor of the box and entirely screened by it, were five cards with backs like those of playing cards and bearing on their faces pictures of the five animals

> ELEPHANT (E)
> GIRAFFE (G)
> LION (L)
> PELICAN (P)
> ZEBRA (Z).

The pictures were in appropriate colours.

On the table in front of (EA) were five cards on which were printed in large, bold type the numbers 1, 2, 3, 4, 5.

## Position of Shackleton

The percipient, Shackleton, sat in the ante-room while he was guessing the cards, in one of the following positions. For the first 18 sittings, between 24th January 1941 and 13th June 1941, he sat on one of the chairs (C), with the experimenter (EP) beside him in front of the fireplace. On and after 14th August 1941, and until 21st December 1941, Shackleton and (EP) sat at a small table towards the far end of the ante-room. On and after 15th May 1942, Shackleton and (EP) sat at a desk (V) (see p. 136).

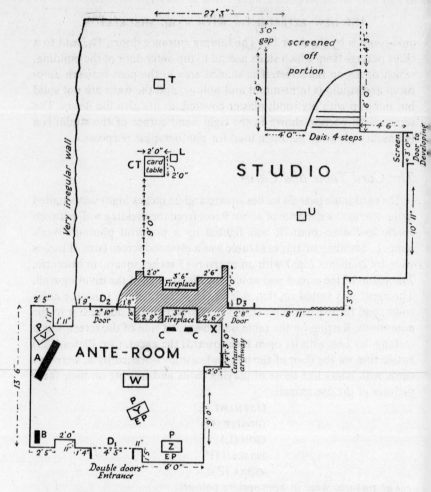

## PLAN OF ROOMS IN THE SHACKLETON EXPERIMENTS

A = Sofa
B = Worktable and stool
C = Chairs before fireplace
X = Seat of photographer's assistant
Z = Table showing position of (P) and (EP) on 14th and 25th August 1941
Y = Position of table on 24th September 1941
W = Position of table on 21st November, 4th and 21st December 1941
V = Desk where B.S. sat from 15th May 1942 to 26th August 1942
T = Position of card table till 21st February 1941
CT = Position of card table on and after 21st February 1941
L = Photographer's lamp
U = Position of R.E. on 5th June 1942
$\left.\begin{array}{l} D_1 \\ D_2 \\ D_3 \end{array}\right\}$ = Doors

136

## Scoring Sheets (See p. 138)

S.G.S. brought to each sitting scoring sheets, foolscap size, each designed to accommodate two columns. For each column there were two divisions: the one on the left was headed G (for guesses), and the one on the right A (for actual cards). The two divisions were divided into 25 rectangular cells, and, for convenience, these cells were numbered at intervals of five. The left hand column with its two divisions of 25 cells will be referred to as the (a) column, and the right hand one with its two divisions of 25 cells as the (b) column. Thus sheet 4(a) means the left hand column (with its two divisions of 25 cells) on the fourth sheet; sheet 4(b) the right hand column (with its two divisions of 25 cells) on the fourth sheet. Before coming to the sitting, S.G.S. filled in the A-divisions of all the sheets to be used by (EA) with a random sequence of the digits 1, 2, 3, 4, 5. In general, S.G.S. prepared these lists from the last digits of the seven-figure logarithms of numbers selected at intervals of 100 from Chambers's Tables, as explained in Chap. VII, p. 106. In some cases, however, Tippett's* random numbers were used. These lists were compiled by S.G.S. at his lodgings in Cambridge, with no one present but himself, and they were kept under lock and key until the day of the sitting. They were then brought to London in a suitcase which was never out of S.G.S.'s sight till the experiment was about to start. At the last moment S.G.S. took the suitcase into the studio, extracted the compiled lists, and handed them to (EA). (P), therefore, who never entered the studio till the experiments were finished, had no opportunity of seeing these sheets before his guesses had been recorded.

S.G.S. also handed Shackleton (P) some empty scoring sheets similar to those in the possession of (EA), and both (EA) and (P) numbered the sheets they were about to use '1', '2', '3', etc. (P) recorded his guesses in the G-divisions on each sheet.

The lists of random numbers were made out in blue-black ink, but (P) found it more convenient to use a pencil in recording his guesses. (P) and (EP) now seated themselves in the ante-room. The door $D_3$ was kept closed. In the earlier experiments, till Sitting No. 10, the door $D_2$ was completely closed also. After Sitting No. 9, however, it was left an inch or two ajar in order to facilitate hearing. From where he sat, Shackleton was quite unable to see either (EA) or the screen, even had the door $D_2$ been wide open. Still less was he able to see the box on the far side of the screen or the agent (A). The purpose of the box was to

---

* Tippett's tables were used on the dates 7th November 1941, 14th November 1941, and 21st November 1941. The total score was 124 in 480 (+1) trials. This corresponds to a CR of 3·2 (odds about 700 to 1).

# SCORING SHEET: NAME B.S.

SHEET 1.  DATE 14 November '41

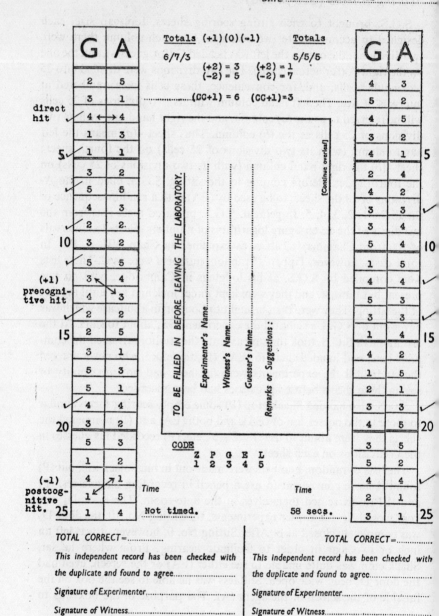

Totals (+1)(0)(-1)    Totals
6/7/3                 5/5/5

(+2) = 3   (+2) = 1
(-2) = 5   (-2) = 7

(CC+1) = 6   (CC+1)=3

[Continue overleaf]

**Left record (G A):**

|   | G | A |   |
|---|---|---|---|
|   | 2 | 5 |   |
|   | 3 | 1 |   |
| direct hit | 4 ↔ 4 |  |   |
|   | 1 | 3 |   |
| 5 | 1 | 1 |   |
|   | 3 | 2 |   |
|   | 5 | 6 |   |
|   | 4 | 3 |   |
|   | 2 | 2. |   |
| 10 | 3 | 2 |   |
|   | 5 | 5 |   |
| (+1) precognitive hit | 3 | 4 |   |
|   | 4 | 3 |   |
|   | 2 | 2 |   |
| 15 | 2 | 5 |   |
|   | 3 | 1 |   |
|   | 5 | 3 |   |
|   | 5 | 1 |   |
|   | 4 | 4 |   |
| 20 | 3 | 2 |   |
|   | 5 | 3 |   |
|   | 1 | 2 |   |
| (-1) postcognitive hit | 4 | 1 |   |
|   | 1 | 5 |   |
| 25 | 1 | 4 |   |

**Right record (G A):**

|   | G | A |   |
|---|---|---|---|
|   | 4 | 3 |   |
|   | 5 | 2 |   |
|   | 4 | 5 |   |
|   | 3 | 2 |   |
| 5 | 4 | 1 |   |
|   | 2 | 4 |   |
|   | 4 | 2 |   |
|   | 3 | 3 |   |
|   | 3 | 4 |   |
| 10 | 5 | 4 |   |
|   | 1 | 5 |   |
|   | 4 | 4 |   |
|   | 5 | 3 |   |
|   | 3 | 3 |   |
| 15 | 1 | 4 |   |
|   | 4 | 2 |   |
|   | 1 | 5 |   |
|   | 2 | 1 |   |
|   | 3 | 3 |   |
| 20 | 4 | 5 |   |
|   | 3 | 5 |   |
|   | 5 | 2 |   |
|   | 4 | 4 |   |
|   | 2 | 1 |   |
| 25 | 3 | 1 |   |

TO BE FILLED IN BEFORE LEAVING THE LABORATORY.

Experimenter's Name...........................

Witness's Name...............................

Guesser's Name...............................

Remarks or Suggestions :

CODE
Z P G E L
1 2 3 4 5

Time                    Time
Not timed.              58 secs.

TOTAL CORRECT=...............          TOTAL CORRECT=...............

This independent record has been checked with the duplicate and found to agree...........................

Signature of Experimenter...........................

Signature of Witness...........................

This independent record has been checked with the duplicate and found to agree...........................

Signature of Experimenter...........................

Signature of Witness...........................

screen the five cards from the view of any person who might conceivably be concealed in the studio or who might be gazing down into the studio through some hypothetical hole in the ceiling. In fact, with the cards inside the box, no one could see them unless he was standing directly behind (A), in which case his presence would be apparent at once.

The five cards were now shuffled by either the agent (A) or the observer (O) if an observer was present. Throughout the experiments S.G.S. and K.M.G. adopted as a cardinal principle the rule that neither (EA) nor (EP) should shuffle the five cards or witness the shuffling. Hence, since (EA) did not know the order of the cards inside the box, he could give nothing away to Shackleton by any inflections of the voice when he gave the vocal signal for Shackleton to write down his guess. Furthermore, since (EP), who sat beside Shackleton, was also unaware of the order, he could not help (P) in any way when the latter recorded his guess. If (EA) looked through the square aperture in the screen, he could see only (A) and the top of the box.

## The Call

At the beginning of the experiment the agent (A) and sometimes the observer (O) shuffled the cards out of sight of the experimenters (EA) and (EP) and laid them faces downward in a row on the floor of the box. (EA) then called to Shackleton in the next room 'Are you ready?' and on receiving the answer 'Yes' from the experimenter (EP) in the ante-room, lifted to the aperture in the screen the printed card bearing the number in the first cell of the A-division of the (*a*) column of the first sheet. (EA) paused for about half a second and then called 'One'. On seeing, say, the number 4 at the aperture, (A) lifted up the fourth card counting from left to right, just far enough for him to see the picture on its face. He then let the card fall back face downwards on the floor of the box, without, of course, disturbing the order of the five cards. On hearing the word 'One', Shackleton wrote down in the first cell of the G-division of the (*a*) column of his scoring sheet the initial letter of one of the animals E, G, L, P or Z. The momentary pause by the experimenter (EA) was to ensure that the agent (A) had lifted the card by the time Shackleton had received the signal. (EP) verified that Shackleton synchronized his recording with (EA)'s calls. While the guessing was in progress, (A) remained absolutely silent. To summarize: (A) or (O), the only persons who knew the order of the five cards, never spoke at all; (EA), the only person who spoke, did not know the order of the cards. The possibility of a code being conveyed by the voice was therefore precluded.

Until Sitting No. 9 (21st March 1941), Shackleton used to shout 'Right' immediately he had recorded his guess; but, after a time, this became unnecessary, since he got into the habit of writing down his guess at the instant he heard (EA)'s serial call, or at an interval scarcely ever exceeding two-fifths of a second after the call. (This was timed by S.G.S. with a stop-watch.)

(EA) now showed the next random number at the hole in the screen, and called 'Two' after a pause of half a second. On seeing the number card at the aperture, (A) lifted the appropriate animal card, looked at it, and let it fall back into its place in the row. Shackleton, on hearing 'Two' immediately recorded his guess in the second cell of his G-division; and so the guessing continued. (EA) called the numbers 1, 2, 3, 4, up to 25 at a rhythmical rate, keeping the intervals as constant as possible. At guess number one (EA) started a stop-clock which he stopped at guess number twenty-five. When the (a) or left hand column of 25 guesses was complete, there was a pause of at least six or seven seconds, after which (EA) shouted 'Next column', and, on hearing (EP)'s 'Right', began again with 'One', 'Two', 'Three', etc., until the right hand, or (b) column of the sheet was run through. The average time taken for a column of 25 guesses worked out at 62·33 seconds, which corresponds to an average interval of 2·6 seconds between successive calls. The actual time for a column of 25 calls varied between limits of about 50 and 80 seconds. This was found to be a comfortable rate of guessing, and we referred to it as the 'normal rate'.

## The Recording of the Code

When the sheet of 50 calls (2 columns) was completed, there was a break of perhaps a couple of minutes for the recording of the code. The experimenter (EA) went round to the other side of the screen, and, watched by the observer (O), or by the agent (A), turned the five cards faces upward without disturbing their order. He then recorded the code at the bottom of the scoring sheet thus (see Plate 4):

$$\begin{array}{ccccc} G & E & Z & L & P \\ 1 & 2 & 3 & 4 & 5 \end{array}$$

This represented the order of the five cards as seen and lifted by the agent, counting from left to right. Shackleton in the meantime remained with (EP) in the ante-room.

Before a start was made on the second sheet, which both (EA) and (P) numbered '2', the five cards in the box were shuffled by (A) or (O), out of sight of both (EA) and (EP), and this was done each time before a new sheet was begun.

1. Experimenter (EA) shows the random number 4 at the aperture in the screen

2. The Agent, Mrs Holding, lifts up and looks at the fourth card in the box counting from left to right

3. Experimenter (EP) (Mr Bateman) watches Mrs Stewart record her guesses

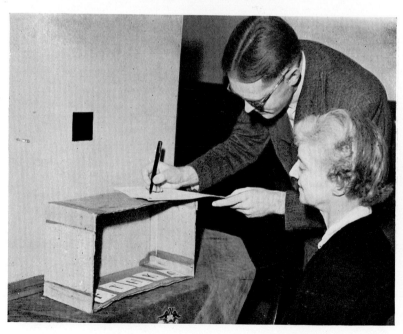

4. Experimenter (EA), having turned the five cards face upward, records the code (FTHKC) on the scoring sheet

## Decoding and Checking

The decoding and counting of successful hits was carried out by (EA), (EP), and (O) with (A) looking on.

(EA) first brought the random number sheets into the ante-room (or Shackleton's sheets into the studio), and laid sheet No. 1 on a table by the side of (P)'s guess-sheet No. 1. One of the experimenters read aloud (P)'s guesses, and, as he did so, (O) or the other experimenter copied down in the appropriate cell of (EA)'s G-column the code number for each of (P)'s letters, which he obtained by referring to the code at the bottom of (EA)'s sheet. As this number was entered, either (O) or the other experimenter checked it, while (A) checked the letter read out by the first experimenter. Thus, each member of the *active* pair was checked by a looker-on. All the decoded numbers were entered in ink. When a column of 25 guesses was filled in on (EA)'s sheet, the numbers of successes were counted in the order

(a) direct hits (0),

(b) precognitive (+1) hits,

(c) post-cognitive (−1) hits,

with, as a rule, at least three persons checking the counts. These numbers were then entered in ink at the top of (EA)'s sheet thus:

$$\frac{(+1)}{6} \Big/ \frac{(0)}{4} \Big/ \frac{(-1)}{3}$$

Ticks were made against the direct hits. The checking was usually done immediately after the last experiment of the day was completed, though in some of the earlier sittings it was done at the end of each sheet, and later on at the end of three sheets. The two experimenters as well as (O) signed their names at the bottom of each scoring sheet.

In the earlier sittings Shackleton often watched the decoding and checking as a passive observer, but after June 1941 he was seldom present at the checking, having left the studio. He would usually return after we had finished, but, as a rule, he was (after June 1941) not told his exact scores. After a successful sitting the experimenters would remark to him 'The results were first-rate today', or something of that sort. If the results were poor, he would be told 'Not so good today'. He was never much depressed by poor scores, but neither was he unduly elated by good scores. His general attitude was one of detachment, and often he seemed quite indifferent to the outcome of his performance. Certainly there was none of that emotional stress which some experimenters have described as existing in their subjects.

In connection with the above method of decoding and checking, it must be understood that many variations and changes of personnel were made in order to discount the criticism that the same two persons, playing the same roles, might be in collusion to falsify the records. All the independent observers without exception were satisfied that the task of checking was performed in a straightforward manner, and many testified to this in writing. The experimenters frequently asked the observer whether he would like to re-check independently some of the higher scores. Professor H. Habberley Price,[1] for instance, himself selected three columns of high scores, and re-checked independently both the decoding and the counting of hits. No errors were found.

Each week a re-check of the decoding and of the counting of hits was carried out by S.G.S. from the original records, and errors were very rare—indeed almost non-existent.

On 14th August 1941, and on several subsequent occasions, Shackleton did not record his own guesses in writing. On these occasions at his own request, five cards bearing the pictures of the five animals were laid on the table in front of him, and, instead of Shackleton writing down his own guess, he merely touched one of the five pictures with a pencil, and the choice was recorded by S.G.S. acting as (EP). S.G.S. noticed that Shackleton always touched the card from two-fifths to four-fifths of a second after the call. We used this method only at Shackleton's request. He said he felt it involved less conscious effort, and was more automatic. The method has the slight draw-back that errors might occasionally arise, through inaccurate recording by (EP) of Shackleton's choice, but S.G.S. is confident that such was not the case.

In most of the forty sittings, Shackleton recorded his own guesses, and we thus had independent records of the card sequences and of the subject's guesses, which could be compared and checked after the sitting was concluded.

It would be futile, therefore, for any critic to suggest that Shackleton's extra-chance scores were due to inaccurate recording of his guesses, since at those sittings in which he made his own records, the odds against chance were of an astronomical order.

One or two variations in the method of checking and decoding may be cited.

(i) On 21st December 1941, Professor C. A. Mace,[1] the psychologist, stood between K.M.G. and S.G.S., so that he could check both the letter read out by S.G.S. and the correctness of the number entered (in ink) by K.M.G. who did the decoding. *He reported no errors*, and the (+1) score was 58 hits in 192 trials, giving odds against chance of 2,500 to 1.

At this sitting the sheets of random numbers were prepared by Mr. C. U. Blascheck, when alone in his lodgings in Cambridge, and posted directly by him in a sealed envelope to Mrs. Woollard of 7 North Hill,

Highgate. A day or two before the experiment, Mrs. Woollard reposted the sealed envelope still unopened to Professor Mace, who brought it with him to the sitting. S.G.S. had no opportunity of seeing the lists of random numbers till the moment of checking. This was a sitting at which Shackleton did *not* record his own guesses, but it would be absurd to suppose that these high odds could have been due to mistakes made by S.G.S. in the recording, unless, indeed, he possessed paranormal powers similar to those of Shackleton, to which he can certainly make no claim.

(ii) On 5th December 1941, Sir Ernest Bennett read aloud Shackleton's guesses, while K.M.G. decoded and entered the numbers (in ink) with S.G.S. looking on and checking her. The agent Miss Rita Elliott was also watching. The (+1) score was 59 hits in 192 trials, with odds of 1,500 to 1 against chance. This was another occasion on which Shackleton did *not* write down his own guesses, but be it noted that the random number sheets had been prepared by Dr. G. D. Wassermann, a mathematician, in his rooms at Cambridge. They were sealed up in an envelope marked 'Not to be opened until the time of the sitting', and posted by Wassermann to K.M.G., who brought the envelope unopened to the sitting. It was opened out of sight of S.G.S. in the presence of Sir Ernest Bennett, the observer. It would be futile again to argue that errors in the recording of Shackleton's guesses could account for this very significant score.

(iii) On 15th April 1943, the entire work of the decoding and entering of numbers and the counting and checking of the hits was carried out by Dr. Donald J. West (now research officer of the S.P.R.) with S.G.S. checking him. The score was 60 (+1) hits in 192 trials, giving odds against chance of nearly 10,000 to 1. At this sitting Shackleton recorded his own guesses in pencil, and any errors in decoding would have to be attributed to Dr. West, and must, moreover, have escaped the vigilance of S.G.S., and have remained undetected by the careful re-check the latter habitually made of all decoding and counts.

It has been shown over and over again that persons with life-long training in habits of accuracy, and especially mathematicians, very rarely make errors, and it is merely ridiculous for sceptics to suggest that the high odds against chance obtained week after week by Shackleton or Mrs. Stewart are to be attributed to errors in the copying of figures or the decoding of letters into numbers.

## *The Duplicate Record Sheets*

The final task at the conclusion of each sitting was the making of duplicates in ink of all the completed scoring sheets. This work was usually shared among K.M.G., S.G.S., and the principal agent Rita Elliott. The experiments had been carried out in war time, and it was felt that the risk of destruction by bombing would be diminished if two sets of records were kept in different towns. After being signed by both K.M.G. and S.G.S., and by any observer who might be present, the duplicates were, in full view of all members of the party, placed in a stamped envelope addressed to Professor C. D. Broad, Trinity College, Cambridge. This envelope was posted in the presence of not fewer than three people in the post-box in Shaftesbury Avenue a few yards from Shackleton's studio. By this time the observer, if any, had usually departed. K.M.G. and S.G.S. then customarily adjourned to a restaurant, where scores were re-checked and plans made for future experiments.

S.G.S. took his set of records back with him to Cambridge or to his home in Essex, as the case might be, and there proceeded to make a complete re-check of both the decoding and the counting of successes. He also counted all precognitive ($+2$) and all post-cognitive ($-2$) hits, and recorded the totals for each column. No error in the whole period of the experiments was ever discovered in the decoding but on one occasion it was found that a single precognitive ($+1$) hit had been overlooked in a count.

The duplicates were kept by Professor Broad for the duration of the war, and were then returned by him to the Society for Psychical Research.

## The Accuracy of the Records

Professor Henry Sidgwick, in his first presidential address to the Society for Psychical Research, said 'We have done all that we can when the critic has nothing left to allege except that the investigator is in the trick. But when he has nothing else left to allege, he will allege that.' So perhaps the last resort of the sceptic would be to suggest that the record sheets were tampered with by the experimenters themselves at the conclusion of the sittings. *Both* experimenters would need to have been in collusion; it would not have been possible for one to have tampered with the figures without the connivance of the other, since both experimenters checked the results together, and affixed their signatures to each sheet, and the duplicates were posted to Professor Broad, in full sight of both experimenters and of the principal agent immediately after they had left the studio.

It cannot be denied that, if both K.M.G. and S.G.S. were bent on trickery, it would have been possible, on those occasions when no observer was present, to make false record sheets and duplicates to agree with them. Many observers were unable to stay long enough to watch the lengthy business of the re-checking and duplication of the scoring sheets; they had trains to catch, other appointments, etc. But this was not the fault of the experimenters, who expected and asked them to remain. On the other hand, many observers, such as Mr. Chibbett, Miss Jephson, Mr. Medhurst, Sir Ernest Bennett, Mr. Rozelaar, Dr. West, *did* stay to the end, and on these occasions the original scoring sheets were directly under their observation from the time of the first checking to the final posting of the duplicates to Professor Broad; they were posted on such occasions by the observer himself. An inspection of the list of scores on occasions when observers were present revealed long runs of highly significant (+1) scores, in which scarcely a single column showed a figure lower than five correct hits.

The experimenters themselves, however, were anxious to have a check, not on their honesty, but on their accuracy. Each separate sheet had involved the checking of 240 pairs of figures for the five counts (−2), (−1), (0), (+1) and (+2); the making of the duplicates was a boring business which might easily have led to carelessness; and all this had to be done at the end of a long day's work, and before a late supper. Still further copying of the totals had to be done for the typing of the lists of scores.

After dividing them into batches, the experimenters therefore posted all the original scoring sheets and a carbon copy of the typed list of scores to the following persons: Mr. Kenneth Richmond, Miss Jephson, Mr. Redmayne, Mrs. Woollard, Mr. Medhurst, Mr. Chibbett, Mrs. Johnstone and Mr. Rozelaar. The first five of these are members of the Society for Psychical Research.

At the same time Professor Broad was asked to post them the corresponding duplicate record sheets in his possession. Each recipient was asked to check all scores in the five categories (−2), (−1), (0), (+1) and (+2) on the typewritten list of scores against the results obtained by actual recounting of the hits on the original scoring sheets. They were also asked to check the totals written in ink at the top of each column, e.g. 6/7/3 (see p. 138), against the records obtained by direct counting. This was important, since any tampering with the figures in the column itself would have necessitated a corresponding alteration in these totals, which were written at the actual time of the sitting in the presence of both the experimenters and any observer who was there. The checker was also asked to compare the original records with Professor Broad's duplicates, and to sign each of the typewritten lists of scores as being in agreement with the original and duplicate. In cases where the checker himself had acted as the observer at any of the experiments, he was asked to examine his signature. The originals were returned to S.G.S. together with the signed lists of scores, and the duplicates were returned direct to Professor Broad.

In all the original scoring sheets so checked over the total period of the experiments fewer than a dozen isolated errors were found, *none of these being in the precognitive groups*. These few errors almost cancelled one another out, and were of no significance whatsoever. There was also a number of not very serious copying errors in the duplicate scoring sheets returned to Professor Broad. Since the duplicates had passed out of the possession of the experimenters it was possible for the latter to make corrections only on the original records, and not on these duplicates.

There were six occasions on which the whole of the checking and entering of figures was carried out by the observer himself, who never lost control of the original scoring sheets from the instant when they were first handed to him to the moment when he posted the duplicates to Professor Broad. Statistically these six occasions alone would be sufficient to establish the existence of a paranormal faculty in Shackleton. On some occasions the observers (including Mrs. Woollard, Mr. Medhurst, Dr. West and Mr. Rozelaar) copied out the totals from the original scoring sheets, and took them home for retention. This was an additional safeguard.

The extreme scarcity of errors in the original records (amounting to about one in a thousand trials on the average) revealed by this re-check must surely testify to the accuracy of the experimenters, and make it extremely unlikely that any important errors arose on those occasions when (EP) recorded Shackleton's guesses for him.

## Methods of Evaluation

Throughout this investigation no attempt was made to count beyond $(-2)$ and $(+2)$ displacements. The scores on $(-2)$, $(-1)$, $(0)$, $(+1)$ and $(+2)$ trials only were considered. As the card sequence was a random one, the expectations on these five types of score are theoretically independent of each other, though the variances (p. 126) are not independent. As we have stated previously, throughout this work the odds against chance corresponding to any deviation $x$ from mean expectation is understood to mean the odds against there being a deviation which lies outside the range $-x$ to $+x$. In other words we estimate our odds on the assumption that we are just as interested in negative deviations as in positive deviations.

Two methods of evaluation were employed.

(a) In a series of $N$ trials the mean expectation of successes is $N/5$, and the standard deviation is $0 \cdot 4\sqrt{N}$. These formulae apply when we are dealing individually with any of the five types $(-2)$, $(-1)$, $(0)$, $(+1)$ or $(+2)$.

(b) The expectation and variance were calculated for each set of, say, 24 $(+1)$ trials or 24 $(-1)$ trials by formulae due to Mr. W. L. Stevens,[2] and the results were summed for all sets. This is perhaps a slightly more accurate method than that described in (a). The scoring of large batches of trials by both methods showed that the standard deviations obtained by Stevens's method were, almost without exception, very slightly less than those given by the formula $0 \cdot 4\sqrt{N}$. We are, therefore, on the safe side in using $0 \cdot 4\sqrt{N}$ for the standard deviation instead of the value given by Stevens's formula, which is tedious to evaluate. But the expectations were found from Stevens's formula.[2] (cf. Appendix J).

The experimenters were most interested in the $(+1)$ scores, and for this type a 'cross-check' was made by the scoring of the (a) G-column of each sheet against the (b) A-column of the same sheet, and the (b) G-column against the (a) A-column. That is the 'guesses' in the left hand 25 trials of the sheet were compared with the 'target'-presentations of the right hand 25 trials and *vice versa*.

Thus in a total of 3,789 $(+1)$ trials at telepathy, working with prepared random numbers at 'normal' rate, with Miss Elliott as agent, the 'cross-check' gave 798 hits which number is not significantly different from the Stevens expectation of $775 \cdot 8$. The actual number of hits made by Shackleton on these 3,789 $(+1)$ trials was 1,101 which exceeds the chance level by $13 \cdot 2$ standard deviations.

# CHAPTER X

# The Main Results with Shackleton

S hackleton started on the new experiments with animal cards on 24th January 1941. The 'sender' was Miss Rita Elliott, who remained the principal agent for a whole year. K.M.G. was not present at the first two sittings, and S.G.S. was the only experimenter. He acted as (EA), and also checked the results with the agent and Shackleton looking on. At the first sitting there were no fewer than 67 hits on 192 (+1) trials compared with a Stevens expectation of 39·7. This is a highly significant result but on the 'actual' or 'target' card there were only 40 hits in 200 trials, the exact number which chance might be expected to produce. The score on 192 post-cognitive (−1) trials was 41, which again is a chance result.

At the conclusion of this first experiment on 24th January, S.G.S. asked Shackleton to keep on reminding himself during the following week that at the next sitting on 31st January he was going to score *direct* (0) hits, and not precognitive hits. Each day during the week S.G.S. kept repeating aloud 'Shackleton will score *direct* hits next Friday.' The suggestions seem to have taken effect, for on 31st January he scored 76 *direct* hits on 200 trials—an excess over chance expectation of 36 and corresponding to odds of more than ten million to one. But on the 192 (+1) trials the score was only 30, which is below expectation.

At the end of the sitting on 31st January S.G.S. asked Shackleton to concentrate during the following week on the idea of scoring (+1) precognitive hits, and S.G.S. also repeated aloud several times a day 'Shackleton will score precognitive hits next week.'

The results of these suggestions were disappointing, but this may have been due to the presence of K.M.G. and Mr. H. Chibbett, both of whom were meeting Shackleton for the first time. It has been noted by Rhine, Tyrrell and others that the effect of the arrival of a fresh personality on the scene is sometimes a temporary lowering of the score. At the third sitting on 7th February Shackleton obtained 39 (+1) hits in 144 trials, which corresponds to odds of about 30 to 1. But, contrary to

148

the suggestion given, he scored 43 hits on the 'target' card in 150 direct trials, a result which is better than the precognitive score, the odds in this case being about 120 to 1.

After this sitting no more suggestions were given, and during the succeeding weeks, in which there was an influx of fresh visitors, the interest of everyone became centred on the remarkable precognitive (+1) scores which Shackleton now continued to produce week after week. The experimenters and visitors talked to Shackleton only of 'precognition'. The effect of all this may have been to direct his extra-sensory faculty into the precognitive channel, from which it scarcely ever strayed for a whole year.

Between 24th January 1941 and 21st December 1941, Miss Rita Elliott acted as agent at nineteen sittings in which prepared lists of random numbers were used to decide which card in the box was to be looked at by the agent. Except on the dates 14th and 25th August 1941, the material for telepathic transmission consisted of pictures of the five animals. On the dates mentioned, however, experiments with the animal pictures were alternated with experiments in which cards inscribed with the associated words TRUNK, NECK, MANE, BEAK and STRIPES were substituted for the corresponding animal pictures. These latter experiments (which will be discussed separately later on) are here included in the grand total of 3,789 (+1) trials. These yielded 1,101 (+1) hits as compared with a Stevens expectation of 775·82. We have therefore an excess of (+1) hits which amounts to 325·18 and corresponds to 13·2 standard deviations. It follows that the odds against the occurrence of a positive or negative deviation of this magnitude are greater than $10^{35}$ to 1. Since, however, the (+1) score was picked out as the best score of the five categories (−2), (−1), (0), (+1) and (+2), the above odds should be divided by five, but this hardly affects their colossal significance. With the exception of the tremendous score on (+1) trials none of the scores has the least significance but for completeness we give them in the following table:

## TABLE 2

### *Prepared random numbers. Telepathy. Normal rate.*
### *Agent: Miss Rita Elliott*

| Category | (−2) | (−1) | (0) | (+1) | (+2) |
|---|---|---|---|---|---|
| Trials | 3,630 | 3,788 | 3,946 | 3,789 | 3,632 |
| Expected hits | 726 | 758 | 789 | 776 | 726 |
| Actual hits | 714 | 768 | 829 | 1,101 | 703 |
| Deviation | −12 | +10 | +40 | +325 | −23 |
| Standard deviation | 24 | 25 | 25 | 25 | 24 |

In the above table the results are all given to the nearest whole number. With the exception of that on (+1) all the deviations are less than twice the corresponding standard deviations. The experiments were all conducted at 'normal' rate. That is, the *average* time for 25 guesses was 62·33 seconds, which corresponds to an average interval of 2·6 seconds between successive calls. Significant successes in (+1) trials were obtained at almost all rates between 50 and 80 seconds for a column of 25 calls. These extremes represent the lower and upper limits for the 'normal' rate.

## Clairvoyance Experiments

The first variation of the PRN method consisted in the introduction, unknown to Shackleton, of sheets of 50 trials during which the agent did not know the order of the five cards in the box, but merely touched their backs at each call without turning them up. A couple of sheets of these 'clairvoyance' tests were interspersed each week more or less randomly among the ordinary 'telepathy' tests. Before starting on a 'clairvoyance' sheet, the agent, Miss Elliott, would shuffle the five cards with her eyes shut, and lay them on the floor of the box without having seen their faces. On a good many occasions the five cards were shuffled by an observer out of sight of the agent and of anyone else in the room. When (EA) showed the random number card at the aperture in the screen, the agent, Miss Elliott, touched the corresponding card without lifting it to look at it. But as there was no other difference in the procedure, Shackleton was kept in ignorance of the fact that a variation had been introduced. Considered as an experiment in pure clairvoyance the test was far from satisfactory. For instance, had the test succeeded, it could have been suggested that the agent might be able to recognize the five cards by noting specks etc. on their backs (though probably the light inside the box was not good enough to make this possible). Had Shackleton obtained any significant degree of success in this admittedly defective test, the experimenters would have gone on to perfect it by sealing up the cards in opaque envelopes. But such refinements proved unnecessary since the 'clairvoyance' tests invariably failed.

Between 24th January 1941 and 28th February 1941, ten sheets of 'clairvoyance' experiments were completed, but the results on all five types of score were entirely negative. For instance, on 500 'actual' card trials the number of direct hits was 98 as compared with an expectation of 100. On the 480 precognitive (+1) trials there were 98 hits compared with the Stevens expectation of 96, while on the 480 post-cognitive (−1) trials there were 106 hits compared with the same expectation 96.

150

The cross-check total of 101 hits on the (+1) trials was also in close agreement with expectation.

Between 24th October 1941 and 21st December 1941, a further series of experiments was carried out, in which sheets of 'clairvoyance' were rigidly alternated (not randomly interspersed) with sheets of 'telepathy'. There was one important difference, however. In this second series Shackleton was told at the start of each sheet of 50 guesses whether he was to try for 'clairvoyance' or for 'telepathy'. Thus (EA) would call out before the first sheet 'Sheet No. 1 telepathy', before the second sheet, 'Sheet No. 2 clairvoyance', before the third sheet, 'Sheet No. 3 telepathy' and so on. The rest of the procedure was the same as in the first series. The regular alternation of the two types of experiment would tend to eliminate any differences due to fatigue and show up clearly Shackleton's reaction to the two kinds of test. Now while the 'telepathy' sheets showed highly significant scores, the 'clairvoyance' results were, on the whole, only what chance might be expected to produce. Thus, on 768 (+1) trials in clairvoyance there were 160 hits, and on 768 (−1) trials 159 hits compared with an expectation of 153·6 in each case. In the five categories there was a just significant critical ratio of 2·12 on the direct hits, but, since this score was chosen as the best score out of five, the result is of no importance as regards over-all significance. It is, however, worthy of mention that, though the total 'clairvoyance' score on this series was without significance, yet on a single occasion, 5th December 1941, Shackleton obtained no fewer than 58 direct (0) hits in 200 trials compared with a chance expectation of 40 (CR = 3·18). But this was an isolated result.

It seems clear, then, that Shackleton failed in 'clairvoyance' tests, whether he was informed of the nature of the experiment or kept in ignorance of it.

It is interesting to compare the 'telepathy' scores in this second series with the alternated 'clairvoyance' scores on the precognitive (+1) trials. On 864 (+1) 'telepathy' trials Shackleton obtained 243 hits, compared with a chance expectation of 174·4 (Stevens), and this corresponds to a critical ratio of 5·84. But on the 768 alternated clairvoyance trials he scored only 160 (+1) hits which exceeds the expected number (156·64) by fewer than 4.

In other words, the 'telepathy' experiments show odds against chance of at least ten million to one, whereas the 'clairvoyance' experiments give results entirely consistent with chance.

Shackleton's failure to succeed in the 'clairvoyance' tests was certainly not due to any lack of confidence. At no time did he so much as hint that he anticipated or feared failure in experiments when the agent did not look at the cards. Apparently he tackled the 'telepathy' and the 'clairvoyance' tests with the same assurance. Nor did he seem aware of any difference in feeling when carrying out the two tests.

In the whole of the clairvoyance work none of his scores in the five categories $(-2)$, $(-1)$, $(0)$, $(+1)$ and $(+2)$ was anywhere near significance.

The striking difference between the 'telepathy' and 'clairvoyance' scores must give pause to those critics who try to maintain that Shackleton's high scores were the result of inaccurate recording, or of faulty statistics, if, indeed, any such critics still exist. Errors in decoding or recording or checking would affect clairvoyance and telepathy scores in roughly the same way. There would be no reason for the occurrence of 'chance' scores in 'clairvoyance' and exceptionally high scores in 'telepathy'. Again, if there were any truth in the suggestion that statistical formulae cannot be applied to large scale experiments in card-guessing, a change in experimental conditions would not affect the question one way or the other.*

Why both Shackleton and Mrs. Stewart should fail under the clairvoyance condition while many of the American subjects have been successful under similar conditions we cannot say, but we may conjecture that it may have something to do with the fact that both Shackleton and Mrs. Stewart showed displacement in their guessing. It will be recalled that in the picture-guessing experiments of the late Dr. C. E. Stuart it was found that in the clairvoyance experiments† the 'compressive' subjects displaced their guesses on to the picture preceding the one the agent was looking at, whereas in telepathy‡ experiments the 'compressives' showed no backward displacement, but scored a little above chance expectation on the actual picture the agent was looking at. This suggests that there is some sort of connection between the telepathy conditions and the direct type of paranormal guessing on the one hand and between the clairvoyance conditions and the displaced type on the other. But what the connection is, or what relevance Dr. Humphrey's findings have to the very different performances of our own subjects, we have no inkling. S.G.S. thinks that Shackleton would be rated by all who know him as an 'expansive' type. He is talkative and sociable, and no one could possibly say he was timid or inhibited. But, as we have mentioned, he also possessed a flair for rapidly sizing up a person's character and temperament, almost at first sight. In this he may have been assisted by his telepathic powers. At the same time he seemed very little influenced by, and generally almost indifferent to, the people

---

* These facts furnish us with a formidable argument against the theories of Mr. Spencer Brown (cf. Chap. XX, p. 350).

† V, 10.          ‡ V, 11.

whom he met. This last characteristic perhaps gives us the clue to why he differed from most card-guessing sensitives in that his rate of scoring was, for the most part, unaffected by the presence of witnesses. He was sensitive to the mental atmosphere surrounding the persons with whom he made contact without being himself emotionally affected by it. But unlike Dr. Humphrey's typical 'expansive' subject, he showed no tendency to score above chance in 'clairvoyance' experiments though, as we shall see later (p. 189), he scored below chance on the (0) or 'target' card over a considerable period in 'telepathy' tests with one particular agent.

## Experiments with Counters

The clairvoyance experiments described above made it highly probable that Shackleton succeeded only when the agent knew the order of the five pictures in the box. The next step was to discover whether the experiment would succeed if, instead of using lists of random numbers prepared before the experiment began, the experimenter (EA) determined the agent's selection of cards by drawing counters from a bag or bowl at random. With this method the choice of cards would be determined during the progress of the experiment by the colours of the counters drawn instead of by a series of numbers already in existence at the start of the tests.

For this purpose 200 bone counters of the same make and size, but in five different colours, were thoroughly mixed inside a cloth bag, there being equal numbers of each colour. It was agreed with the agent, Miss Elliott, that the five colours stood for the digits 1–5 in the following order: white = 1; yellow = 2; green = 3; red = 4; and blue = 5.

In order to assist the agent, five counters with colours in the above order from left to right were placed in a row on top of the box containing the cards, so that, when the experimenter (EA) showed, say, a red counter at the aperture in the screen, (A) would merely have to lift up the card directly beneath the red counter before her. In actual practice the association between the card positions and colours is rapidly memorized, so that the appearance of a colour at the aperture results in the agent's almost automatic selection of the correct card. After an abortive effort by S.G.S., who proved to be far too slow in extracting the counters at the required speed, this task was allotted to K.M.G., who was much more successful in presenting the counters at a uniform and 'normal' rate. The recording of the counters in the A-column of a scoring sheet as they appeared was, as a rule, entrusted to S.G.S., who translated them mentally into the corresponding digits.

On 14th March 1941, however, in K.M.G.'s absence, Miss Ina Jephson selected the counters. In the first two experiments, on 7th March and March 14th, (EA) drew the counters from a cloth bag, replacing each counter in the bag after it had been exposed at the aperture in the screen. After the sitting on March 7th, K.M.G. wrote a short description of her method of extracting the counters. She said:

'I arranged the bag so that the counters were easily accessible. I then dipped each hand in alternately and showed a counter at the screen-aperture with one hand while the other hand was already delving in the bag for the next counter. At intervals I hesitated just long enough to give the bag a quick shake and always picked out counters from all corners, and above and below, in order to avoid picking the same counters up twice as far as possible.'

On and after March 21st K.M.G. found it more practicable to place all the counters in an open bowl. In order to avoid conscious selection, which would destroy the desired random character of the presentation, she stood up, looking straight over the top of the screen and selected the counters with each hand alternately by touch alone and without looking at the bowl. After presenting each counter at the aperture she let it fall back into the bowl. Now, although this method of selection appears to give approximately equal numbers of each of the five colours when the extraction is done at 'normal' speed, this is certainly no longer the case when the speed of calling is doubled, as it subsequently was. Even at a comfortable 'normal' rate it is doubtful whether the distribution is strictly 'random' in the sense that it would satisfy all the theoretical criteria for randomness. But when the rate of selection of the counters is increased to, say, 35 seconds for a run of 25 from the usual time of 62 seconds, the numbers of the different colours chosen become very unequal. This is probably due to the fact that at the increased speed there is not sufficient time for the experimenter's hand to delve into all parts of the bowl as described in K.M.G.'s note quoted above. If, therefore, there happens to be, say, an excess of white counters on the surface of the bowl, white counters may be picked up more frequently than those of the other colours. However, there is some compensation for this in the fact that Stevens's method of working out the expectation of hits, which we have used throughout, takes into account the unequal distribution of the five symbols in a run of 25 calls.

In their *Introduction to the Theory of Statistics* (p. 339) Yule and Kendall[1], say:

'Sight is not the only sense which may bias a sampling method. In certain experiments counters of the same shape but of different colours were put into a bag and chosen one at a time, the counter chosen being put back and the bag thoroughly shaken before the next trial. On the face of it this appears to be a purely random method of drawing the counters. Nevertheless, there emerged a persistent bias against counters of one particular colour. After a careful investigation, the only explanation seemed to be that these particular counters were slightly more greasy than the others owing to peculiarities of the pigment and hence slipped through the sampler's fingers.'

This observation has a certain relevance to the point under discussion.

A *machine* which produced a random sequence of presentations at the required rapid rate would, of course, have served the purpose of the experimenters better than the bag or bowl of counters. At first it was thought that an ingenious machine designed by Mr. Geoffrey Redmayne,* based essentially on the principle of the roulette wheel, would meet all requirements. It could be used to generate a random sequence of five numbers or pictures or symbols of any sort. But, unfortunately, owing to the time taken for the wheel to come to rest, the interval between successive presentations would have exceeded five seconds, and this rate with counters had proved to be too slow for Shackleton to produce successful results.

Moreover, human volition does not enter into the working of a machine in the same way as it is manifest when a person draws counters from a bag or bowl. The sampler can, for instance, exercise choice as to the corner of the bag in which to feel for his counter. But if, as in Mr. Redmayne's machine, he has merely to press a button to set the wheel in motion, he does not possess the same degree of freedom. Had a mechanical selector been available, the experimenters would certainly have made use of it, since a *random* sequence was very desirable for their immediate purpose, though the introduction of an element of human choice into 'precognitive' experiments raises a very intriguing problem.

As K.M.G. showed the counters at the hole in the screen, S.G.S. recorded the corresponding digits 1–5 in the appropriate cell of the A-column of his scoring sheet. During the first four sittings with the counters, S.G.S., while recording, sat by the side of the box in such a position that he could not see the five cards. But in subsequent sittings at which counters were used he sat behind the agent in such a position that he could not only record the counters, but was able, at the same time, to observe whether the agent lifted the correct card. As in all the experiments, the only person to speak a single word was (EA), who did not know, and could not possibly see, the order of the cards. While K.M.G. and S.G.S. were occupied with the counters in the studio, an observer acted as (EP), sitting beside Shackleton in the ante-room.

* XV, 3.

## The Results with Counters

Apparently the new method by which the experiment was conducted with counters instead of with lists of numbers prepared beforehand had no effect whatever on the nature of the results or on the degree of success. With Miss Elliott acting as agent, Shackleton still continued to score on precognitive (+1) presentations at the same high rate of success. Between 7th March 1941 and 3rd January 1942, Miss Elliott acted as agent on eight occasions on which counters were shown at 'normal' rate. On 1,578 (+1) trials Shackleton scored 439 hits, compared with a Stevens expectation of 321. This gives a critical ratio of 7·4 with odds against chance of nearly $10^{11}$ to 1. It is of interest to note that the 'cross-check' (see p. 147) gave a total of 327 (+1) hits which is in excellent agreement with the Stevens expectation.

It will be noticed that the total number of (+1) trials, 1,578, is not an exact multiple of 24. The reason is that on 18th April 1941, Dr. Wiesner, who was acting as (EP) on this occasion, noticed that in one column Shackleton hesitated at call No. 20 and got completely out of step. The last six (+1) trials, therefore, were not taken into account. The scores on the other four categories (−2), (−1), (0) and (+2) were all close to chance expectation and call for no comment.

## Experiments with Counters at Rapid Rate

On 21st March 1941, when Mr. Kenneth Richmond* (then editor of the *Journal* of the Society for Psychical Research) acted as (EP), an important discovery was made. After Shackleton had completed three sheets of guesses at the 'normal' speed, with an average interval between successive calls of 2·8 seconds, someone suggested that the experiment with the counters should be speeded up, so as to reduce the interval to about half its previous value, if this proved to be practicable. In order to facilitate this rapid rate of presentation, K.M.G., who had been drawing counters from the cloth bag, emptied them into the bowl, and drew them out with alternate hands as described on p. 154.

Mr. Richmond sat beside Shackleton to see that he kept in step, noting hesitations and gaps, if any, and using a stop-watch. S.G.S. sat next to the agent by the side of the box, so that he could not see the cards, and recorded the counters. It was impressed on Shackleton that he must keep in step at all costs. If, on hearing the call to write down the initial letter in a certain cell, he found his response was not quick enough for him to write down the letter in time, he was instructed to

* XI, 12.

leave that cell a blank, so that he would be ready to fill in the next cell when its serial number was called.

The new experiment was a strain on all concerned. After three sheets of guesses were completed, the experimenters stopped, and checked the results. Everybody expected the experiment would be a failure, and, indeed, we found only chance scores on the categories (−1), (0) and (+1), although the preceding experiments on the same day at 'normal' speed had yielded a significant score on precognitive (+1) trials. Then it was suggested that a count should be made on the (+2) precognitive trials. When this was done, it was at once obvious that Shackleton had been scoring significantly above chance expectation on (+2) instead of on (+1) presentations. In other words, when the speed of calling was approximately doubled, his 'precognitive' faculty shifted from the (+1) card and fastened upon the one which immediately followed it.

In order to make sure of their discovery, the experimenters did three more sheets of guesses at the same rapid speed (after giving Shackleton fifteen minutes' rest). The results confirmed the previous observations.

For the six sheets at 'rapid' rate the average interval between successive calls was 1·44 seconds—equivalent to an average time of 34·6 seconds for 25 calls. In the last three sheets Shackleton left a few blank spaces here and there. On the 280 (+1) trials done on this first occasion the number of hits was 57, compared with a Stevens expectation of 56·4. But on the 265 (+2) trials there were no fewer than 84 hits, compared with the Stevens expectation of 53·6. This gives a critical ratio of +4·67, and corresponds to odds of more than 50,000 to 1 when the score is selected as the best in the five categories considered.

The experiments with counters at 'rapid' rate with Miss Elliott as agent were continued for four sittings. In all, a total of 794 (+2) trials gave 236 hits, while the Stevens expectation was only 159·4. The corresponding odds against chance amount to more than a hundred million to one. On the other hand, the total of 831 (+1) trials at rapid rate on the above occasions yielded only 154 hits, compared with a Stevens expectation of 167.[*]

The scores on the categories (−2), (−1) and (0) were all close to the chance expectations.

## Experiments at Slow Rate

Between 6th June 1941 and 14th November 1941, experiments were carried out in which successive calls were separated by an interval of

---

[*] We have here another argument against the theories of Mr. Spencer Brown. If ESP is due to non-randomness, why should the change in the speed of calling affect the results?

just five seconds, as timed by a stop-clock. At the first of these sittings counters were used, but on the other occasions prepared random numbers were employed. Whenever this slow rate was in operation, Shackleton grew very irritable, saying that it was useless for him to continue, and complaining that it was enough to drive him mad. Invariably he failed to achieve a significant score of any kind at the 'five seconds' rate. Suggestions that he would eventually succeed seemed to have no effect.

On the four occasions a total of 768 (+1) trials yielded only 157 hits, compared with a chance expectation of 151·7, a result that is without any significance. Nor were any of the scores in the other four categories, (−2), (−1), (0) and (+2) significant.

On two of the four occasions batches of 50 trials at the 'slow' rate were regularly alternated with batches of 50 carried out at the 'normal' speed. The striking difference between the results under the two conditions is apparent from an inspection of the following table:

TABLE 3

|  | (+1) Trials | (+1) Hits | Expectation (Stevens) | Critical ratio |
|---|---|---|---|---|
| Slow | 384 | 74 | 75·5 | less than 1 |
| Normal | 384 | 112 | 77·3 | 4·43 |

Thus, at the 'five seconds' rate the score is almost exactly what might be expected by chance, but on the alternated batches at 'normal' rate the odds against there being at least one of the five categories with a critical ratio as high as 4·43 exceed ten thousand to one.

## Experiments with the Agent Mr. J. Aldred

At the end of December 1941, Miss Elliott took up a full-time war job, which left her with little leisure for helping with the experiments. During the early winter months of 1942, Shackleton considered that the studio was too cold for experiments to be carried out in the evenings, especially as his health was not as good as usual. The investigation was therefore abandoned until the beginning of May 1942 when work was begun with a fresh agent, Mr. J. Aldred,* who had been one of the principal agents in the 1936 experiments. When working with Aldred in these earlier tests, Shackleton had scored about equally well on both (+1) and (−1) guesses. It was, therefore, of interest to discover whether, with Aldred as agent, Shackleton would continue to score significant results only on (+1) (precognitive) trials, or whether the (−1) (postcognitive) scores would now be significant as well.

* VII, 1.

Throughout the nine sittings at which Aldred acted as agent, cards bearing the initial letters E, G, L, P, Z of the five animals instead of the animal pictures were used, since it had been found during the experiments with Miss Elliott that this change did not affect the rate of scoring on (+1) trials. Counters were also abandoned in favour of lists of random numbers. For the first three sittings (May 8th, 15th, 22nd) K.M.G. was absent, and her place was taken by R. G. Medhurst, a mathematician, who himself did all the work of decoding and counting of hits on the above dates.

At the very first sitting on May 8th, there were signs of a change in the nature of the results with the advent of the new agent. On 192 (−1) (post-cognitive) trials Shackleton scored 52 hits, which was promising, while, on the same number of (+1) trials, his score was only 46, a result that is only slightly above chance expectation. These eight sheets of guesses were done at the 'normal' rate, but, in addition, there were three columns of 25 calls, during which the speed was slowed down to 5 seconds between successive calls. After guess No. 20 in the third column, Shackleton, who had been growing more and more irritated, threw down his pencil, saying that it was a waste of time for him to continue with the 'slow' tests. There were only chance results at the slow rate on all five categories.

At the further sittings carried out in 1942 at 'normal' rate with Aldred as agent, the precognitive (+1) scores became highly significant as well as the post-cognitive (−1) scores. Thus, at the four sittings (May 8th–August 26th) a total of 720 (+1) trials yielded 203 hits, and the same number of (−1) trials, 207 hits, compared with an expectation of nearly 144 in each case. Thus Shackleton was scoring about equally well on both precognitive (+1) and post-cognitive (−1) trials. The above figures correspond to 5·4 and 5·8 standard deviations, and the odds against there being *at least two* of the five categories (−2), (−1), (0), (+1) and (+2) with deviations as high as 5·4 standard deviations work out at approximately $3 \times 10^{11}$ to 1, i.e. astronomical odds.

When working with Aldred as agent in 1936, using Zener cards, Shackleton* obtained 5·38 per cent of true cognitions (i.e. successful guesses not due to chance) on (+1) and (−1) trials taken together. In the present 1942 series the corresponding figure was 10·59 per cent of 'true cognitions'. Surprisingly, however, this difference is *not* significant, even though one percentage is almost double the other. There is no satisfactory evidence that Shackleton in his work with Aldred had improved since 1936.

* VII, 1.

## Experiments at Rapid Rate

Now that Shackleton had re-established post-cognitive (−1) scoring, a characteristic which had been absent from his guessing for a whole year, an interesting question presented itself. When the rate of calling was speeded up to about double the 'normal' rate, would there be a displacement of the post-cognitive (−1) hits corresponding to the displacement of precognitive (+1) hits which took place with Miss Elliott as agent? The results show that this is what actually happened. On the three occasions (22nd May 1942, 5th June 1942 and 6th January 1943) experiments were carried out at 'rapid' rate, lists of random numbers being used instead of counters. As before, cards bearing the initial letters of the five animals were employed. The modified procedure on all three occasions was as follows:

The screen, which normally stood on the card-table, was removed, and the five cards which bore the numerals 1–5 were arranged in order on the *top* of the box, which was in its ordinary place on the table. The agent, Mr. Aldred, sat in the usual position, and laid his five letter cards in a row faces downward inside the box out of sight of (EA) and (EP). (EP) sat with Shackleton at his desk in the ante-room and the latter had before him five 'letter' cards similar to those in front of the agent. (EA) stood facing Aldred on the near side of the box, with his prepared lists of random numbers. He called 1, 2, 3, etc., up to 25 at a rapid rate, and, as he called each serial number, he touched with a pencil the number card on top of the box corresponding to the figure on his prepared list. As Aldred saw the numeral touched with (EA)'s pencil, he instantly jerked up the corresponding card inside the box, looked at it and dropped it into its place again. As Shackleton heard the serial number of the call, he instantly touched with a pencil one of the five letters E, G, L, P, Z in front of him. (EP) recorded the letter in the appropriate cell of the G-column on the scoring sheet.

The experiment went without a hitch on all three occasions; there were no gaps, and Shackleton was never out of step. As Aldred was new to the 'rapid' technique, on each of the first two occasions the actual experiment was preceded by a rehearsal in which (EA) and Aldred took part, using the previous week's lists of random numbers. During this trial run S.G.S. sat by the box to verify that Aldred was able to synchronize the lifting of the cards with (EA)'s calls at the required rapid rate.

The average intervals between successive calls on the three occasions were 1·37 seconds, 1·39 seconds and 1·44 seconds. The results are given in Tables 4 and 5 below.

## TABLE 4

### (+1) and (−1) scores (rapid rate)

| Precognitive | | | Post-cognitive | | |
|---|---|---|---|---|---|
| Trials | Hits | Expected | Trials | Hits | Expected |
| 552 | 126 | 111 | 552 | 112 | 110 |

## TABLE 5

### (+2) and (−2) scores (rapid rate)

| Precognitive | | | Post-cognitive | | |
|---|---|---|---|---|---|
| Trials | Hits | Expected | Trials | Hits | Expected |
| 529 | 149 | 106·5 | 529 | 151 | 103 |
| Critical ratio = 4·62 | | | Critical ratio = 5·21 | | |

A glance at these tables shows that, at the 'rapid' rate of calling, the (+1) and (−1) hits are quite without significance, and have been replaced respectively by (+2) and (−2) hits.* This, however, is an oversimplification. The fact is that, on the first occasion the two effects did appear to proceed simultaneously, and there were moderately significant scores on both (+2) and (−2) trials. On the second occasion, however, there was a very significant score on (+2), but only a chance score on (−2). And finally, on the last occasion, there was a chance score on (+2), but a tremendous score (critical ratio = 6·23) on (−2). But on no occasion was either the (+1) or the (−1) score significant.

The violent switch over to (−2) on the last occasion is very remarkable. There was, however, an interval of seventeen weeks between the second and third occasions, during which Shackleton had had a good rest.

The fact that Shackleton's *psi* faculty could still flare up to a peak represented by 6·23 standard deviations on only 184 (−2) trials, two years after the beginning of the experiments, testifies to the strength of his paranormal ability.†

Mr. Rozelaar took away with him a list of the total scores in each of the five categories (−2), (−1), (0), (+1) and (+2). He also compared each original scoring sheet carefully with the corresponding duplicate, and himself posted the duplicates to Professor Broad.

---

* Here is another formidable argument against the theory that ESP is due to the fact that tables of random numbers do not behave in accordance with ordinary probability theory.

† On this occasion Mr. L. A. Rozelaar, M.A. (Senior Lecturer in French at Queen Mary College, London University), who acted as (EA), wrote: 'I carried out every step of decoding and checking with S. G. Soal checking every step of the process. The agent did not speak during the guessing, nor did I notice any signs of his signalling by shuffling of feet, coughing or in any other manner. I inspected and recorded the code at the end of every 50 guesses.'

## Was there Prediction of Future Events?

If lists of random numbers were in existence at the start of an experiment, it would be unnecessary to assume that Shackleton was predicting a future event when he scored significantly on the (+1) card. It would be possible for him to succeed by employing either telepathy or clairvoyance to ascertain certain facts existing in the present. By telepathy from (EA)'s mind, or by clairvoyance, he could learn what was the next number on the list. And by telepathy from the agent, or by clairvoyance, he could obtain knowledge of the order of the five cards in the box. By combining these two bits of information he would be able to say what animal picture the agent would look at next. When, however, coloured counters are drawn by touch from a bag or bowl the problem is more complicated. Since, however, in most of the experiments with counters K.M.G. drew them out of a bowl with alternate hands, it might still be possible to explain away the apparent prediction of a future event by supposing that Shackleton exercised clairvoyance or a combination of clairvoyance and telepathy upon an existing situation. For, at the instant when Shackleton wrote down his guess, and K.M.G.'s right hand was holding a counter to the hole in the screen, her left hand might already have selected the next counter. Shackleton would know by clairvoyance the colour of the counter which would be shown next at the aperture, and by clairvoyance or telepathy from the agent he would know the order of the cards in the box. He could, therefore, deduce the (+1) card from the facts belonging to the existing situation. One difficulty in the way of this hypothesis is that Shackleton never at any time showed that he possessed the gift of clairvoyance. We might perhaps dispense with the assumption of clairvoyance on the part of Shackleton or K.M.G. by supposing that the latter was able to recognize certain colours subconsciously by *touch*. That is the various pigments might possess a slightly different feel. In the experiments especially designed to test clairvoyance he failed completely.

But when we try to explain the (+2) displacement in the experiments with counters at 'rapid' rate, the hypothesis seems to break down completely. For, when Shackleton makes his guess at, say, the instant when K.M.G.'s right hand is holding a counter to the aperture, and her left hand is delving in the bowl for the (+1) counter, the (+2) counter is not known until the right hand has returned to the bowl and made a selection.

It is not easy, therefore, to see how Shackleton could have deduced the (+2) symbol from existing data.

A more recondite possibility, however, suggests itself. Having obtained by telepathy from the agent the order of the cards in the box, could Shackleton, as he recorded his guess, have influenced the sub-conscious mind of K.M.G. in such a way that the *next* counter she drew tallied with the symbol Shackleton had just written down? In the case where the counters were taken from a closed bag, we might have to suppose, in addition, that K.M.G. herself used clairvoyance in selecting the colour implanted in her subconscious mind by Shackleton. When the counters were in an open bowl, she might, in spite of the fact that she looked steadily over the top of the screen, know enough about the positions of various counters to be able to select the right colour without using clairvoyance. It is true, of course, that K.M.G. was blissfully unaware of any influence from Shackleton, but in everyday life it may well be that we often imagine that we are exercising free choice when, in reality, we are acting under unconscious compulsions of various kinds.

The experimenters thought it advisable, in view of the above suggestion, to carry out two special tests in order to discover whether Shackleton could influence K.M.G.'s selection by touch of counters from a bowl. In these experiments the ordinary agent was absent, and the box with the five cards was not in use.

The first such experiment on 9th May 1941, was conducted as follows: Dr. Wiesner (EP) sat in the ante-room with Shackleton, who had in front of him the five differently coloured counters. He was also given a number of scoring sheets whose A-columns had been previously filled in by S.G.S. with random digits 1–5. Dr. Wiesner shuffled the five counters so that they stood in a row in any haphazard order, the order being changed after the completion of each sheet of fifty calls. Shackleton touched the counter whose position in the row corresponded to the random number on his sheet. He was checked by Dr. Wiesner. As he touched each counter, Shackleton called out 'Right'. On hearing this signal, K.M.G. in the studio immediately chose a counter from the bowl while looking straight over the top of the screen, just as she did on ordinary occasions in the counter experiments. K.M.G. let the counters drop back one by one into the bowl, the contents of which she stirred up at frequent intervals as usual. S.G.S., seated on the other side of the screen in the place normally occupied by (A), recorded the *numbers* standing for the five colours as the counters appeared at the aperture. After four sheets had been completed, the sheets of random numbers were decoded into colours according to the code records for each sheet kept by Dr. Wiesner. The sheets filled in by S.G.S. during the experiment were similarly decoded into colours, and the number of successes in each of the five categories (−2), (−1), (0), (+1) and (+2) was counted. In every category the number of hits agreed closely with the chance expectation. For instance, in 192 (+1) trials K.M.G. scored 41 hits, as compared with 38·4, the expected number, and in 184 (+2) trials she scored 32 hits, compared with an expectation of 36·8. There was, in fact, not the slightest sign that Shackleton had influenced K.M.G. in her choice of the counters. The calls were made at about the 'normal' rate.

Perhaps the chief objection to this control experiment is that Shackleton was not exercising free choice, as he presumably did when he wrote down his animal symbols in an ordinary experiment. The colour he tried to make K.M.G. select was rigidly determined by the number on the list. Shackleton, therefore, may not have been acting with his usual spontaneity. Moreover, he was *consciously* trying to influence K.M.G. The psychological conditions undoubtedly were very different from those which obtained in an ordinary 'precognitive' experiment.

In the second test on 7th August 1942, no lists of random numbers were employed.

Shackleton sat at his desk in the ante-room with five coloured counters in front of him arranged in the order

W, Y, G, R, B,

the capitals denoting the initials of the five colours. Shackleton touched the counters one by one with a pencil at 'normal' speed, and, as he did so, called aloud the serial numbers 1, 2, 3, up to 25. S.G.S. sat opposite him, and recorded the numerical position of each counter in the row as it was touched, counting from Shackleton's left to right. K.M.G. sat in the studio at the card-table with a friend, Mrs. Wykeham-Martin. In front of K.M.G. was a bowl containing 245 counters, there being equal numbers of each of the five colours. On hearing the serial number of the call, K.M.G., who sat throughout with her eyes closed, drew out a counter, letting it fall back in the bowl. The corresponding number (in the order W, Y, G, R, B) was recorded in the A-column of a scoring sheet by Mrs. Wykeham-Martin. At the end of each column of 25 calls, there was a pause of from 30 seconds to a minute, during which K.M.G. thoroughly reshuffled the counters in the bowl. Then the work was resumed until ten sheets were completed.

The sequence of 500 counters drawn by K.M.G. appears to satisfy the usual tests* of a random distribution, but Shackleton's selections were very far from being a random set.

Except in the category (+2) all the scores achieved by K.M.G. were in good agreement with chance expectation. But in 460 (+2) trials there were 112 hits, compared with 92, the number to be expected. There is,

---

* There was approximate equality in the numbers of the five symbols, and the numbers of runs of 2, 3 or more of the same symbol were in agreement with theoretical expectation.

thus, a positive deviation equivalent to 2·33 standard deviations, but this cannot be regarded as significant since the (+2) score is chosen as the best score in the five categories. Hence the odds against chance have to be divided by five, and amount to no more than 10 to 1. Thus the experiment affords no conclusive evidence that Shackleton could influence K.M.G.'s selection of counters from the bowl. But here again this second control experiment is not really satisfactory, since Shackleton knew that he was attempting an entirely different feat from that which he performed in his ordinary routine. It would perhaps have been better if he had been led to believe that he was *guessing* the counters shown by K.M.G. in the other room instead of trying to influence her.

On the other hand, the theory that Shackleton scored his (+1) or (+2) hits by being influenced by a future event, i.e. the image which was to enter the agent's mind in about three seconds' time, has much to support it. It affords a satisfactory explanation of the conversion of (+1) hits into (+2) hits at the 'rapid' rate of calling. We must suppose that Shackleton possesses a span of telepathic precognition which ranges between 2 and 3½ seconds into the future, or possibly between 2 and 4 seconds. If the object of presentation is closer to his 'present instant' than, say, two seconds, it is perhaps too near in time for him to perceive it, and so he cognizes the next object which is within his span. We cannot, of course, attempt to fix too accurately the upper and lower limits of this supposed span of precognition, but the fact that Shackleton invariably failed to cognize telepathic presentations five seconds ahead of his 'present instant' strongly suggests that the upper limit is about 3½–4 seconds. All that it is permissible to affirm is the probable existence of an optimum span of prehension.

It is an interesting hypothesis to suppose that our percipient developed a fixed precognitive time-*habit*, engendered originally by the 'normal' rate of calling, to which he had become accustomed during the earlier experiments. If his prehensive span into the future remained fixed when the rate of calling was doubled, his successes would then fall on the (+2) trials instead of on the (+1).

It seems highly probable that whatever theory is invoked to explain the apparent precognitive effect in the 'counters' experiments must account also for the same effect observed when prepared lists of random numbers were used, for there appears to be little or no difference in the degree of success obtained by the two methods.

Now, if we wish to avoid the assumption of precognition, we must suppose that Shackleton was, in the case of either method, able to obtain by telepathy or clairvoyance the order of the cards in the box. Since, however, he failed in experiments designed to test clairvoyance, it must be assumed that he got the order of the five cards from the agent's mind. But the agent, in most cases, shuffled the cards without looking at their faces, or the cards were laid faces downward in the box by another person. The agent, therefore, would only learn this order after lifting and looking at several cards. For instance, after lifting the card corresponding to the first number on the list, she would be unable to provide Shackleton telepathically with any very precise information about the picture on the card in the particular position indicated by the next number on the list, except, of course, in the infrequent case of a repeat. If, therefore, Shackleton was succeeding in getting the (+1) card by first obtaining the next number on the list from (EA)'s mind and the card order from (A)'s mind, we might reasonably expect to find that the first three or four (+1) guesses on each sheet were, on the whole, far less successful than the later guesses made at a time when (A) was in full possession of the order of all the card-pictures. It is conceivable, however, that this effect might be offset by a decline in the success-rate as we proceed down the column.

A fair test, therefore, would be to compare the score on the first four trials of the first or (a) column with that on the first four trials on the second or (b) column of the same sheet. It will be remembered that the agent did not reshuffle the five cards in the box until the end of the second column. At the end of the (a) column there was a pause of a few seconds to give Shackleton a breather before beginning again. At the start of the (b) column the agent would know the order of the cards, and Shackleton would be making a fresh beginning.

Actually, however, an examination of the records revealed that Shackleton, while working with the agents Miss Elliott and Mrs. Albert at 'normal' rate (either with counters or with prepared lists of numbers), scored on the first four trials of the (a) columns 127 (+1) hits, as compared with 138 (+1) hits on the first four trials of the (b) columns. The expected number in each case would be 132·5. The difference between the two scores, +11, is quite without significance, since, with Yates's correction, $\chi^2 = 0.377$. Thus, so far as this test goes, the result affords no evidence for the hypothesis that Shackleton was deducing the (+1) card from facts known to anyone at the moment when he made his guess. In fact, even on the first *two* trials only there is no significant difference between the (a) and the (b) columns.

That the personality of the agent plays a part in the process is clear from the fact that, except for a single occasion, Shackleton obtained only precognitive successes when working with Miss Elliott, while with Aldred both precognitive and post-cognitive effects were produced. With a third agent, Mrs. Albert, who came on only two occasions, Shackleton obtained (+1) successes only, as in the case of Miss Elliott.

In fact, on 432 (+1) trials with Mrs. Albert as agent he scored 139 hits, compared with a Stevens expectation of 88·6. This gives a positive deviation which exceeds 6 standard deviations, and corresponds to odds of more than a hundred millions to one. In none of the other categories was the score anywhere near significance. There were no experiments at 'rapid' rate with this agent, and prepared random numbers were in use throughout.

In addition to the three successful agents, Miss R. Elliott, Mrs. G. Albert and Mr. J. Aldred, eight other persons acted as agent, but Shackleton had no success with them.*

In all, 1,152 (+1) trials at 'normal' rate were made with the eight agents but these yielded only 222 hits which is only slightly below the Stevens expectation of 233·5. Among the unsuccessful agents were Mrs. Basil Shackleton, K.M.G., Dr. Wiesner and S.G.S.

As regards K.M.G., there was an earlier occasion (21st February 1941) on which she was apparently a successful agent. On this date, after Miss Elliott had acted as agent for four sheets of guesses, K.M.G. took her place, while Miss Elliott watched K.M.G. Miss Elliott sat about three feet away, but in a position where she could certainly have seen the cards in the box if she had chosen to do so. It is quite possible, therefore, that Miss Elliott was, all unwittingly, the agent on this occasion, though she reported that she was watching K.M.G. the whole time and did not look at the cards. There is, however, an interesting difference between results scored with K.M.G. as agent and those previously obtained earlier in the sitting with Miss Elliott as agent. In fact, on the 192 (+1) trials with Miss Elliott as agent the score was not significant (CR = +1·84), but the score on 200 trials on the actual or target card was just significant (the odds are about 40 to 1 when it is regarded as the best score in the five categories).

But when K.M.G. took Miss Elliott's place at the box, there was a score of 61 in 192 (+1) trials, and a chance score on the target card. The odds against getting this (+1) score by chance, when it is regarded as the best score out of five categories, amount to 2,000 to 1.

It may be that, even if Miss Elliott was the unconscious agent in this case, K.M.G. did perhaps have some influence on the result, although on a later occasion (25th April 1941) when K.M.G. was again the agent, Miss Elliott being absent, there were no significant scores of any kind. We cannot, of course, draw conclusions from such a limited number of guesses.

* The fact that the nature of the result depended on the agent is difficult to reconcile with Spencer Brown's hypothesis.

## *Theoretical Considerations*

The outstanding feature of Shackleton's guessing is his general inability to receive the image at the instant when it is clearly focused in the agent's mind. There are many indications from mediumistic studies that it is those ideas just below the threshold of the sitter's consciousness, or on its fringe, which have the best chance of being transferred to the medium's mind. In his sittings with the spiritualistic medium, Mrs. Blanche Cooper,* S.G.S. frequently noticed that, when he asked for a name, this would seldom be given at the moment when he was consciously thinking of it. A little later in the sitting, when he was thinking about something else, Mrs. Cooper would volunteer the name correctly. It was as if the image had to sink back into the unconscious part of the sitter's mind before it became available for telepathic transference to the medium. If we confine ourselves to the post-cognitive effect observed when Aldred was the agent, it would seem that the image had to fade out of the latter's conscious mind for about three seconds before it had reached a subconscious level favourable for its transmission to Shackleton's mind. And the results on the (−2) displacement indicate that the interval necessary for the image to sink to the right level was remarkably constant with this agent. It may even be that the rate of fading to the optimum level varies with the agent, and this might possibly explain why there were no (−1) or (−2) displacements with the other successful agents Miss Elliott and Mrs. Albert. Conceivably with some persons this sinking back of the image into the subconscious is far less rapid than it is with others. Thirty seconds might be required instead of three. If ever another Shackleton appears on the scene, it would be of great interest to experiment systematically with different persons as agents, and with intervals between successive calls ranging from $1\frac{1}{2}$ seconds up to several minutes. It would, of course, be much harder to explain the precognitive time effects by a similar theory. We might suppose that the agent has become aware of the future image of the card at some subconscious level of his mind a few seconds before this image becomes clearly focused at the conscious level. The image then requires time to pass up through various levels in the subconscious on its way to the conscious, and at some stage in this ascent it is in a ripe state for being transferred to Shackleton's subconscious.

Such a theory would, however, do nothing to remove the fundamental difficulty, which is to understand how the agent's unconscious was able to register an event before it had actually happened. We should merely be supposing that the agent, and not Shackleton, was the person

* VI, 4.

who exercised precognition. It may be that we are all in touch with future events in our own lives at the unconscious level, but that normally such fore-knowledge never reaches our conscious minds.* Perhaps it requires the telepathic faculty of a Shackleton to bring it to light.

Perhaps, however, the most plausible hypothesis of a psychological kind that has relevance to the Shackleton effects is that of 'the specious present', advanced by the late Mr. H. F. Saltmarsh† in 1934. It is generally accepted by psychologists that there is no such thing as an instantaneous mental experience. Every act of perception, or of imagining, occupies a small but finite interval of time. We are not fully conscious of an event until it has faded a little into the past. So far as our mental experience goes, there is no sharp dividing line which separates the present from the past. Now Saltmarsh suggested that this short interval of time, over which every act of awareness is spread, embraces not only a fragment of the past but also a little bit of the future. The actual extent of an individual's 'specious present', as it is called, may vary with his state of mind. When he is alert, it will be shorter than when his attention is diffused. In other words, the more sharply conscious and awake he is, the briefer will be the duration of an act of perception. It might therefore be reasonable to suppose that, as one recedes from the fully conscious state to the deeper subconscious levels of the mind, there will be an increasing spread in what we experience as the 'present moment', and this spread will embrace more of the future as well as more of the past. Now there is very good reason to believe that extra-sensory cognition takes place at subliminal levels of the mind. It is, therefore, quite possible that a mental event which, for the conscious self, is either in the past or the future, may, for a subconscious level, be within the span of the present. If, then, we assume that in persons like Shackleton there is a free traffic way connecting the conscious with the unconscious parts of the mind, it would, on Saltmarsh's hypothesis, be possible for a future event to be known to our present consciousness. Saltmarsh's theory is probably of more interest to the psychologist than to the metaphysician. Actually it explains very little. It leaves unanswered how we become aware of an event which has not yet happened. Yet we should hesitate to suppose that an event in the future can influence or cause a present event. May it not be as Dr. Wassermann suggests that world events have pre-existing mental patterns, and that it is these patterns, and not the events themselves, which we contact in cases of precognition? Themselves timeless, these patterns are in the process of realizing themselves in time. Perhaps,

---

* This would seem to imply that physical events are the realizations of timeless mental patterns which are neither created nor destroyed.

† VI, 1.

as Wassermann suggests, the latent patterns of all possible events pre-exist—both those that will be realized and those that will never become actual. He thinks that an infinity of mental patterns is associated not only with particles of living matter but with every fundamental particle in the universe.

The evolutionary process suggests the pre-existence of well-defined patterns which realize themselves bit by bit at the moments when appropriate molecular assemblies become available. It is difficult to suppose for instance that the neurons of the speech centres in Man were the result of chance mutations alone. Wassermann thinks that natural selection and chance mutations are insufficient to explain evolution; there is in addition a tremendous drive inherent in the patterns themselves, which are pushing towards physical embodiment against all obstacles.

According to Bergson the future is being created at every moment but Wassermann believes that it is all latent in the womb of the present. There is no creation but only a development of patterns which are eternal and indestructible.

According to this view, the behaviour of the molecules in a human body is only partly determined by the laws of quantum theory; there are superimposed on these quantum effects psycho-kinetic influences produced by the urge of the striving patterns.

The only meaning that could be given to human freedom is that we are free when our desires are in harmony with the unconscious urge of the developing patterns.

It may be that we are unconsciously in touch with the mental patterns of all possible events in the universe, but an avoidance drive prevents the vast majority of such patterns from becoming conscious. Those patterns which have achieved realization in time appear to us as memory but only rarely do the unfulfilled patterns of future events escape the vigilance of the avoidance drive and reach the level of consciousness.

We might, of course, ask how it is that Shackleton, for instance, was able to single out from the infinite pool of latently existing patterns just the one which was going to be realized in a few seconds' time in the form of a specific event, namely the turning up of a certain card by the agent. But this is the old problem of singularization which has been encountered so often in clairvoyance and in telepathy. Now singularization is also a feature in the recall of memories. How, for instance, does it come about that by a mere act of attention one of us, S.G.S., is able, out of myriads of unconscious memory states, to single out the ones which refer to the day twenty years ago when he broke an ice-axe on the

Blümlisalp glacier and to the following day when he climbed the First with his friend Tom Jones, and the succeeding days on which it rained incessantly. Probably singularization is a fundamental property of psychological drives—a law of nature for which it would be futile to seek an explanation.

It seems to us that Wassermann's view of precognition does something at any rate to clarify the situation. We no longer need to ask such questions as how can causation work backwards in time, or how can a future event influence a present event. Nor need we postulate extra dimensions of time for which we have no empirical evidence whatever.

## The Theories of Hinton, Dunne, and Broad

Most of the theories which have been advanced to account for the fact of precognition begin by postulating that time is a kind of space. There are obvious analogies which will occur to everyone. Events in time can be arranged in order just like the milestones, the villages, and the trees, along a straight road. As we travel to the Essex coast from London, Romford comes before Brentwood, and Billericay after Brentwood. In like manner the Romans landed in England before the Saxons and the Normans after them. In other words, we can, if we do not examine the question too closely, set up a one to one correspondence between happenings in time and the points on a straight line. Events, however, are not like abstract points on a line, because they possess duration or extension in time. Even a flash of lightning is not instantaneous, but lasts for a fraction of a second. Here is a house, a rectangular object in three dimensions, but, as was pointed out by the Time-traveller in H. G. Wells's[4] irresponsible romance, it is meaningless to talk of an *instantaneous* house. The house has been standing perhaps for fifty years, and it may last for another twenty years. In addition to the three dimensions of length, breadth and height, the house has another dimension extending along the time-stream.

Now the mathematician C. Hinton thought of all objects and events, past, present and future, as being spread out along the time-dimension. Our brains and bodies are also extended in time. In other words, our bodies are four dimensional objects, and our appearance at, say, the age of 40 is merely a three-dimensional section of our four-dimensional reality.

Hinton[5] thought of our human consciousness not as a thing having extension in time like the material being, but either as an unextended something or as a two-dimensional film which moved along the time dimension from the cradle to the grave. More accurately he would have

171

to think of consciousness as moving along the temporal extension of the brain, and scanning the brain states as it proceeds.*

According to this theory of Hinton, past events as well as future events exist in the eternal present of a static universe. As Eddington remarked: 'Events do not happen; we only meet them in our passage.'

It is no doubt picturesque to think of our consciousness as a car with rear lights but no head-lights speeding along a dark road. We sit within a little circle of bright light which we call our present moment. Behind us is the stretch of road over which we have travelled, faintly illuminated by memory, but ahead all is silent and dark. Future events in our life are already 'there' waiting to be caught up by our little spot-light. Such images are romantic but apt to be misleading.

It was upon this probably erroneous conception of Hinton that J. W. Dunne† based his celebrated theory of precognition. Dunne's theory has been shown by Professor C. D. Broad[10] and other philosophers to be an unsound logical construction, but it could possibly be modified so as to avoid the infinite regress of times and observers which is its most objectionable feature. In very brief outline the theory runs as follows: Dunne starts off with Hinton's idea of the spotlight of our normal consciousness moving along the brain-track in a four-dimensional world. The changing series of three-dimensional sections which our consciousness encounters gives the illusion of passing time and also the illusion of motion in the three-dimensional world. Dunne then argues that this shifting of attention from one aspect to another of the apparently changing three-dimensional universe must take place in a real time. Now just as the original time of the waking self is, in reality, a dimension of space so the introduction of this new time must be justified by the addition of a fifth spatial dimension to the universe and the creation of a second conscious observer who is capable of moving in the five-dimensional world. Motion in the fifth dimension gives the illusion of time to this new observing consciousness, which, according to Mr. Dunne, slavishly follows the normal waking consciousness along the original track of sense impressions so long as this latter consciousness is functioning. But during sleep, or after physical death, when the normal consciousness is out of action, this second observer is free to flit backwards and forwards along the whole stretch of sense-data and mental images along the brain track between the points of birth and death. This track, which to the normal consciousness is an illusory time, appears as a

* There seems some confusion here. For consciousness is not an entity. It is merely the empirical state of a mental pattern, and mental patterns may be conscious or unconscious. A mental pattern cannot move or *scan* anything.
† VI, 3.

fourth dimension of space to the second observer. The second consciousness is therefore not only able to relive the past life of the waking consciousness, but it can also, by turning its attention to that part of the track which is still in the future for the normal consciousness, precognize events in this future. But according to Mr. Dunne it can do much more than this. The second consciousness can create new and significant mental experiences by blending pieces of imagery chosen from different periods of the individual's life. No doubt much of the glamour with which Dunne's theory was invested for the general public originated in these rather fanciful suggestions. This kind of creation, according to the theory, happens in dreams, but less romantic people see in dreams —for the most part—only the muddled workings of memory.

But the second observing consciousness must also have a 'real' time in which to produce its mental jugglery, and hence a sixth dimension of space and a third observer must be conjured into existence, and so it goes on *ad infinitum*. The process is never complete until we reach 'the observer at infinity', but, as there is no last term in an infinite progression, the theory, as it stands, breaks down.

All the 'observers' except the normal waking consciousness, which ends at death, are immortal. Each 'real' time becomes a dimension of space for the observer next in the hierarchy.

Professor Broad, however, has pointed out that, in order to explain precognition along Mr. Dunne's lines, the infinite series of times and observers are not required. In fact, only five dimensions of space are needed.

Theories employing four or more dimensions of space are of frequent occurrence in mathematical physics, and there would be nothing unorthodox in the application of multi-dimensional space to the study of the human mind. But when we come to theories which postulate that time has more than one dimension, we are on less safe ground.

Professor Broad thinks that precognition resembles a memory that works forwards instead of backwards rather than a direct perception of physical events. He has himself suggested the hypothesis that time has a second dimension which is at right angles to the linear dimension that we experience through our normal consciousness.

According to this theory, events would be symbolized not by points on a line but by lines or areas in a plane. A happening which may be in the future as regards the time dimension of our normal consciousness may already be in the past with regard to the second dimension of time. If, therefore, we possess an extra-sensory consciousness which is capable of appreciating those ghostly fields of time which lie to the left or right of the linear track, we may become aware of an event before our normal consciousness has reached it.

Very roughly we may represent this diagrammatically as follows:

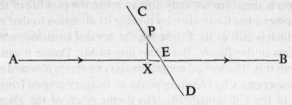

Let AB represent the world line along which our normal consciousness, according to Hinton, moves from birth to death. Let CED denote the extension of the event E into the second dimension of time which lies at right angles to AB. Normally we should not become aware of this event until our consciousness arrives at the point E. Nevertheless, the extra-sensory consciousness which can look to the right or left of AB may perceive the event P from the point X, that is before the normal conscious-ness reaches E. If then the extra-sensory faculty, which is not confined to the track AB, is able to communicate with the normal consciousness, the latter will appear to have performed an act of precognition.

This is admittedly an extremely crude presentation of the theory, but we do not suppose that Professor Broad himself pins very much faith on this notion of a second dimension of time at right angles to the first. Indeed, attempts to think of time in terms of geometry, or to regard it as a kind of space, are in all probability mere nonsense. It is better for us to refrain from theorizing than to allow ourselves to be misled by the ideas of Hinton, Dunne and their followers. A worth-while theory is unlikely to appear until a great deal more experimental work has been done on the subject of prevision. At present there is insufficient confirmation by experiment that non-inferential precognition really exists, though there is a certain amount of evidence which suggests that it is a possibility.

But as C. T. K. Chari[7] has pointed out, when occultists talk glibly of consciousness 'moving' along metaphysical world lines of particles stretched out statically in a hyper-space they are indulging in a 'vast *ignoratio elenchi*'. There is in fact no philosophical justification for the introduction of the 'moving now', which has made such an appeal to the popular imagination.

Alexander Horne[7] has remarked that as soon as we introduce the idea of 'motion', though it be only of consciousness, the problem of time re-asserts itself, for without time no motion is conceivable. To cite Chari again: 'The whole attempt to assimilate time to *motion* (of con-sciousness) is ill-conceived and is the sign of philosophical immaturity.'

But even if the idea of a universe consisting of rigid material threads stretched out in a four-dimensional space was acceptable to modern thought, this would not justify Dunne in his contention that by an act of will the moving observer is able to alter the future course of events by a lateral displacement of the world lines which lie ahead of his moving 'now'. For, as Horne has pointed out, such a displacement would involve a time-motion in an *impossible* direction and would violate Hinton's whole conception, which is that time is simply our experience of the motion of our consciousness *along* the direction of the world lines of brain particles. But this is only one of the many muddles which ensue from the confused thinking of Hinton and Dunne.

# CHAPTER XI

# Secondary Findings with Shackleton

I n the present chapter we shall discuss under various headings some of the less important results which follow from the experiments with Shackleton.

## (a) The Material of Transmission

For the first nine sittings with Shackleton, the agent, Miss Elliott, looked at the pictures of the animals, but at Sitting No. 10 on 28th March 1941, without informing the percipient that there was any change, S.G.S. substituted for the pictures five plain white cards on which were printed in block letters the initial letters E, G, L, P, Z of the animals' names. This did not affect the success of the experiment in any way, for in 192 (+1) trials with counters at normal rate there were 57 hits, while at rapid rate, 173 (+2) trials yielded 54 hits. These scores, which correspond to critical ratios of 3·18 and 3·88 respectively, are of about the same order of significance as those obtained when pictures were employed.

With the agent J. Aldred, initial letters were used successfully throughout.

At his visit to the studio on 6th June 1941, Professor H. H. Price of Oxford suggested that it would be of interest to discover whether the experiment would succeed if the material for transmission were to consist of words having associations with the five animals instead of pictures or initials. Accordingly, on 14th and 25th August 1941, S.G.S. arranged for the agent's use five white cards in the centres of which were printed the words BEAK, MANE, NECK, STRIPES and TRUNK in large block capitals—words having obvious associations with PELICAN, LION, GIRAFFE, ZEBRA and ELEPHANT. The same words were printed at the tops and bottoms of the cards in smaller characters so that the agent Miss Elliott would recognize the card immediately it was lifted from the floor of the box. Shackleton was never shown these cards, which S.G.S. took home with him at the end of each sitting.

During these two sessions S.G.S. regularly alternated the ordinary 'picture' cards with those bearing the 'associated words' in batches of 50 calls. Thus, on 14th August during sheets 1, 3, 5, 7 the agent looked at the pictures, while for sheets 2, 4, 6, 8 she looked at the 'associated words'. (EA) would call out 'First sheet—Pictures', 'Second sheet—White cards', etc., so that, while Shackleton knew that there was *some* change, he was kept in ignorance of its nature. The results were as follows: On the 336 (+1) trials at normal speed with pictures there were 94 hits, while with the same number of (+1) trials with 'associated words' there were 89 hits. Fisher's method for small samples was employed in order to estimate whether or not the difference between the two scores was significant. The actual difference is only 5 hits, and it was found that a larger difference than this might be expected to occur by chance alone in about two out of every three such experiments.

We can safely conclude that the 'associated words' proved quite as successful as the 'pictures'. It seemed very probable that any symbols which the agent interpreted as meaning Elephant, Giraffe, etc., would serve just as well. In the subsequent work with Mrs. Stewart we found further confirmation of this conjecture (see p. 255).

## (b) Perception versus Memory

A series of experiments was carried out in order to ascertain whether 'sight' of the card at each call was a help to transmission, or whether the results would be equally good if the agent merely remembered the order of the five cards without lifting and looking at the card when the random number was shown at the aperture in the screen. In other words, would transference be as successful when it was from the agent's memory content alone as when there was, in addition, perception of the initial letter at each call?

The first experiment of this kind was carried out on 26th August 1942, with Mr. Aldred acting as agent. Before the test we explained to Shackleton what we were trying to discover. During the (*a*) (or first) column of each sheet Aldred lifted the cards in the box and looked at them one by one as usual, thus getting to know their order; but during the succeeding (*b*) (or second) column the agent merely touched the backs of the cards as the random numbers were shown by (EA) without lifting them or looking at their faces. The order of the five cards in the box remained the same until the end of the (*b*) column, when the cards were reshuffled as usual by the agent. The experiment was done at the normal rate, and the *combined* scores on (+1) and (−1) trials were counted.

Thus, on 192 (+1) and (−1) trials taken together in which Aldred

N                                      177

lifted and looked at the cards there was a total of 60 hits, whereas on the 192 (+1) and (−1) trials in which Aldred merely touched the backs of the cards, there was a total of 53 hits.

Using Fisher's method for small samples, we should expect a greater difference than the actual difference (7) of the scores to occur about once in every two such experiments. It would appear then that the perception of the card-symbol at each trial does not help success. The result was confirmed by a repetition of the experiment on 8th April 1943, which was held in the rooms of the S.P.R. at 31 Tavistock Square, London, W.C.1. In this case Mr. Aldred was again the agent, and the other conditions remained the same. On 192 (−1) and (+1) trials taken together in which Aldred lifted and looked at the cards individually there was a total of 61 hits and on the 192 (−1) and (+1) trials in which he touched the backs of the cards without looking at them there was a total of 62. Obviously the difference is of no importance.

## A Variation of the 'Lift and Touch' Experiment

At a sitting held at the rooms of the S.P.R. on 15th April 1943, an interesting variation of the above experiment was tried. J. Aldred was again the agent, and Mr. D. J. West was invited to assist at the experiment. Before each sheet of 50 guesses was done, the agent shuffled the five cards (initial letters) and laid them faces *upward* on the floor of the box. He then gazed at the cards for about 15 seconds, studying their order. The cards were then turned faces downward without any alteration of their order, and, as each random number was shown at the aperture in the screen by (EA), the agent merely touched the back of the corresponding card without lifting it or looking at its face. Throughout the guessing therefore, Aldred had no direct perception of the faces of the cards but only memory of their order. Shackleton recorded his own guesses in pencil. All the sheets were signed by both experimenters (Mr. West and S.G.S.), but all the decoding, checking, counting of hits, and duplicating were done by Mr. West alone with S.G.S. watching. Mr. West posted the duplicate sheets to Professor C. D. Broad, and took away with him a private record of scores in the three categories (+1), (0), (−1).

The results were highly significant on both (+1) and (−1) scores. Out of 192 (+1) trials there were 60 hits, and 192 (−1) trials yielded 53 hits. These correspond to critical ratios of 3·86 and 2·65 respectively.

This experiment, which is the last reported in the Soal-Goldney series, became the basis of a routine method two years later in our work with Mrs. Stewart.

## (c) *Experiments with Non-Random Sequences*

Dr. C. A. Mace, now Professor of Psychology at Birkbeck College, University of London, who witnessed the Shackleton experiments on 21st December 1941, made the suggestion that it would be of interest to discover whether Shackleton would succeed with a series of prepared numbers not chosen haphazardly or at random, but pre-arranged in some improbable order. On the three dates 15th May 1942, 22nd May 1942, and 12th August 1942, it was arranged that among the sheets of random numbers (made in the usual way from tables) should be inserted a single column of 25 calls in which the first 12 numbers were all the same digit and the last 13 the same (but different) digit. Shackleton was given no hint that these 'doctored' columns differed in any way from the others. The results of the experiment (with Shackleton's guesses translated into numbers 1–5) are given below in Table 6. The first column is not as successful as the other two.

TABLE 6

### *Experiments with Non-Random Digits*

(i) 15*th May* 1942 (*Normal rate*), Sheet 1, Col. (*b*).
    Card    555, 555, 555, 555;    333, 333, 333, 333, 3.
    Guess  233, 444, 332, 445;    413, 233, 454, 333, 1.

(ii) 22*nd May* 1942 (*Normal rate*), Sheet 1, Col. (*b*).
    Card    111, 111, 111, 111;    333, 333, 333, 333, 3.
    Guess  335, 111, 531, 113;    145, 333, 433, 355, 2.

(iii) 12*th August* 1942 (*Normal rate*), Sheet 2, Col. (*a*).
    Card    333, 333, 333, 333;    111, 111, 111, 111, 1.
    Guess  343, 125, 333, 312;    535, 211, 151, 121, 1.

On all three occasions J. Aldred was the agent. It will be seen that the total numbers of 'direct' (0) hits are

7 (first occasion)
12 (second occasion)
13 (third occasion)

In example (i) Shackleton does not seem to respond until the second half of the column.

There are two ways in which we can examine the matter. In example (i), for instance, the relevant digits are 5 and 3. We may count how many 5's and 3's there are in the 'correct' part of the column and how many in the 'wrong' part. As 5 and 3 were guessed 12 times, we might expect 6 relevant digits to be in the 'correct' part and 6 in the 'wrong' part. Similarly for the other examples. Thus, altogether, there are 32 relevant digits in the 'correct' part and only 13 in the 'wrong' part, whereas chance would predict equal numbers (22·5) in each part.

A simple contingency table (with Yates's correction) gives $\chi^2 = 7·20$, with corresponding odds of more than 150 to 1 against the results being due to chance.

We may, however, proceed as follows: When, as in example (i), a 5 is presented a large number of times, we may ask ourselves: Does Shackleton tend to guess the digit more frequently than he does on ordinary occasions? From the totals given for each of the five digits on the guess-columns of his scoring sheets we may, on the assumption that Shackleton's guesses are fairly randomly mixed, estimate the number of times the digit 5 would be expected to occur in a column of 25 calls, and similarly in the case of all the other relevant digits. A contingency table based on this method of estimation gives $\chi^2 = 23·19$, with corresponding odds of more than 600,000 to 1.

There seems little doubt that repetition of the same symbol a large number of times by the agent causes Shackleton to guess that symbol with increased frequency.

## (d) Multiple Determination

We saw that in 1936 Shackleton was producing significant scores on both the precognitive (+1) card and the post-cognitive (−1) card. The interesting question then arose: When the (0) card, i.e. the 'actual' card, was sandwiched between two cards bearing the *same* symbol, would the influence of the (+1) image and that of the (−1) image tend to reinforce each other? In other words, should we expect to get a significantly larger proportion of (+1) hits, and similarly of (−1) hits in the case when the (0) symbol was sandwiched between like symbols than when the symbols on either side were unlike? A method[1] was devised to deal with this problem, and it was found that, while Mrs. Stewart's 1936 records showed no sign of the effect, those of Shackleton showed that reinforcement was probably operating to a slight degree.

Since with Rita Elliott as agent there were only (+1) effects, the question could not be re-opened in 1941, and it was only when, a year later, Shackleton began to produce significant scores on both the (+1) and (−1) cards that the problem could be further investigated. Two different methods were utilized, one being that suggested by Professor H. Robbins (mentioned in Chapter VIII) and the other due to Mr. A. M. Walker[1] of Manchester* University. Both methods, when applied

---

* Of the two methods that of Mr. Walker would appear to be safer than Professor Robbins's method, to which objections have been recently made.

by Dr. J. G. Pratt of Duke University in co-operation with Dr. T. N. E. Greville of Washington, demonstrated conclusively[2] that in the 1942-3 experiments with J. Aldred as agent there was a high degree of reinforcement in the case of the multiply-determined (MD) guesses.

For the technical details the reader may consult two papers in the Duke University *Journal of Parapsychology*, Vol. 15, 1951, by Pratt and Greville[1, 2] respectively.

Not only was there a much higher proportion of $(+1)$ and $(-1)$ hits on card patterns of the type

$$\begin{matrix} O \\ O \end{matrix} \qquad \begin{matrix} + \\ S \end{matrix}$$

than on card patterns such as $\begin{matrix} O \\ O \end{matrix}$ when the

experiment was conducted at the normal speed, but at the 'rapid' rate of calling, which resulted in significant $(+2)$ and $(-2)$ hits, there was also highly significant reinforcement on patterns such as

$$\begin{matrix} L \\ G \\ \to E \\ P \\ L \end{matrix} \quad or \quad \begin{matrix} L \\ L \\ \to E \\ G \\ L \end{matrix} \quad or \quad \begin{matrix} L \\ G \\ \to L \\ L \\ L \end{matrix} \quad or \quad \begin{matrix} L \\ L \\ \to L \\ L \\ L \end{matrix}$$

as contrasted with patterns such as

$$\begin{matrix} L \\ G \\ \to E \\ P \\ Z \end{matrix}$$

in which the $(+2)$ and $(-2)$ guesses were not multiply-determined. (The horizontal arrow denotes the point where Shackleton made his guess.)

Thus at the 'rapid' rate of calling it was the $(+2)$ and $(-2)$ images which reinforced each other so as to produce a significantly larger proportion of $(+2)$ and $(-2)$ hits. It is of interest to note that the evidence for reinforcement in the case of $(+2)$ and $(-2)$ patterns was even stronger than in the case of the $(+1)$ and $(-1)$ patterns. In fact the Robbins method applied to the $(+1)$ forward displacement gave odds in favour of reinforcement amounting to 5,000 to one, but, when applied to the $(+2)$ forward displacement, when the tempo was 'rapid', the odds in favour of the reinforcement effect in the case of MD guesses were as high as 20,000 to 1.

The reader may form an estimate of the strength of the reinforcement in the case of the $(+2)$ and $(-2)$ guesses when he learns that on a total of 60 multiply-determined patterns there were no fewer than 35 $(+2)$ hits, which is over 58 per cent, whereas on the 170 patterns which were not multiply-determined, there were only 49 (+2) hits, which is only about 29 per cent.

As Dr. Pratt[2] writes in the above-mentioned paper:

'The reinforcement effect in displacement is one of the most striking instances of improvement in ESP performance that has yet been observed. If we can find out what caused Shackleton to do so much better when he had the particular situation in the target order presented by a multiply-determined pattern, we may be able to generalize to other situations and bring about similar improvements in scoring in other subjects, even those for whom displacement is not the primary ESP effect.'

Dr. Pratt goes on to say that the phenomenon of reinforcement indicates that ESP is not an all or nothing act of perception comparable to, say, visual perception under conditions that are either quite favourable or totally unfavourable to sight. For, if ESP were a complete perception of the correct target in every case in which it occurs, there would be no need for reinforcement and no opportunity for reinforcement to show up in the results.

What is clear is that ESP is not concerned entirely with isolated targets, but that its effects are in relation to patterns and configurations in the target sequence. When we come to study the records of Mrs. Stewart, we shall see how her scoring is affected by patterns of quite a different kind.

## (e) Can Shackleton Pre-judge his Success or Failure?

Perhaps the most discouraging and perplexing aspect of the extra-sensory process is its unconscious nature. The fruits of the faculty are garnered into consciousness, but the undergrowth of supporting stems is matured in darkness and seemingly inaccessible to introspection. Were there some peculiar feeling or some sense of certainty which accompanied the emergence of authentic impressions, the percipient could withhold his guesses until this feeling appeared. It would then be possible to discriminate between the hits that were due to ESP and those that were the offspring of chance. At present, ESP is not in the true sense a form of cognition, because the subject has no inkling of how he arrives at his impressions; it is more akin to guessing. If only some means could be found, such as a drug, which would bring the whole process into the light of consciousness, progress would be rapid.

When Shackleton expressed the opinion that certain of his guesses felt better than the rest, it was of importance to ascertain whether or not his belief corresponded with reality. Owing to the rapid rate at which all guessing was done it would have been quite impracticable for him to have graded his guesses A, B, C, D according as he felt them to be 'very good', 'good', 'indifferent' or 'bad'. Any attempt to impose such a grading would probably have ruined the experiments. However, as he went along, Shackleton, from time to time, volunteered comments, and marked a sequence of, say, five guesses, as being probably better than the rest. Sometimes he would mark a whole column of 24 (+1) trials as 'jolly good'; or 'this felt good'; or 'this felt better than the rest', etc. Such marked groups occur on most dates between 24th January 1941 and 14th August 1941. After the latter date he ceased to mark his guesses or express verbal opinions about special groups. We have therefore counted all such marked (+1) guesses at 'normal rate' which were registered between 24th January 1941 and 14th August 1941, whether these occurred during telepathy tests or clairvoyance tests, and irrespective of the person acting as agent (i.e. work with all agents is included in the counts). In the absence of a proper grading of all guesses, the method can be regarded as only a very rough one, but it affords no evidence that Shackleton was able to pre-judge successful hits.

Actually, out of a total of 396 marked (+1) guesses he scored 100 hits, while out of 4,683 unmarked trials he obtained 1,331 hits. A simple contingency table (with Yates's correction) shows that there is no significant difference between the proportions of hits on marked and unmarked trials ($\chi^2 = 1.66$).

Shackleton, then, like most other ESP subjects, has no normal knowledge of whether his guesses are right or wrong.

## (f) Has Shackleton's Rate of Scoring any Relation to the State of his Health?

We mentioned on p. 133 that Shackleton does not normally enjoy good health, and, on account of this fact, we made no systematic records of his state of health at each sitting. On certain occasions, however, he did complain of feeling exceptionally unwell, and a special note was made at the time. The scanty information in our possession may be best put into tabular form.

### Scoring in Relation to Health

[*N.B.*—By percentage of 'true cognitions' is meant* the percentage of hits most probably *not due to chance*. For (+1) work at normal rate with Miss Rita Elliott as agent this percentage is 10·9 while with J. Aldred as agent on the (+1) and (−1) scores combined (at normal rate) it is 10·6.]

* Cf. Appendix B, 12.

## TABLE 7

| Date | Shackleton's remarks | Percentage of true cognitions |
|------|----------------------|-------------------------------|
| 7.2.41 | The percipient complained at the start of a 'bad hang-over' from the previous night, when he had been to a party. | 8·85 |
| 14.3.41 | Before starting Shackleton complained of feeling unwell and advised that if the results were not good after the first two sheets, we ought to stop the experiment. | 17·53 |
| 18.4.41 | Shackleton reported that he did not feel like getting good results, as he felt tired after the very bad 'blitz' of two days earlier, 'but of course one can't say for sure.' | Normal rate 8·51 Rapid rate 10·96 |
| 23.5.41 | Before the experiment Shackleton complained that kidney trouble had been bad during the past few days, and that he was still in pain. | 15·34 with agent Miss Rita Elliott. 24·48 with agent Mrs. Albert. |
| 10.10.41 | Shackleton was in a bad humour from the start. He complained of feeling exasperated after a heavy day's work. | Chance results only. |
| 7.11.41 | After the results were found to be chance results, Shackleton said this was the first day for some time that he had been free from pain. | Chance results only. |
| 14.11.41 | Before starting Shackleton said he was suffering from severe kidney trouble, and did not expect good results as he was in pain. | 10·16 |
| 16.1.42 | Shackleton was in a bad humour and was feeling ill. He also complained of the cold weather. | Chance results, but the agents were new. |
| 15.5.42 | Shackleton was in a wrought-up state. Before the start of the experiment, Shackleton, who had been kept waiting owing to the lateness of J. Aldred the agent, remarked: 'You know my nerves are in a terrible state, and doing this sort of thing is absolute torture. . . . I am completely tired and run-down, and am going away for a day or two.' | (+1)  6·25. (−1) 12·20. |

| Date | Shackleton's remarks | Percentage of true cognitions |
|------|----------------------|-------------------------------|
| 5.6.42 | Shackleton was in a very irritable state owing to J. Aldred the agent being half an hour late again. Before the checking, he said his mind was so disturbed that he felt sure the results would be just chance results. | Rapid rate (+2) 13·72 (−2) Chance results. |

An inspection of the above remarks* and the corresponding scores certainly suggests that, on several occasions when Shackleton had made complaints of ill-health, bad nerves, etc., he nevertheless made a very high score; and so far as the limited data go, there seems no reason to connect failure with ill-health. Opinion, however, as to whether illness affects ESP scoring is far from unanimous. Mr. Tyrrell,† for example, reported that while his subject Miss Johnson was suffering from a severe cold her score fell sharply to the level of mere guessing, and the same thing appears to have happened during Dr. Rhine's experiments with Mrs. Garrett. In the case of Mrs. Stewart we have no information with regard to the influence of states of health on her scoring, since she never seems to have been ill on any of the evenings when experiments were carried out. She frequently made high scores, however, on days when she complained of feeling tired. The well-known medium, Mrs. Annie Brittain, once told S.G.S. that she often gave her most successful sittings when she was feeling tired and overworked.

## (g) Two Agents in Opposition

On 23rd May 1941, a new line of research was initiated which we shall return to in Chap. XIV where the subject is pursued in greater detail.

During the first part of the sitting held on the above date, Miss Elliott acted as agent for 200 calls at normal rate, lists of random numbers being used. Throughout these 200 calls Dr. Wiesner acted as (EP) and S.G.S. as (EA) while Mrs. Albert sat by the side of the box in a position from which she could not see the five cards.

On 189 (+1) trials Shackleton obtained 61 hits, with corresponding odds against chance of about 10,000 to 1. After these results had been decoded and checked, a special experiment was carried out.

Miss Elliott and Mrs. Albert were each handed four small cards on which were inscribed the following codes:

* IX, 1.          † VI, 13.

185

| *Miss Rita Elliott* | | | | | *Mrs. G. Albert* | | | | |
|---|---|---|---|---|---|---|---|---|---|
| G | L | E | P | Z | L | G | P | Z | E |
| P | E | Z | G | L | L | Z | P | E | G |
| P | E | L | G | Z | Z | G | P | L | E |
| G | E | L | P | Z | Z | P | G | L | E |

These are so arranged that no letter in any one of Miss Elliott's four codes is the same as the letter in the corresponding position in any of Mrs. Albert's four codes. The two agents were asked to select any *three* from their four codes in any order, unknown both to S.G.S. and to Dr. Wiesner. Shackleton, who remained in the ante-room, and knew nothing whatever of the proposed experiment and the arrangements being made in the studio, was merely told that for the next three sheets of guesses Mrs. Albert was to be the agent. He was given no hint that while Mrs. Albert sat behind the screen in the usual position, Miss Elliott would be seated a few feet farther back with a second set of five animal picture cards in front of her. The two agents were asked to select their codes privately in any order, and to change from one code to another at the end of each sheet of 50 calls. The two sets of codes being mutually exclusive it followed that when (EA) showed, say, the number 4 at the aperture in the screen, both agents would lift and look at the fourth card in the row counting from left to right, and hence at every call they would be looking at *different* animal pictures. From where she was sitting Miss Elliott could see the random numbers as they appeared at the hole in the screen. S.G.S. acted as (EA).

The two agents, having each selected a code from the four available on their cards, arranged their five picture-cards in the order indicated by the code; the cards were as usual laid faces downward on the floor of the box or table. The experiment then proceeded in the usual way, and (EA) recorded the codes for each agent at the end of the sheet. Two more sheets of guesses were completed, different codes being used by the two agents for the three sheets, and the results for all the sheets were then decoded, counted and checked.

At each call the agents were competing in opposition. The outcome of the experiment was that Miss Elliott failed to influence Shackleton, who, on the other hand, made very successful contact with Mrs. Albert. Shackleton had been told that Mrs. Albert was the agent and things happened just as if Miss Elliott had not been present.

The difference between the two sets of scores is very striking. Thus for (+1) hits we have:

| Agent | Sheet No. | 5a | 5b | 6a | 6b | 7a | 7b | Total |
|---|---|---|---|---|---|---|---|---|
| Mrs. G. A. | — | 8 | 10 | 11 | 10 | 10 | 8 | 57 |
| Miss R. E. | — | 4 | 3 | 4 | 3 | 5 | 6 | 25 |

There is, of course, no question with such scores as to who was the real agent. For Mrs. Albert the critical ratio is 5·45, which corresponds to odds against chance amounting to considerably more than two million to one. The score with Miss Elliott is a chance score. A similar phenomenon is often observed when two persons sit in the same room with a mediumistic sensitive. If the medium is told at the beginning of a successful sitting that visitor X is to be the sitter and visitor Y the note-taker, she will make contact with X and not with Y, and the information which is forthcoming generally will apply to the circumstances of X and not to those of Y.

## (h) Decline Effects and Negative Scoring

It has been frequently noticed in experiments with cards or dice that the first few guesses are better than those which follow. In a run of 25 calls the subject often scores at a higher rate on the first five or ten trials than on the remaining twenty or fifteen. Sometimes, however, there is an improvement towards the end of the run after a falling off in the middle sections, and the scoring graph may present the appearance of a U-shaped curve. Such decline and recovery effects during the run can of course be investigated statistically only by the counting of the total score for each of the 25 positions over a large number of runs. Miss Jephson* thought the decline in scoring which she noticed in her own experiments was due to some kind of mental fatigue, but it is more likely to be the result of a loss of interest or of spontaneity on the part of the guesser. It may also happen that when the subject is near the end of his task—say in the last five trials—there is a revival of spontaneity or of interest in the work, which produces a spurt of recovery in the final guesses.

This decline during the column of 25 calls is, we shall see, a highly significant feature of Mrs. Stewart's guessing, but curiously it is absent throughout the work with Shackleton. In fact, if we work out the distribution of the 1,755 (+1) hits Shackleton obtained in all 'telepathy' experiments done at normal rate with the agents Miss Elliott, Mrs. Albert, K.M.G.(?), and Dr. C. E. M. Joad, we find that, within the limits of random sampling, these hits are equally spread over the 24 positions in the column. The same is true of the 343 (+2) hits produced at 'rapid' rate with the agents Miss Elliott and J. Aldred.

There is, however, a decline in rate of scoring within the experimental session itself.[4] For example, the first page at a sitting shows, on the average, a higher (+1) score than the last page. Thus, if we pool the

* II, 9.

'telepathy' experiments done at normal rate with the agents Miss Elliott and J. Aldred, we find that on 46·08 'first page' runs* the average (+1) score is 7·77 per run, while on an equal number of 'last page' runs the average is only 6·60 hits per run. The odds against there being such a difference by chance are about 200 to 1.

Similarly the 90·24 runs which belong to the first half of a sitting show a somewhat higher rate of scoring than do the 90·24 runs of the second half. In fact, the average (+1) score per run declines from 7·38 to 6·62, the odds against chance being in this case about 100 to 1.

It is curious to note that although the above batch of data, taken on the whole, provides no evidence of significant scoring on the 'target' or (0) card, yet, even on this card, there is a suggestive decline from an average of 5·67 per 25 on the first pages to an average of 4·65 on the last pages. In this case the odds against the decline's being due to chance amount to no more than 80 to 1. One might perhaps have expected to find that a falling off in the (+1) score would be compensated by a rise in the (0) score, but such is not the case.[4]

Again, in the (−1) scoring at normal rate with J. Aldred as agent, although the total number of runs (11·52) is small, there is a quite significant decline from the first half-session to the second. The score falls from an average of 7·81 to 6·01 per run, the odds in this case being more than 250 to 1. The decline in the (−1) score from first to last pages is suggestive, but not very significant.

Speaking generally, we can say that the decline in scoring noted during the experimental session with Shackleton is not to be explained as a shift in attention from one category to another, but rather suggests an all-round falling off in ESP functioning.

We have said that the spacing of hits within the column of 25 occurs, with Shackleton, in a random or haphazard fashion. He shows no tendency to crowd his (+1) hits into any special regions of the scoring sheet, and in conformity with this finding is the fact that the numbers of runs of 1, 2, 3, 4, etc., consecutive (+1) hits are in close agreement with the chance expectations for such runs. For instance, in the case of the 1,755 (+1) hits mentioned above, the number of 'isolated' successes or 'singletons' is 884 which is remarkably close to the expected number 883·29.

## A Case of 'Negative' Scoring[5]

It was noted first by Dr. Rhine,† and subsequently by other experi-

---

* By a 'run' we mean 24 (+1) trials with no carry-over from the end of a column to the start of the next.

† III, 1.

menters, that, when card-guessing subjects became tired or bored, their scores fell not only to the chance level but sometimes significantly below it. That is to say, the guesser made a much smaller number of correct hits than he would be expected to make if no factor but blind chance was operating. Now if he persistently gets the wrong card, it seems reasonable to suppose that at some level of his mind he possesses some knowledge, perfect or imperfect, concerning the card he is consciously trying to guess. He might, for instance, be aware subconsciously that the card was a lion, and then from some perverse motive suppress this image and permit only one of the other four symbols to emerge into consciousness. On the other hand, the guesser might know nothing about the card except that it was *not* an elephant. If, in this case, his subconscious mind wished to avoid the right card, it could do so by allowing 'elephant' to emerge. There is one remarkable example of 'negative' scoring on the target or (0) card to be found in Shackleton's work with the agent J. Aldred. The effect is absent from the 1936 experiments with this agent, but it persists right through the 1942–3 sittings, and occurs not only in the tests carried out at 'normal' rate but likewise in those done at the 'rapid' rate.

Omitting the experiment on 7th August 1942, at which no agent was present, the one on 26th August 1942, at which Zener cards were used, and the three columns where non-random lists of presentations were employed (p. 179), we have, in all, 69 columns of 25 guesses at the (0) or target card, the equivalent of 1,725 trials. On these 'direct' targets the expected number of correct hits is 345, whereas we counted only 281. The *deficiency* of 64 hits is the equivalent of 3·85 standard deviations, and (as an isolated result) the odds against its being due to chance are about 8,000 to 1. Since, however, the batch was selected from a grand total of 11,852 (0) trials the true odds would be round about a thousand to one. We think there is little doubt that the effect is a genuine one, but its interpretation is obscure. We know that it occurred in the last nine recorded sittings with Shackleton, and it may have heralded the decline of his powers which set in during the latter part of 1943.

Of the 69 columns mentioned above, 23 were guessed at 'rapid' rate and the remaining 46 at 'normal' speed.

It must be borne in mind that all the time this below-chance scoring on the (0) card was in progress Shackleton was making high positive scores on the (+1) and (−1) trials at 'normal' speed and on (+2) and (−2) trials in experiments at the 'rapid' rate. There does not, however, appear to be any correlation between the positive displacement scores and the 'negative' scoring on the target card.

S.G.S.[7] was at first of the opinion that the negative scoring on the

189

main target was due to a psychological reaction on the part of Shackleton, which led him to change his call after scoring a precognitive (+1) hit. The change of call was, in fact, a response by his subconscious to a successful precognition. It is clear from the accompanying diagram that, if Shackleton changed his guess after a (+1) hit, he would score automatically a *miss* on the next 'direct' target.

Thus:

| Guesses | Cards |
|---------|-------|
| O | S |
| + ⟶ | O |

A further examination of the question by Dr. J. G. Pratt, *however, showed that, even after *misses* on the (+1) target, there was a significant negative deviation on the next main target. S.G.S., in his preliminary analysis, had omitted to take into account the subject's individual tendency to change his call in the data considered as a whole.

The most reasonable interpretation, then, of the negative deviation is that it represents a *psi*-effect which is independent (or largely independent) of the successful scoring on the (+1) and (+2) targets.

Rhine found in some cases that below-chance scoring could be induced when a high-scoring subject was asked to try to get every guess wrong. Thus, at a time when his best percipient, Hubert Pearce,† was averaging about eight hits per twenty-five trials in telepathy tests, the latter was asked to aim consciously at low scores during a batch of 275 trials. For this short series Pearce obtained an average score of only 1·81 hits per run of twenty-five. This drop in the scoring level is tremendously significant. It will be noted that the low average score (1·81) is about as much below the chance level (5) as the previous high average (8) is above it, and herein lies a curious paradox. When a subject scores above chance expectation, we may reasonably assume that he knows completely a certain number of the cards by telepathy or clairvoyance, and in addition gets one-fifth of the remaining cards right by chance. Of these remaining cards he presumably knows nothing. One might be tempted to suppose that, when the same person is scoring significantly below chance expectation, he knows completely a certain number of cards by ESP, and gets these wrong by the simple expedient of calling wrong symbols in place of the right ones, so that his actual score will be one-fifth of the remainder about which he is completely ignorant. Now it is easy to see that, if the below-chance effects are produced by the rejection by the guesser of symbols whose values he knows exactly, he would, using five-symbol cards, have to employ four times as much ESP ability in order to produce a given negative deviation as he would normally employ in scoring an equal positive deviation.

This is best seen by an example. Let us suppose that a person knows five cards by ESP in guessing through a pack of twenty-five Zener cards. If he calls correctly the five cards which he knows, his most probable score will be 5 plus one-fifth of 20, i.e. 9. His percentage rate of true scoring will be $\dfrac{\text{No. of cards known by ESP}}{25} \times 100$, i.e. $\dfrac{5}{25} \times 100$, i.e. 20 per cent, and his positive deviation from 5 (the chance expectation) is $9 - 5$, i.e. 4.

Now suppose that he is trying to score below chance level with another pack of 25 cards. If his deviation is, this time, 4 below expectation, his actual score is $5 - 4$, i.e. 1. To obtain this 1 he would, on the average, have to make blind guesses at 5 cards about which he knows nothing. It follows therefore that if he has been working in the same way as when he was scoring above chance, he must have known completely by ESP, $25 - 5$, i.e. 20 cards, and substituted wrong symbols for each of these 20. That is to say, his percentage rate of true scoring is now $\dfrac{20}{25} \times 100$, i.e. 80 per cent, which is four times as large as when he scored the same deviation (4) above chance expectation.

If then, we wish to avoid the improbable hypothesis that the subject's ESP ability has suddenly been quadrupled, we are bound to assume that, when he is making significant negative scores, his subconscious does not merely reject symbols which it knows perfectly.

Conceivably it might know, for instance, that the card is *not* a circle; calling 'circle' would then register a miss. This would imply a lesser degree of ESP than would be necessary for perfect knowledge. Rhine[10] has discussed various psychological factors and experimental situations which appear to induce negative or below-chance scoring in individuals and groups. The evidence adduced of causal relation is, perhaps, often suggestive rather than conclusive. It is claimed that, when subjects are given ESP tasks which they feel to be impossible, they often produce negative scores. For example, in certain of Rhine's* precognition experiments with mechanically selected cards, a group of adults produced a negative deviation of 239 in a series of 27,700 trials, a result which is amply significant. A similar experiment conducted with a group of children at the same time gave a fairly significant positive deviation. It is suggested that the adults deemed their task to be an impossible one, while the children regarded their own as merely a game, and were free from any intellectual misgivings about it.

* VI, 7.

There is also a certain amount of suggestive evidence that group tests with cards sealed up in envelopes frequently lead to significant or almost significant below-chance results, more especially in cases where the guessers are frustrated by delay in being told their scores, as happens, for instance, when the tests are conducted through the post. But there are so many exceptions—the Jephson sealed envelope experiments, for example—that it is difficult to feel certain about such findings.

Dr. Gertrude Schmeidler's* 'sheep' and 'goats' experiment, however, produced very rigid and conclusive evidence that a hostile intellectual attitude towards ESP, or a strong belief that it is unlikely to occur under the existing conditions of the experiment, leads, in general, to negative scoring. But, as we have seen (p. 71), personality factors are also involved, and the socially well-adjusted 'goats' were responsible for the major share of the negative deviation observed.

It will be recalled (p. 66) that in her clairvoyance experiments with drawings Dr. Humphrey† found that the 'compressive' subjects produced a significant negative deviation while in the same test the 'expansives' tended to score somewhat above chance expectation. When, however, the telepathic condition was not excluded, the situation was reversed, and it was the 'expansives' who made a significant below-chance score.‡

But 'expansion' and 'compression', as estimated by the tests employed do not appear to measure permanent personality traits, since Dr. Humphrey found that subjects who had registered as 'expansives' in one experiment were graded as 'compressives' in a later test.

When we come to examine the work of Mrs. Stewart, we shall consider quite a different kind of negative scoring which does not manifest itself as a grand total of hits significantly below chance expectation, but is directed upon certain target patterns and not upon others. This has turned out to be one of the most interesting and distinctive features of her guessing, and appears to be the result of a strong personal motivation.

## Do the Shackleton Experiments Admit of a Normal Explanation?

Nearly ten years have elapsed since the publication of the Soal-Goldney§ report on the powers of Basil Shackleton, and it was only to be expected that a few ingenious critics should have tried to find 'normal' explanations for his remarkable feats. We mean by 'normal' explanations attempts to show how the results could have been obtained without the postulation of extra-sensory perception. It is, of course, the

* V, 22.     † V, 13.     ‡ V, 14.     § IX, 1.

apparent precognition of the next card, or the next card but one, which proves the chief stumbling block to the would-be critic. However, one or two such attempts have been made, but, it is generally agreed, with little, if any, real success.

A suggestion through correspondence was made to S.G.S. by Mr. C. E. M. Hansel, a psychology student at Cambridge, that, if Basil Shackleton and the agent were in collusion, the latter, if not properly supervised, might, during the experiment, alter the order of the five 'animal' cards in the box. If, for instance, the agent (A) and the percipient (P) had agreed beforehand that (+1) 'precognitive' hits were to occur in positions 9, 14, 19, 24 of the scoring column, they might arrange for (P) to call, say, G, L, Z, P in these positions. Having ascertained the order of the five cards in the box during the first few trials, the agent would, at call No. 10, shift the card bearing the symbol G into the position indicated by the experimenter (EA) controlling the agent (A) at the hole in the screen. At call No. 15, (A) would shift the card bearing L into the position corresponding to the current random number, and so on. This method, if not skilfully carried out, would lead to a piling up of 'hits' in certain positions of the scoring sheet, and probably to a deficiency of hits in the first five places—that is before the agent had much chance to learn the order of the five cards. As a result of a prolonged examination of the record sheets Mr. R. C. Read, of St. Catharine's College, Cambridge, failed entirely to discover any evidence that such a method was actually employed. He wrote: 'Nothing was discovered which was different from what one would expect, with the exception, of course, of the final result; in that (P) scored significantly high on the card one ahead, and nothing was found in the nature of a clue to a normal explanation of the results obtained.' S.G.S. found, indeed, that there was no significant deficit of hits on even the first two places in the (a) column.

The experimenters have no hesitation in asserting that in many of the successful experiments at which an observer watched the agent, this method would not have been possible. Lack of space prevented Mrs. Goldney and S.G.S. from publishing in the report every minute detail of every experiment. But if, for instance, the reader will turn to p. 127 of the report he will read that Miss Ina Jephson sat at the experimenter's table during sheets 1–3 and shuffled the cards before each fifty calls *out of sight of both the experimenter (EA) and the agent (A)*. On p. 83 she writes: 'I am also satisfied that (the agent) Miss Elliott turned up the correct card indicated by the printed random number held at the little opening in the screen by S.G.S. (acting as (EA) ).' In fact, the agent and (EA) moved to a distant part of the room while Miss Jephson shuffled the cards so that there was no opportunity whatever either *before* or *during* the experiment for the agent to alter their order.

The (+1) score for these sheets was equivalent to +3·74 standard deviations.

The 'Chronicle'* of the Shackleton experiments shows that Mr. Chibbett, for instance, the observer on 14th February 1941, took identical precautions. As the sole functions of the observer when he watched (A) were to listen for signals and to satisfy himself that she turned up the correct cards, he sat, of course, where he could see the cards. (The CR for the (+1) score was 6·09 with 240 trials.)

Further, the method suggested by Mr. Hansel does not satisfactorily explain (i) the sudden and unexpected appearance of (+2) precognitive results when the rate of calling was doubled without any previous warning to either (P) or (A), and (ii) the phenomenon of multiple determination (p. 181), now satisfactorily established by sound statistical procedures. Actual collusion between Shackleton and the three agents was very improbable since the agents were well-known to one or other of the experimenters.

No critic has yet suggested that everything was pre-arranged between Shackleton, the experimenters and the agent before the sitting. Such supposed pre-arrangement would, however, have been upset by the fact that on many occasions it was the outside observer (O) who shuffled the five cards at the beginning of each sheet of fifty calls. Moreover, on such occasions (O) sat by the side of (A), and had the cards in view from the moment of shuffling till the end of the series of, say, 150 calls. Highly significant results were obtained under such conditions. As mentioned above, during the shuffling by (O), (A) and (EA) moved away to a distant part of the studio and returned only when (O), who remained in his seat at the card-table, intimated that the cards were ready.

Mr. Kenneth Richmond,[12] one time editor of the S.P.R. *Journal*, wrote:

'On the occasions when I was witness of the procedure at the experimenter's table, I myself shuffled the cards before each experiment out of sight of the experimenter, who thus had no opportunity till the experiment was ended of knowing in what order they were placed before the agent.'

In order to meet the possible suggestion that S.G.S., who prepared the sheets of random numbers, might be in collusion with (P) and (A), it was arranged that on three occasions these sheets should be compiled privately by an outside person who would post them directly to Mrs.

---

* The *Chronicle* was not published but a copy can be seen at the rooms of the Society for Psychical Research.

Goldney or to Mrs. Woollard, a member of the Society for Psychical Research who assisted with the experiments for some time. The details are given on pp. 83–84 of the report* itself. All three such tests were brilliantly successful.

## Auditory and Visual Signals

All the independent observers testified that the results were not due to any kind of signalling, direct or indirect, between the agent and Shackleton. In the first place, the rapid and uniform rate of the calling precludes the successful use of such signals. If Shackleton were receiving visual signals, it would soon be obvious to the experimenter sitting next to him, for he would have to keep looking up from his scoring sheet. Further, it is not the card turned up by (A) that would have to be signalled but the card that is one ahead. Shackleton could not leave any gaps in his scoring sheet to be filled up later, since (EP), who was frequently the independent observer, was watching him all the time. He had to fill in cell No. 11, say, immediately after hearing call No. 11.

Mr. Kenneth Richmond* has perhaps said the last word on the impossibility of Shackleton's receiving any *visual* aid. He wrote: 'It is obvious that, even if he had a television set before him giving a plain view of each card as it was selected (by the agent), he would have been no better able to note the succeeding cards before they were selected.'

Dr. B. P. Wiesner,* consulting biologist, wrote:

'It seems to me that the obvious explanations (signals) are fully excluded both by the set-up and by the consistent manner in which the experiment was performed.'

As regards *auditory* signals by the agent, all the observers who sat next to (A) while she was turning up the cards testified most emphatically to the fact that she never spoke, whispered, coughed, scraped her feet, moved her chair, or acted in any way which even the most suspicious could look at askance, or which could convey any coded information. Each independent observer was specially warned at the outset to be on the look-out for whispers and other sounds, but not one reported hearing such sounds.

Mr. H. Chibbett,* a most sceptical observer, wrote:

'Miss E. (the agent) kept silent during the whole of each experiment. There was no whispering or muttering on her or anybody else's part.'

Miss Ina Jephson,* an S.P.R. Council member, wrote:

'I saw no sign of a code between any of the people involved, and heard no unnecessary talking, coughing, or whispering.'

* IX, 1.

Professor C. A. Mace,* the eminent University of London psychologist, wrote: 'Visual and auditory signals were, I think, adequately precluded.'

Professor H. Habberley Price*, Wykeham Professor of Logic in the University of Oxford and ex-President of the S.P.R., wrote:

'I should like to say that, as far as I can judge, the methods you have adopted are perfectly water-tight and fool-proof. It seems to me impossible that the percipient should obtain the knowledge of the card that is being shown, in any 'normal' manner; still less of the card which is going to be shown a few seconds later.'

Sir Ernest Bennett,* a member of the S.P.R. Council, wrote:

'I am convinced that no exchange of signals, audible or visual, was possible between agent and percipient, and that under the conditions which prevailed any form of collusion was ruled out.'

## An Untenable Theory

We shall now deal very briefly with a theory which is so preposterous as to be hardly worth refuting. This is a 'double whispering' theory, put forward by a young man, Mr. D. H. Rawcliffe,[13] in an inadequate book† that abounds in errors of fact and important omissions of relevant details. Rawcliffe, obviously a mere novice in psychical research, reverts to the now discredited hyperaesthesia of hearing hypothesis by which to explain away telepathy.

Briefly, he supposes that, as the experimenter (EA) at the screen calls aloud the series of 'signal' numbers 1 to 25, he manages at the same time either to whisper the *next* number on the list or to 'tag' on to the serial number the initial consonant of the next number. The agent on the other side of the screen is supposed to 'pick up' this whisper subconsciously, to *translate* it into the corresponding animal's name, and whisper this name (or its initial) again under her breath. Shackleton, seated 18–20 feet away, in the next room, subconsciously picks up this whisper and writes down the corresponding letter. At the rapid rate of calling the experimenter, for some unknown reason, whispers not the next number but the next number but one on his list, and the complicated series of exchanges and translations and receptions has to be accomplished in about one second and a half!

Needless to say, the author, who has never seen a Shackleton experiment, makes no offer to give a practical demonstration!

* IX, 1.

† *The Psychology of the Occult*, D. H. Rawcliffe, London, Derricke Ridgway, 1952.

We shall now briefly dispose of Mr. Rawcliffe's ill-considered theory.

(i) Is it credible that *seven* experimenters, some of whom had not the slightest knowledge of the results to be expected when they first visited the studio, should one and all whisper the next or adjacent numbers on the list? And would *all seven* be completely unaware that they were whispering? With all seven persons Shackleton succeeded brilliantly, and though in his book the author admits that unconscious whisperers are *rare*, he is now faced with the contradiction that almost everyone exhibits this peculiarity!

(ii) Though the agent's whispers are so faint that even the observers looking out for them and sitting close beside her fail to notice them, yet Shackleton about twenty feet away in another room successfully picks them up. There is not a scrap of satisfactory experimental evidence for such extensive auditory hyperaesthesia, and we are certain it would not be revealed by the most sensitive microphone.

(iii) When batches of 50 trials were alternated at the slow rate of one call every five seconds with batches at the normal speed, the experiments at the slow rate failed completely, whereas the increased interval should have given more scope for the whispering!

(iv) Why, when the new agent, Mr. Aldred, came on the scene, did all the experimenters, to whom he was a complete stranger, start whispering the number one or two places *behind* as well as that one or two places ahead?

(v) We shall see that it is absolutely impossible to reconcile the results of the Stewart experiments with *any* theory of whispering.

(vi) If the agent whispered faintly the initial letters of the five animals' names E, G, L, P, Z, we should surely expect under the difficult conditions in which Shackleton worked—the loud drowning noise of the experimenter's calling—that he would often mistake P for E or G. If, on the other hand, the agent whispered the *names*, he would surely confuse 'pelican' with 'elephant' to a significant degree.

But an examination of the records fails to reveal any such systematic mishearing of similar sounds.

(vii) The critic fails to notice that it is expressly stated on p. 39 of the Soal-Goldney* report that during the whole of the first nine sittings with Shackleton *both* doors between studio and ante-room were completely closed. Only from the tenth sitting onwards was one of the doors left slightly ajar. On the whispering theory we ought to find a marked increase in the scoring rate on and after Sitting No. 10. But an inspection of the results shows clearly that the first eight sittings were definitely

* IX, 1.

more successful than the next eight done under similar conditions except that the door was slightly ajar.*

But the whole hypothesis is so exceedingly impracticable that we need not give it any further attention.

It is safe to say that, had any parapsychologist advanced so contradictory and flimsy a theory to establish some case of ESP as that of Mr. Rawcliffe, he would have been laughed to scorn.

---

* Sitting No. 9 was a 'counters' experiment and hence is omitted from consideration. For details see Chap. XX, p. 347.

CHAPTER XII

# The New Work with Mrs. Stewart

D uring the war Mrs. Stewart was evacuated to Upton-on-Severn
in Worcestershire, and it was impossible to arrange any further
experiments with her until her return to Richmond in the
summer of 1945. When the Soal-Goldney report was published, S.G.S.
sent her a copy, and she wrote saying that she was willing to try further
experiments on her return home. The excellent review by Professor
C. D. Broad[1] of the Shackleton experiments in *Philosophy* (November
1944), and the great publicity achieved for the report by the efforts of
Professor Ifor Evans, then Principal of Queen Mary College, showed
that the findings had aroused considerable interest in academic circles.
S.G.S. therefore thought the time ripe to ask lecturers from his own
college to take part in the new experiments. In the Shackleton series
the assistants had been drawn almost exclusively from the S.P.R., but
it now seemed highly advisable that the evidence should be made to
depend largely on the testimony of persons of a different academic
training. F. Bateman, M.Sc., an old pupil of S.G.S., had read an account
of the experiments and had written to the latter about them. As S.G.S.
knew him to be meticulously accurate and reliable and a very competent mathematician, it was thought that no better choice of a colleague
could be made. S.G.S. therefore wrote to Mr. Bateman inviting him to
take part in the new series of experiments which he proposed to carry
out. The invitation was gladly accepted. In the Shackleton experiments,
the whole burden of the counting of hits, the carrying out of elaborate
classifications of the data, the application of statistical formulae, etc.,
had fallen entirely on S.G.S., and excellent as his old friend and col-
laborator Mrs. K. M. Goldney, M.B.E., had shown herself to be in all
other aspects concerning the experiments, she could not afford him
much aid in the laborious work of statistical computation. It was more
important than ever that S.G.S. should have a colleague of this kind since
the preparation of fresh syllabuses and new courses of lectures in his
professional work at Queen Mary College left him with even less leisure
than he had had during the war.

199

Since the experiments, with very few exceptions, had to be conducted at Mrs. Stewart's home in Richmond, which is at a considerable distance from the station, a journey of two and a half hours had to be made for every one of the 120 odd experiments carried out at Richmond.

Moreover, since Mrs. Stewart was available only in the later evening, it meant that S.G.S. reached home at Prittlewell usually in the early hours of the morning, and the strain was almost equally severe on F.B.

## General Lay-Out of the Experiments

It was decided in August 1945 that the set-up of the experiments should approximate as closely as possible to that of the Shackleton series. With the exception of two sittings held at the Royal Free Hospital and five of the six experiments of the London-Antwerp series, the rest of the Stewart experiments (123 sessions) were carried out in Mrs. Stewart's home at Marchmont Road, Richmond, Surrey. Three rooms on the ground floor were usually available; a very large lounge, a fair-sized kitchen and a large hall. Two doors opened into the large lounge, one from the kitchen, and the other from the hall (see plan). The door between the lounge and the kitchen was in fact double, one door opening into the lounge and the other into the kitchen. In most of the tests Mrs. Stewart, the percipient (P), sat at a table in the kitchen with an experimenter (EP) who watched her as she wrote down her guesses. Very occasionally, when no (EP) was available, she sat alone. On three or four occasions (P) sat in the hall with (EP). The agent or agents and a second experimenter (EA) sat in the lounge with the screen and cards. The screen, which was three feet square and had a 3-inch square hole in its centre, stood on a small table. On the side of the screen remote from the wall which divided kitchen and lounge, sat the agent (A) and on the table in front of him was a cardboard box placed on its side so that the open end faced him. On the floor of the box were five lexicon cards chosen from the same pack which bore on their faces the initial letters of the names of the five animals: elephant, giraffe, lion, pelican and zebra. Pictures of the animals were not employed, and this is a variation from the usual Shackleton experiment. The five letters E, G, L, P, Z were constantly used until the autumn of 1947. From mid-October of that year Mrs. Stewart's scoring remained at a chance level for some weeks, and an inspection of her guesses showed that she had been repeating mechanically such combinations as P E G , L E G, etc. Accordingly, in November 1947, the symbols on the lexicon cards were changed to C = camel; F = fox; H = horse; K = kangaroo; T = tiger;

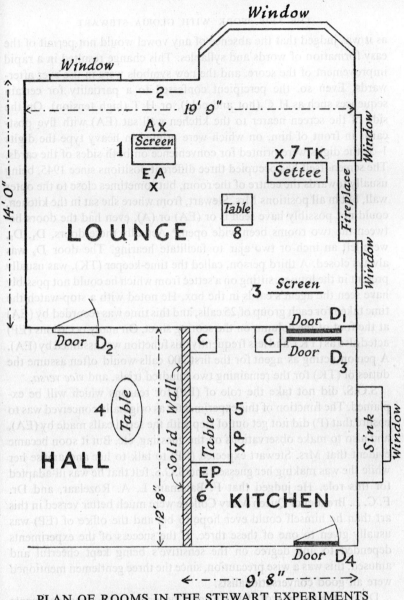

PLAN OF ROOMS IN THE STEWART EXPERIMENTS

1 = *Usual* position of screen with (A) and (EA)
2 = *Occasional* position of screen
3 = Position of screen in TTN(*x*)L experiments
4 = Position of 'cards agent' in T2SCTN experiments
5, 6 = Usual position of (P) and (EP)
7, 8 = Settee and small table at which 'opposition' agents and (TK) (time-keeper) sat
C, C = Cupboards

as it was judged that the absence of any vowel would not permit of the easy formation of words and syllables. This change resulted in a rapid improvement of the score, and the new symbols were in use ever afterwards. Even so, the percipient confessed to a partiality for certain sequences such as H C (hot and cold), or H T (high tension). On the side of the screen nearer to the kitchen wall sat (EA) with five postcards in front of him, on which were printed in heavy type the digits 1–5; the digits were printed for convenience on both sides of the cards. The screen itself has occupied three different positions since 1945, being usually towards the centre of the room, but sometimes close to the outer wall, but in all positions Mrs. Stewart, from where she sat in the kitchen, could not possibly have seen it or (EA) or (A), even had the doors between the two rooms been wide open.* Actually these doors, $D_1$, $D_3$, were left an inch or two ajar to facilitate hearing. The door $D_2$ was always closed. A third person, called the time-keeper (TK), was usually present in the lounge, sitting on a settee from which he could not possibly have seen the agent's cards in the box. He noted with a stop-watch the time taken for each group of 25 calls, and this time was recorded by (EA) at the foot of the column on the scoring sheet. On many occasions (EP) acted also as (TK), and less frequently this function was assumed by (EA). A person acting as agent for the first 200 calls would often assume the duties of (TK) for the remaining two hundred trials, and *vice versa*.

S.G.S. did not take the role of (EP) for reasons which will be explained. The function of this experimenter as originally conceived was to ensure that (P) did not get out of step with the serial calls made by (EA), and also to make observations on the guessing, etc. But it soon became evident that Mrs. Stewart expected (EP) to talk to her and amuse her while she was making her guesses, and S.G.S. felt that he was ill-adapted for this role. He judged that F. Bateman, L. A. Rozelaar, and Dr. F. C. L. Brendel of Queen Mary College were much better versed in this art than he himself could ever hope to be, and the office of (EP) was usually given to one of these three. If the success of the experiments depended to any degree on the sensitive's being kept cheerful and amused, this was a wise precaution, since the three gentlemen mentioned were all good conversationalists.

During the autumn of 1949 we actually conducted some experiments to test whether (P) scored at a significantly higher rate while (EP) kept up a continual stream of amusing banter than when (EP) preserved a grim silence (Chap. XVII, p. 302). One would have expected, on the whispering hypothesis, that (P) would fail miserably owing to the drowning of

---

* The *normal* distance between (P) and (A) was 18 feet but on many occasions the distance was 20 feet.

the assumed faint whispers from the agent, but nothing of the sort happened. When continuous conversation was kept up at her table she scored neither more nor less brilliantly than when complete silence was maintained.

What the experiment showed conclusively is that conversation, though continuous and mixed with loud laughter, did not interfere over thousands of trials with the working of ESP, and this provides no support for the sub-vocal whispering theory.

Like Shackleton, Mrs. Stewart writes down the five initial letters almost automatically without waiting for any visual image to enter her mind.

## The Object of the Experiments

The primary object of the new experiments was something quite different from a mere demonstration of the existence of telepathy; it was rather to find out something about it. The Shackleton work had convincingly established the reality of extra-sensory perception, and it had put beyond question the soundness of our technique. Unfortunately, there are some psychical researchers who possess so little of the scientific spirit that they cannot conceive of anything beyond an endless repetition of the same experiment under more and more stringent precautions and in the presence of more and more witnesses.

We heartily agree with Dr. Thouless that such an attitude is detrimental to all real progress. Having once formed a technique which satisfactorily eliminates sensory cues, let us follow it by all means, but after this there is no point at all in spending one's precious time in convincing sceptics who often do not want to be convinced, and whose presence makes everyone uncomfortable. It is far better to get together a small group of people who work harmoniously in an atmosphere free from suspicion and constant doubts of one another's honesty.

The acceptance of facts about ESP by the scientific world depends in the long run on the observation of similar facts by a large number of independent investigators, and not at all upon the honesty of individual experimenters. A case in point is the phenomenon of displacement. Quite a number of parapsychologists, both in England and in America, have encountered this peculiarity of the ESP function, and it is now well on the way to general acceptance.

We have not, therefore, in these new experiments concentrated on ultra-rigorous precautions against fraud on the part of the *experimenters,* for, after all, if the experimenters (academic people) are not to be trusted, there is no point whatever in their doing experiments. The future will decide whether or not their work is sound.

There has been great care taken in the checking of records and in the elimination of sensory cues, but we have not thought it worth while to copy out duplicate record sheets and post them to some independent person, as was done in the Shackleton experiments. Our chief reason for doing this in the earlier experiments was the not unreasonable apprehension that, if we had only one copy, the sheets might be destroyed in an air-raid. On the other hand, even more time has been spent by F.B. and S.G.S. on the repeated checking of score sheets and on the correction of slips in the decoding and the counting of hits than was given to the Shackleton records.

Moreover, in a certain number of the Shackleton sittings Shackleton did not record his own guess, but pointed to one of five cards or spoke its initial letter aloud, and it was actually recorded by (EP). There was, of course, a majority of sittings at which he did write down his own guesses, but in the case of Mrs. Stewart all her guesses were entered by herself on the score sheets.

In addition to the numerous agents, the persons who have assisted us most frequently with the conduct of the experiments are Dr. F. C. L. Brendel and Mr. L. A. Rozelaar, both of Queen Mary College. Dr. H. S. Allen visited us on several occasions, and other members of Queen Mary College who assisted are Dr. Hugh Blaney, Dr. G. E. Newell and Dr. W. J. Hickinbottom.

An old friend and one-time fellow student of S.G.S., Mr. R. A. M. Kearney, B.A., helped us on several occasions. All our visitors were satisfied that the experiments were carried out in a careful manner.

Our chief aim was to observe the effects when we varied the conditions of the experiment, and to make bold innovations. At the same time when a new condition has led to unexpected success, we have, where possible, continued experimenting with this condition until the statistical significance of the results was beyond all question.

## The Conduct of the Experiments

With very rare exceptions 400 trials were made at each sitting. The scoring sheets used were almost identical with those of the Shackleton experiments. Each sheet provided space for two columns of 25 guesses, the left-hand column being known as the (a) column and that on the right as the (b) column. Each column was divided into two sets of 25 cells, the left-hand set G for the subject's guesses and the right-hand set A for the actual card presentations. Before an experiment the A-columns of eight sheets were filled in by S.G.S. with a random series of the digits 1 to 5. These were taken from a large pool that had been compiled about the year 1943 by Mr. R. O. Williams from seven-figure logarithmic tables. The instructions given to the compiler who volunteered for this work, but who never met Mrs. Stewart or saw any of her records, are those fully described on p. 106.

With regard to a particular pattern (1, 2, 1) we subsequently found a certain deficit in its frequency compared with expectation, which will be mentioned later, but as will be shown, this has not altered the expectation or variance of the direct hits with which we are primarily concerned in Mrs. Stewart's work (see Appendix E, p. 382). The sheets were kept by S.G.S. in his case until just before the experiment started.

The first half-hour of each sitting was usually devoted to conversation of a general kind having no connection with parapsychology, and to this practice we attached considerable importance, because it relieved undue tension, which many experimenters believe is inimical to the emergence of ESP.

And now to describe a typical experiment involving a single agent.

When all is ready, (P) is handed eight empty scoring sheets and five lexicon cards on which the animals' initials are printed, or five pictures of the animals to serve as reminders of the range of choice. She then goes with (EP) into the kitchen to her usual table, and writes her name and the date at the head of each sheet in ink, having numbered the sheets 1 to 8. (EA), (TK), and any other person present, having seated themselves in the lounge, the agent, who is visible to (EA) only through the hole in the screen, shuffles his five lexicon cards with eyes shut and lays them in a row *faces upward* on the floor of the box.

(TK) starts his stop-watch immediately, and (A) is told to begin looking at his cards. He is asked to make no conscious effort to remember their order, though it often happens that he does remember it throughout the sheet of fifty trials. When, say, 30 seconds are up, (TK) calls: 'Turn over', and (A) turns the five cards faces downward without disturbing their order. (EA) then announces to Mrs. Stewart the name of the agent (unless for a special reason this is to be kept secret). (EA) now calls to Mrs. Stewart 'Sheet No. 1'. He looks at the first entry in the A-column of his sheet, presents the corresponding random number at the hole in the screen, pauses from one-half to one second, and calls aloud the serial number 'one'. On seeing the random number at the aperture, (A) *touches the back* of the corresponding card in the row, counting from left to right. The card is not lifted or looked at as in the earlier experiments with Shackleton. Quite early in the new series we discovered that the present method worked perfectly. On hearing the serial number 'one' (P) writes down one of the five initial letters in the first cell under G in the (*a*) column of her first sheet, and she immediately calls 'Right'. (EA) then presents the next random number on his list at the aperture, pauses again, and calls the serial number 'two'. (A) touches the *back* of the appropriate card, and (P) writes down her initial letter in the second cell of her G-column, and calls 'Right'. And so the experiment proceeds until the first or (*a*) column of 25 guesses is completed. There is then a pause of a few seconds during which (TK) calls out the time taken for the column of 25 calls. If the experiment is at 'normal' rate, the time for a column will average about 58 seconds, but may vary between 48 and 75 seconds as extreme limits. This procedure is known as TTN(30), which is interpreted to mean: *telepathy; touch; normal* rate of calling; *30* seconds' exposure of the cards to the gaze of the agent.

Having recorded the time, (EA) calls out 'Next column', and the experiment proceeds as before, the subject calling 'Right' after entering each guess.

At the end of 50 calls (EA) takes his random number sheet to the other side of the screen, and (A) turns his five cards faces upward.

(EA), *always watched by* (*A*), records the code in the upper part of his scoring sheet thus:   P   G   Z   E   L
                                                                                              1   2   3   4   5

The agent is asked to check the record.

At the end of each sheet the agent reshuffles the five cards with his eyes shut, and again lays them faces upward on the floor of the box. The whole procedure is then repeated for the second sheet.

On completion of the last sheet, (EP) brings the eight sheets of guesses into the lounge, and Mrs. Stewart, who seldom sees the checking, goes into the kitchen to prepare tea. By means of the code on each sheet of random numbers, the subject's guesses of animal names are decoded into numbers 1–5, and entered in ink in the appropriate G-column. Three or four people take part in this decoding or watch it; usually they are the two experimenters, the time-keeper, and an agent. Ticks are placed opposite correct hits on the (0) or target card, and the total score is written in ink on the sheet with the other details of the experiment. When Mrs. Stewart returns to the lounge, she is usually told her score, and praised if it is significant.

As an example of the decoding we give F.B.'s chronicle for the sitting on 9th December 1946:

'Decoding by F. Bateman checked by Mrs. J. O. Stewart (a relative by marriage of the percipient).

'Dr. Brendel checked S.G.S. as he read out Mrs. Stewart's guesses.'

(The total score on this occasion was 118 in 400 trials.)

During a large part of the 4½ years' work S.G.S. travelled back with F.B. to Liverpool Street, and in the train the record sheets were re-examined and discussed. F.B. took them home and carefully re-checked all the scores, and in addition counted and recorded the displacement hits as far as $(+2)$ and $(-2)$. These he recorded as shown below:

| (a) | (b) |
|-----|-----|
| 3/4/8/2/5 | 2/3/7/1/6 |

In each row of five, the centre number denotes hits on the target (0) card. That just to the left of the centre is the precognitive $(+1)$ score, and that on the extreme left the precognitive $(+2)$ score, while those on the right of the centre are the post-cognitive $(-1)$ and $(-2)$ scores in this order.

The record sheets were then returned to S.G.S. who made a second recount. They were later sent once more to F.B. for a thorough re-check. The various details and conditions of each sitting were recorded by F.B., or sometimes by S.G.S. in consultation with F.B., on the scoring sheets themselves, either during the sitting or, if we were pressed for time, in the train immediately afterwards. Before leaving the house, each sheet was signed at the bottom by both experimenters and often by one of the principal assistants.

If F.B. was unable to attend, S.G.S. took the sheets home, and re-checked only the hits on the direct target. S.G.S. then sent the sheets by post to F.B., who re-checked the hits on the target card, and counted the displacement scores.

From the records on the scoring sheets, F.B. prepared a complete chronicle of the experiments.

## The First Experiments

When S.G.S. began work again with Mrs. Stewart on 3rd August 1945, he naturally expected to obtain the displacement phenomena which he had discovered in the records of the 1936 experiments. He was also interested to ascertain whether, like Shackleton, Mrs. Stewart would fail under the clairvoyance conditions, i.e. when the agent had no knowledge of the order of the five cards until after the experiment. It was therefore disappointing to find that the first sitting yielded no clear evidence of precognitive displacement, but gratifying to obtain a high score on the target card.

The agent, on this occasion, was Miss W. Hewson, who, after S.G.S.'s broadcast in July, had written saying she would like to be present at a telepathy experiment, as she believed she possessed some ESP ability. On the off-chance that she might turn up S.G.S. sent her an invitation for 7.30 p.m. on 3rd August, and when he arrived at Marchmont Road she was there waiting—a complete stranger to both Mrs. Stewart and

S.G.S. The only other person present that evening was Mrs. J. O. Stewart, whom S.G.S. had met in 1936. This lady acted as (EP) for Mrs. Stewart, and the pair sat at a table in the kitchen. S.G.S. explained to (P) that the letters E, G, L, P, Z stood for the five animals, elephant, giraffe, lion, pelican, zebra, and she was provided with five picture cards to remind her of the range of choice. The table on which the screen stood was placed near the centre of the lounge, and Miss Hewson sat on the side remote from the dividing wall between kitchen and lounge. S.G.S. acted throughout as (EA). In this initial experiment no box was used, and the cards, after having been shuffled by (A), were laid in a row on the table faces downward. As S.G.S. showed the random numbers at the hole in the screen, the agent either lifted and looked at the corresponding cards, or touched their backs, as in the Shackleton series.

For sheets 1, 3, 5, 7 the agent lifted and looked at the cards, but for sheets 2, 4, 6, 8 she shuffled the five cards with her eyes closed, and only touched their backs when she saw the numbers at the aperture. Mrs. Stewart was not told whether the condition during any sheet was the 'telepathic' or the 'clairvoyant' condition. In fact, the word 'clairvoyance' was not mentioned to her till the end of the sitting.

After the completion of the eight sheets, Mrs. Stewart's guesses were decoded into numbers and entered in the G-columns of the sheets of random numbers by Miss Hewson. S.G.S. took no active part in this, but checked her as she made the entries. We checked only the direct (0) score and the $(+1)$ and $(-1)$ displacement scores.

The results were rather surprising.

For sheets 1, 3, 5, 7 the numbers of hits on the target card for the successive runs of 25 were: 12, 12, 6, 6, 8, 9, 7, 7, giving a total of 67/200. The result is unquestionably significant with odds against its being due to chance—even when considered as the best score in five categories—of about 60,000 to 1. The only other score of interest was a post-cognitive $(-1)$ score of 55/192, which looked very promising. Unfortunately, at the next and later sittings the post-cognitive results were not significantly above chance expectation.

At this first sitting the (0) or 'target' score on the 'clairvoyance' tests (sheets 2, 4, 6, 8) bordered on significance (51/200), but this promise was not fulfilled at any later sittings. The calling was not timed on this first occasion, but the rate was roughly 'normal'.

The telepathy technique described above we shall refer to as TLN, i.e. *telepathy*; *lifting* and *looking* at each card; *normal* rate of calling. The clairvoyance method will be known as CTN, i.e. *clairvoyance*; *touching* backs of cards; *normal* rate of calling.

At the second sitting, held on the evening of 8th August 1945, the agent was again Miss Hewson. This was the occasion of F.B.'s first visit, and he acted as (EP), sitting at a table with Mrs. Stewart in the hall. The screen and card-table were in the lounge near the centre of the room. S.G.S. acted as (EA), showing the random numbers at the aperture, and Mrs. J. O. Stewart was (TK), sitting in the lounge where she could not see either agent or cards.

This time clairvoyance (CTN) sheets were *randomly* mixed with telepathy (TLN) sheets, and not rigidly alternated as in the first experiment. Again Mrs. Stewart was not told whether the telepathy or clairvoyance condition obtained during a sheet.

At the end of the eight sheets the decoding and entering of scores was done by F.B., checked by Miss Hewson. (TK) and (P) stood close by, waiting for the results and looking on.

The target card score for the 'telepathy' sheets (Nos. 1, 2, 5, 6) was again quite significant (58/200), but lower than at the first sitting. None of the (+1), (−1), (+2) or (−2) displacement scores even approached significance.

The clairvoyance sheets (Nos. 3, 4, 7, 8) yielded a total score on the target card of only 42/200, which is what chance might be expected to produce. Though classed as 'normal', the rate of calling was exceptionally slow compared with the average.

It appeared that Miss Hewson was more interested in her personal spontaneous experiences than in card-guessing, and she did not visit us again. This was a pity, because she seems to have been an excellent agent.

As the sittings went on, the failure of the precognitive results we had hoped for to materialize was a bitter disappointment. On the involuntary whispering hypothesis of Rawcliffe,* it is a little difficult to see why S.G.S. could not have produced them by whispering the number on the list that was one ahead of that shown at the aperture! We were, however, amply compensated by the steady persistence week after week and year after year of the extra-chance score on the target card, which ran a remarkably constant average of nearly seven hits per 25 over a period of four years.

## Telepathy and Clairvoyance

At thirteen sittings scattered throughout the whole period of the series of experiments we mixed four telepathy sheets with four clairvoyance sheets. The first five sittings were devoted entirely to this type of experiment, and in these there were no means by which Mrs. Stewart could guess whether a sheet was intended for telepathy or for clair-

* XI, 13.

voyance, as the only difference lay in the fact that the agent lifted and looked at the cards in the first type of experiment, and in the second merely touched their backs without knowing their order in the row. Mrs. Stewart was not even told that any of the sheets would be devoted to clairvoyance tests. In only the first of these five sittings were the conditions rigidly alternated, but during the last four sittings clairvoyance sheets were randomly interspersed among telepathy sheets, there being four of each kind.

In these first five sittings 1,000 telepathy trials yielded no fewer than 305 hits on the target card (an excess of 105 above chance expectation), whereas the 1,000 clairvoyance trials gave only 207 direct hits, which is only 7 above expectation. That is to say, the telepathy tests were tremendously significant, while the clairvoyance score was just what chance might be expected to produce.

At each of these five sittings the ordinary TLN technique was employed. That is, the agent lifted and looked at each individual card when the random number was shown at the aperture. But at the other eight sittings the new TTN($x$) method was used for the telepathy sheets. In this method the agent gazed at the five cards laid faces upward in a row before each sheet for a given time $x$ seconds, then turned them faces downward, and merely touched the back of a card when a random number was shown at the aperture (cf. p. 205).

Though the same interval of $x$ seconds was allowed to precede each clairvoyance sheet, it is just possible that on some occasions Mrs. Stewart in the other room may have heard S.G.S. give his instructions to the agent to start looking at the cards. One cannot, therefore, be quite certain that Mrs. Stewart was not sometimes aware that a given sheet was not a telepathy sheet.

Only at Sitting No. 120 was Mrs. Stewart told before each sheet the exact nature of the test. On this occasion the telepathy score was 51/200 and the clairvoyance score 37/200, so that there is still a complete failure to score under the clairvoyance condition.

For the whole 13 sittings there were seven occasions on which telepathy and clairvoyance were rigidly alternated, and six on which the two conditions were randomly mixed.

The 2,600 telepathy trials yielded a total of 707 hits on the target card—an excess of 187 above expectation, corresponding to the critical ratio of 9·17 with odds against the result being due to chance of the order $10^{19}$ to 1.

On the other hand, the 2,600 clairvoyance trials gave only 509 hits as compared with the expected number (520). This is clearly a chance result. The reader will grasp that it is absolutely impossible to reconcile such meaningful results with the theory of Mr. Spencer Brown that ESP is a mere statistical artifact.

None of the (+1), (−1), (−2) or (+2) displacement scores in the clairvoyance experiments was significant.

There seems, then, little doubt that, like Shackleton, Mrs. Stewart does not succeed in clairvoyance experiments, but only scores above chance expectation when the agent knows the order of the cards.

Why these two subjects should differ from the majority of those investigated in America, who appear, on the whole, to score equally well under the telepathic and clairvoyant conditions, is a mystery.

It is worth noting, however, that one of Rhine's early percipients, George Zirkle, did well at telepathy but badly in clairvoyance tests. There was no evidence, so far as we know, however, that Zirkle, like Mrs. Stewart and Shackleton, had ever produced significant displacement scores.

## The New Technique

In the popular conception of an experiment in telepathy the agent, or sender, closes his eyes, pictures the object he wishes to transmit as vividly as he can, clenches his hands, tenses his muscles, contracts his brows, and strives with all his might to project the image in the direction of the receiver. Does this make for success? Probably not. Is it even necessary for the agent to be consciously thinking of the image at the instant when he transmits it? Definitely not. For the first five sittings with Mrs. Stewart we followed the method so largely used with Shackleton, known here as the TLN method. That is, the agent, when he saw a random number at the aperture, lifted the appropriate card sufficiently for him to see the letter on it, and then let it fall face downwards into its original position in the row.

But at Sitting No. 6 in this series we tried out a variation which we found worked every bit as well as the old method, and this was subsequently adopted as a routine technique. The new procedure is as follows: The agent shuffles the five cards and lays them faces downward on the floor of the box. At a signal from the time-keeper, the agent turns all the cards faces upward and looks at them for a prescribed period of, say, 30 seconds. He makes no effort whatever to remember the order of the five cards, but when the 30 seconds are up, at a signal from (TK), he turns all the cards faces downward again without disturbing their order in the row. Now when the experimenter (EA) shows, say, the digit 4 at the aperture in the screen, the agent merely touches lightly with his finger the fourth card, counting from left to right. The experimenter then gives the serial number of the call for Mrs. Stewart to record her guess. Hence the agent is seldom thinking consciously of the letter on the card at the instant he touches its back. The agent, we found, was frequently unable to repeat correctly the order of the five cards when questioned during the interval between columns (a) and (b), or at the end of the sheet, especially if taken unawares.

Sometimes, however, he did remember it perfectly.

The first occasion on which we tried this new technique in the Stewart experiments was at Sitting No. 6 on 29th October 1945, when F.B. was the agent. On this occasion F.B. reported that he remembered the cards as he touched their backs. The direct score was not very striking (50/200). However, at Sitting No. 7, when the same technique was employed, we obtained with Mrs. Y. Hales as agent a score of 52/200, and with F.B. as agent a score of 51/200, so that it was clear that significant scores were being produced with the method.

Sittings 8, 9, 10 were devoted to a comparison of the 'lift' (TLN) and the 'touch' (TTN(30)) methods.

At each of these sittings sheets 1, 3, 5, 7 were TLN experiments, while for sheets 2, 4, 6, 8 the new TTN(30) method was used. The total score for the old method (TLN) was 157/600, while that for the TTN(30) method was 154/600. It does not need any statistical evaluation to conclude that the methods are equally effective.

Our next step was to reduce from 30 seconds to 5 seconds the interval during which the agent gazed at the five cards while they lay faces upward.

At Sittings 11 and 12, the agent was F.B., and for sheets 1, 3, 5, 7 the cards were exposed to his gaze for only 5 seconds, after which interval he was told to turn them faces downward. He then touched their backs as the random numbers were presented. For sheets 2, 4, 6, 8, he looked at the row of cards for 30 seconds. F.B. reported that during the TTN(5) experiments he did *not* remember the order of the cards. For the TTN(5) tests the total score was 111/400, and that for the TTN(30) was 101/400. Applying Fisher's method for small samples, we find no significant difference between the two rates of scoring $(0.4 > P > 0.3)$.*

Thus, even when the time during which the cards are exposed to the agent's gaze is as short as five seconds, there appears to be no serious diminution in the success of transmission.

---

* This means that a larger difference between the two scores might be expected to arise by chance alone between three and four times in every ten.

## Other Timing Experiments

At Sittings 48 and 49 we introduced another variation. For sheets 1, 3, 5, 7 the agent, Mrs. Y. Hales, shuffled the cards with her eyes shut, and laid them faces downward in a row on the floor of the box. At a signal from Mr. Kearney (TK), she lifted the cards successively, glancing rapidly at each card, and letting it fall face downwards into its place. The whole operation took about 5 seconds. The experiment then proceeded as with the TTN(30) method.

We shall call the new method TTNS(5) where S stands for *in succession* and N as usual for the *normal* rate of calling.

For sheets 2, 4, 6, 8 the TTN(30) method was employed. The TTNS(5) experiments gave a total score of 108/400, while the TTN(30) score was 126/400. Fisher's method for small samples shows that there is no significant difference in the two scoring rates ($0.3 > P > 0.2$).

It would appear that two conditions are necessary for the success of such experiments. The order of the five symbols must have been registered in the subconscious mind of the agent, and a signal must be given letting the subconscious mind of the agent know which symbol is the target.

## Experiments Which Failed

At Sittings 56 and 57 we tried a variation which seems to have created confusion in the agent's mind. At this period, October 1948, we were using lexicon cards bearing the letters C, F, H, K, T, these being the initial letters of the names of the five animals camel, fox, horse, kangaroo and tiger. The procedure was as follows: The agent shuffled the cards with eyes shut, and laid them faces downward in a row on the floor of the box. He then looked at them in succession, rapidly letting each card fall face downward as he did so, the operation taking $x$ seconds, where $x$ was 3 or 4.

The experimenter (EA) then, in rapid succession, presented to the agent's gaze $y$-1 other permutations of the five symbols; the showing of each sequence took $x$ seconds. The experiment then proceeded as in the TTN technique, the agent merely touching the back of a card when the random number was shown at the aperture. The method will be called TTND$y(x)$, where the letter D stands for *different* codes.

On 3rd September 1948, sheets 1, 3, 5, 7 were devoted to this method (TTND4(3)), but unfortunately no record was kept of the three code arrangements presented to (A) by (EA). Sheets 2, 4, 6, 8 were ordinary TTN(30) experiments. The agent on this occasion was F.B., while S.G.S. acted as (EA).

While the ordinary TTN(30) test produced the brilliant score of 60/200 on the target card, the rapid presentation test gave only a chance result 36/200 It seems probable that the rapid presentation of the three new codes following immediately upon the agent's code (by which the results were scored) caused confusion.

At Sitting No. 57 on 1st October 1948, in sheets 2, 4, 6, 8 we followed the technique TTND3(3), while sheets 1, 3, 5, 7 were done by the usual TTN(30) method. On this occasion a record was preserved of the codes presented rapidly by (EA). The agent throughout this sitting was Miss J. Edis. F.B. was (EP) and sat with (P) in the kitchen. S.G.S. was (EA) and sat with (A) in the lounge. The decoding was carried out by F.B. and Miss Edis working together. First, on the code given by the order of the five cards in the box, code (i), the TTND3(3) score was only 37/200, while the ordinary TTN(30) method produced a score of 56/200 which is significant.

The score on sheets 2, 4, 6, 8 by the first of the additional codes presented by (EA), code (ii), was only 38/200, and by the second (or last), code (iii), it was 49/200, which, though not significant, is an improvement. We did not, however, find time to continue with this method. On the two sittings taken together the TTN(30) method produced a total score of 116/400 (critical ratio = 4·5), while scored by the 'box' code the rapid presentation of different codes produced only a chance score of 73/400 which is only 7 below the expected number 80.

What seems clear is that the agent's original code is wiped from the slate of his subconscious mind, as it were, by the immediate impact of the succeeding codes.

## Is it Necessary for (P) to Keep in Step with (EA)?

Early on in the new series Mrs. Stewart had once or twice suggested to the experimenters that she felt sure she would succeed if she wrote down a column of 25 guesses, the agent having first shuffled the five cards and laid them faces downward in the box. Immediately after she had recorded her guesses (EA) was to present to (A) the random numbers at the aperture at normal rate. We were very sceptical about this plan, but we tried it out at Sitting No. 13 on 11th January 1946.

Mrs. Stewart sat in the kitchen with F.B. In the lounge were Mrs. Y. Hales, the agent, S.G.S. (EA), and Mrs. J. O. Stewart, who sat by the fire. Some time after the experiment had started, Mrs. M. Johnstone arrived accompanied by a friend, Mr. A. Costa. The two visitors sat on the settee, where they could not see the agent or the cards.

Sheets 1, 2, 3, 4 were done as follows: At a signal from S.G.S. (P) wrote down a column of 25 guesses very rapidly in about 20 seconds. The agent had shuffled the five cards and laid them faces downward in the box before she began. Immediately Mrs. Stewart gave the signal that she had finished, (EA) started showing the random numbers on his *first* scoring sheet at the aperture. Mrs. Hales lifted and looked at the cards, letting each card fall back into its place as in the usual TLN method. The code was recorded by S.G.S., and the agent reshuffled her five cards. Mrs. Stewart then wrote down rapidly a second column of 25 guesses, and the procedure was repeated. Sheets 5, 6, 7, 8 were a control series carried out by the usual TLN method.

The 'special' method gave, as we expected, a chance score of 37/200 (expected number = 40), but the ordinary 'lift and look' method at normal rate produced the brilliant score of 59/200 (critical ratio = 3·35 nearly, with odds of about 1,200 to 1).

The decoding was done by F.B. assisted by Mrs. Hales and Mrs. Johnstone. F.B. also acted as (TK).

Two years later, however, Mrs. Stewart thought she would succeed if, starting a column with (EA), she wrote down her guesses in her own time, i.e. if she failed completely to keep in step with the presentation of random numbers at the aperture.

F.B., when acting as (EP), had at times noticed that Mrs. Stewart tended to write down her guesses a little before (EA) called out the serial number of the guess, e.g. she might write down her twentieth guess when (EA) was calling 'nineteen'. He formed the opinion that Mrs. Stewart occasionally perceived the letters in runs of three or four at a time, and he thought that she might be more successful if she were allowed to write down her guesses in her own time.

At Sittings 50 and 51 held on 1st March and 19th March respectively in the year 1948 we carried out experiments to test this belief. The following procedure was adopted. S.G.S., acting as (EA), called 'one' at the beginning of each column and then remained silent until he had presented the 25 random numbers at the hole in the screen. On presenting the last number he called 'right'. Mrs. Stewart in the kitchen started when (EA) called 'one', and wrote down her 25 guesses in her own time. When she had finished her column (EP) called 'right'.

On each occasion sheets 2, 4, 6, 8 were done by this method, while sheets 1, 3, 5, 7 were ordinary TTN(30) experiments, in which (EA) called aloud the serial numbers and Mrs. Stewart kept in step.

We shall refer to the new variation as TTN(30)OT, the final pair of letters denoting that (P) did the experiment in her *own* time. The meaning of the prefix TTN(30) will by now be familiar to the reader.

At the first of the two sittings the agent was Mrs. Y. Hales, F.B. was

(EP), and Mr. R. A. M. Kearney the time-keeper. On that occasion Mrs. Stewart seemed a little put out; she had not been expecting to have to do an experiment and she had been asked at very short notice.

When (P) had finished writing down her 25 guesses, (EA) was calling 10 on sheet 2(*a*), 15 on 2(*b*), 21 on 4(*a*), 19 on 4(*b*), 19 on 6(*a*), 18 on 6(*b*), and had already finished calling 25 on 8(*a*) and 8(*b*).

At the second sitting (No. 51) Mr. R. A. M. Kearney was agent and Dr. F. C. L. Brendel was (EP). S.G.S. acted as (EA). (P) and (EP) were in the kitchen, and the others in the lounge. The decoding was done by Dr. Brendel, checked by Mr. Kearney. When (P) had finished writing down her 25 guesses, (EA) was calling 20 on sheet 2(*a*), 18 on 2(*b*), 21 on 4(*a*), 22 on 4(*b*), 24 on 6(*a*), 23 on 6(*b*), 21 on 8(*b*), and had already finished about one second earlier on 8(*a*).

Now for the results. The ordinary TTN(30) technique yielded 110 direct hits in 400 trials (with odds exceeding 5,000 to 1). But the TTN-(30)OT method, in which (P) was clearly out of step, gave only 88 hits in 400 trials, which is merely a chance result. Keeping in step with the serial numbers called by (EA) would appear therefore to be an essential condition for success. None of the displacement categories yielded any significant results.

In the TTN(*x*) technique in which the agent gazes at the row of five cards for *x* seconds, turns them faces downward again, and thereafter touches their backs as the random numbers are presented, we obtained highly significant results for $x = 5, 10, 15$ and $30$, the only values* we have used. The totals of hits and trials for simple uncomplicated TTN(*x*) experiments are set out below.

TABLE 8

| Value of x | Total trials | Direct hits | Critical ratio |
|---|---|---|---|
| 5 | 600 | 165 | +4·59 |
| 10 | 1,200 | 349 | +7·86 |
| 15 | 1,000 | 294 | +7·43 |
| 30 | 16,800 | 4,220 | +16·59 |

## Experiments at the Rapid Rate

It will be recalled (Chap. X, p. 157) that, when, with Miss Rita Elliott as agent, we speeded up the rate of calling to nearly double the normal rate, Shackleton ceased to score significantly on the (+1) card, but apparently shifted his ESP focus on to the card two places ahead. Similarly with Mr. J. Aldred as agent both the (+1) precognitive and the (−1) post-cognitive scores fell to the chance level at the rapid rate

* An isolated TTN(3) experiment at Sitting 46 gave only chance results. See p. 225.

of calling, and significant (+2) and (−2) scores appeared in their place.

We were therefore curious to discover what would happen when we speeded up the experiment with Mrs. Stewart, whose extra-chance scores at the normal rate were confined apparently to the contemporaneous or (0) card.

Sittings 14–18 inclusive in the early months of 1946, were devoted almost entirely to this question.

On these five occasions sheets 1–4 were conducted at a rapid rate, so that the average time occupied by 25 calls was reduced from about 58 seconds to 35·3 seconds. This high speed was maintained over forty columns with remarkable consistency, and the standard fluctuation from the average was only 2·9 seconds. Throughout, a TTR(10) technique was employed. (R signifies *rapid* rate as opposed to normal rate of calling.) At such a rapid speed we had to dispense with (P)'s calling 'right' after each guess. Mrs. Y. Hales was the agent at each sitting except the last, when F.B. took her place.

At Sittings 14–17 inclusive sheets 5–8 were devoted to ordinary TTN(10) experiments. The average time for a column of 25 calls in these normal rate experiments was 58·97 seconds with a standard fluctuation over 32 columns of 3·7 seconds.

And now for the results. At the rapid speed of calling the extra-chance score on the (0) card disappeared, and in its place a highly significant score on the card *one behind*, i.e. the post-cognitive (−1) card, was observed. In fact, the 1,000 (0) trials at rapid speed yielded only the chance score of 191 hits, which total is only 9 below expectation. On the other hand, on the 960 post-cognitive (−1) trials there were no fewer than 273 hits, which gives a positive deviation of 81 above the expected number (192). The critical ratio is 6·54, and if the (−1) score is considered as the best in the five categories, the odds against this result being due to chance exceed a hundred million to one.*

Whether the effect is the result of a psychological 'lag', or a true temporal displacement, is uncertain. It might well be that Mrs. Stewart registered the impression of the card in her subconscious mind at the instant when the agent focused it, but that this impression required a second or so to emerge into her normal consciousness. Since, however, the (+1) precognitive displacement observed with her in 1936 was probably of the nature of a time displacement, there is at least the possibility that the present effect is similar in type to the forward (+1) displacement which she produced in that year.

* It is worth noting that had Mrs. Stewart been successful with the TTN(30)OT experiments of the preceding sections, the results would have contradicted those of the TTR(10) tests. But we have consistency here which would not be expected if ESP were an artifact.

None of the other displacement categories in this rapid series shows any significance. It may be added that the 32 columns of ordinary TTN(10) experiments done on the same occasions as those at rapid rate yielded for direct hits a score of 238/800 (a positive deviation of 78, the equivalent of more than six standard deviations), while the post-cognitive (−1) score was 137/768, a result of no significance.*

The agents Mrs. Hales and F.B. on March 11th and March 18th respectively, both recorded that they did not remember the order of the cards as they touched their backs, while the rapid experiment was in progress. The total (−1) score for these two occasions was 101/384—a quite significant result (CR = 3·09).

* These highly significant and very consistent changes from (0) to (−1) scoring cannot be explained as being due to defects in accepted probability theory. They are obviously the result of changes in the experimental conditions and they constitute a challenge to Mr. Spencer Brown's inadequate hypothesis. So do also the TTN(30)OT experiments described on pp. 214–16.

# CHAPTER XIII

# The 'Split Agent' Experiments

T he striking success of the TTN technique suggested to S.G.S. a novel experiment. The plan was to use two agents or transmitters, each of whom had been individually successful when working with Mrs. Stewart. From the lay-out of our experiment it is obvious that two pieces of information are required before the animal name which is to be transmitted can be specified. One is the order of the five animal cards in the box, and the other is the random number shown at the aperture in the screen. The intention now was to allow each agent to possess only one of these bits of knowledge. When standardized, the experiment proceeded as follows. Mrs. Stewart sat with (EP), as usual, in the kitchen. One of the agents known as the 'screen agent' sat behind the screen in the lounge, but the animal letter cards were removed from the box and replaced by a row of five blank cards.

The second agent, usually referred to as the 'cards agent', sat alone in the hall with five lexicon cards bearing the animal initials. These he was asked to shuffle and lay in a row faces downward on the table. He then turned them faces upward, and gazed at them for a prescribed number of seconds 10, 15 or 30, as the case might be. After the expiration of the interval, he turned the five cards faces downward again, and took no further part in the experiment till the end of the sheet.

When the cards agent had completed his task, and Mrs. Stewart was ready to begin, (EA) presented the random numbers as usual to the screen agent, calling aloud as he did so the serial numbers 1–25. As each number was presented at the aperture, the screen agent merely touched with a finger the corresponding blank card, counting from left to right. Mrs. Stewart on hearing the serial number, wrote down as usual the initial letter of an animal name in the correct space of her scoring sheet, answering 'right' as she did so. At the end of the sheet of fifty calls, the experimenter (EA) entered the hall, and, watched by the cards agent, recorded on his sheet the order of the five animal initials. (EA) then returned to the lounge, the cards agent reshuffled his five cards, and (EA) took up his next sheet of random numbers, the experiment proceeding as before. The checking was done in the usual way at the end of eight sheets.

Except on a few special occasions Mrs. Stewart was informed of the nature of the experiment, and told the names and functions of each agent at the outset. Sometimes the roles of the two agents would be interchanged at the end of 200 trials, or another person would be substituted for one of them.

The experiments of this type did not always succeed but, taken as a whole, the eleven occasions on which this method was used yielded results that were significant beyond all question.

We shall refer to the above technique as T2SCTN($x$) which means: *telepathy* with *two* agents; a *screen* agent and a *cards* agent; carried out at *normal* rate; with the cards agent looking at the five cards for a period of $x$ seconds, and the screen agent *touching* the backs of five blank cards when he was shown the random numbers.

Since the cards agent in the hall was not concerned with the serial numbers called aloud by (EA), the door between lounge and hall was (except on one or two occasions that were noted) kept completely closed. This meant that Mrs. Stewart was isolated by a solid wall from the cards agent, and thus a double whispering hypothesis is rendered extremely improbable.

## The Experiments

A preliminary test of the above method was carried out on 18th March 1946. On this occasion the cards agent and the screen agent were both in the lounge. The table on which the screen rested was placed in the centre of the room. F.B. was the screen agent for sheets 5–8, while Mrs. Y. Hales, the cards agent, sat at a small table near the fire with her back to the screen, so that she could not see the random numbers presented at the aperture by S.G.S. (EA). Since F.B. had his back to Mrs. Hales, he could not see her five cards. Mrs. Stewart sat in the kitchen alone. The decoding was by F.B., checked by Mrs. Hales.

This was a T2SCTN(30) experiment, and the direct score was 62/200 (odds 10,000 to 1). Since, however, the two agents were in the same room, we shall ignore the result of this first test.

At the next sitting, No. 19, held on 1st April 1946, we again tried out the method under much improved conditions. During sheets 5–8 Mrs. Stewart sat in the kitchen with (EP), who on this occasion was Miss B. Jacobs, a research student from Bedford College, London. Mrs. Hales, the cards agent and (TK), sat alone in the hall. The screen agent F.B.

sat at a table in the middle of the lounge, and S.G.S. acted as (EA). Mrs. J. O. Stewart sat in the lounge near the fire. The decoding was done by F.B. checked by Mrs. Hales and Miss Jacobs. It is specially noted that the door between lounge and kitchen was completely closed during this evening's work so that we can reasonably assume that involuntary whispering was ruled out.

This was a T2SCTN(10) experiment. Sheets 1–4 were devoted to an ordinary TTN(10) experiment in which Miss Jacobs was the agent and F.B. was (EP). The test with two agents gave a score on the target of 54/200, while that with the single agent yielded 53/200. These results, when considered separately, are of only border-line significance but when taken together (107/400) are definitely significant (CR = 3·37.) Miss Jacobs met Mrs. Stewart as a complete stranger. She reported that during sheets 1–4, when she was the agent, she was unable to recall the order of the five cards in the box.

## The Agents Exchange Roles

In the preceding experiments F.B. had acted as screen agent and Mrs. Hales as cards agent. At the next two sittings, Nos. 20 and 21, held on 17th April and 29th April 1946, the same pair of agents worked together with their parts interchanged.

At Sitting No. 20 F.B. sat in the hall alone with the five cards during sheets 5–8, while Mrs. Hales sat at the screen in the lounge. Mrs. Stewart was in the kitchen with Mr. L. A. Rozelaar who was (EP). Mrs. J. O. Stewart, who took no part in the work, sat in the lounge near the fire. The results were decoded by F.B., checked by Mrs. Hales and Mr. Rozelaar.

The score, however, was only 49/200, and is not actually significant. This was a T2SCTN(10) experiment. Sheets 1–4, however, with Mr. Rozelaar as the sole agent, had yielded a significant score of 58/200 (CR = 3·18).

At Sitting No. 21 sheets 5–8 were devoted to a T2SCTN(30) experiment in which F.B. sat alone with the cards in the *kitchen* while Mrs. Hales was at the screen in the lounge. (P) sat with Dr. J. H. Blaney in the *hall*. The door between *kitchen* and lounge was closed and the hall door about an inch ajar to facilitate hearing. F.B. decoded the results, checked by Dr. Blaney and Mrs. Hales. This time the score was 56/200.

During sheets 1–4 Dr. Blaney, who met Mrs. Stewart as a complete stranger, acted as agent in an ordinary TTN(30) experiment in which she scored the brilliant total of 63/200 (odds of 16,000 to 1). Blaney reported that he did not remember the order of the five cards except during the first sheet.

Taking Sittings 20 and 21 together, we have for the two-agent experiments a total of 105/400 (giving a critical ratio of 3·1). There is some reason to believe that, with F.B. and Mrs. Hales, the experiment succeeds whichever plays the role of screen agent, since the difference between the two scoring rates 49/200 and 56/200 is not significant.

## Another Combination of Agents

At Sitting No. 26 on 12th June 1946, we carried out a T2SCTN(30) experiment with Mrs. Hales as cards agent alone in the hall, and Mr. L. A. Rozelaar as screen agent in the lounge. Mrs. Stewart sat with F.B. in the kitchen. In the checking at the end of sheet 8, S.G.S. read aloud Mrs. Stewart's guesses, watched by Mr. Rozelaar, while F.B. decoded and entered the figures, checked by Mrs. Hales. The direct score (sheets 5–8) was 62/200, equal to the best recorded so far for this type of experiment (odds of 10,000 to 1).

It is of considerable interest to add that sheets 1–4 on this evening were devoted to an experiment carried out over the telephone between two houses 150 yards apart. Mr. Rozelaar was the agent, and throughout the experiment (A) and (P) were situated at distances of 10 feet and 8 feet respectively from their instruments. The score was again brilliant (60/200). [For further details see Chap. XVI, p. 277.]

Rozelaar and Mrs. Hales are, without doubt, two agents with whom Mrs. Stewart made some of her best scores, and it appears that in combination they are equally successful.

## A Variation

Up to this point Mrs. Stewart had been given warning that two agents were to be employed, and told before she began who were the cards and screen agents. At our next T2SCTN experiment (Sitting No. 39 held on 19th May 1947) we let her suppose that F.B. at the screen was the sole agent during sheets 1–4. She was unaware that Dr. F. C. L. Brendel had slipped silently into the hall with the five lexicon cards. Nor is it probable that she was expecting T2SCTN, because eleven months had elapsed since we had done any tests of this kind. F.B. was in the lounge sitting at the screen with his five blank cards, and Mrs. Stewart was in the kitchen with Mr. David Makgill as (EP). At the close of each sheet of 50 trials, S.G.S., acting as (EA), slipped away very swiftly but silently into the hall in order to record Dr. Brendel's code.

At the end of sheet 4, S.G.S. called out to Mrs. Stewart: 'This is a new experiment with two agents. Mr. Bateman will look at the numbers behind the screen, and Dr. Brendel in the hall will look at the five cards. You must divide your attention between them.'

Decoding was done at the end of sheet 8 by F.B. checked by Dr. Brendel. Throughout, the method used was T2SCTN(15).

It was found that on sheets 1–4, during which (P) was unaware that two agents were operating, Mrs. Stewart's score was only 29/200, a result below chance expectation, while on sheets 5–8, when she was fully aware that two agents were employed, she made the brilliant score of 60/200 (odds against the result being due to chance exceed 2,000 to 1).

From this experiment it appears probable that, in order to succeed, (P) must be informed that two agents are being used. That is, her conscious mind must be oriented towards the two agents. Unfortunately, we were prevented by accident from confirming this conjecture.

As 'control', Mr. D. A. Stewart, sitting in the lounge by the fire in such a position that he was unable to see the five blank cards inside the box, wrote down his guesses as the serial numbers were called by (EA). Mr. Stewart did not fully understand what Dr. Brendel was doing in the hall, as he had not previously attended a T2SCTN experiment. His score for sheets 1–4 was 37/200, and for sheets 5–8 41/200, giving a total of 78/400, which is only two below chance expectation.

We intended to repeat this variation at Sitting No. 42 on 27th October 1947, but, unfortunately, a hitch occurred. Before starting on her first sheet, Mrs. Stewart in the kitchen with Mr. David Makgill was given the impression that Mrs. Hales, sitting at the screen in the lounge, was the sole agent. She was unaware that Dr. Brendel had slipped silently into the hall with the five cards. Unluckily, in a pause at the end of sheet 2, S.G.S., wishing to make sure that Brendel in the hall had finished looking at his cards, called out 'Brendel, are you ready?' This, of course, gave the game away, and Mrs. Stewart realized that two agents were at work.

We continued with the experiment, however, until the end of sheet 4. Before starting on sheet 5, F.B., who had been up till now in the lounge, acting as (TK), went into the hall to take over Dr. Brendel's part as cards agent. Brendel returned to the lounge as (TK) for sheets 5–8. Mr. Makgill was (EP) throughout the evening. Mrs. Stewart was not told of the change in the cards agent, though she might easily have deduced it. The technique throughout was T2SCTN(30). The decoding was done by F.B., Mrs. Hales and S.G.S. working together. The score for sheets 1–4 was only 48/200, and that for sheets 5–8 40/200—the exact number predicted by chance. There is, however, a very good reason for the total failure of this experiment.

Mrs. Stewart's work fell to about chance level for several weeks in the autumn of 1947. Thus, Sitting No. 41 with TTN(30) was also a failure. At Sitting No. 43 with TTN(30) she made only chance scores. An examination of her guess sheets revealed that she had got into a mechanical habit of repeating certain sequences of letters such as LEG, PLEG, GP, EG, LE, etc. For example, the sequence GP occurred no fewer than 52 times in the eight sheets of Sitting No. 42, and LEGP 15 times.

We decided, therefore, at Sitting No. 43 to use the letters C, F, H, R, T, these standing for camel, fox, horse, rabbit and tiger. However, at Sitting No. 44 we substituted K (kangaroo) for R, and the five letters C, F, H, K, T were used at all subsequent sittings. There was an immediate improvement at Sitting No. 44 on 24th November at which the highly significant score of 116/400 was produced in a TTN(15) experiment with Mrs. Soal as agent. Thereafter, the scores fell again to chance level for the next three sittings, but this may have been due, in part, to the introduction of a new agent, Mr. R. A. M. Kearney.

At Sitting No. 47 on 2nd February 1948, we again tried the T2SCTN variation. In sheets 1–4 Mrs. Stewart was led to infer that Mrs. Y. Hales at the screen in the lounge was the sole agent, but, unknown to her, Mr. Kearney went quietly into the hall with the five cards. Mrs. Stewart was in the kitchen with F.B. who acted as (EP) and (TK) throughout the evening.

At the end of sheet 4, S.G.S. called out to Mrs. Stewart: 'We will now try a new experiment with two agents. Mrs. Hales will look at the cards in the hall and Mr. Kearney will look at the numbers through the screen.'

The results were checked by F.B., S.G.S., and Mrs. Hales working together. The technique was the rather unusual T2SCTN(5) method.

Unfortunately, the experiment yielded only chance results. Sheets 1–4 gave a score of only 29/200, and sheets 5–8 the quite insignificant score of 45/200. It might well be that the Kearney-Hales combination was an unfavourable alliance.

## The Kearney-Morgan Experiments

Although Mrs. Stewart had told us that she felt she would not get good results with Mr. Kearney as agent, she did obtain a good score with him at Sitting No. 51 on 19th March 1948, when he acted as sole agent for sheets 1, 3, 5, 7 in a TTN(30) experiment. On this occasion the score was 58/200, quite a significant one. We have seen, however, that he failed when co-operating with Mrs. Y. Hales who is a first-rate agent. Kearney had also failed when acting as agent in our only TTN(3) experiment at Sitting No. 46 on 19th January 1948, on which occasion the score for sheets 1–4 was 40/200.

At Sitting No. 52 on 23rd April 1948, Dr. Louise Morgan, a well-known journalist on the staff of the *News Chronicle*, visited us, and took part as agent in an ordinary TTN(30) experiment. Dr. Brendel was (EP), and sat in the kitchen with Mrs. Stewart. Mr. Kearney in the lounge was (TK). The checking was done by Dr. Brendel assisted by Mr. Kearney and Dr. Morgan. The latter proved herself an excellent agent, for the score was 109/400 (critical ratio = 3·6).

At the next sitting, on 30th April, Dr. Morgan came again, and this time co-operated with Mr. Kearney in a T2SCTN(30) experiment.

For sheets 1–4 Dr. Morgan sat at the screen in the lounge, while Mr. Kearney was in the hall with the five cards. Dr. Brendel (EP) sat in the kitchen with Mrs. Stewart. Mr. Kearney also acted as (TK).

During sheets 5–8 Mr. Kearney was the screen agent and Dr. Morgan in the hall was the cards agent. Dr. Morgan timed herself as she looked at the cards for 30 seconds before each sheet began. The decoding and entering of figures was done by Dr. Brendel checked by Mr. Kearney. Mrs. Stewart was told the nature of the experiment, and the names and functions of the agents at the commencement of the sitting. She was also informed of the change in roles at the end of sheet 4.

The score for sheets 1–4 was 56/200, and that for sheets 5–8 was 59/200. The total score for the evening's work, 115/400, is highly significant (CR = 4·37), and there is obviously no significant difference of the scoring rate arising from the exchange of roles by the two agents.

## The T2SCLN Method

In the two final experiments of the 'split agent' series we used a slight modification of the ordinary technique. The cards agent, instead of shuffling and looking at his row of cards for a prescribed number of seconds, shuffled them, laid them in a row faces upward, and looked at them for the whole period during which (EA) called the serial numbers 1–25. The screen agent touched the five blank cards, as usual. At the end of each sheet (EA) went into the cards agent's room to record the code on his random number list, and the five cards were reshuffled before the next sheet was begun. This was the only change.

The above method was employed only at Sittings 119 and 121, and at this late stage of the investigation Mrs. Stewart's scores had fallen to the chance level with all techniques. We need, therefore, mention the results only very briefly.

At Sitting No. 119 on 16th September 1949, the two agents were Mr. R. Whelan and Mrs. Whelan, friends of Mrs. M. Holding (see Chap. XIV, p. 239). For sheets 1-4 Mr. Whelan was screen agent, but for sheets 5-8 the screen agent was Mrs. Whelan. Mrs. Stewart was told the names and functions of the agents. The score for sheets 1-4 was 36/200, and that for sheets 5-8 45/200.

At Sitting No. 121 on 23rd September 1949, the agents were Mrs. M. Holding and Mr. R. Whelan. For the first four sheets the screen agent was Mrs. Holding, and for the last four sheets Mr. Whelan played this role. Mrs. Stewart was again told who were the two agents and what were their functions. For sheets 1-4 the score was 45/200, and that for sheets 5-8 was 46/200. In fact, both sittings were complete failures.

## Summary of Results

Omitting the first very successful sitting on the grounds that the two agents were in the same room, we have, in all, 3,200 trials which yielded 759 direct (0) hits. This is an excess over chance expectation of 119, the equivalent of 5·2 standard deviations, with corresponding odds which far exceed two millions to one. There can be no question then that, despite the sittings which gave only chance scores, the 'split agent' experiments have, on the whole, been a striking success.

The mechanism of the process itself is veiled in obscurity. That it involves a complex interaction among the personalities of three individuals seems fairly certain.

We find the Kearney-Hales combination a complete failure, while the Kearney-Morgan association succeeds brilliantly. On the other hand both Hales-Rozelaar and Hales-Bateman are excellent combinations.

From Sitting No. 39 there is striking evidence that Mrs. Stewart herself must be made consciously aware of the existence of the two agents before the experiment can succeed. It is a pity that we were unable to confirm this finding by further experiment.

The last four sheets of Sitting No. 39 show conclusively that the experiment may succeed when both agents are men. It may even be that the subconscious minds of the two agents temporarily combine, as it were, to form a single mind which presents the card-image to Mrs. Stewart's subconscious mind as a completed entity, so that she has not to put together two separate fragments of information. But if this is the case, why did she fail when she was unaware that two agents were operating? It is hopeless to attempt to answer any such questions, and scores of sittings devoted entirely to this one type of experiment would be necessary to obtain even a glimmer of a solution. We need hardly say that, if Mrs. Stewart had continued to produce extra-chance scores, we should have carried out many more experiments on this fascinating theme. But while she was at her best, there were other questions in which we were interested and which claimed our time.

# CHAPTER XIV

# Agents in Opposition and Conjunction[2]

In the present chapter we discuss such questions as the following: What happens when two agents focus at the same time on different cards? Does the percipient, Mrs. Stewart, pick up now an image from one agent and now an image from the other? Or does she ignore one of the agents and receive only the thoughts of the other? And in the case of the latter alternative, what determines her choice of one agent in preference to the other?

Again, when two or more agents focus at each trial on the *same* card symbol, are the results, in general, any better than in the case when only one of the agents focuses on the symbol? We have no cut and dried answers to these questions, and such tentative conclusions as we have been able to draw can clearly apply only to the case of Mrs. Stewart; it is possible that different findings might be reached in work with other subjects.

The experiments are really a continuation and amplification of an experiment which Mrs. K. M. Goldney and S.G.S.* carried out with Basil Shackleton on 23rd May 1941. For a description of this experiment the reader is referred to Chap. XI, p. 185. The main finding was that, when the two agents looked at different cards at each trial, Shackleton made contact with the person who he thought was the agent, and apparently ignored the other person who was operating unknown to him.

This, then, was the starting point for our new experiments with Mrs. Stewart.

In the present series, in which two or three agents were employed simultaneously, one agent sat in the lounge on the far side of the screen, with his five cards in the box, and he is usually referred to as the 'screen' agent. The second agent sat with his five cards either on the settee or at a low table usually on the same side of the screen as (EA), from which he was able to see the random digits held up by (EA) to the hole in the

* IX, 1.

screen. When two agents were employed in addition to the screen agent, care was taken to place them (especially in 'opposition' experiments) so that no agent could see another's cards. If there was any danger of this, some opaque object was placed between the agents concerned.

If there are two agents working in conjunction (i.e. focusing at each trial on the *same* card symbol), the screen agent first shuffles and lays out his five cards in a row in the box, and the second agent then arranges his own cards in the same order on his table.

If the agents are in opposition, they are provided each with a small card on which are written four different arrangements of the five letters. Each agent is told by (EA) to arrange his cards for each sheet of trials according to one of the four orders shown on his code card. These arrangements are such as to produce conflicting codes in all cases, no matter which arrangements the agents choose. As each arrangement is used, the agent crosses it off his code card, and it is not used again. The agents are asked to select their codes in any order they please. Thus the arrangements might be as follows:

|  | Screen agent |  |  |  |  | Second agent |  |  |  |  |
|---|---|---|---|---|---|---|---|---|---|---|
| (i) | H | K | C | F | T | K | C | F | T | H |
| (ii) | F | K | H | C | T | T | C | K | H | F |
| (iii) | H | T | C | F | K | K | F | T | H | C |
| (iv) | F | T | H | C | K | T | F | K | H | C |

It follows at once that, whichever pair of arrangements the agents select as the orders for their five cards, when the experimenter (EA) shows, say, the number 3 at the aperture, they will be focusing on *different* letters.

At the end of each sheet the screen agent in a *conjunction* experiment reshuffles his five cards, and the other agents arrange their five cards to agree with those of the screen agent.

In the case of an *opposition* experiment, each agent selects another code from his list, and crosses out the one he has just used.

Throughout this series the TTN($x$) technique was used without exception. That is, the agents did not lift and look at their cards one by one, but turned them faces upward at the start of each sheet, gazed at them for $x$ seconds, and then turned them faces downward again, touching the backs as the random numbers were shown.

At the end of each sheet in an opposition experiment, (EA) recorded first on his random number list the screen agent's code, and then recorded that of the second agent some way lower down on the list.

When the first four sheets had been completed, there was usually a change in technique, and Mrs. Stewart (as a rule) was told the nature of this change before starting on sheets 5–8.

The results were decoded and checked at the end of sheet 8, and in the decoding for an experiment with two or more agents, in opposition, the screen agent's code was applied first, the other codes being covered by a piece of paper so as to prevent confusion. The decoded numbers for the screen agent were usually entered in the G-column, and those for agents 2 and 3 on the right of the screen agent's record, but not all those who have decoded have followed this plan. The total scores for the five categories were written over the top of each column, those for the screen agent being above the scores for agent No. 2, and so on, as shown below.

|  | (a) | (b) |
|---|---|---|
| Screen agent | 3/4/8/2/5 | 2/3/7/1/6 |
| Second agent | 1/5/3/7/4 | 5/4/5/3/6 |

# I. *Opposition Experiments*

An opposition experiment with two agents is referred to as T2OTN($x$), which means: *telepathy*; *two* agents in *opposition*; the *touch* method; *normal* speed; cards exposed to the agents' gaze before each sheet for $x$ seconds. Similarly T3OTN($x$) denotes an opposition experiment in which three agents focus different cards at each trial.

Our first experiment with two agents in opposition took place at Sitting No. 31 on 18th November 1946. Before starting, we told Mrs. Stewart—after she had gone into the kitchen with (EP)—that for sheets 1–4 there would be two agents, but she was not told that they would be in opposition. As the idea of agents in opposition had never been mentioned to her, it is very probable that she thought the two agents were seated at the screen looking at the same cards. Possibly, however, she imagined that a 'split agent' experiment was intended. She was told, however, the names of the two agents, F.B. and Mrs. Y. Hales, and on previous occasions she had scored highly significant results with both of them working separately or in co-operation.

At the end of sheet 4 she was told that for sheets 5–8 F.B. would be the agent, but she was not informed that Mrs. Hales would still be working in opposition to him. She would naturally suppose that F.B. was to be the sole agent for sheets 5–8.

The procedure was T2OTN(30). Mr. David Makgill was both (EP) and (TK). The screen agent was F.B. and the 'opposition' or second agent was Mrs. Y. Hales. Checking and decoding were carried out by F.B., S.G.S., Mrs. Hales and Mrs. J. O. Stewart, working together.

Mrs. J. O. Stewart sat by the fire while the experiments were in progress, without taking part, but watched the checking.

And now for the results. For sheets 1–4 the (0) score with the screen agent (F.B.) was 35/200, which is merely a chance score, but that with the opposition agent (Mrs. Hales) was 54/200 (CR = 2·47) which is, only suggestive (odds of 74 to 1).

For sheets 5–8 the score with the screen agent (F.B.) was 54/200, again suggestive, while with the opposition agent (Mrs. Hales) it was 43/200 which is a purely chance result.

The experiment was suggestive, but not conclusive. It does seem probable that any contact or 'rapport' made with Mrs. Hales during sheets 1–4 was broken by the suggestion that F.B. was to be the agent for the last four sheets. But why did Mrs. Stewart aparently make rapport at the start with Mrs. Hales in preference to F.B.? Quite possibly because Mrs. Hales was a friend of longer standing.

At the next sitting, No. 32, held on 25th November 1946, Mrs. Stewart in the kitchen was told by (EA) that for sheets 1–4 F.B. and Mr. L. A. Rozelaar were to be the agents, but it was not mentioned that they would work in opposition. (P), however, quite probably guessed that the agents, as in the experiment of the previous week, would be in opposition. She had on previous occasions obtained highly successful results when working with Mr. Rozelaar alone as agent.

At the end of sheet 4, (P) was told that for sheets 5–8 Mr. Rozelaar would be the agent, but it was not mentioned that F.B. would continue to work in opposition to him. It is quite possible, however, that (P) may have guessed that this was indeed the case.

During sheets 1–4 Mrs. Stewart sat in the kitchen with Mrs. Hales, who was both (EP) and (TK). The screen agent was Mr. Rozelaar and the second agent F.B.

For sheets 5–8 precisely the same conditions obtained as in the case of the first four sheets. The checking was done by F.B., Mr. Rozelaar and S.G.S., working together.

For sheets 1–4 with the screen agent (Rozelaar) the score was 49/200 and with the second or opposition agent (F.B.) it was 42/200. But for sheets 5–8 the score with the screen agent (Rozelaar) rose to 59/200, while that with F.B. was only 31/200.

If we combine the results of Sittings 31 and 32, we find that with the screen agent Mrs. Stewart scored only 84/400 on sheets 1–4, i.e. merely a chance result, while on sheets 5–8 she scored with the screen agent, i.e. the agent to whom her attention had been directed, 113/400 (with odds against this result being due to chance of more than 6,000 to 1 when the score is chosen as the best of the four).

On the other hand, with the second agent she made on sheets 1–4 only the dubious score of 96/400 (CR = 2·00), and on sheets 5–8 the purely chance score of 74/400.

What is remarkable about these two sittings is that, after Mrs. Stewart's attention had been directed by (EA) towards the screen agent, her score leaped up from a purely chance score of 84/400 to the highly significant level of 113/400.

## Continuity Experiments

We shall now describe five experiments which gave what is rare in this field—reasonably consistent results. The method was to allow Mrs. Stewart to work for the first 200 trials with a single agent who was, except in the one case of Dr. Allen, well-known to her, and with whom she had scored significantly in the past. At the end of sheet 4, a second agent, known to her, was brought into opposition with the first agent, and the two agents operated with conflicting codes for the next 200 trials (sheets 5–8). Mrs. Stewart was frankly informed before starting that a named person would be the sole agent, and at the end of sheet 4 she was told that for sheets 5–8 a second named agent would be brought into opposition with the first. Usually, the first agent sat at the screen during the whole experiment and the second agent at a small table from which he could see the random numbers as they were presented at the aperture, but he could not see the screen agent or the cards in the box. As explained previously, at every trial during sheets 5–8 the two agents were focusing on different cards. During sheets 1–4 we used the TTN(30) method, and during sheets 5–8 the T2OTN(30) procedure.

The details and results of the five experiments are given below.

### FIRST EXPERIMENT. SITTING NO. 58, 4TH OCTOBER 1948

In this experiment, contrary to the usual procedure, the first agent, Mrs. Hales, sat at the screen during sheets 1–4, but then moved to a small table for sheets 5–8; whereas the opposition agent, Mrs. S. G. Soal, sat at the screen during sheets 5–8.

Mrs. Stewart sat in the kitchen with F.B. who was (EP) throughout. No times were taken, but the rate of calling was approximately normal. For sheets 5–8 each agent was given four codes on four slips of paper, and asked to use them in any order, but not to use the same code twice. The decoding and checking were done by F.B., Mrs. Hales and S.G.S., working together. For sheets 1–4 Mrs. Stewart scored with the first agent, Mrs. Hales, 56/200 (CR = 2·83), and for sheets 5–8 she scored with Mrs. Hales a not very different score of 53/200 (CR = 2·30).

But with the opposition agent, Mrs. Soal, (P) scored only 41/200, which is a purely chance result.

SECOND EXPERIMENT. SITTING NO. 62, 18TH OCTOBER 1948

On this occasion the first agent, Mrs. Soal, sat at the screen throughout the eight sheets while the opposition agent, Mrs. Hales, sat during sheets 5–8 at a small table with her five cards. F.B., acting as (EP), sat with Mrs. Stewart in the kitchen throughout the experiment. Mrs. Hales acted as (TK) for sheets 1–4, and was then relieved by Mrs. J. O. Stewart.

(P) was told at the start of the experiment that Mrs. Soal would be the only agent for sheets 1–4, but after the sitting she told us that she was under the impression that Mrs. Soal and Mrs. Hales were in opposition the whole time.

The checking was done by F.B., Mrs. Hales and S.G.S. working together.

For sheets 1–4 Mrs. Stewart scored with the first agent, Mrs. Soal, 47/200, which is without significance, but for sheets 5–8 her score with Mrs. Soal rose to the brilliant level of 61/200 (CR = 3·71).

With the opposition agent, Mrs. Hales, her score was only 37/200 for sheets 5–8, a purely chance result.

The contrast between the performances of these two agents in Sittings 58 and 62 is very striking indeed. When Mrs. Soal was opposition agent, (P) made no contact with her whatever, and when Mrs. Hales was in opposition, she in turn was ignored.

THIRD EXPERIMENT. SITTING NO. 64, 25TH OCTOBER 1948

In this experiment Mrs. Hales and Mrs. Soal were again the agents. For sheets 1–4 Mrs. Soal, at the screen in the lounge, was the only agent, and during sheets 5–8 Mrs. Hales was brought into opposition to her. Mrs. Stewart was in the kitchen with F.B. who acted as (EP). The calling was not timed, but the rate was approximately normal. Checking was by F.B., Mrs. Hales and S.G.S. working together.

Mrs. Soal began again with the not significant score of 47/200 in sheets 1–4, and this rose to 51/200 for sheets 5–8. Mrs. Stewart's total score with Mrs. Soal as agent was 98/400 which is only of borderline significance. The score with the opposition agent Mrs. Hales on sheets 5–8 was only 36/200, and this is a purely chance result.

FOURTH EXPERIMENT. SITTING NO. 65, 29TH OCTOBER 1948

On this occasion, in addition to S.G.S., there were present three members of the staff of Queen Mary College. During sheets 1–4 Dr. H. S. Allen was the sole agent, sitting at the screen, and for sheets 5–8 Dr. F. C. L. Brendel was brought into opposition with Allen, who still sat at the screen.

Mrs. Stewart sat in the kitchen with Mr. Rozelaar, who acted as (EP). The time-keeper throughout was Dr. Brendel. Checking was done by Dr. Allen, Dr. Brendel, Mr. Rozelaar and S.G.S. working together.

Strange to say, Mrs. Stewart began with a quite insignificant score while working with Dr. Allen in sheets 1–4, but apparently she 'warmed up' with this agent during sheets 5–8, and her score rose to 56/200 (CR = 2·83).

The score with the opposition agent, Dr. Brendel, 42/200, was a purely chance result.

FIFTH EXPERIMENT. SITTING NO. 68, 10TH DECEMBER 1948

At this last experiment of the series Mrs. Edis, who rents part of Mrs. Stewart's house, was the sole agent for sheets 1–4, sitting behind the screen. For sheets 5–8 Dr. Brendel was brought into opposition with Mrs. Edis. Mr. Rozelaar was (EP) throughout the sitting and sat in the kitchen with Mrs. Stewart. Dr. Brendel was (TK) throughout. The results were decoded and checked by Dr. Brendel, Mr. Rozelaar and S.G.S., working together.

For sheets 1–4 Mrs. Stewart's score with Mrs. Edis as agent was 50/200, and this score rose to 54/200 in sheets 5–8. The total score with Mrs. Edis as agent was 104/400, which yields a positive deviation of exactly 3 standard deviations, and is therefore significant (odds of 370 to 1).

On the other hand, the score with Dr. Brendel, the opposition agent, for sheets 5–8, was only 38/200, a chance result.

## Summing up of the Results

For the five experiments taken together the total score on the target card with all first agents for sheets 1–4 amounts to 244/1,000. This yields an excess over chance expectation of 44; the critical ratio is 3·48, and the corresponding odds against chance are about 1,800 to 1.

For sheets 5–8 with the same first agents Mrs. Stewart's score is 275/1,000. This gives an excess over chance expectation of 75, which is the equivalent of 5·9 standard deviations, and the corresponding odds are of the order of $10^8$ to 1.

It must be borne in mind that the opposition score is not independent of the first agent's score. For if (P) scores a hit with the first agent, she must score a miss with the opposition agent. If, however, (P) scores a miss with the first agent, the probability of her scoring a hit with the opposition agent is 1/4 and not 1/5.

Now the total score on the target card with the opposition agents in sheets 5–8 was 194/1,000. But since the score with the first agents was 275/1,000 in sheets 5–8, the expected number of hits with the opposition agents is $\frac{1}{4}$ (1,000 − 275), i.e. 181·25, with standard deviation equal to $\sqrt{(\frac{1}{4} \times \frac{3}{4} \times 725)}$, i.e. 11·66. The observed or actual deviation is 194 − 181·25, i.e. 12·75.

Thus the excess over chance expectation for the opposition score is only just greater than the standard deviation, and is entirely without significance. It is easily seen that the scores for the individual agents in opposition are all without significance.

The upshot of this series seems quite unequivocal. Mrs. Stewart scored significantly above chance when working with the first agents as sole agents, and she continued to score significantly with them when a second agent was brought into opposition. There is not the slightest sign that she made any contact whatever with the opposition agents. The 'rapport' established with the first agent apparently causes her to ignore the second agent completely. At first sight it might appear that (P) was doing even better with the first agents *after* the opposition agent had been introduced, but the difference between the mean scores per 25 before and after opposition is 6·87 − 6·10, i.e. 0·77, which is not in any way significant. There is, however, a discernible tendency for the score with the first agent to begin rather badly, and then jump up in sheets 5–8.

It should be pointed out that, with every one of these opposition agents, Mrs. Stewart had at some time or other made highly significant scores when working alone with the agent; it was not at all a question of the opposition agents being poor transmitters; all of them proved themselves to be very good.

And how very difficult it is to reconcile these extraordinary findings with the theory that so-called telepathy is nothing else but the picking up of involuntary whispers uttered by the agent!

If this theory were true, we ought to find evidence that Mrs. Stewart is so confused with whispers proceeding from both agents that either she fails to score significantly at all, or else she scores somewhat above chance expectation with each of them. We certainly should not expect one of the agents to be completely ignored. The percipient was almost the same distance from each agent, and there was nothing in the situation which would enable her to hear one agent better than the other. Indeed, the first agents sitting behind the screen were a little farther away from Mrs. Stewart than were the opposition agents in front of it.

## II. *Agents in Opposition and Conjunction*

We shall now describe experiments in which two, or sometimes three, agents were working part of the time in conjunction and the remainder in opposition. The conditions of some of these experiments were not so satisfactory as might have been desired, for it was often impossible to arrange for two *good* agents to be present at the same sitting, and frequently a poor agent had to be put into conjunction with or opposition to a good agent. For this reason, the results are not so illuminating as they might otherwise have been.

We shall first describe four experiments in each of which two or three agents worked in opposition for four sheets and in conjunction for the other four sheets. Opposition and conjunction sheets were rigidly alternated. Since each experiment has distinctive and peculiar features of its own, individual treatment of the four sessions is advisable.

### (i) SITTING NO. 92, 18TH MARCH 1949

The agents were Mrs. M. Holding, who sat in the usual place behind the screen, and Mr. W. Harwood, who was placed at a small table behind the screen with the screen on his left as he faced the kitchen. Mrs. Holding had in the past proved herself an excellent agent. This, however, was Mr. Harwood's first visit to Marchmont Road, and afterwards he did not prove to be a good agent for Mrs. Stewart.

For sheets 1, 3, 5, 7, the agents were in conjunction. The procedure is designated T2CTN(30), which means: *telepathy*; *two* agents in *conjunction*; the agent *touching* the backs of the cards; *normal* rate; *30*-seconds' exposure to the agents' gaze before the start of each sheet.

For the sheets 2, 4, 6, 8 the two agents were in opposition: T2OTN-(30). On this occasion Mrs. Stewart sat alone in the kitchen. S.G.S. was both (EA) and (TK). Checking was done by S.G.S., Mr. Harwood and Mrs. Holding working together. Before each sheet (EA) told Mrs. Stewart whether the experiment was a 'conjunction' or 'opposition' test, and she was also given the names of the agents.

The conjunction score was 52/200, which is not quite significant (CR = 2·12).

In the opposition experiment (sheets 2, 4, 6, 8) Mrs. Stewart made with Mrs. Holding the brilliant score of 59/200 (CR = 3·36), but with Mr. Harwood she obtained only 33/200, which is a purely chance result. On the eight sheets the score with Mrs. Holding was 111/400; the corresponding odds are more than 8,000 to 1. Apparently Mrs. Stewart made no contact with Mr. Harwood.

236

## (ii) SITTING NO. 99, 29TH APRIL 1949

This was a most interesting, if puzzling, experiment in which three agents took part. These were (i) Mr. W. Harwood, who sat in the usual place behind the screen; (ii) Dr. Brendel, who sat at a small table slightly behind the screen with the screen on his left as he faced the kitchen; and (iii) Mrs. M. Holding who sat at another similarly placed small table with the screen on her right. Mrs. Stewart sat alone in the kitchen. She was told before each sheet whether the three agents were to be in conjunction or in opposition, but her attention was not directed to any particular agent. That is to say, although she knew that all three visitors were agents, no names were mentioned by (EA).

For sheets 1, 3, 5, 7 the three agents were in opposition, working with codes which were always in conflict. This was a T3OTN(30) experiment. For sheets 2, 4, 6, 8 the three agents had their cards arranged in the same order, so that at each trial they focused on the same symbol. The procedure was T3CTN(30). Each agent was sitting so that he could see the random numbers as they appeared at the aperture. In order to prevent agents (ii) and (iii) from seeing each other's cards, an opaque screen was placed between them. Checking was done by Dr. Brendel assisted by Mrs. Holding and S.G.S.

The results were very curious.

The conjunction score was only 44/200 which is merely a chance result. But on the opposition sheets (1, 3, 5, 7) Mrs. Stewart made with Dr. Brendel the very brilliant score of 61/200 (CR = 3·71). On the other hand, her score with Mrs. Holding, who is normally a first-rate agent, was only 38/200, and with Mr. Harwood she obtained 35/200. The latter scores are merely chance scores.

Dr. Brendel's result is highly significant even when selected as the best of four results, for the odds against its being due to chance are still more than 1,200 to 1. This was Dr. Brendel's first visit after an absence of several months. Mrs. Stewart manifested great delight at his appearance, and she had asked S.G.S. on many previous occasions why Dr. Brendel did not come to the experiments any more. He had, in the past, made himself very useful in putting up shelves, etc., in the house, as he is an expert woodworker. This pleasurable reaction to his surprise visit may have put Mrs. Stewart *en rapport* with him to the exclusion of Mrs. Holding, who normally is the better agent.

What, however, is inexplicable, is that this rapport with Brendel appears to have been abruptly broken at every conjunction sheet, and resumed again at each opposition sheet. For at each conjunction sheet the score dropped to about the chance level. It would appear almost as if the efforts of the other two agents somehow temporarily interrupted the rapport between Dr. Brendel and Mrs. Stewart when all three began to focus on the same symbol.

This curious observation, needless to say, is absolutely incompatible with the whispering hypothesis. If Brendel was the only whisperer, why on earth should he whisper only on the *odd* sheets, and never on the *even* sheets? But if the other two agents were whispering as well as Brendel, or if only the good agent, Mrs. Holding, was whispering, then the conjunction sheets ought to have shown an extra-chance score at least approximating to significance. But this conjunction score is only 44/200 —that is 4 above chance! None of the agents changed position during the whole eight sheets of the experiment.

## (iii) SITTING NO. 101, 6TH MAY 1949

The agents on this occasion were Mrs. M. Holding, who sat behind the screen, and Mr. W. Harwood who sat slightly in front of the card-table with the screen on his left. Between the agents a small vertical screen was placed. S.G.S. acted as (EA) and (TK). Mrs. Stewart was alone in the kitchen. Checking was done by S.G.S., Mr. Harwood and Mrs. Holding, working together. For sheets 1, 3, 5, 7 the agents were in opposition, and were provided with conflicting codes. The procedure was T2OTN(30).

For sheets 2, 4, 6, 8 they were in conjunction: T2CTN(30). Mrs. Stewart was informed by (EA), before starting each sheet, whether the agents were in conjunction or opposition, but no special attention was directed to either of them by the speaking of the names of the agents.

The conjunction score was 60/200 (CR = 3·54). In the opposition experiment Mrs. Stewart's score with Mrs. Holding was 54/200 (CR = 2·47), but that with Mr. Harwood was only 31/200, which is merely a chance result.

The difference between the conjunction score and that with Mrs. Holding when in opposition is not significant when Fisher's method for small samples is applied. This gives $0·7 > P > 0·6$. It seems probable, therefore, that Mr. Harwood contributed nothing to the conjunction score, and that (P) made contact only with Mrs. Holding.

It might be suggested by some sceptic that, since there was no (EP) sitting by Mrs. Stewart, she could have left her seat, peeped through the crack in the door, and seen the cards of the two agents as they lay faces upward, and that she might have continued to watch the random numbers shown by (EA). The snag is that this theory would not account for the opposition score with Mrs. Holding (54/200), who was quite out of sight behind the screen with her cards inside a box.

(iv) SITTING NO. 103, 13TH MAY 1949

This was an experiment with three agents. These were (i) Mrs. M. Holding, seated behind the screen, (ii) Mr. Ray Whelan, at a small table slightly in front of the screen with the screen on his left, and (iii) Mrs. Ray Whelan, on the settee.

S.G.S. was (EA) and (TK). Mrs. Stewart sat alone in the kitchen. For sheets 1, 3, 5, 7 the three agents were in opposition: T3OTN(30), and for sheets 2, 4, 6, 8 they were in conjunction: T3CTN(30).

This was the first visit of Mr. and Mrs. Whelan, who are friends of Mrs. Holding.

(EA) told Mrs. Stewart before each sheet who were the agents, and whether they were in opposition or conjunction, but her attention was not drawn especially to any one of them.

The conjunction score was 53/200 (CR = 2·30).

In the opposition sheets Mrs. Stewart made the quite significant score of 57/200 with Mrs. Holding (CR = 3·01), but with Mr. and Mrs. Whelan the scores were only 28/200 and 36/200 respectively.

The difference between the conjunction score and the opposition score with Mrs. Holding when tested by Fisher's method for small samples is not significant (0·7 > P > 0·6).* It seems probable, therefore, that in the conjunction experiment Mrs. Stewart made contact only with Mrs. Holding. Mr. Ray Whelan subsequently, when tested alone, proved himself to be a good agent, but Mrs. Whelan was not successful. Here again, though Mrs. Stewart was alone in the kitchen, it would be absolutely impossible to account for the high score 57/200 with Mrs. Holding, who was completely hidden behind the screen, with the cards in a box, even if we were to suppose that (P) was watching through the crack in the door the whole time!

## Summary of the Results

If we take the grand total of the *highest* opposition scores on each of the four occasions, we have an aggregate of 231/800 (CR = 6·28), and the total for the conjunction scores is 209/800, (CR = 4·33). We find that the difference between the two rates of scoring is not significant (P = 0·16). It seems probable that, having chosen one of the opposition agents, Mrs. Stewart continues to work only with that agent during the conjunction experiment. There is certainly no evidence that, when agents are in conjunction, the score improves, as it might be expected to do on the whispering hypothesis.

* This means that a larger difference between the two scores might be expected to arise by chance alone between six and seven times in every ten.

## Two First-rate Agents in Conjunction

At Sitting No. 94, 25th March 1949, we obtained very striking evidence that, even when two brilliant agents are in conjunction, the score does not improve. On this occasion Mr. A. M. Walker (a statistician of Manchester University) sat in the kitchen with Mrs. Stewart while she made her guesses for sheets 1–4, but she was alone for sheets 5–8. The agents were Mrs. Y. Hales and Mrs. M. Holding. S.G.S. was (EA) and Mrs. Holding (TK).

Before beginning sheets 1–4 Mrs. Stewart was told that Mrs. Hales would be the sole agent. Before the start of sheet 5 she was told that the agents would be Mrs. Hales and Mrs. Holding in conjunction. Mrs. Hales sat behind the screen throughout, and Mrs. Holding at a small table in front of the screen with the screen on her left.

For sheets 1–4 Mrs. Stewart made with Mrs. Hales a very brilliant score of 63/200 (CR = 4·06). The procedure was TTN(30).

The conjunction score for sheets 5–8 was 50/200 (CR = 1·77).

The results were checked by Mrs. Holding and S.G.S., working together, and were re-checked later by S.G.S. and F.B.

The interest here lies in the fact that we had two excellent agents focusing on the same card at each trial, one of them, Mrs. Holding coming in fresh at the start of sheet 5. But there is no improvement in the score, and actually the two rates of scoring are not different to a significant degree ($P = 0·1$ approx.).

On the whispering hypothesis we might reasonably expect that Mrs. Holding would, in sheets 5–8, be whispering cards not always, or even generally, in the same positions on the scoring sheet as those selected by Mrs. Hales and the resulting score ought to have been an exceptionally high one. But actually it is not as high as when Mrs. Hales was 'whispering' alone!

## Further Experiments

### SITTING NO. 96, 1ST APRIL 1949

It was decided that during sheets 1–4 Mr. W. Harwood should be tested by being allowed to work alone as agent with Mrs. Stewart. The procedure was TTN(30). Mrs. Stewart sat in the kitchen with Mrs. Holding's son as (EP), and Mrs. Stewart was told before starting that Mr. Harwood would be the sole agent. S.G.S. acted as (EA).

At the start of sheet 5 Mrs. Stewart was told that for sheets 5–8 Mr. Harwood, who sat at a small table slightly in front of the screen with the screen on his left, would work in conjunction with Mrs. Holding, who sat behind the screen.

The score with Mr. Harwood as sole agent was 31/200, a purely chance result. The conjunction score for sheets 5–8 was 51/200 (CR = 1·94).

The improvement in the score, estimated by Fisher's method for small samples, is just significant ($P = 0.01$ approx.). It seems probable that it was due to the introduction of the good agent, Mrs Holding. From the result of this test and those of Sittings 92, 99 and 101, it seems likely that Mr. Harwood is a poor agent for Mrs. Stewart.

## SITTING NO. 90, 11TH MARCH 1949

We are not concerned here with sheets 1–4 on this date, since they were devoted to a long-distance experiment between Richmond and Cambridge, for details of which the reader is referred to Chap. XVI, pp. 278–84. But sheets 5–8 (T2CTN(30) ) and 9–12 (T2OTN(30) ) were experiments in which two agents took part. These were (i) Mrs. M. Holding, sitting behind the screen, and (ii) Mr. Leonardi, a friend of Mrs. Holding, sitting at a small table slightly behind the screen with the screen on his left.

Mrs. Stewart's son, Mr. Alan Stewart, acted as (EP) throughout, and assisted S.G.S. in checking the results. Mrs. Stewart was told by (EA) before sheet 5 that for the next four sheets the two agents would be in conjunction, and before sheet 9 that they would be in opposition for sheets 9–12.

The conjunction score was 54/200 (CR = 2·47), and in the opposition experiment Mrs. Stewart scored 49/200 with Mrs. Holding and only 34/200 with Mr. Leonardi. The difference between the conjunction score and that obtained with Mrs. Holding in opposition is not significant ($P = 0.5$). There is no reason to think that Mr. Leonardi, who was on his first and only visit, contributed anything significant to the score in the conjunction experiment.

## SITTING NO. 105, 20TH MAY 1949

Our object in sheets 1–4 was to discover whether Mr. Ray Whelan would succeed when working alone with Mrs. Stewart. Mrs. Stewart was told before starting that he was to be the sole agent. (P) was in the kitchen sitting by Mr. W. Harwood who was (EP). Mrs. Holding acted as (TK), seated on the settee, and by her side was Mrs. Whelan. S.G.S. was (EA) throughout. The procedure was TTN(30).

At the end of sheet 4, (P) was told that three agents, (i) Mr. Whelan, behind the screen, (ii) Mrs. Whelan, on the settee, and (iii) Mrs. Holding at a small table in front of the screen with the screen on her right, would be in conjunction for sheets 5–8. The procedure was T3CTN(30).

R
241

Checking was by Mrs. Holding, Mrs. Whelan and S.G.S. working together.

For sheets 1–4 the score with Mr. Whelan was 55/200 (CR = 2·65). This is quite a usual rate of scoring with a successful agent for a series of only 200 trials.

The conjunction score for sheets 5–8 was 48/200.

The difference between the score with Mr. Whelan as sole agent and the conjunction score is not significant ($P = 0·38$). There seems no reason to suppose that Mrs. Holding contributed anything to the conjunction score.

The total score for the sitting, 103/400, is significant (CR = 2·87).

## SITTING NO. 115, 8TH JULY 1949

Mrs. Stewart had returned from Antwerp the previous day. The two agents on this occasion were Mr. Ray Whelan, at the screen, and Mrs. Ray Whelan, on the settee (see p. 201). Mrs. Stewart was in the kitchen throughout the experiment with Mrs. Holding who acted as (EP). S.G.S. acted as both (TK) and (EA).

Before starting, Mrs. Stewart was told that the agents would be in conjunction for sheets 1–4, and at the end of sheet 4 she was informed that the same agents would be in opposition for the last four sheets.

The checking was done by S.G.S., Mrs. Holding, Mr. Whelan and Mrs. Whelan working in pairs.

The conjunction score was 52/200 (CR = 2·12). In the opposition experiment Mrs. Stewart scored 49/200 with Mr. Whelan, and only 37/200 with Mrs. Whelan. The difference between the conjunction score and the opposition score with Mr. Whelan is not significant, and it is probable that Mrs. Whelan contributed nothing to the conjunction score. This is confirmed by the results of the next two sittings.

## SITTING NO. 116, 15TH JULY 1949

At the start of the experiment Mrs. Stewart, after she had gone into the kitchen with Mr. Harwood (EP), was told that Mrs. Whelan would be the agent for sheets 1–4, but she was *not* told that Mr. Whelan would be in opposition to Mrs. Whelan, so that she must have thought that Mrs. Whelan was the sole agent. At the end of sheet 4, Mrs. Stewart, who supposed Mrs. Whelan to have been the only agent, was now told that Mr. Whelan would, for sheets 5–8, be put into conjunction with Mrs. Whelan.

Mrs. Holding was (TK) throughout, and there was also sitting in the lounge a friend of Mrs. Stewart, Mr. Saffery, who watched but took no part in the experiment. Mrs. Whelan sat behind the screen, and Mr.

Whelan at a small table slightly in front of the screen with the screen on his left.

The checking and decoding were done by S.G.S., Mrs. Holding, Mr. Whelan and Mrs. Whelan, working together.

In sheets 1–4 Mrs. Stewart scored with Mrs. Whelan 41/200, a chance result, and with Mr. Whelan 44/200, which is also to be attributed to chance.

But in the conjunction experiment the score was 56/200 (CR = 2·83), and this is significant.

The results of this sitting are of considerable interest. In sheets 1–4, with the agents in opposition, it would seem that (P) did not make contact with either of them. She presumably failed with Mr. Whelan, who is a moderately good agent, because she imagined Mrs. Whelan to be the only agent and therefore was unaware that Mr. Whelan was operating. But why did (P) fail with Mrs. Whelan also? We suspected the answer to be that Mrs. Whelan is a poor agent, at least for Mrs. Stewart. After (P)'s attention had been drawn to Mr. Whelan at the end of sheet 4, the score leaped into significance. The results of the next sitting make it seem very probable that our conjecture was right, so that it is unlikely that Mrs. Whelan contributed anything of significance to the conjunction score.

## SITTING NO. 117, 22ND JULY 1949

The object of this sitting was to test the hypothesis that Mrs. Whelan is a poor agent. For sheets 1–4 Mrs. Whelan was the sole agent, sitting behind the screen. Mrs. Stewart was in the kitchen with Mrs. Holding who acted as (EP). Mr. Whelan on the settee was (TK) and S.G.S. was (EA). For sheets 5–8 Mr. Whelan was the sole agent and Mrs. Whelan (TK).

Before commencing each series, Mrs. Stewart was told the name of the agent, and assured that only one agent was in action.

In order that Mrs. Whelan should have every chance, she was allowed to take first turn as agent while (P) was fresh. The procedure throughout was TTN(30). The checking was carried out by S.G.S., Mrs. Holding Mr. Whelan and Mrs. Whelan working in pairs.

Mrs. Stewart's score when working with Mrs. Whelan was 39/200 which is just one below chance expectation.

But when working with Mr. Whelan, her score was 63/200, a very high score (CR = 4·06). If we consider this as an isolated score, the odds against such a result being due to chance are about 15,000 to 1.

The results show clearly that (1) Mrs. Stewart did not make any contact with Mrs. Whelan; (2) Mr. Ray Whelan is a very good agent; and

(3) Mrs. Stewart was in excellent form at this sitting. These findings lend confirmation to our conjectures about the results of the previous sitting.

In addition to the experiments described in detail in this chapter, one other conjunction test was carried out at Sitting No. 123 on 30th September 1949. At this period Mrs. Stewart's scores had fallen to chance level and the results are recorded here merely for the sake of completeness.

The procedure was T2CTN(30) throughout the sitting. The agents in conjunction were Mrs. Holding, behind the screen, and Mr. R. H. Whelan at a small table about four feet away from the screen on the left of it and slightly in front, the screen being now in the centre of the lounge. Mrs. Stewart sat in the kitchen with Mrs. Whelan who was (EP). Checking was by Mrs. Holding, Mr. Whelan, Mrs. Whelan and S.G.S., working in pairs. (P) was told that the agents were to be in conjunction.

The total direct score was 78/400, which is just 2 below chance expectation, and is of no significance whatever.

## Summary of Results

Let us now consider the combined results of the ten sittings at which two or more agents were in conjunction for 200 trials out of the 400 trials of each experiment.

In seven of these sittings the same agents were in opposition for the remaining 200 trials. In the other three sittings a single agent operated alone without opposition for 200 trials, and was brought into conjunction with a second agent for the other 200 trials. For these ten sittings, we have, for the total conjunction score, 520/2,000 (CR = 6·71). The sum of the *highest* opposition scores and the scores of the single agents is 522/2000. Thus there is almost no difference between the two totals, which include the scores when there was rigid alternation of opposition and conjunction conditions as well as those when the two conditions were not alternated in blocks of 50. All this evidence, then, goes to show that, in all probability, only the agent who scores significantly in the opposition experiment, or the successful single agent, plays any essential part in Mrs. Stewart's success in the conjunction experiments.

Indeed, the main effect of all these experiments is to bring us back to something akin to the old notion of 'rapport' between agent and percipient in a telepathy experiment. But when we use the term 'rapport' we mean no more than to suggest that Mrs. Stewart, subconsciously, directs her attention exclusively to *one* of the two agents and ignores the other *temporarily*.

When two agents, equally good, work simultaneously with Mrs. Stewart, we find no evidence whatsoever which supports the suggestion that she picks up now an image from one agent, and now an image from the other. On the contrary, everything points to the conclusion that she attaches herself temporarily to one agent, and ignores the other. This is certainly not what one would expect if telepathy were nothing more than a picking up of casual whispers from the persons who are focusing on the cards. The conditions of the experiments are, indeed, not such as to encourage the agents to whisper the names or initials of the five animals. If a person concentrates consciously on a task such as gazing at the figure on a card, he may be liable to reinforce his visual perception with a sub-vocal accompaniment, but under the TTN condition the agent, as a rule, does not even form memory images as he touches the backs of the cards at intervals of three seconds. It would, of course, be another problem if the agent were gazing hard at a diagram for an interval of a minute or so. But there is, so far as we are aware, no experimental evidence that, under the very different conditions of the present technique, the agents whisper anything whatever. However, we shall later on meet with phenomena in Mrs. Stewart's work which are absolutely incompatible with *any* whispering hypothesis.

The 'rapport' of which we spoke as existing between Mrs. Stewart and some particular agent may be determined, for instance, by the experimenter's telling her that X is the agent, while she is kept in ignorance that a second person Y, is working in opposition to X. When Mrs. Stewart actually knows consciously that there are two agents working in opposition, she appears to choose one and totally ignore the other. If she has been previously working with X as sole agent, the rapport temporarily established with X persists even after a second agent Y, equally good, has been put into opposition to X.

When no suggestion has been made to her by the experimenter that X is to be preferred to Y and Z, she seems to make her own choice by a kind of auto-suggestion. This emerges very clearly in Sitting No. 99, when three agents worked together in opposition and conjunction for alternate blocks of fifty trials. Normally, Mrs. Holding has proved herself to be a more consistent and a higher-scoring agent than Dr. Brendel, but apparently the emotional reaction to Brendel's surprise visit set up a rapport with him to the entire exclusion of Mrs. Holding. Mrs. Stewart's subconscious mind does not appear to make any rational choice, but blindly obeys the experimenter's suggestion or an auto-suggestion.

In Sitting 116, merely because the experimenter suggested to her that Mrs. Whelan was the agent, Mrs. Stewart seems to have tried ineffectually to make contact with the weak agent, entirely ignoring the fact

245

that a good agent Mr. Whelan was available. Then, when Mr. Whelan's name had been mentioned to her, she apparently abandoned the futile attempt to make contact with Mrs. Whelan's thought, and established instead a successful *rapport* with Mr. Whelan.

These results are not in accord with the findings of Whately Carington[1] in his seventh picture-guessing experiment. He says in his book *Telepathy* (2, p. 70): 'If several experimenters work concurrently, or substantially so, as in my seventh experiment, subjects are no more likely to hit originals prepared and displayed by their own experimenter than those prepared and displayed by others; the process does not depend on any "rapport" in the sense in which the term is commonly understood. . . .'

We have the greatest admiration for Carington's work in this field, but we cannot help feeling that he, too, often drew his conclusions from statistical results of only marginal significance. In his efforts to extract the last ounce of information from his data, he sometimes overlooked the paramount necessity for repeating an effect over and over again before coming to a conclusion.

In any case, it seems quite clear that in our own experiments, Mrs. Stewart did not pick up card images indiscriminately from a number of agents who were focusing simultaneously on the same or different cards.*

---

* An experiment in which two agents looked simultaneously at the Zener cards of two different packs was reported by J. D. MacFarland in *J. of Parapsychol.* Vol. 2 Sept. 1938. One of the two senders, J. D. MacF., had previously been highly successful when working alone with selected subjects, but the other, Mr. Dale Hutchinson, had obtained nothing but chance results with such subjects. It was arranged that the two experimenters sat together in front of an apparatus consisting of five electric bulbs by means of which a guesser in a room two floors above signalled his guess. The subject knew that two agents were using different packs. The guess series were recorded independently by J.F. and D.H. and each re-checked the target series of the other. In a total of 7,650 GESP trials made by five good percipients, the deviation on D.H.'s target was only +44, a chance result, but that for J.F. was +394, the equivalent of 11 standard deviations. This difference between the 'good' and 'poor' agent we present as a problem for Mr. Spencer Brown.

# CHAPTER XV
# Experiments to Demonstrate Pure Telepathy

The early investigators, including Frederick Myers, ascribed most of their paranormal experiences to telepathy, by which term they envisaged the direct action of one mind upon another without the intermediary of the normal sensory mechanisms. Minds they regarded as immaterial entities, not subject to the laws of physics, and they found little difficulty in supposing that one incarnate mind could affect another directly, or even that a discarnate mind could sometimes infiltrate thought into one still linked to a human body. Science, it was felt, was incapable of dealing with anything but the material world, and mind belonged to the province of metaphysics or of religious philosophy. Since mind was in its essence immaterial and non-spatial, there was no fundamental difficulty in the supposition that a person could have a telepathic hallucination of a dying friend on the other side of the world.

Hence it came about that psychical researchers like Myers, Gurney, Hodgson and the Sidgwicks, paid very little attention to the faculty of clairvoyance for which there was held to be little satisfactory evidence. In order to make contact with the physical world, mind had to make use of the sensory apparatus of the nervous system, and no one could conceive how a person could obtain any direct knowledge of material objects without the use of his own or someone else's sense organs.

If the alleged clairvoyant perceived, not the sensory qualities of material objects, but their structure as inferred by the nuclear physicist, it is almost impossible to conceive how he could possess the experience necessary to translate this recondite knowledge into the familiar descriptions by which we recognize objects in everyday life.

There were, of course, difficulties in the supposition that one mental pattern could influence another without the use of the ordinary sensory channels of communication, but the early investigators did not feel that there was any logical or metaphysical impossibility in such an idea. A

247

man was able to think even when he had lost the use of one or more of his senses. A blind man could still see in his mind's eye things he had seen before he became blind. It was argued that a person who had lost the senses of sight, hearing, taste, and smell might still be able to think about a proposition of Euclid, even though he was unable to communicate his thoughts to another person. The human brain, as Bergson[1] taught, was not a generator of consciousness, but a canalizing agent whose purpose was rather to inhibit the flow of thought and concentrate it at particular points as the solution of our immediate practical problems required.

It would be true to say that most of the evidence for the paranormal collected by the pioneers of psychical research pointed to a telepathic rather than a clairvoyant interpretation. It was difficult to suppose that an objective faculty of clairvoyance was responsible for the numerous cases in which the percipient had a vivid impression that a distant friend or relative was involved in some physical crisis, or was undergoing some painful experience. For why should the faculty confine itself so narrowly to the disaster which had overtaken this friend, and ignore entirely other things which were happening in the vicinity? Or why should the percipient not see what was happening in the house next door?

Was it not far more likely that, in his agony, the distant friend subconsciously directed towards the percipient a telepathic impulse so strong that it was able to break down the normal barriers of resistance in the latter's mind, and force itself upon his attention?

Until the late twenties and early thirties of the present century, few investigators who carried out experiments in telepathy thought it worth while to take serious precautions to exclude the possibility that their results might be explained by clairvoyance. We have seen that Coover* (1912–17) did not realize that his 'control' experiments, in which no-one looked at the cards, could be vitiated by the possible exercise of clairvoyance by his guessers. With hardly an exception, experimenters in telepathy allowed their agents to look at material objects such as playing cards, printed numbers, etc.

The evidence for clairvoyance was deemed to be so slender as to render absurd any precautions to exclude it. The publication of Miss Jephson's† clairvoyance experiments with playing-cards was disturbing, but when Besterman, Jephson and S.G.S.‡ undertook an extensive series of experiments with the cards enclosed in sealed envelopes without obtaining any evidence for the faculty, it seemed probable that certain of Miss Jephson's percipients, working at home and perhaps using soiled cards, either had sent in only their best scores or had unconsciously

* II, 1.        † II, 9.        ‡ II, 11.

identified certain cards from marks on their backs. It was not until such carefully controlled series as the Pearce-Pratt* series and the Martin and Stribic† experiments were put on record that the tables were completely turned. The clairvoyance issue could now no longer be shelved. How, for instance, was one to explain by telepathy the feats of Martin and Stribic's subject C.J. who guessed through a pack of cards from top to bottom, and scored consistently above chance, even though the pack was hidden from him by a screen? In America, successful experiments in clairvoyance became the rule rather than the exception.

As a last resort, a critic might suppose that in the screened experiments of Martin and Stribic the experimenter identified the *top*‡ card of the pack by means of some irregularity on its back, and transferred the image by *telepathy* to the percipient on the other side of the screen. Or he might put forward the still more far-fetched suggestion that the experimenter *whispered* the name of the top card. But even if this happened with perfect regularity, it would not account for the average of *seven* hits per 25 achieved by C.J. It was conclusively shown, moreover, that the hits were distributed more or less uniformly throughout the pack, and the significant results were not to be attributed to heavy scoring on the top and bottom cards. And such a suggestion would not apply at all to the Pearce-Pratt experiments, in which experimenter and guesser were in different buildings.

## Hypothesis of Precognitive Telepathy

Carington's§ experiments and those of Soal and Goldney¶ strongly suggested, even if they did not prove, that a person might be aware of the future content of another person's mind without the use of rational inference based on present knowledge. Here, then, was an explanation which might enable us to circumvent the immense philosophical difficulties which any belief in clairvoyance seemed to entail. True, the acceptance of non-rational precognition would involve fresh difficulties almost as great, but the hypothesis of a single faculty of telepathy which operated independently of space and time would surely be preferable to the assumption that there were two distinct kinds of paranormal cognition—one which apprehended mental events, and the other physical objects. Moreover, it seemed perhaps less incongruous to suppose that a mind could apprehend directly a mental image belonging to another

---

* III, 2.   † III, 4, 5.
‡ The experimenters state definitely that they were very careful to ensure that the *bottom* card was not seen.
§ VI, 22.   ¶ IX, 1.

mind than to assume that a mind was able to apprehend a physical object without the intervention of a nervous system.

The majority of the clairvoyance experiments with Zener cards could now be explained on the hypothesis that there was an act of precognitive telepathy on the part of the guesser. It could be suggested that he did not apprehend directly the physical designs on the cards; instead, he became aware of *future* mental events which would occur in the minds of whoever compared the card-order with the order of the percipient's guesses.

The hypothesis, however, had its own peculiar difficulties. If clairvoyant subjects were capable of performing such remarkable feats of precognitive telepathy while they were doing what were ostensibly clairvoyance experiments, it would not be unreasonable to expect them to succeed equally well when they were asked, say, to predict the future order of a pack of cards that would be shuffled and looked at in a minute's time. Yet, while high-scoring clairvoyance subjects were not so very uncommon in America, those who made high scores in tests expressly designed to test precognition were excessively rare.

But, more important, types of clairvoyance experiments had been designed which seemed to preclude the possibility that the guesser went ahead in time to the moment when the experimenters checked the records. It will be recalled (Chap. VI, p. 85) that, in Mr. Tyrrell's* experiments with his electrical aparatus, the guesser scored very significantly above chance expectation, even when the possibility of precognitive telepathy appears to have been ruled out. With the commutator in action, the agent never knew which of the five lamps he was lighting when he pressed any particular key. Furthermore, the automatic recorder merely marked successes and failures on the tape, but made no record of *which* box was responsible for each success or failure. The mind of the guesser, therefore, would gain no useful information by going forward in time† to the moment when the experimenter examined the recording tape. All he would learn would be whether the particular guess he was about to make would be right or wrong; he would have no guidance as to which box he must open to secure a success.

At first sight one might argue that the guesser could score a hit by going forward in time to the instant when he himself perceived the lamp alight in one of the boxes. But the guesser has to *make* his choice before its outcome can be predicted. Thus, as far as we can see, he cannot be guided by any present knowledge of the result of his choice. Mr. Tyrrell himself, apparently, was not happy about this argument, since he

* VI, 13.

† The reader will understand that we are here using metaphorical language.

suggests that, to make the experiment conclusive, the lamps should be completely hidden from the guesser's sight, so that after each trial the latter remains ignorant of whether he has made a hit or a miss. But if, as Broad[2] seems to think, the argument is sound, we shall have to agree that Tyrrell has demonstrated clairvoyance to a high degree of significance, and by a method which excludes the possibility of precognitive telepathy.

A machine for the testing of pure clairvoyance has also been constructed by Mr. Denys Parsons. In this device counters in five different colours are employed. The counters are shuffled out of sight, and emptied into the machine, so that they lie inside a vertical tube, one above the other, in an order unknown. The guesser operates a five-way switch, and presses a lever which causes the lowest counter in the column to fall into one of five concealed compartments, according to the position in which he sets the switch. The five compartments are coloured, and a disc which falls into a compartment of its own colour scores a success.

At the end of 100 trials the compartments are opened, and the numbers of discs of correct colour are counted. Since it is impossible for the checkers to gain any clue as to the order in which the discs fall, it does not appear possible that the results could be explained by precognitive telepathy.

So far as we are aware, however, no one has yet obtained any significant results by the use of this machine.

Another experiment designed to eliminate the possibility of precognitive telepathy is the 'chutes' experiment recorded by Drs. Humphrey and Pratt[4] in the *Journal of Parapsychology*, December 1941. In this test a large number of Zener cards was taken, and each card was enclosed in an opaque sealed envelope. There were five chutes, each provided with a kind of letter-box opening, and on each letter-box was pinned one of the five Zener symbols. The guesser was asked to drop each envelope into the chute whose symbol he thought matched the card enclosed. The envelopes fell down the chutes into five boxes, but, in the falling, the order in which the envelopes were dropped into the chutes was not preserved. The boxes were in another room, and were unobserved by either the guesser or the experimenters. In order to check the success of this experiment, the investigator had only to count the number of correct cards which fell into each box.

Actually the evidence for clairvoyance was indirect, for there were significantly fewer correct guesses than chance would predict. There was, in fact, a negative deviation which, selected as the best of five experimental results gave odds of 1,000 to 1 against chance. The assumption underlying the experiment was that the guesser, when about to drop, say, the tenth envelope into a chute, would be unable to obtain from the mind of the person who ultimately opened the envelope the fact that this tenth envelope contained, say, a circle, since, when the checker opened it, he could not know that it was the tenth envelope, owing to the change in the original order. All that the guesser could obtain by precognitive telepathy from the checker's mind was that ultimately each box would contain so many squares, circles, etc., and this would be of little or no assistance to him in identifying the card in the particular envelope he was holding. But the assumption that the envelopes were indistinguishable from one another does not seem to have been true in this particular experiment, since each envelope had affixed to it a band of brown paper on which a code combination was written. If, therefore, the guesser noted the combination Q12 on an envelope before he dropped it into one of the five chutes, he could obtain by precognitive telepathy from the mind of the checker who ultimately opened the envelope the fact that Q12 contained, say, a circle. But even had the envelopes borne no code numbers, certain of them might have been distinguished by, say, prominent specks on their faces or backs. We have plenty of evidence that persons with good eyesight and good visual memory are able to recognize a plain new postcard after it has been mixed with several others of similar make. Even new playing-cards can be distinguished by means of specks and irregularities on their backs. To make the experiment completely satisfactory as a demonstration of pure clairvoyance, it should have been carried out in the dark, and the envelopes should have been dropped into the chutes by guessers who wore gloves.

In the autumn of 1945 Dr. Rhine[5] put forward the rather startling view that the experimental evidence for telepathy was much weaker than that for clairvoyance. In his opinion, telepathy proper had not been satisfactorily established. It is, of course, true that, whenever material representations such as cards, pictures, etc., of the thoughts to be transmitted are employed, a successful experiment might be attributed to the operation either of telepathy or of clairvoyance. But Rhine went much farther than this. Even if no actual cards or other physical objects were looked at by the agent as he tried to transmit his thoughts, the experiment might still be highly inconclusive. To take an actual case, let us consider an experiment carried out with Mrs. Stewart at Sitting No. 27 on 18th June 1946. On this occasion, Mr. L. A. Rozelaar was the agent throughout. For sheets 2, 4, 6, 8 the five Lexicon cards were in the box, and the experiment was an ordinary TTN(15) test. But before the start of each of the sheets 1, 3, 5, 7 the cards bearing the initials of animal names were removed, and five white blank cards were substituted for them. Mr. Rozelaar was asked to make up in his head an arrangement of the five letters which was easy to memorize, such as P, E, L, G, Z. At the time no record was made of the code selected; nor was it whispered or spoken aloud. The agent simply imagined the five letters to be printed on the five blank cards. When, say, a 3 was presented by (EA) at the aperture in the screen, (A) touched the third white card bearing the imaginary letter L. Not until Mrs. Stewart had completed her fifty guesses did the agent divulge to (EA) the code, and the latter then recorded it on his first sheet of random numbers. The agent then invented another code in his head, and again imagined the letters, say, L, E, G, P, Z, on the five white cards. Mrs. Stewart sat in the kitchen throughout, with F.B. acting as (EP). Mrs. Y. Hales was also present in the lounge.

Decoding was by F.B., checked by Mrs. Hales. Mr. Rozelaar checked S.G.S. as he read aloud Mrs. Stewart's guesses. We called this new method TN (*telepathy* at *normal* rate).

For sheets 1, 3, 5, 7 (TN) the score was 60/200, and the corresponding odds against chance are about 2,000 to 1.

For sheets 2, 4, 6, 8 in which actual cards were used, the score was 58/200. Thus there is hardly any difference in the two rates of scoring.

But does the TN experiment exclude the possibility of clairvoyance? Dr. Rhine would answer: No, because *precognitive clairvoyance* is still a possibility. For the record of the code written by S.G.S. at the end of a block of fifty trials was a *future* physical object for Mrs. Stewart. While she was guessing, say, the seventh card, she might have obtained the number shown at the aperture by *clairvoyance in the present*, and the code by *precognitive clairvoyance*; and she might by putting these items together in her mind have discovered the letter the agent was thinking of at the seventh trial. All this, of course, may sound very far-fetched—more especially as Mrs. Stewart did not succeed at all with ordinary clairvoyance tests. We may be reasonably certain that she was, in fact, getting her information from Rozelaar's mind, but Dr. Rhine would still argue that the experiment, in a strict sense, was inconclusive.

The next step, clearly, was to invent a method which would ensure that the percipient's mind could not range ahead, as it were, into future time, in order to make use of a written or spoken record.

Dr. R. H. Thouless suggested the use of a list of random numbers 1–5. The agent associates *mentally* with each digit one of the five Zener symbols or the name of an animal. Before starting the experiment he thinks of a number between 0 and 4 inclusive, but makes no written record of it; nor does he speak it aloud. At each trial he adds this number to the random number on his list *mentally*, and, if the sum exceeds five, he subtracts five in his head. The resulting digit determines the symbol he will think of at any particular trial. The subsequent decoding of the percipient's symbols into numbers must be performed mentally by the agent, and no ticks must be placed opposite hits. Nor must the agent betray any hesitation, or pause unduly when he encounters a success. Otherwise he may produce an objective series of signs of which the guesser might avail himself by means of precognitive clairvoyance. The agent carries the number of hits in his head to the end of the column, and records the total only. Needless to say, the digit which was added mentally to each random number must never be recorded or divulged to any person at any future time.

The main objection to the method just described is that the results of an experiment would depend entirely upon the accuracy and honesty of a single person—the agent. For independent checking of scores the number that was added to each random digit must be communicated to a second person. This difficulty, however, is easily surmounted if the agent has a friend with whom he shares certain memories. For instance, he may say to this friend: 'The number to be added is given by the size of the family which you will recall when I mention the word "walnuts" .' The friend, if he remembers the incident, may reply: 'I understand perfectly', or use some similar phrase which gives nothing away. The reference, of course must be one that conveys nothing to the guesser.

The credit for the carrying out of a pioneer experiment on these lines must go to Miss Elizabeth McMahan[8] of the parapsychology laboratory at Duke University. The precautions she took in order to eliminate the possibility of precognitive clairvoyance were very thorough, as were also her safeguards against involuntary whispering. Judged merely by the total deviation, which was only +16 in a series of 6,500 trials with Zener symbols thought of by the agent, who was Miss McMahan herself, the results were of no significance.

But the fifth and last experiment of the series was of a different type from the others, and yielded results which were very suggestive of the operation of telepathy. The subjects for this experiment had been previously divided into two groups A and B. In group A were those who had scored somewhat above chance level in a previous clairvoyance test, and who, in addition, had been rated as 'expansives' according to the Elkisch* technique, and were further classed as psychologically 'secure' by the Maslow test. In group B were those who in the same clairvoyance test had made low scores, and who were rated as 'compressives', and, in addition, were psychologically 'insecure'. Since it had been found that 'expansives' at one time may change into 'compressives'

* V, 8.

at another, Miss McMahan re-assessed her subjects with regard to these two characteristics, and made the necessary modifications in the composition of groups *A* and *B*.

In the new telepathy test it was found that 700 trials made by the group *A* subjects yielded a *negative* deviation of 14, while the 1,000 trials made by group *B* showed a *positive* deviation of 34. The odds against there being such a marked difference in the scores of the two groups work out at about 300 to 1. (But see footnote on p. 55.)

When the result of this last experiment is combined with those of the first four, a chi-squared test shows that the odds against the occurrence by chance of such a high value for the sum of the five chi-squared values are about a hundred to one. The significance, however, is almost entirely due to the success of the fifth experiment. It is of interest to note that group *A*, which had scored *above* chance level in the original clairvoyance test, now yielded a negative deviation in the pure telepathy experiment. This is in line with the findings of Dr. Humphrey in her early work on 'expansives' and 'compressives'.

When all is said, however, Miss McMahan's experiment was suggestive, but far from conclusive. This was only to be expected, since throughout she was working with persons who possessed only weak ESP powers or none at all. It seemed to us, therefore, well worth while to carry out a similar experiment with Mrs. Stewart, our high-scoring subject.

## Description of the Experiment

Since our main object in doing this experiment was to eliminate precognitive clairvoyance, it will be necessary to disguise some of the details of the code. Otherwise we might still ruin the whole affair. Now it so happened that F.B. and S.G.S. had at one time belonged to a certain society. Of those members of this society whom we mention below, it is safe to say that Mrs. Stewart knew nothing. Among the prominent members of the society were five men, four of whom were well-known to both F.B. and S.G.S., and the other only to S.G.S. These five men were compared by S.G.S., on account of certain very marked physical and mental characteristics, to the five animals used in the experiments. S.G.S. knew beyond all doubt that F.B., who was to act as agent, could, by making use of certain veiled hints, easily identify four of the men, and discover the other by a process of elimination.

In August 1946, S.G.S. sent F.B. a package which contained a copy of Dr. Rhine's[5] article *Telepathy and Clairvoyance Reconsidered*, together with the published comments of Professor Broad, Dr. Thouless, and others, on the article.[7] The package also contained a sealed envelope.

F.B. was asked to study carefully the printed articles on the elimination of clairvoyance before he opened the envelope. In the sealed envelope was a list of five names, each having some connection with a surname of one of the five men; the names were in random order. The actual surnames were thus disguised but not so much that F.B. would be unable to recognize them. For instance, to take a fictitious example, Mr. Rose might be called Mr. Flower. No mention was made of the name of the society to which the men had belonged.

On a separate sheet of paper were veiled hints about the habits of the human counterparts of the animals. For instance: 'This pelican delighted in water-sports', to give another imaginary example. The order of the hints for the four animals had also been randomized. F.B. was asked to identify the fifth animal by elimination. When he had identified all five, he was to be careful to make no written records whatever, and he was not to mention the matter to any living person, not even to members of his own family. He was then to send S.G.S. a brief note saying 'I have been successful', or words to that effect.

A few days after despatching the parcel, S.G.S. received such a note stating briefly that F.B. was certain of the identifications, and that the conundrum had amused him, but giving no details.

Shortly before the actual experiment, S.G.S. had printed on five blank cards, in ink, the initial letters, or first two letters, of the surnames of the five men. These cards were substituted for the ordinary 'animal' cards in the actual experiments, which took place in the first three sittings held in the autumn of 1946.

Throughout, the TTN(30) technique was used, and this type of test was called TTN(30)E, where E stands for the *elimination* of clairvoyance.

At the start of each TTN(30)E test, Mrs. Stewart was told nothing of the special nature of the experiment, and she was left to infer that we were doing an ordinary TTN(30) experiment with a single agent. Nor was she told at any time that cards with the initials of men's names were being used instead of the initials of the five animals.

At the first experiment held on 10th October 1946, Mrs. Stewart sat in the kitchen with Mr. L. A. Rozelaar, who acted as (EP). Mrs. Y. Hales (TK) was in the lounge sitting where she could not see the agent or the cards in the box. F.B. was agent throughout sheets 1–8, and S.G.S. was (EA).

As is usual in TTN(30) tests, (A) looked at the faces of the cards for 30 seconds, and afterwards turned them faces downward. He then touched the backs of the cards indicated by the random numbers shown at the aperture in the screen.

When the 400 guesses were completed, Mrs. Stewart and the other members of the group were told by S.G.S. that the experiment had been a special one, and would require a different method of checking but nothing beyond this. F.B. was handed the eight sheets of random numbers 1–5, and also the eight sheets on which Mrs. Stewart had made her guesses at the initials E, G, L, P, Z of the five animals' names. F.B. then retired with S.G.S. into the hall, and F.B. checked *mentally* Mrs. Stewart's guesses against the list of random numbers 1–5, making use of the code which had been recorded on the sheet by S.G.S. in the usual way. F.B. wrote nothing whatever on the random number sheet except the *total* of hits for each column. Displacement hits were ignored entirely for this experiment. At this first sitting, however, F.B. made some slight movements with his fingers to assist him in counting hits. At the two subsequent sittings devoted to the test F.B. made no finger movements. No ticks were made opposite hits.

S.G.S. then took all the sheets home, and re-checked the decoding and counting, using the same laborious method. The totals for four columns out of sixteen differed slightly from those given by F.B. The sheets on which there was disagreement were posted back to F.B., who again re-checked his decoding and counts.

At the second sitting on 21st October 1946, only sheets 5–8 were devoted to TTN(30)E. Mrs. Stewart was again in the kitchen with Mr. R. Devereux acting as (EP). Mrs. Y. Hales, (TK), sat in the lounge. Mr. David Makgill sat reading in the lounge, but took no part in the experiment. F.B. was again the agent, and S.G.S. acted as (EA).

F.B. and S.G.S. retired to the hall at the end of sheet No. 8, and, as before, F.B. decoded the guesses, and counted hits mentally, writing nothing on the random number sheets except the total score for each column.

On this occasion, having been warned, F.B. was careful not to make any movements with his fingers. The whole process was afterwards re-checked by S.G.S., using the same methods, and this time there was perfect agreement on every column.

Sitting No. 30, on 4th November 1946, was again devoted entirely to TTN(30)E. This time Mr. L. A. Rozelaar was (EP), sitting in the kitchen with (P). As before, F.B. did the first decoding and counting of hits in the hall. S.G.S., who was watching him, could detect no finger movements or other indications that a hit was being counted. The results were re-checked independently by S.G.S. alone, and three columns out of sixteen showed different totals. These were decoded and counted again by F.B. and agreement was reached. During this sitting Mr. Rozelaar talked to Mrs. Stewart while she was writing down her guesses in order to distract her conscious attention. It was thought the distraction might result in better scores. This was the first occasion on which an experimenter deliberately sought to keep the percipient's conscious mind engaged.

Finally it should be noted that at the end of the last sheet of a TTN-(30)E experiment S.G.S. (EA) always collected from the box the five cards bearing the men's names and put them in his pocket. They were never left behind at the house.

After agreement had been reached between F.B. and S.G.S., the scores of the three experiments were found to be (i) 112/400, (ii) 53/200, (iii) 127/400.

For the three sittings, Nos. 28, 29, 30, the total score is 292/1,000. This corresponds to an average of 7·3 direct hits per 25 trials sustained over 1,000 trials, or 40 runs. The excess above chance expectation is 92, and the corresponding odds against there being such a deviation by chance are more than $10^{11}$ to 1.

It should be observed that the highest score was made on the last occasion after F.B. had become practised in controlling his gestures with a view to suppressing any objective signs that a hit had been noted. Indeed the last score is the highest made by Mrs. Stewart during the whole course of our experiments with her.

It seems not unreasonable to suppose that the possibilities of both contemporaneous and precognitive clairvoyance were excluded in these tests, and that the source of the information obtained by Mrs. Stewart was the conscious or unconscious mind of F.B.

## The Status of Telepathy

Frederick Myers[13] thought of telepathy as a direct communication between one mind and another, but nowadays we are not so certain that there is an entity called the mind which can function as a unit isolated from the brain. The latest researches into the physiology of the brain teach us that the mental processes which result from consciousness are accompanied by complex patterns of electrical impulse, which radiate through a vast net-work of fibres embedded in the cerebral cortex. By means of the electro-encephalograph characteristic changes in the rhythm of these impulses can be detected when a person is set to do, say, a problem in mental arithmetic. When the problem is solved, the normal rhythms are restored again. We are still, however, a long way from any proof that a one-to-one correspondence exists between patterns in the brain and specific thoughts. No one at present, from inspection of an electro-encephalogram, could deduce that a person was thinking of, say, Snowdon. Nor are there any very sound reasons for the assumption that, when two persons excogitate the proof of the theorem of Pythagoras, the circuits traced out by the electrical disturbances in their brains even remotely resemble each other.

We know that in sense perception the appearance of mental patterns is accompanied by the firing of neurons in the cortical network. It is inappropriate to use causal language here, since our notion of cause is derived from the action of one physical system on another. Causal happenings are expressed in the language of space-time differential equations. But a mental experience and a physical happening such as an electrical impulse in the brain belong to different orders of existence which cannot interact. A mental pattern is essentially qualitative, and not quantitative like a physical phenomenon. We cannot imagine any language in which interaction between the two could be described. All we can say is that mental experience and cortical activity are correlated and this correlation would seem to be one of the irreducible facts of nature which defy all analysis. We have presented in Chapter XX, p. 339, a few of the arguments which tell against the hypothesis that there is any strict isomorphism between mental and cortical events. Nevertheless, in sense perception at least, the correspondence must be fairly complete or otherwise chaos would result in our lives.

Thouless and Wiesner[11] have suggested that sense perception is a universally familiar, though special, case of the correlation between mental patterns and physical events which occurs in cases of clairvoyance. There is this difference: that sense perception is mediated through the nervous system while in clairvoyance the nervous system is dispensed with. But the correlation in one case is no more to be explained than in the other. If this view is true it implies that it is useless to search for a mechanism by which to explain clairvoyance. For whether we postulate a physical or a mental mechanism we shall reach, in the end, the unbridgeable divide which separates the mental and the material.

Moreover, like sense-perception, clairvoyance is a non-inferential means of obtaining knowledge of physical events. We gather useful information about the external world without knowing what is happening inside our brains.

But Thouless and Wiesner[11] have also suggested that telepathy may be a particular case of clairvoyance, and not a direct correlation of mental states.

Just as I have mental patterns which correspond to my own brain states, I may on occasion receive mental patterns which are correlated to the brain activity of another person. In other words non-inferential clairvoyance may be operating and its object may be an alien brain.

If this is a possibility it means that the experiments described in this chapter, designed to eliminate clairvoyance, do not, in fact, obviate one particular kind of clairvoyance.

If PK is a fact of nature, other possibilities suggest themselves. The agent's mental patterns may excite neurons in the receiver's brain and the corresponding mental images may be similar to those of the agent. This may be considered improbable but it is at least a possibility.

To mention an even more remote possibility, the agent's mental patterns might activate his own cortex and this excitation might be accompanied by similar mental patterns in the *percipient's* mind.

So far as we know such theories could not be tested by experiment.

Although we have no knowledge whatever of how the mental processes of *A* can affect those of *B* without the use of the ordinary channels of sensory communication, we consider that it is still useful to retain the term *telepathy* to cover all those cases in which *A* obtains an extrasensory knowledge of the mental content of *B* which cannot be explained by the assumption that *A* has paranormal access to some objective record in past, present, or future time.

It has to be admitted that many mediumistic cases suggest the operation of telepathy rather than that of clairvoyance.

A good example is the case of *John Ferguson*,* recorded by S.G.S. in 1921, and published in the *Proceedings* of the Society for Psychical Research, Vol. XXXV, 1925, p. 523. At two sittings with the medium Mrs. Blanche Cooper held early in November 1921, a communicator manifested who gave the name of John Ferguson, and claimed to have connections with an address at 'Westcott' Road in the town of Brentwood (Essex). S.G.S. had never visited Brentwood, though he had travelled through its railway station almost daily for many years. At subsequent sittings with the same medium, 'John Ferguson' said that he had died from a chill contracted in a boating accident on March 3rd 1912, at the age of 33 years. He also mentioned that he had a brother Jim, ten years younger than himself, and still living. He went on to describe a house in Brentwood situated in a street, with trees on each side, whose name began with H. The houses in this street were quite large with gates painted dark red. The family living there was musical, and they kept fowls. After the sitting at which 'Jim' was mentioned, S.G.S. suddenly recalled that, when he was 13 years old, he had known a boy of about his own age and in the same class at the Southend-on-Sea High School, whose name was Jimmy Ferguson. S.G.S. knew little about Jimmy's family, but was aware that his father was an Army schoolmaster at Shoeburyness, though he had never heard of a brother

* VI, 4.

John. A comparison of ages and dates convinced S.G.S. that it was not impossible for the Jimmy Ferguson of the séance to be the one he had known. At the next sitting these conjectures were startlingly confirmed by the medium's 'control' 'Nada' and by 'John Ferguson' himself. The latter now volunteered the information that his father was not a soldier, but used to help soldiers—'maps and compass'. 'Nada' identified Shoeburyness by saying 'Boom, boom—he makes a noise like big guns—the noise would break all the windows. Big guns in the sea.' As an artilleryman in the First World War, S.G.S. well knew that the duties of an Army schoolmaster included the teaching of map-reading and the use of the prismatic compass. From this point onwards the sitter, S.G.S., felt almost certain that he was on the track of the Jim Ferguson he had known at Southend.

A week or two later, on November 28th, S.G.S. visited Brentwood for the first time, and discovered that there was, about a mile away from the centre of the town, an avenue called Highland Avenue in which were large houses standing in their own grounds with gates painted dark red. Nearby, at the bottom of the hill, was a street of workmen's houses called Warescott Road (pronounced Wesscott Road). S.G.S., however, did not at this stage make any enquiries at Brentwood about a John Ferguson. He began to wonder what was the connection between the two streets. At the following sitting 'John Ferguson' said he was now able to give the name of the street which began with H, and volunteered the name 'Highland', which was heard clearly by both S.G.S. and Mr. A. L. Gregson, who was present. S.G.S. asked what was the connection between Warescott Road and Highland Avenue, and was told 'Enquire for Ethel—Ethel is the link.'

After meditating upon this for several days, S.G.S. conjectured that 'Ethel' was probably a servant maid, who worked at one of the large houses in Highland Avenue, but lived with her people in a small house in Warescott Road. At the next sitting 'John Ferguson', speaking, as usual, in staccato, 'Jingle-like' periods, gasped out the words: 'Ethel Lloyd—the young person in Warescott Road—maid to the family in Highlands—went there to help every day', etc. Another detail given was the existence of two unusual looking gas-lamps at the top of Warescott Road, and S.G.S. had noticed these on his visit.

On 12th December 1921, S.G.S. growing rather tired of the case, paid a second visit to Brentwood, and was told by the postmaster that no John Ferguson had lived in Highland Avenue for at least ten years; and this was confirmed by a visit to the Registrar of Births and Deaths. There appeared to be no Fergusons connected with Brentwood. S.G.S., however, out of curiosity, visited Highland Avenue again, and was struck by the name of one of the houses—'Paglesham' which was then empty. This name was that of a fishing village a few miles from Southend, and well-known to the sitter. On consulting an old directory of Brentwood, S.G.S. found that this house was occupied in 1914 by a certain 'Captain Shoesmith' (pseudonym) of the Royal Naval Reserve. At the next sitting S.G.S. taxed 'Ferguson' with telling untruths about his having lived at Brentwood, but the latter cunningly denied that he had used the words 'lived there', but maintained that he had actually said: 'Enquire at Brentwood.' He now said that he and his brother Jim had paid visits to a friend in Highland Avenue, with whom they joined in amateur music-making.

A little later on, 'Ferguson' volunteered the information that this friend at Highland Avenue was a 'naval man', which confirmed another conjecture made by S.G.S., that John Ferguson might have met 'Shoesmith' at Shoeburyness, since the Navy works in close co-operation with Coast Defence.

Better still, the name 'Shoeshine' was given—a close approximation to 'Shoesmith'. When S.G.S. demanded 'Now tell me the name of Shoeshine's house!', the voice replied: 'It's where cowslips grow in cockle-beds.' This was very extraordinary, because S.G.S. had often seen the cockle-beds at Paglesham, and the name itself means 'cowslip-meadow'. S.G.S. had often wondered where the cowslips grew, though he had found plenty of cockle-shells in the beds left dry by the receding tide.

S.G.S. addressed a letter to Captain Shoesmith's old address in Highland Avenue, marking it 'Please Forward'. In this letter he gave a brief account of the sittings, and asked the Captain whether he could throw any light on the matter. In due course he wrote from Plymouth saying that he had never known a John Ferguson, and that none of the details had any meaning for him.

'John Ferguson', who maintained that he had spent some years at Pollockshields, in Glasgow, working with his brother Jim as a motor engineer, declared after much questioning that he was buried in a large cemetery near the city. S.G.S. bought a map of Glasgow, and found that there were some fourteen cemeteries in or around the city. The two which were nearest to the district of Pollockshields were called 'Janefield Street' and 'South Necropolis'. A day or two after purchasing the map, S.G.S. had another sitting with Mrs. Cooper, at which he again enquired of 'Ferguson' the name of the cemetery. He was at first unable to give it, but some minutes later, when S.G.S. was no longer holding the names of 'Janefield Street' and 'South Necropolis' in his mind, the communicator jerked out 'South Necrop'.

S.G.S., therefore, wrote to the keeper of this cemetery, requesting that he would make out a list of all John Fergusons who had been buried there since the year 1890 with the dates of death, and note particularly whether any child named Amy Ferguson was interred in the same grave. 'John Ferguson' had, at an early séance, claimed that he had had a small daughter Amy, who had died at the age of five, and that father and daughter were buried in the same grave. When the list arrived, it appeared that John Fergusons in the South Necropolis were as plentiful as blackberries in autumn, but there was no man of that name who had died on 3rd March 1912, and no Amy Ferguson anywhere. S.G.S. never identified the 'John Ferguson' of the sittings, nor was he able to trace the Jimmy Ferguson he had known at school.

Apart from the unsolved mystery of the medium's getting the name of an obscure street in Brentwood, and what afterwards proved to be a correct description of Highland Avenue, the most satisfactory interpretation of this remarkable case is to suppose that it was largely a joint fabrication at the subconscious level by the minds of Mrs. Cooper and S.G.S. In this telepathic collaboration, the fictitious John Ferguson confirmed one by one the unspoken conjectures made about him by S.G.S. Clairvoyance on the part of Mrs. Cooper is not a satisfactory hypothesis, because S.G.S. neither spoke aloud nor recorded in writing his conjectures until after they had been verified by the medium at a subsequent sitting. Even precognitive clairvoyance is improbable, since, had there been no confirmation of the things he imagined about John Ferguson, S.G.S. would certainly never have bothered to make any record of them, or to mention them to anybody. Thus the conjecture had to be 'right' before it could even become a target for precognitive clairvoyance.

The telepathic collaboration was extremely successful for the reason that S.G.S., for a time at any rate, believed whole-heartedly that the communicating entity was in reality the brother of the boy he had known at school. S.G.S. was at that time anxious to obtain a genuine 'spirit' communication which could not be explained away as a case of telepathy from his own mind. The 'Ferguson' case—if it proved eventually to be founded on fact—would provide just the kind of evidence the sitter needed, for many of the details volunteered by the communicator were definitely outside the memory content of S.G.S. The subconscious mind of Mrs. Cooper was doubtless just as anxious to supply the type of case the sitter demanded. But clearly, if nothing that was given at the sittings could be verified, S.G.S. would soon lose interest. The little flame of excitement in the sitter's mind must not be allowed to die down for want of fuel. The bits of fuel supplied by the medium consisted of her confirmations of successive conjectures made by the sitter.

Each such confirmation reassured him that, after all, he was on the right track, and would eventually run his quarry to earth. Thus, both the medium and the sitter had strong motives for keeping up the telepathic game as long as possible.

The case is a mine of evidence, all tending to show that the names and incidents volunteered by Mrs. Cooper, when not pure inventions of the medium, had their main source in the sitter's mind. Thus the name of the cemetery, the name of the house in Highland Avenue, the name of Ferguson's 'friend', and even the name 'Highland' itself, were not forthcoming until S.G.S. himself had acquired the information.

But once the bubble was pricked, once it was clear to the conscious mind of S.G.S. that John Ferguson was apparently no 'spirit', but a mere figment of the unconscious, he disappeared as suddenly as he had come. Week by week he had appeared at each sitting, strong and confident, never making statements that conflicted with his earlier ones. He had a subtle answer ready for any attempt to trap him. The object of all this subconscious collaboration was clearly to deceive the *conscious* mind of the sitter. When, at the end, this became no longer possible, 'John Ferguson' collapsed immediately into a confused and feeble ghost.

During this series of sittings, S.G.S. noticed again and again that the names volunteered by Mrs. Cooper were seldom forthcoming at moments when the sitter was holding them clearly in his conscious mind. The name would usually be given when he was thinking of something quite different, and when he was not expecting it. This would support the belief that complexes in the sitter's mind are more easily transmitted while they remain in the unconscious. Possibly, by becoming conscious, ideas lose the potential energy which may have to be expended when they pass into another mind.

Ehrenwald,* in his discussion of telepathy and schizophrenic deterioration, seems to have reached a similar conclusion. He writes: 'I pointed out that the conditions for the origin of telepathy are beyond the control of the experimenter. They are likely to occur at moments when he is off his guard and unprepared to pay them the necessary attention. On the other hand, the phenomena will generally fail to materialize once his attention is focused on them. This peculiar elusive behaviour of telepathic occurrences is particularly marked in schizophrenic patients under clinical conditions, and anyone expecting to find them on his daily hospital round as a matter of routine may be sorely disappointed.'

There are several other remarkable cases reported by Dr. Osty, in which a sensitive does not succeed apparently in getting the objective

* V, 7.

facts about a lost jewel, or a missing relative, which her client is so earnestly seeking, but merely a reflection of the client's own secret beliefs and conjectures as to what has happened.

Indeed, it would be true to say that professional mediums and clairvoyants, in 90 per cent of cases, 'read' their sitters' minds, and only very rarely tell them anything which they do not know, or which is not in their memories. In the study of mediums it is telepathy which forces itself on the attention; true clairvoyance is a much rarer faculty.

It is, perhaps, a pity that Dr. Rhine had little or no experience with high grade psychical sensitives before he embarked on his work with Zener cards. He might then have realized the strength of the case for telepathy in a truer perspective.

## Shackleton and Telepathy

There can be little doubt that telepathy from the agent is the most plausible, as well as the simplest, interpretation of the Shackleton experiments. Dr. Rhine,[5] however, has disputed this. His first suggestion was that Shackleton may have failed in the clairvoyance tests (Chap. X, p. 150), because he was inhibited by his own belief that clairvoyance was impossible. But when it was pointed out by those who had assisted at the experiments that Shackleton was just as confident with regard to clairvoyance as he was about telepathy, Dr. Rhine quite rightly abandoned this position. In fact, neither Shackleton nor any of the experimenters were biased in favour of telepathy. Both K.M.G. and S.G.S. are quite certain that Shackleton would have felt sure of succeeding in *any* paranormal experiment, however hopeless it might seem to others. He tried experiments with Mr. Denys Parsons's clairvoyance machine with as much enthusiasm as he had shown in the previous tests with S.G.S., but without success.

Dr. Rhine[6] then went on to suggest that, in our ordinary clairvoyance tests, some personal element may have been lacking which was vital to success. That is, he thought that the presence of an agent who looked at the cards was, in the case of Shackleton, perhaps an indispensable condition. The argument seems to us somewhat far-fetched. For, even in the clairvoyance experiments, the agent was still in her usual position in front of the cards. She touched their backs when the random numbers were shown at the aperture. The only difference, in fact, was that she did not know the order of the five animal pictures.

Moreover, if Shackleton was succeeding by means of clairvoyance in the experiments in which the agent looked at the cards, why should he be successful with only three agents out of about a dozen?

Again, we have seen that, when we substituted a fresh agent, Mr. J. Aldred, for the original agent, Miss Rita Elliott, the whole character of the displacement suddenly changed. With Miss Elliott, Shackleton scored significantly only on the (+1) or (+2) cards, whereas with Mr. Aldred he scored about equally well on the (−1) and (+1) cards. This fact alone emphasizes the part played by the personality of the agent, and strongly supports the telepathic theory that the mind of the agent, and not the pictures on the cards, was the true source of Shackleton's information.

It is, moreover, a formidable obstacle to the hypothesis of Mr. Spencer Brown that ESP is due to a hitherto unrecognized defect in probability theory. Had Mr. Brown put forward his hypothesis a quarter of a century ago it might have been worthy of serious attention. But ESP is no longer a mere effect of marginal significance. There have been so many gifted subjects who have produced persistent high scoring over long periods of time, and so many cases in which changes in the physical or psychological conditions of the experiment have been accompanied by consistent changes in the rate or character of the scoring, that it is no longer possible to attribute ESP to any kind of statistical artifact whatsoever.

# CHAPTER XVI

# Long-Distance Experiments

Experiments in telepathy in which agent and percipient are separated by hundred of miles have not been, on the whole, conspicuously successful. This is probably due to psychological causes. The guesser may feel that he is isolated and out of touch with the sender, or that he has lost the sensation of rapport. This is especially true if he has to wait for several days before hearing the results of the test. George Zirkle, one of Dr. Rhine's most successful subjects for pure telepathy, confessed, when trying a test with Miss Sarah Ownbey at a distance of 165 miles, that his usual sense of rapport with this lady had completely left him. Zirkle felt he was not going to succeed, and the results justified his pessimism.

In the summer of 1933, however, one of Rhine's subjects, Miss May Turner,* made three very remarkable scores in a pure telepathy experiment with the sender, Miss Ownbey, 250 miles away. Miss Turner, at Lake Janaluska, had arranged to guess at Zener symbols thought of by Miss Ownbey, who remained in Durham, North Carolina. No actual cards were used, and the agent chose her symbols mentally in groups of five, and concentrated on each symbol for five minutes. When the group of five symbols had been 'transmitted', she recorded it on paper, and constructed another group in her head. The experimenters, who had synchronized their watches, agreed to do twenty-five trials at a specified time on each of eight days. It had been arranged that agent and percipient should send their records at the end of each day's work to Dr. Rhine, but, unfortunately, a misunderstanding seems to have arisen. For, while Miss Ownbey delivered her lists of symbols to Dr. Rhine without delay, Miss Turner posted her guesses for the first three days' work to Miss Ownbey. The scores for these first runs were phenomenal, being 19, 16, 16. It is only fair to point out, however, that Miss Ownbey did not receive Miss Turner's list of guesses until she had dispatched her own records to Dr. Rhine. And when Miss Ownbey gave Dr. Rhine the

* III, 1, 2.

lists she had received from Miss Turner, these lists were indubitably in the latter's handwriting and in her own ink, and at the foot of the lists of symbols was additional information, also in Miss Turner's hand. Since, therefore, Miss Ownbey dispatched her own records before receiving those of Miss Turner, we shall have to accept the results of the experiment, or assume that the two experimenters were in collusion.

Miss Ownbey was at that time a graduate assistant of unblemished reputation in the psychology department at Duke University; and it is unusual, to say the least, for a young person of this standing to fake experiments at the outset of her career.

After the third sitting, Miss Turner posted her records to Dr. Rhine, but, unfortunately, the subsequent scores of 7, 7, 8, 6, 2 are not by themselves significant. In the last five runs the interval between successive symbols was reduced from five minutes to three minutes, but otherwise there seems to have been no obvious change in the conditions of the tests.

A month later, a second series of pure telepathy experiments was organized, with Miss Turner and Miss Ownbey now separated by a distance of about 300 miles.

The scores for the five runs were not, however, significantly different from what chance might produce, being 6, 4, 6, 3, 5.

The detailed lists of symbols employed by the agent in these experiments have been published,[1] and empirical cross-checks reveal no indications that sender and guesser had similar mental preferences in ordering their sets of five symbols.

The very high scores produced by the first three runs of the Janaluska experiment remain a mystery. A mere fluke of chance could scarcely be responsible for their occurrence.

But it is worth noting that Professor Gardner Murphy[2,3] has recorded a not dissimilar case. A woman student from Hunter College, named Lillian Levine, visited the rooms of the American Society for Psychical Research in New York in order to take part in some tests with Zener cards. In one room sat Mrs. Laura Dale with packs of cards which had been randomized by means of tables of numbers, and with her was Dr. Ernest Taves, who witnessed the experiment. Miss Levine sat in another room in front of a signalling apparatus with five keys. As Mrs. Dale exposed the cards one by one, the guesser pressed a key which indicated to the experimenters in the other room which symbol she had chosen.

Now, in one run of 25, Miss Levine got the first 15 cards absolutely correct, and the odds against this result being due to chance work out to about thirty thousand millions to one.* But there was nothing at all remarkable about Miss Levine's guessing apart from this single run.

The subject was put through a psychological cross-examination as to her feelings and mental attitude while she was making this remarkable run, but little of interest was revealed. According to her account of the matter, the percipient saw crosses and waves in the protuberances of the radiator, or in the patterns of the carpet, somewhat as a person sees faces in the fire, or visions in a crystal, though she was not in any state of trance or of deep abstraction. She was also given a Rorschach ink-blot test, but again nothing unusual was discovered about her personal motivations or inhibitions. No light was shed on what had happened to Miss Levine during those few moments, but who can doubt that some change in her mental orientation had occurred, which she was unable either to describe or to recapture?

It may well be, as Professor Gardner Murphy[3] has suggested, that extra-sensory perception is not primarily a function of the individual personality, but something that emerges essentially from an intra-personal relation. That is to say, it results from some peculiar relations which exist at the subconscious level between the personalities of the percipient, the agent, and the experimenters. It may be that, unless the group in which the sensitive is working is such as to favour the setting-up of the right sort of intra-personal relations, ESP does not take place. And after these relations have been established, it is probably useless to tear the subject away from her intra-personal environment, plant her among a set of strangers, and still expect ESP to function as before. Thus it is possible that Miss Turner, like Miss Levine, was able to establish, for a brief period, some subconscious contact with her agent that was closer and more vital than the normal relations of everyday life.

In a third series of thirteen runs carried out in August and September 1933, Miss Ownbey was the agent and George Zirkle the subject, the two being separated by a distance of 165 miles. The pure telepathy method described above was again employed, and a single run of 25 trials was completed on each working day. But once more the experiment was a failure. The 325 trials yielded 72 hits, which is only 7 above expectation.

---

* Using a formula given in W. Feller's *Probability Theory and its Applications* (p. 267) we find that the probability of getting an unbroken run of 15 successes *anywhere* in a sequence of 25 trials works out to $2 \cdot 9 \times 10^{10}$.

## The Zagreb-Durham Experiments[4]

Dr. Karl Marchesi, a medical practitioner living in Zagreb, Jugoslavia, communicated to Dr. Rhine in the year 1939 the results of some clairvoyance tests in which Dr. Marchesi himself had been the percipient. In these tests the pack was guessed through from top to bottom, with the guesser standing about ten feet away from the cards.

A series of 5,000 trials with this DT (down through) technique gave an excess of hits above chance expectation of 279, which is the equivalent of 9·86 standard deviations. Rhine was so impressed by the tremendous significance of these results that he arranged for Dr. Marchesi to guess in Zagreb the order of packs of cards set up at Duke University, some 4,000 miles away. This is probably the longest distance over which a clairvoyance experiment has been tried.

Each experiment consisted of ten runs of 25 guesses, and, in preparation, the Duke University experimenters, on the day before the test, shuffled thoroughly ten packs of ordinary Zener cards, and put them into boxes. The ten boxes were placed in order along a north-south line, so that pack No. 1 was at the south end of the line. The packs were in position by 5 p.m., local time, on the day preceding the experiment, and were left undisturbed until 1 p.m. on the following day. The card order for each pack was then recorded, and the cards were reshuffled in readiness for the next experiment. Since there is a difference of six hours between Durham and Zagreb time, this arrangement ensured that Dr. Marchesi was able to record his guesses at any hour up to 7 p.m. on the day of the test. He was not informed as to the precise orientation of the ten packs, and presumably he was expected to discover by extra-sensory perception the order in which they were to be taken. The first set of 125 runs was done in August 1939, and after that came a gap of four months. Two other sets of 90 and 103 runs were carried out in January and February, 1940, respectively, while the final batch of only 35 runs was not done till May 1940. After this the threat of war to Jugoslavia supervened, and the experiments had to be abandoned. Dr. Marchesi did not mail his guesses to Dr. Rhine until the end of the series.

On the grand total of 353 runs, or 8,825 individual trials, the number of (0) hits amounted to no more than 23 above chance expectation. This is not in any way significant, being less than one standard deviation. It is curious, however, that the last sub-series of 35 runs gave a critical ratio of +2·87, which, *as an isolated result*, is significant.[4]

On the whole, however, the experiment failed to provide any direct evidence for extra-sensory perception. There is, nevertheless, some evidence of a more recondite character that some factor other than chance

270

was at work. This depends on the comparison of two statistics known as the 'run' salience and the 'segment' salience. The 'run' salience gives us an estimate which tells us whether or not the guesser is scoring at a higher (or lower) rate on the first and last five trials of the run of 25 than on the middle fifteen. If he is scoring at a significantly higher rate on the first and last five trials taken together than on the central group, the percipient's record is said to show *terminal* salience. That is to say, his ESP functions best at the beginning and end of the run of 25, and falls off towards the middle. If, on the other hand, he scores at a higher rate in the middle of the run than at its ends, he is said to exhibit *middle* salience.

Now card-guessers, as a rule, naturally think of a run of 25 trials as being broken up into five successive groups of five trials. Most scoring sheets, in fact, have a thick line drawn after trials Nos. 5, 10, 15, 20, 25. Thus the guesser tends to envisage his work of guessing at the 25 targets as a succession of smaller tasks, each consisting of five trials. Now it has been found in many cases that *terminal* salience in the whole run is often accompanied by terminal salience within segments of five. And, similarly, *middle* salience in the run and in the segment are frequently associated. That is, if a person tends to make higher scores at the start and finish of the run, he will likewise do better on the first and last guesses of the segment than on the middle three. Thus we are able to calculate two statistics, one called the RSR or 'salience ratio for the run', and the other the SSR or 'salience ratio for the segment'.[5, 6, 7]

Now, if nothing but blind chance is responsible for the hits scored by the guesser, these two ratios will be quite independent of each other. A tendency to make high scores at the start and finish of the run would not by itself produce a similar effect in that smaller unit, the segment, nor *vice versa*. In other words, the two effects would show no significant correlation. An exceptionally high RSR would not generally go with a correspondingly high SSR. But, if we found that the two ratios went up and down together very consistently, this would provide evidence that some factor other than chance was in operation. It would show that the guesser's peculiarities in distributing his hits in the run of 25 were reflected also in the segment of 5.

In addition, therefore, to computing the RSR and the SSR, we must work out another statistic known as the covariance ratio. From this we can estimate the extent to which the first two ratios vary together.

Now the 353 runs guessed by Dr. Marchesi showed, on the whole, what has been called middle salience. That is, the rate of scoring on the middle fifteen trials was higher than that on the first and last five trials, except for a few runs at the beginning of the series of experiments.

What is important, however, is the high degree of positive correlation between the RSR and the SSR values, which holds throughout the four sub-series. If the two statistics are compared for each sub-series, the covariance ratio works out at +4·05, and the odds against our getting such a high degree of dependence by chance alone are about 7,000 to 1.

The reader will naturally ask: How can we argue that ESP has been at work during this long-distance experiment when the total number of hits is insignificantly above chance expectation? What real meaning can be attached to the recondite effect we have just described? To explain these facts we must envisage the possibility that alternations of positive and negative scoring take place *within the run itself*. We have, indeed, overwhelming proof that our gifted subject, Mrs. Stewart, was scoring below chance expectation on some kinds of target patterns, and above chance level on the other patterns. In her case, the positive scoring clearly had the upper hand, and easily prevailed against the negative scoring. But with subjects who display a much lesser degree of ESP ability, the two tendencies operating within the run may be more evenly matched, and may cancel each other, so that, on the whole, there is no significant extra-chance deviation. This oscillation from positive to negative scoring, feeble though it may be, can probably be detected in cases where salience exists in both the run and the segment scoring, even when the run-salience and the segment-salience are each separately too small to be significant.

Besides acting as subject himself, Dr. Marchesi suggested to Dr. Rhine that ten Duke University subjects should try in Durham to guess packs of ESP cards set up at pre-arranged times by Dr. Marchesi in Zagreb. On each of ten days Dr. Marchesi laid out in his office ten packs of Zener cards in two rows of five, and each of the ten guessers at Duke University recorded his guesses for the ten packs. Thus on every one of the ten occasions the different subjects were guessing at the same packs, and, this fact rather complicates the strict statistical evaluation of the results. Dr. Marchesi sent to Dr. Rhine the records of his target lists, and the checking was done at Duke University. A rough evaluation of the results shows that not one of the Duke subjects obtained a significant critical ratio in his 2,500 trials, and on the grand total of 25,000 guesses made by all the percipients there was an excess of only 88 over chance expectation, which is but a trifle greater than the standard deviation itself. Nor was there any significant covariance between RSR and SSR. Thus the experiment in the reverse direction must be regarded as a failure. A more accurate evaluation would probably make little difference to the result.

## *The Second Zagreb-Durham Experiment*[8]

Seven years later, at the close of the Second World War, the Duke University workers were able to resume their correspondence with Dr. Marchesi. At the latter's suggestion three series of tests were planned; in two of these the packs of cards were to be guessed by Dr. Marchesi, while they were *in situ* at the Durham laboratory, but in a third series he was to record his guesses a day before the packs were shuffled and set up. The last mentioned experiments were, therefore, of a precognitive type. The three series were conducted between 18th November 1946 and 16th January 1947, with breaks of a few days between series.

On each day at 5 p.m. Eastern Standard Time each of ten packs of Zener cards was shuffled, and its card order recorded on a scoring sheet by Miss McMahan. Each pack was then replaced face downwards in its box, and the ten boxes, with lids on, were placed standing on end in a row against a wall so that the cards all faced east towards Jugoslavia. The boxes were numbered 1–10. Above each box the corresponding record sheet of the cards it contained was pinned to the wall. The cards were left undisturbed till 1 p.m. the following day, at which time they were reshuffled in readiness for the next experiment. The first two series comprised a total of 244 runs (6,100 trials), while the precognitive series, in which Dr. Marchesi made his guesses for packs that were to be shuffled and set up a day later, consisted of 110 runs (2,750 trials). The subject sent his lists of guesses at the end of the last series to Duke University.

The results of none of the series taken separately were anywhere near significance, but, on the grand total of 354 runs (8,850 trials), there was an excess of hits on the target card of 89, which is equivalent to 2·37 standard deviations, and corresponds to odds against chance of about 50 to 1.

These results, therefore, being of only borderline significance, are far from conclusive.[8]

Both the runs and segments showed middle salience, but in neither case was it significantly above the chance level. Nor was there any significant covariance between RSR and SSR, which was such a striking feature of the earlier experiment.

In Jugoslavia psychical research was, according to Dr. Marchesi, at this time frowned upon by the authorities, and it required no little courage on his part to contend successfully against the many obstacles put in his way.

## Distance Experiments with Drawings

In experiments at a great distance it would appear that the transmission of material such as drawings, to which the guesser is able to make a free response, has generally been more successful than attempts with cards or numbers, where the subject's choice is very restricted. We have already given an account of Carington's* successful group experiments with pictures pinned up in a room at Cambridge. In these tests 68 of the guessers were in Holland, another 31 in Edinburgh, and 12 as far away as Duke University in North Carolina. It is of interest to note that the highest rate of scoring was achieved by the small batch in North Carolina, who were the farthest from Cambridge. It will be recalled that the final odds against chance for these experiments were given by Carington as approximately 7,000 to 1.

## The Austin-Dallas Experiments[9]

Another very successful experiment with drawings was carried out in 1940 by a young physicist, Mr. J. H. Rush, of Duke University, at that time working for his Ph.D. degree, and Mrs. A. Jensen, who was a resident of Dallas in Texas. In 1938 both had been unsuccessful in ESP tests with Zener cards. The new experiments were conducted between April and August 1940, with Mr. Rush in Austin, Texas, and Mrs. Jensen usually at Dallas, 200 miles away. In certain of the tests, however, Mrs. Jensen was 500 miles from Austin. The experiments took place on four successive evenings each week between 10.30 and 11 p.m.; for the first quarter of an hour Mr. Rush was the sender and Mrs. Jensen the receiver, but during the last fifteen minutes the roles were reversed. Each person, when acting as sender, drew a sketch of a simple object such as a flower-pot with a red tulip in it, or a drawing of a bottle labelled 'Conc. Acid Nitric, $HNO_3$'; or occasionally the target was verbally specified by such a phrase as: 'I am sending you the *moon*.'

Each sender used what appealed to his fancy at the moment, and a weakness of the procedure was that the targets—unlike those of the Carington tests—were not chosen at random. At the end of each week's work Mr. Rush and Mrs. Jensen exchanged their sheets of drawings and the responses by post. In sending, Mr. Rush tried to hold in his mind a clear visualization of the test object, at the same time 'willing' that it should reach the percipient. In receiving, Mr. Rush often sat in darkness, made his mind a blank, and waited for impressions to develop in

* VI, 22.

his mind's eye. He confessed that his chief difficulty was to prevent himself from interfering by conscious reasoning with the autonomous growth of the first vague imaginings that entered his mind.

Mrs. Jensen was unable to describe her subjective state with any clarity, but insisted on the necessity for relaxation and a certain focusing of attention during the experiments.

On some occasions the receiver failed to get a response, or was prevented from participating in the test, but, altogether, there were 50 trials in which the receiver produced either a sketch or an unambiguous verbal impression. In 21 of these 50 trials the transmitter was Mrs. Jensen, and in the remainder, Mr. Rush.

Mr. Rush copied the drawings and targets on to index cards which were sent to Duke University. Two had to be discarded, and the remainder were divided chronologically into twelve groups of four target sketches and the four responses to these targets.

Judges, who did not know which response was intended for which target, were asked to match in order of resemblance each response against each of the four targets in the group, and then again each target against each of the four responses. According to the degree of similarity, a 'weight' was accorded to each matching, these weights ranging from 1 to 4. The weights assigned to each of the two matching operations, 'targets against responses' and 'responses against targets', would have a total chance expectation of 10, i.e. of 20 for both operations. When evaluated by means of 'Student's' $t$-test, the odds against the hypothesis that the observed resemblances between target and response were due to chance worked out at 500 to 1.

The two sets of judgments involved in the matching showed a correlation of $+0.67$, which indicates fairly good agreement ($P = 0.02$).

It is very interesting to notice that the great majority of the resemblances were similarities of *form* rather than of content or meaning. In a single instance—that of the tulip in a flower-pot—Mrs. Jensen actually sketched an unmistakable flower-pot with a two-leaved flower growing in it, but in most other cases the actual concept eluded the receiver, who obtained only a more or less striking impression of the geometrical line or shape of the original. For example, when the target was a pair of spectacles, Mrs. Jensen drew a child's train with two *oval* wheels. For a many-toothed gear wheel she drew a number of conical outlines like inverted V's. For a watch with a concentric circle on its face she drew what looked like a row of four rifle targets with rings, together with a curved piece of chain.

It would seem as though what the percipient received was a fragmentary impression of shape, to which her conscious mind gave a wrong interpretation, and this in turn prevented the full development of the image in her mind's eye. This tendency to register the form rather than the meaning was a marked feature in the Usher and Burt experiments (Chap. II, p. 19). In the present tests the almost exclusive preoccupation with line and shape makes less serious the non-random method by which the targets were selected. Strictly speaking, we cannot call this a laboratory experiment, but the results were evaluated by a sound scientific procedure, and there is no reason at all to suspect the good faith of the two persons concerned in the actual conduct of the tests.

## Distance Experiments with Mrs. Stewart

### (1) TESTS OVER THE TELEPHONE

It was clear that the American experiments over long distances with Zener cards had achieved only a meagre and limited success, and it seemed, therefore, worth while to try similar experiments with Mrs. Stewart, in order to obtain, if possible, more conclusive evidence. As a beginning, we thought it wise to try first an experiment over the telephone, during which she would still be able to hear the experimenter's voice calling out the serial numbers 1–25.

At Sittings Nos. 24, 25 and 26 the sender was in the house of Mrs. Y. Hales which was situated about 100 yards away, as the crow flies, from Mrs. Stewart's house in Marchmont Road. For the first test, held on 22nd May 1946, the screen was not available, and Mrs. Y. Hales, the agent, sat with her five cards in the hall at a small table opposite S.G.S. F.B. stood at the telephone, three feet away from the table. The experiment was of the TTN(30) type, and, before each sheet, S.G.S. went out of the hall, and F.B. turned his back while Mrs. Hales shuffled the cards, looked at them for the prescribed 30 seconds, and laid them faces downward in a row. She then touched their backs as S.G.S. showed her the random numbers. As S.G.S. showed each random number, F.B. paused for half a second, and called the serial number into the telephone. Mrs. Stewart sat alone in her own house, holding the telephone with one hand, and writing down her guesses with the other. Mrs. Hales also acted as (TK). At the end of eight sheets the experimenters returned to Mrs. Stewart's house, and the results were decoded and checked by F.B., Mrs. Hales and S.G.S. all sitting at the same table.

The experiment was a failure, as the score on the target was only 83/400, as compared with the chance expectation of 80.

Lack of success was possibly due to the fact that (P) had to manipulate the telephone herself as well as record her guesses, and this may

276

have produced some mental disturbance. This conjecture is supported by the subsequent experiments, which were very successful.

At the second test on 29th May 1946, Mr. L. A. Rozelaar was the agent sitting in Mrs. Hales's house behind the screen with the five cards in the box as usual. S.G.S. was (EA), and Mrs. Hales, sitting about three feet away from the screen on the same side of it as S.G.S., called the serial numbers into the telephone as the random number cards were presented to Mr. Rozelaar. On this occasion F.B. held the telephone in Mrs. Stewart's house and Mrs. Stewart, 8 feet away, heard each serial number called by Mrs. Hales, and recorded her guess. As she did so, F.B. called 'Right' into the telephone. At the end of sheet No. 8, the experimenters and agent returned to Marchmont Road with the sheets of random numbers. The decoding and checking was done as follows: S.G.S. read aloud Mrs. Stewart's guesses, checked by Mr. Rozelaar, while F.B. decoded the guesses and entered the figures, checked by Mrs. Hales. The score on this occasion was 103/400 (critical ratio = 2·88).

At the third and last telephone experiment, held on 12th June 1946, Mr. Rozelaar was again the agent, seated behind the screen with the box and cards in Mrs. Hales's house. S.G.S. acted as (EA), but this time Mrs. Hales sat on the stairs with the telephone, *ten* feet away from Mr. Rozelaar. This was carefully measured by S.G.S. before leaving the house. As before, F.B., in the house at Marchmont Road, stood with the telephone at a distance of 8 feet from Mrs. Stewart, and held the instrument so that she could hear the serial numbers. As she wrote down her guess, F.B. called 'Right' into the telephone. Sheets 1–4 only were devoted to this type of experiment, and the decoding and checking was done at Marchmont Road. As on the previous occasion, S.G.S. read aloud (P)'s guesses, checked as he did so by Mr. Rozelaar, while F.B. decoded and entered the figures, checked in his turn by Mrs. Hales. The score this time was 60/200; the odds against this score being due to chance are 2,000 to 1. S.G.S., in his Myers Memorial Lecture,* reported inaccurately that in the last two tests Mrs. Stewart was 10 feet away from F.B.'s receiver. At the time of the lecture F.B.'s chronicle was not available, but F.B. afterwards assured S.G.S. that the distance on both occasions was 8 feet.

On the total of 1,000 trials for the three telephone experiments (P) scored 246 hits. The odds against her getting such a result by chance are about 3,400 to 1.

It is of great interest to observe that on the last occasion, when the distance between agent and telephone receiver was increased from 3 feet to 10 feet, the rate of scoring was even higher than in the second

* XV, 10.

experiment. Indeed, with (A) and (P) at distances of 10 and 8 feet respectively from their telephones, the score obtained (60/200) represents Mrs. Stewart almost at her best. This is quite contrary to what one would expect if unconscious whispering by the agent was the source of her success. It is well known that whispers, even when audible and quite distinct, are extremely difficult to get over a telephone. But when the whisperer is 10 feet away from the receiver into which another person is bellowing serial numbers, and the person who tries to pick up the whisper is 8 feet away from her instrument at the other end of the line, can one regard the whispering hypothesis as anything but a fanciful absurdity invoked only by those who will go to any lengths to discredit extra-sensory perception?

## (2) THE CAMBRIDGE-RICHMOND EXPERIMENTS[10]

Our first series of long-distance experiments, in which the agent was at Cambridge and the percipient at Richmond, Surrey—a distance of more than fifty miles—was a failure, for which, however, some fairly obvious reasons may be suggested. The tests were arranged with the assistance of Mr. C. E. M. Hansel, at that time secretary of the Cambridge University Society for Psychical Research. Synchronization was effected by means of the 7 p.m. time signal (B.B.C. Light Programme) and the use of stop-watches. The material of transmission consisted of the initial letters C, F, H, K, T of the names of the five animals, camel, fox, horse, kangaroo and tiger, printed on five cards taken from a lexicon pack. Before each sitting, Mr. Hansel, in Cambridge, filled in the A-columns of four of our ordinary scoring sheets with random numbers 1 to 5 obtained in the usual way from tables. Four sheets, or 200 guesses, were done at each of eight weekly sittings.

The method by which the experiment was conducted at the Cambridge end was similar to that described in Chapter XII, p. 205, except that it was not necessary to separate the agent (A) and the experimenter (EA) by a screen. At least three persons were present at each test. These were the agent, who looked at the cards, the time-keeper, who called aloud the serial numbers 1–25 at intervals of two seconds and the experimenter, who indicated to (A) which card he was to lift and look at. On some occasions an observer was also present. The five lexicon cards were laid in a row before the agent, and opposite each card was placed a small card bearing one of the digits 1–5; the small cards were so placed that the agent saw them in increasing numerical order, counting from left to right. (EA) was provided with the list of random numbers and with a ruler, with which he pointed to the number of the card which he wanted the agent to lift and look at momentarily.

At the commencement of each sitting, the agent shuffled his five cards, and laid them faces downward in a row before him. It was arranged for 'zero' time to coincide with the last pip of the time signal. The experimenter had his finger on the first random digit of his first sheet, and at zero plus 60 seconds he indicated with his ruler the card the agent was to lift and look at. The experimenter then lowered his finger to the second number on the list, and at zero plus 62 seconds he pointed with his ruler to the card which corresponded with the second number. Thus the cards were exposed at intervals of two seconds, and the agent gazed at the initial letter for a little under two seconds before letting the card fall back into its place. At the end of the 25th exposure, there was an interval of 10 seconds, and when the seconds pointer of the watch had reached 60 again, the experimenter indicated the first random number in the second column of his sheet, and the exposures were made at intervals of two seconds. There was thus a 10-second interval between columns and between sheets. At the end of the fourth sheet the experimenter or agent recorded on his first scoring sheet the order of the five cards, which had remained unchanged during the experiment, thus:

$$\begin{array}{ccccc} T & H & F & C & K \\ 1 & 2 & 3 & 4 & 5 \end{array}$$

The lists of random numbers were in triplicate. One copy was posted to S.G.S. as early as possible after the experiment, and another to Professor C. D. Broad, while the third was retained by Mr. Hansel.

At the Richmond end of the experiment Mrs. Stewart was provided with scoring sheets already numbered 1–8, each sheet being triplicated by means of pages of carbon paper that had been placed between the sheets. At zero plus 60 seconds S.G.S. called aloud 'One', and Mrs. Stewart wrote down in the first space of the G-column of her first sheet the letter she thought the agent was looking at. At zero plus 62 seconds S.G.S. called 'Two', and Mrs. Stewart wrote down another letter in the appropriate cell. In the 10-second interval which followed the end of the 25th exposure she was warned, 'Get ready for the next column', or 'Have the next sheet ready', as the case might be.

A few minutes after the completion of the fourth sheet (200 guesses), Mrs. Stewart, by way of comparison, was asked to carry out a 'control' experiment of another 200 trials with Mrs. M. Holding as agent. The two were in adjoining rooms, the door between them being slightly ajar to facilitate hearing. In the control experiment S.G.S. acted as (EA), and as usual was separated from (A) by the screen with the aperture, at which the random numbers were presented at normal rate. The chief object of this control experiment was to discover whether or not Mrs. Stewart's faculty was working on this particular day.

At the end of the checking of the results of the control experiment S.G.S. left the house, and posted in the first box on his way to the station one copy of Mrs. Stewart's guesses to Mr. Hansel and a second copy to Professor Broad, retaining the third himself. The checking of results in the distance experiment was thus done independently by S.G.S. and by Mr. Hansel. The random number sheets were usually received by S.G.S. from Mr. Hansel by 5 p.m. on the following day.

At the last two of the eight sittings the interval between successive exposures was, by arrangement with Mr. Hansel, increased from two seconds to three seconds, with an interval of 45 seconds between each two columns of 25 trials.

F.B. was prevented by pressure of work from attending any of the sittings but he re-checked all the results afterwards.

## The Conditions of the Experiments

We shall now describe the conditions of the eight experiments.

All the Cambridge sittings were held at 59 Park Street, the lodgings of Mr. Hansel, and the Richmond sittings as usual at 18 Marchmont Road.

For the first test, on 21st January 1949, the agent was Mr. V. Idelson, and neither the name of the agent nor the precise location of the experiment in Cambridge was known either to Mrs. Stewart or to S.G.S.

For the second test on 28th January 1949, owing to Mr. Idelson's failure to put in an appearance, the agent had to be Mrs. Molyneux, Mr. Hansel's landlady, but this change was unknown to anyone present at Richmond at the time of the experiment.

Before the third experiment on 4th February, Mrs. Stewart was told that the agent would be Mrs. Molyneux, and was also given the address at Cambridge. In addition she was provided with a photograph of Mrs. Molyneux which was placed in view on the mantelpiece during the experiment for (P) to look at if she so desired. At the fourth, fifth and sixth experiments Mrs. Molyneux was still the agent, and her photograph remained on the mantelpiece in Mrs. Stewart's house. A few minutes before the fifth experiment on February 17th, Mrs. Stewart was shown a photograph of the card-table at Cambridge with an old violin resting on it.

Before the sixth experiment on February 24th, (P) was provided with a detailed sketch of the room at 59 Park Street, and a written description of the manifold objects in this room. In these, however, she appeared to take little interest. Nor did she often lift her eyes to the picture of Mrs. Molyneux.

The object of this progressive enlightenment of Mrs. Stewart with regard to the conditions which obtained at Cambridge was to put Whately Carington's association theory of telepathy to the test.

Carington* supposed that mental events such as ideas and images exist in their own right, and are not synonymous with chemical and electrical events which take place in human brains. He looked on a mind as consisting of a large number of elementary constituents—sense data and images. Images are of the same nature as sense data, only less vivid and constant, and Carington* used the word 'psychon' to cover both sense data and images.

Certain tensions and relations exist between the members of a psychon system, and this is what we mean when we say that the system is conscious. Those groups of psychons in which tensions are particularly strong at a given instant would constitute the normal consciousness of the mind, while the more quiescent groups would constitute its subconscious.

Carington supposed that the subconscious psychon systems of different minds have no relation to physical space, and that they form one large system or common mind. This concept of an all-embracing subconscious mind composed of individual minds is, of course, an old one which goes back to the mysticism of ancient India, but Carington made it sound more plausible in a scientific sense by basing it on Bertrand Russell's atomic theory of consciousness.

Carington next* assumed that the laws of association of ideas operate within the common subconscious mind just as they do in individual minds. In a telepathy experiment the agent or sender associates the object he is trying to transmit with the general idea of the experiment. This idea of the experimental set-up is, however, also present in the mind of the distant percipient or receiver. This mutual idea is therefore likely by association to conjure up from the common subconscious into the consciousness of the guesser the impression which the agent is trying to transmit.

Now Carington* suggested that the more the agent and percipient share ideas associated in the agent's consciousness with the object to be transmitted, the better the experiment ought to succeed.

If the theory is true, we ought to find that when we provide the percipient with more and more of the images and ideas with which the object to be transmitted is linked in the agent's mind, the more likely it will be that one or other of these ideas will call up the object by

* XIV, 1.

association into the percipient's conscious mind. Suppose, for example, that the agent is trying to transmit the idea of a rabbit. He is perhaps looking at a toy rabbit, and near it on the table is a bottle of medicine. The two objects become temporarily associated in his mind, and also, according to Carington, in the larger subconscious formed by the psychon systems of agent and percipient. If, therefore, we provide the percipient with a similar bottle of medicine, this ought to call the idea of 'rabbit' into his conscious mind. And if the rabbit is associated in the agent's mind not only with the bottle but with, say, a pair of spectacles lying on the table and an orange, and we arrange for the percipient to have these objects before his eyes, then there ought to be a still better chance of his thinking of 'rabbit'.

It was for this reason that we provided Mrs. Stewart first with a photograph of the agent, then with a photograph of the violin which rested on the card-table at Cambridge, and finally with a detailed sketch of the other objects in the room.

We must inform the reader without delay that the device did not succeed. We did not find Mrs. Stewart's score rising from the levels of chance into the higher regions of significance. It began at chance level, and remained there during the eight experiments. But it would seem to us that association might have little chance to work in cases like the present when the symbols focused by the agent are being changed every two or three seconds. After, say, a hundred cards have been called, it is difficult to believe that association would have much efficacy in causing the percipient to think of, say, a fox in preference to any other of the five symbols. The violin on the card-table would have forged associative links in the agent's mind of equal strength with all five animal names. When the agent is concentrating for some minutes or hours on a single object, the association theory becomes more plausible.

It might, however, be worth while to try an experiment in which five *different* objects, one allotted to each of the card-symbols, were presented to the agent at the same time as the corresponding cards, and in which these same objects were presented in the same order to the guesser. It might give association a better chance to work. Yet if highly successful results can be obtained in card-guessing experiments carried out at a rapid rate, so that association can scarcely be a factor of much importance, this would seem to throw serious doubt upon the truth of Carington's theory.

But there are doubtless other influences, quite as potent as contiguous association, which govern the recall of images from the subconscious. The ideas which emerge most frequently into our conscious minds are those around which our emotional interests are centred. If we see a tall church spire, that is associated in our minds with a great many things—with church bells, religious services, English history, and so on ; but if we happen to be enthusiastic mountaineers we are more likely to think of the Matterhorn than of any of these. This suggests that we might choose for our agent a person with five dominant interests which were also interests of the percipient, and employ cards bearing symbols representative of those interests.

## Résumé of Results

After the sixth experiment S.G.S. suggested to Mr. Hansel that a change of agent seemed advisable, since Mrs. Stewart had been unsuccessful with Mrs. Molyneux. Accordingly, for the last two experiments on March 4th and March 11th, Mr. J. C. Reynolds was the agent. S.G.S., however, did not know the name of the new agent until after the seventh experiment, and it was not told to Mrs. Stewart at all.

The scores for the eight experiments of 200 trials each were : 31, 31, 40, 39, 35, 43, 39, 40. These give a total score of 298/1,600, a result which is 22 below chance expectation and of no significance (CR = −1·38).

There is, however, little doubt that Mrs. Stewart's faculty was functioning on at least four of the eight occasions in the control experiments with Mrs. Holding as agent in the adjoining room. The scores for the eight control tests of 200 trials each were : 53, 53, 55, 45, 49, 43, 47, 54. The total score is 399/1,600, which is 79 above chance expectation (320), and corresponds to a critical ratio of 4·94, with odds against chance of about a million to 1.

It is clear, then, that Mrs. Stewart succeeded with Mrs. Holding, but failed completely with the three Cambridge agents. One obvious and probably vital difference between the Cambridge-Richmond tests and the control tests with Mrs. Holding lies in the fact that, whereas Mrs. Stewart had already met Mrs. Holding in the autumn of 1947 and liked her, she had made no personal contact whatever with any of the Cambridge agents or with the experimenter, Mr. Hansel. Then there was the unfortunate sudden change of agent after the first experiment, which was not anticipated by the Richmond group. It is true that Mrs. Molyneux was agent for four sittings in succession, but she may have been a very bad agent. Again, when Mr. Reynolds was substituted for Mrs. Molyneux at the seventh sitting, no one at Richmond knew even his name.

But quite apart from any question of the agent, there is another factor which may have completely disrupted this series of experiments. By an unfortunate oversight the experimenters omitted to test the two stop-watches for synchronization. S.G.S. subsequently discovered that, unless the watches are of the highest quality, one watch may gain or lose on the other by as much as two or three seconds in the interval of twelve minutes, or thereabouts, occupied by the experiment. This means that the agent and percipient may have been quite out of step. There were, however, no significant −1, +1, −2 or +2 displacement scores, though on a single occasion, one column showed a total of 13/24 precognitive (+1) hits.

It seems clear, then, that the conditions at the Cambridge end of the experiment were distinctly unfavourable for success. From the start, and throughout the series, neither Mrs. Stewart nor any other member of the Richmond group had made any personal contact with the Cambridge agents, and this may well have been the decisive reason why the experiment failed.

## (3) THE LONDON-ANTWERP EXPERIMENTS[10]
### (Sittings Nos. 109–14 inclusive)

When we learned that Mrs. Stewart had made arrangements to leave England for five weeks' holiday in Belgium in 1949, we decided to make the most of the opportunity by carrying out some long-distance experiments. Mrs. Stewart was due to leave on June 3rd, but she informed us that, during the first fortnight, she would be staying at hotels, where she might have great difficulty in obtaining suitable helpers or a quiet room provided with a wireless set. However, by June 17th she would be settled at the home of a friend, Mr. J. Beyleman, at Merksem, near Antwerp. We were assured that this gentleman was very interested in psychical research and could be relied upon, if given suitable instructions in writing, to carry out his task with the stop-watch. The time of year was rather unfortunate, since both F.B. and S.G.S. were engaged on other urgent work. F.B. himself was unable to attend any of the experiments, and S.G.S. could do so only at great inconvenience and sacrifice of time. Moreover, S.G.S. wasted a great many hours which he could ill afford in trying to obtain two stop-watches which synchronized efficiently over the twelve minutes which each experiment would occupy. After considerable trouble he found a pair of watches of good scientific make which, when tested repeatedly over a period of twelve minutes, differed from each other by approximately half a second. The watches were tested both before and after the experiments.

The failure of the Cambridge-Richmond[10] tests had impressed us with the importance of employing agents with whom Mrs. Stewart had succeeded brilliantly in the past, and with whom she was on friendly terms. We therefore decided to employ as agents Mrs. Yvonne Hales and Mrs. M. Holding, since both ladies had proved themselves first-rate senders for Mrs. Stewart. Mrs. Hales, a professional pianist, who was an intimate friend of Mrs. Stewart, had been a main prop of the experiments since 1945. Mrs. Holding had first written to S.G.S. in 1945, offering her services, but she did not visit us until the autumn of 1947, when on two occasions she acted as agent, but without success. At that time, however, Mrs. Stewart's powers were in temporary eclipse. It was obvious that Mrs. Stewart liked her and was attracted by her vivacity. Mrs. Holding came on a third occasion and posed for a photograph which appears in the printed Myers Memorial Lecture* of 1947. No sitting, however, was held on that visit. When, therefore, S.G.S. again invited her assistance in January 1949, Mrs. Holding was well acquainted with Mrs. Stewart. She immediately showed herself to be a successful agent, and became one of the most loyal supporters of the experiments. Regularly every Friday after a day's work in an office she travelled several miles to assist us. As an agent, we consider Mrs. Holding to be about on a par with Mrs. Hales.

It was decided that the first experiment should take place at 7 p.m. on 17th June 1949, and that experiments should thereafter be carried out at the same hour on each Monday and Friday evening until Mrs. Stewart's return to England. It was arranged that Mrs. Hales would be the agent on the Monday evenings, sitting in her house at 22 Denbigh Gardens, Richmond, about 100 yards away, as the crow flies, from Mrs. Stewart's home in Marchmont Road. By kind permission of Mr. and Mrs. W. Harwood, friends of Mrs. Holding, the experiments on Friday evenings were to take place at Mr. Harwood's flat at 71 Jermyn Street, London, S.W.1., and Mrs. Holding was to be the agent. Mrs. Stewart had never visited this address, though she had frequently visited Mrs. Hales's house.

Exactly 200 guesses were to be carried out each evening; it was felt that the customary 400 would impose too great a strain on the experimenters.

It was next decided that there would be a three-second interval between successive calls. S.G.S. would take charge of the stop-watch at the London end, while Mr. Beyleman at Merksem would use the second watch, which had been carefully synchronized with the first. It was also resolved that we should revert to the old TLN method† in which the agent, having shuffled the five cards and laid them faces downward in a row, lifts each card on seeing the random number, glances at the face of the card, and immediately lets it fall back into its place in the row.

S.G.S. was to act as time-keeper (TK). He would call out the serial

* XV, 10. See also Plates 1, 2 and 4.
† This series was designated TLNA, where A stands for Antwerp.

numbers 1–25 at intervals of three seconds. A second person (EA), seated at the same table with (TK) and (A), would have in front of him five cards on which were printed in thick type the numbers 1, 2, 3, 4, 5. This person (EA) would have a finger of his left hand (or a small strip of card) resting just below the random number on the scoring sheet to be used at the next serial call. On hearing the serial call from (TK), (EA) would touch the corresponding number card with his right hand, and, on seeing this number, the agent would lift up, glance at, and let fall the card in the row which corresponded to this number, counting from left to right. After making his touch, (EA) would immediately slide his finger or piece of card one cell downwards on the scoring sheet, so that it rested just below the number next to be used. The interval between the 25th call of one column and the first call of the next was to be 18 seconds so that the timing of the calls would be made easier.

After preliminary practice, it was found that the two operations, (EA)'s touching of the number card and (A)'s lifting of the card bearing the initial letter of the animal's name, if smartly carried out, would together occupy less than two seconds.

In order to ensure that Mrs. Stewart in Merksem should not write down her initial letter before the agent had looked at her card, allowance had to be made for this two seconds' delay. Zero time was to be on the last pip of the 7 p.m. time signal on the B.B.C. Light Programme, and Mrs. Stewart was instructed to tune in to this programme several minutes before 7 p.m. At zero time both S.G.S. and Mr. Beyleman were to start their stop-watches. At zero plus 28 seconds, S.G.S. would call the serial number 'One', and Mr. Beyleman would call 'One' at zero plus 30 seconds. Mrs. Stewart was instructed to write down her first guess *immediately* she heard the serial call. If this occupied about one second, the conditions should ensure that she had not made her guess before the agent in London or Richmond had lifted her card. At zero plus 31 seconds S.G.S. called 'Two', while Mr. Beyleman called 'Two' at zero plus 33 seconds, and so on.

Everything depended on the carrying out of the operations smartly and without a hitch. With the exception of one not very important lapse, to be mentioned later, there was no hitch whatever at the London end. Exactly how the experiment went in Merksem we cannot say with certitude, but the successful results would suggest that it went reasonably well.

## The Experiments

For the first experiment on June 17th there were present Mrs. Holding

(A), Mrs. W. Harwood (EA), and S.G.S. (TK). The group assembled at 6.30 p.m. in the flat at 71 Jermyn Street, and some time was spent in preliminary practice. S.G.S. had previously practised a good many times with the stop-watch in order to familiarize himself with the readings. That day S.G.S. had prepared from tables four sheets of random numbers in ink in his own handwriting.

A few minutes before the experiment was due to start, the agent, Mrs. Holding, shuffled the five letter-cards four times in succession with her eyes shut, thus obtaining four 'codes', one of which was written on each of the four sheets of random numbers. The four codes were also copied in order on to a small card which was handed to the agent.

During the 18-second interval between the end of one sheet and the start of the next, Mrs. Holding changed the order of her five cards to agree with the code on the following sheet. The experiment went off without a hitch—the operations of calling, touching and lifting being carried out with perfect precision. When 200 calls had been made, (A), (EA) and (TK) signed their names in ink at the foot of every sheet of random numbers, and Mrs. Harwood wrote the date in ink under her name. This practice was rigorously adopted at each of the six experiments. Mrs. Stewart's guess sheets were each headed by her name and the date in ink in her own handwriting, and signed at the foot by the experimenter, Mr. J. Beyleman. Mrs. Stewart's guesses were all written down in ink, and she placed her four sheets in a strong gummed envelope together with an accompanying note, affixed a seal, and addressed the envelope to S. G. Soal, at Queen Mary College. The envelope was then dispatched by registered air mail to England. On receiving each envelope S.G.S. locked it up unopened in a drawer of his desk at Queen Mary College, from which it was never removed till it was taken straight to F.B.'s office for checking.

The second experiment was carried out on June 20th at the house of Mrs. Hales in Richmond, Surrey. On the day of the experiment four sheets of random numbers were dictated to S.G.S. from tables by Dr. H. S. Allen, a mathematician at Queen Mary College. On each sheet Dr. Allen wrote in ink 'Prepared by H. S. Allen, 20th June 1949', but the figures themselves were in S.G.S.'s handwriting in ink.

Mr. T. Hales on this occasion acted as (EA) and Mrs. Hales as (A). Preliminary practice was given to Mr. Hales. The experiment again proceeded without a hitch. Each sheet was signed at the bottom by T. Hales, Y. Hales and S. G. Soal; Mr. and Mrs. Hales wrote the date in ink under their signatures. During the experiment Mr. and Mrs. Hales and S.G.S. all sat at the same table, and, as in the previous test, Mrs.

Hales shuffled and laid out the five cards four times in succession before the start, in order to obtain her four codes, which she copied in order, on to a slip of paper. Mr. Hales used a slip of card to slide down the sheets of random numbers. The other details were as described in the planning of the experiments.

After the envelopes containing Mrs. Stewart's guesses for the first two experiments had been received by S.G.S., he removed them from his drawer at Queen Mary College at the first opportunity and took them straight to F.B.'s office in Burlington Gardens, together with the sheets of random numbers. The envelopes were first inspected and then opened by F.B. Each guess sheet was placed by the side of the corresponding sheet of random numbers on a table, and Mrs. Stewart's guesses (all written in ink) were decoded by F.B. into the numbers 1–5 by means of the code written on the sheet of random numbers, and these numbers were entered by F.B. in the empty guess-column of the sheet. S.G.S. took no part, but sat watching F.B. When all the (0) hits had been counted and ticked off, and the totals estimated for each experiment, F.B. took charge of both the random number sheets and those containing Mrs. Stewart's guesses. F.B. then took the sheets home to count the $(+1)$, $(-1)$, $(+2)$, and $(-2)$ hits at his leisure.

In the first experiment with Mrs. Holding as agent, the (0) score was 63/200, which represents Mrs. Stewart at her most brilliant.

For the second experiment with Mrs. Hales as agent it was 58/200.

Thus for the first two experiments we have a total score of 121/400, which corresponds to a critical ratio of 5·12, with odds against the result being due to chance of the order of two millions to one.

After such an unexpected result we were elated, and we sent Mrs. Stewart a congratulatory telegram and later a letter.

The third experiment was held at 71 Jermyn Street, S.W.1., on June 24th, on which occasion Mrs. Holding was the agent, while Mrs. Harwood acted as (EA), and S.G.S. took charge of the stop-watch. The procedure was the same in all details as in the first experiment but, immediately after we had finished, Mrs. Holding remarked that she felt sure the results would not be very good. She had a feeling that something had gone wrong, and when F.B. later came to check up the result, he found the total was only 46/200, a purely chance score.

## Change of Location of Agent[10,11]

Before she left England Mrs. Stewart had been informed that on Monday evenings the agent would be Mrs. Hales, located at 22 Denbigh Gardens, Richmond, and that on Friday evenings Mrs. Holding

288

would transmit from 71 Jermyn Street. We now decided, without telling Mrs. Stewart, to carry out the fourth experiment on June 27th in her own home at Marchmont Road, with Mrs. Hales still the agent. Since Mr. T. Hales could not be present on this occasion, we arranged for Mrs. Holding to come and act as (EA).

Four sheets of random numbers had been prepared from tables on the day of the experiment by F.B. in ink in his own handwriting, and on each sheet he had written in ink: 'Random numbers chosen by F. Bateman.' Each sheet of random numbers was signed by Mrs. Holding and Mrs. Hales, and the latter wrote the date in words under her signature. As usual, Mrs. Hales chose four codes before the start of the experiment by shuffling the five cards with her eyes closed. These codes were recorded at once on the scoring sheets and copied on to a small card. They were checked by Mrs. Hales.

When the sealed envelope containing her guesses for this sitting was received from Mrs. Stewart, the two envelopes for this and the preceding sitting were removed from the drawer at Queen Mary College at the first opportunity and taken immediately to F.B. at his office. As before, the results were decoded and entered by F.B. in ink on the random number sheets without any assistance from S.G.S.

The score for the fourth experiment was 59/200 as compared with the 58/200 obtained in the second experiment when Mrs. Hales was at 22 Denbigh Gardens. Clearly the slight change in location unknown to Mrs. Stewart did not affect the score.

As has been previously mentioned, the score for the third experiment was found to be only 46/200, which is a chance result.

We next decided, without informing Mrs. Stewart, to shift the fifth experiment due on July 1st from 71 Jermyn Street, S.W.1., where she expected it would be held, to the home of Mrs. Holding at 13 The Crescent, Dollis Hill Lane, London, N.W.2, which is at a distance of 5 miles from Jermyn Street. On this occasion Mrs. Holding was the agent, and Mr. Ray Whelan acted as (EA). Four sheets of random numbers had been prepared on June 29th in readiness for this sitting by Dr. Hugh Blaney, a mathematician of Queen Mary College. The figures were taken from tables and entered by Dr. Blaney in ink in his own handwriting. He had also written in ink on each sheet: 'A-list prepared by me—29/6/49. Hugh Blaney'. Neither Mrs. Stewart nor S.G.S. had previously visited the house at Dollis Hill. Mr. Whelan shuffled the five cards and made out the four codes to be used in the experiment a few minutes before we started. He was also asked to check the code records on the random number sheets. Of this day's work Mrs. Holding predicted: 'Not very good, about 50.'

Each sheet was signed by Mrs. Holding and Mr. Whelan, and the latter recorded under his signature in ink the date, 1.7.49.

Mrs. Holding's prediction was this time wrong, for when F.B checked the score, it was 63/200, and exactly the same as that obtained in the first experiment with Mrs. Holding sitting at 71 Jermyn Street. Again we see that change of location, even to a place that was completely strange to the percipient, had no effect on the score.

## A Long-Distance Opposition Experiment[10]

In Chapter XIV we have described a considerable number of tests in which two agents were in opposition (i.e. at each call they were looking at or focusing on different cards). For our sixth and final long-distance experiment we decided, without telling Mrs. Stewart, to try an opposition experiment with Mrs. Holding and Mrs. Hales acting as the two agents. As this last experiment was to fall on a Monday, July 4th, Mrs. Stewart would naturally suppose Mrs. Hales to be the agent, and to impress this belief on her mind, S.G.S. sent her a letter two days before the experiment, reminding her that the agent for July 4th would be Mrs. Hales.

The two agents were put into opposition by means of conflicting codes as described in Chapter XIV. Thus one agent might arrange her cards in the order H T K C F, while those of the other could be F C H K T. Consequently, when (EA) is pointing to the random number 3, say, the first agent will look at K and the second at H. The experiment was held at 22 Denbigh Gardens, the place expected by Mrs. Stewart.

Unfortunately, on this occasion there was no one present to act as (EA), and S.G.S. had to perform the functions of both (TK) and (EA). He managed this by reading off every three seconds a *random* number from the sheet instead of a *serial* number. To do this successfully, he kept the forefinger of his left hand just below the number which was next to be called. On hearing, say, 'Five', the agent simply lifted and looked momentarily at the fifth card in her row. The two agents sat apart at opposite ends of the table, with their sets of five cards arranged in conflicting codes. Before the start of the experiment, S.G.S. had shuffled the five cards four times in succession with his eyes shut, so as to obtain the four codes to be used by Mrs. Hales. From these four arrangements, conflicting codes were constructed for Mrs. Holding. Each agent was provided with a small card on which were written her codes for the four sheets. Change of code was effected as usual during the 18-seconds interval between sheets. To take account of the second which was saved by the use of this variation of the ordinary method,

S.G.S. made the first call at zero plus 29 seconds instead of zero plus 28 seconds.

One hitch occurred which might have been serious but for the prompt action of Mrs. Hales. At the commencement of sheet No. 2, S.G.S., in a moment of distraction, started to call the serial numbers 1, 2, 3. . . . Mrs. Hales called in a flash 'Read the numbers!' Her quick mind had realized what was happening. S.G.S. pulled himself up sharply, and came in all right on the fourth call with the correct *random* number.

The random number sheets for this experiment had been compiled by S.G.S. from tables, and entered in the A-columns in ink in his own handwriting. Each sheet was signed by S.G.S., and by both Mrs. Holding and Mrs. Hales, who entered the date 4/7/49 under their signatures.

Mrs. Stewart brought the guesses for the final sitting back with her to England, and handed them to S.G.S. in a gummed and sealed envelope on July 8th, on which date a sitting was held at her house. This and the previous envelope were as usual taken unopened to F.B.'s office where he decoded the guesses and entered the figures in the G-columns, watched by S.G.S.

The scores for the final (sixth) experiment were as follows:

| Agent | Score | Critical Ratio |
|---|---|---|
| Mrs. Hales | 56/200 | 2·83 |
| Mrs. Holding | 29/200 | —1·35 |

This is a typical result for an opposition test. The sensitive's mind was consciously directed towards Mrs. Hales, and apparently *rapport* was established with her, and not with Mrs. Holding, though the latter is normally almost as good an agent as Mrs. Hales.

At first sight the score of 29/200, obtained with Mrs. Holding, may appear abnormally low, but, as explained in Chapter XI, it is a logical consequence of the high score, 56/200, obtained with Mrs. Hales. In fact, the expected score with Mrs. Holding is not $\frac{1}{5} \times 200$, i.e. 40, but $\frac{1}{4}(200 - 56)$, i.e. 36. Thus the actual score with Mrs. Holding (29) is only 7 below chance expectation, as compared with a standard deviation of $\sqrt{\frac{1}{4} \times \frac{3}{4} \times 144}$, i.e. 5·2. Thus the negative deviation is not at all significant.

## Totals for the Six Experiments[10]

Considered as a whole, these six experiments are extremely significant. If we include the score of 29/200 obtained with Mrs. Holding as agent in the final test, we have on the (0) card a total score of 374/1,400 and hence a positive deviation from chance expectation of 94. This corresponds to odds against chance which exceed a hundred millions to one.

Strictly, the sixth experiment in which the two opposition scores are no independent, should be excluded from the grand total. If this is done the deviation on the total number of (0) hits in the first five experiment is equivalent to 7·03 standard deviations, so that the odds against chanc exceed $10^{11}$ to 1.

The critical ratios for the five categories are as follows; Mrs. Hold ing's opposition score is here included.

| Post-cognitive | | Direct | Precognitive | |
|---|---|---|---|---|
| (−2) | (−1) | (0) | (+1) | (+2) |
| −2·4 | −0·80 | +6·3 | +1·6 | −1·8 |

Apart from the (0) score the only score which approaches significanc is the post-cognitive (−2) score. This is a below-chance score, but, sinc it is chosen from four displacements, the odds against there being a least *one* of the four values as high as 2·4 do not exceed 15 to 1.

The reader may ask: How do these London-Antwerp scores, obtaine at a distance of 200 miles, compare with those which Mrs. Stewar produces when she and the agent are in adjoining rooms?

To answer this query, let us look at the scores she made on the si Monday evenings immediately prior to her visit to Belgium when Mr Hales in the next room was the agent. These scores, starting with th sitting on Monday 25th April 1949, and ending with that on Monda 30th May 1949, were: 62/200; 59/200; 58/200; 57/200; 35/150; 78/25C

The scores in the London-Antwerp series with Mrs. Hales as ager were: 58/200; 59/200; 56/200. Those with Mrs. Holding as agent were 63/200; 46/200; 63/200; 29/200.

It does not need a mathematician to decide, and correctly, that thes are scores of precisely the same order as those made by Mrs. Stewar with the agent in an adjoining room. In fact, if we omit Mrs. Holding opposition score of 29/200, the total scores for the long-range and short range tests are 345/1,200 and 349/1,200 respectively. Thus the result are almost identical. We can safely conclude, then, that when the dis tance between the agent and the percipient is increased to 200 mile Mrs. Stewart's rate of scoring is not affected. And we need not seriousl consider the whispering hypothesis since it clearly cannot explain th London-Antwerp experiments, and it would be absurd to postulate i specially in order to explain the results obtained with the agent in th next room.

Finally, we will take the opportunity to deal with a possible criticisn It might be suggested that, as Mrs. Stewart sent her records to S.G.S he could have steamed open the envelopes and resealed them again. H might thus have altered either Mrs. Stewart's lists of guesses or th figures in the lists of random numbers before he took them to F.B. t be checked. Now these lists of figures, as well as Mrs. Stewart's lists of initial letters, have been shown to five members of the Council of the Society for Psychical Research, and they all agree that both the letters and the figures are exceptionally clear and free from alteration. In order to obtain a total positive deviation of 94, S.G.S. would have had to make a very large number of alterations if Mrs. Stewart's hits had been due to chance, and it is quite impossible for him to have done this without leaving obvious traces.

Further, it will be recalled that for the fourth and fifth sittings of the series the random number lists are in the handwriting of F.B. and of Dr. Blaney respectively, and on every page the compilers made a statement in their own handwriting. In addition, each sheet is signed and dated by the two assistants taking part. The score on these two sittings alone is 122/400, which is the equivalent of 5·2 standard deviations, with corresponding odds of nearly five millions to one. To have *remade* these eight sheets so cleverly as to deceive the compilers and signatories, or to have remade Mrs. Stewart's lists of guesses, would, to say the least, have been a formidable feat of forgery.

Every figure in the lists of random numbers is perfectly clear, There is only a single number crossed out—a 'seven', written in error by Dr. Blaney, that was corrected to a 'four' and initialled by him. Mrs. Stewart's guesses are also perfectly clear without a single alteration. There were four or five decoding errors detected by F.B. on re-checking, and he has initialled each alteration in the G-column. Only one of these registered a direct hit where there was no hit before. Any person who ventures to suggest that S.G.S. could have altered the records before they were checked by F.B. will find it difficult to make his case, since both the compilers of the lists and Mrs. Stewart would testify that there has been no tampering with their records or signatures. Nor would it be wise for such a critic to suggest that F.B. and S.G.S. were in collusion, since there is the high-scoring 'Blaney' record (63/200) to be disposed of as well as the indubitable signatures on every sheet of the persons who assisted at the experiments.

In fact, the critic would be driven to assume that S.G.S. was in collusion with Mrs. Stewart, who herself was in collusion with Mr. Beyleman. But as Mrs. Stewart made extra-chance scores on dozens of occasions when such collusion would not have helped her at all, the assumption of a solitary act of conspiracy designed to produce evidence for long-distance telepathy would be far-fetched in the extreme.

So far as the results of the present experiment go, they suggest that distance up to 200 miles is no hindrance to success in a telepathy test. We do not know whether success would diminish, or disappear altogether at much greater distances. We certainly are not in a position to say that telepathy is independent of distance, for there has not been enough systematic experimental work to settle the question one way or the other.

The complete failure of the Cambridge-Richmond tests does suggest, however, that personality linkages are more important than a moderate spatial separation.

# CHAPTER XVII

# Miscellaneous Experiments with Mrs. Stewart

## (1) *Playing-Cards and Five-Symbol Cards*

### (Sittings Nos. 91, 93, 95, 97, 98, 100, 102, 104, 106, 108)

As we have seen in the early chapters of this book, much of the pioneer work in extra-sensory perception was carried out with the use of playing-cards, and we have discussed at some length the disadvantages which attend experiments with this type of material. (See Chap. III, p. 26.) Tests with playing-cards are, however, from a statistical standpoint, more sensitive than those with five-symbol cards. For the small chance ($p = 1/52$) that the card will be guessed absolutely correctly at any trial, makes the standard deviation for a given number of trials low compared with what it is with five-symbol cards, for which $p = 1/5$. If, therefore, the subject scored at the same intrinsic rate with playing-cards as with, say, Zener cards, he would need to do a much smaller number of guesses to obtain the same degree of significance.

It was of interest, therefore, to discover whether Mrs. Stewart would score at anything like the same intrinsic rate with playing-cards as she scored with the five animal cards.

### THE METHOD

For each evening's work the A-columns of four sheets were filled with random numbers 1-52 taken from Fisher's tables, and those of another four sheets with random numbers 1-5 compiled in the usual way. Code numbers 1-52 were arbitrarily assigned to each of the fifty-two playing-cards, and the codes were listed in a book. From a large stock of playing-cards, all of identical make and design, four packs of 50 cards each were made up—one for each of the four sheets—and the packs were ordered from top to bottom in accordance with the lists of random numbers. Each pack was put into an envelope, and the envelopes were numbered 1–4 to indicate the order in which they were to be used by the agent.

The plan was to alternate playing-cards with five-symbol cards in sheets of fifty. Thus on four of the ten evenings, sheets 2, 4, 6, 8 were devoted to playing-cards, and sheets 1, 3, 5, 7 to five-symbol cards. On the other six evenings the odd sheets were given up to tests with playing-cards.

Mrs. Y. Hales was the agent for both playing-cards and five-symbol cards, except at Sitting No. 98 on 25th April 1949, when she was absent and Dr. H. S. Allen was the agent.

Mrs. Stewart found it difficult at first to adapt herself to the playing-cards, and had to think before writing down her guesses. On the first four occasions (Sittings 91, 93, 95, 97), (P) herself controlled the timing, so that the agent did not lift the next card off the pack until Mrs. Stewart had called 'right'—the signal that she had recorded her guess. Thus at the first sitting she took sometimes as long as 127 or 128 seconds to get through a column of 25 guesses. As she became used to the play-ing-card symbols, she succeeded in reducing the time for a column to about 80 seconds, and, starting with Sitting No. 98, we adopted the following standard procedure. (EA) called out the serial numbers 1–25 at three-second intervals, timed by a stop-watch he was using. Before commencing a sheet of 50, (A) took the appropriate pack from its envelope, and laid it face downwards on the floor of the box. As (EA) called the serial numbers, (A) lifted off the cards one by one, looked at the value on the face of the card, and then deposited it face downwards on another pile. A column of 25 trials now occupied exactly 75 seconds.

At Sitting No. 98 and at subsequent sittings, the screen was in position 2, near the window (see plan of room), and (A) was on the window side of the screen. The alternate five-symbol sheets were the usual TTN(30) experiments.

Checking the playing-card tests was done as follows. One person read aloud Mrs. Stewart's guesses, giving the full title of each card-symbol. A second person called aloud the corresponding code number from the code-list, which he had in front of him. F.B. entered the code number of the guess in the appropriate cell of the G-column of the scoring sheet. The decoding was re-checked at leisure.

## THE RESULTS

In the 2,000 trials with playing-cards there were 78 guesses that were absolutely correct, compared with a chance expectation of $\frac{1}{52} \times 2,000$, i.e. 38·46. Mrs. Stewart thus obtained about double the number of hits she might be expected to get if only chance had been at work.

With $p = \frac{1}{52}$ the standard deviation is 6·14, and this gives a critical ratio of 6·44, with corresponding odds of more than 500 millions to one against the chance hypothesis. In this case, owing to the enormous significance of the deviation, there is no point in applying any correction to the error arising from the use of 'normal' tables, as we did in Coover's experiment.

But on the 2,000 trials with the five-symbol cards she scored 549 hits, which is an excess of 149 above the number to be expected by chance. The standard deviation in this case is 17·89, and we get a critical ratio of 8·33 and corresponding odds exceeding $10^{15}$ to 1. Magnificently as she has scored on the playing-cards, she has done even better with the five-symbol cards.

When a person guesses at cards, we might suppose that the actual score obtained consists of those hits which are the result of chance and those which are due to ESP. This hypothesis, however, presupposes a certain theory as to how ESP works. It assumes that certain of the cards are known completely by a faculty which we call extra-sensory perception, and that the others are not known at all, but that some of these are hits by chance only. The theory can be, and has been, queried. Indeed, it is easy to envisage an alternative possibility. It might be, for instance, that ESP is not confined to certain cards, but is operating at every guess throughout the run. If, for example, at each trial ESP told the percipient that the card was *not*, say, an elephant, this would increase his probability of guessing the card correctly from one-fifth to one-quarter. He would still score significantly above chance without *knowing* any of the targets completely.

But assuming that the *first* theory is correct, then, though we cannot say in any given experiment how many of the correct hits are due to ESP alone, we can yet estimate a 'probable' value for the number of hits due to ESP. This number we may call the 'intrinsic' score. In Appendix B, 12 we have shown how to calculate this intrinsic score, though, as we have hinted, the logic of the proceeding is full of flaws, and we use the formula only in default of a better method.

We may, then, define the percentage rate of intrinsic scoring, I, as

$$\frac{100 \times \text{intrinsic score}}{\text{Total number of guesses}}.$$

Applying the formula in the Appendix, we find from the above experiment that for the 2,000 five-symbol trials the intrinsic percentage is 9·31, while for the 2,000 trials with playing-cards it is only 2·02.

This means, roughly, that when Mrs. Stewart is guessing at the five animal initials (C, F, H, K, T) she *knows* by ESP about one card in every eleven, but when she is guessing at playing-cards, she knows only about one card in fifty.* In other words, her *true* scoring rate is about four times as high with the five-symbol cards as with playing-cards.

We have still to show that the difference between 9·31 per cent and 2·02 per cent, large though it appears, is not a mere sampling fluctuation. To do this, we estimate from the data themselves the observed variance per 25 trials of the intrinsic scoring percentages for five-symbol cards and for playing-cards. The variance for the five-symbol cards is relatively large, and works out at 139·7, but that for the playing-cards is comparatively small, being only 8·41.

Hence the variance of the difference of the two percentage rates is (139·7 + 8·41)/80, i.e. 1·85. The standard deviation of the difference is $\sqrt{1·85}$, i.e. 1·36. Hence the actual difference 9·31 − 2·02, i.e. 7·29, is equivalent to 5·3 standard deviations, and the corresponding odds against there being such a difference by chance are about ten millions to one. There can, therefore, be no question that Mrs. Stewart scored better with the five-symbol cards than with playing-cards, and it would appear that Dr. Rhine was completely justified in his innovation of substituting Zener cards for playing-cards in ESP experiments.

### THE SEPARATE ASPECTS OF PLAYING-CARDS[3]

When a person guesses at cards bearing five geometrical symbols or the initials of five animal names, he is either right or wrong, but, in the case of a playing-card chosen at random from a pack of 52, the guesser may be only partly right, as when, for instance, he says King of Spades for King of Hearts. Or he may get the value and the suit wrong, but guess correctly that the card is a red and not a black one.

The probability of his guessing correctly the value is 1/13, the suit 1/4, and the colour 1/2. Now an interesting feature of Mrs. Stewart's work with playing-cards is that her ESP faculty appears to cognize the card as a unitary object. In other words, when she is employing ESP and not merely guessing, she gets the card completely correct. There is no significant excess of cases when the card is correctly cognized, say, for colour or suit only, but missed as a whole.

The following simple analysis will make this clear. On her 2,000 trials Mrs. Stewart got the card completely right just 78 times, but some of these hits were produced by chance and not ESP. Using the method described in Appendix B, 12 with $p = 1/52$ instead of $p = 1/5$, we find that the most likely number of hits due to ESP is 40·3. These are necessarily right as regards colour, suit, and value, and it is on the remaining 2,000 − 40·3, i.e. 1,959·7 trials that we must base our chance expectations for colour,

* The actual number of *hits* on a pack of 50 playing-cards varied between 0 (19 times) and 3 (twice).

suit and value, taken separately. These expectations are: colour, 979·8; suit, 489·9; and value, 150·7.

Now on the whole 2,000 trials the actual hits were counted and found to be: colour, 1,024; suit, 516; and value, 176. After subtracting 40·3 from each of these totals, we obtain the following comparison of expected and observed values to the nearest whole number.

|          | Colour | Suit | Value |
|----------|--------|------|-------|
| Expected | 980    | 490  | 151   |
| Observed | 984    | 476  | 136   |

The deviations from chance expectation are +4, −14 and −15 respectively. The standard deviations for colour, suit, and value, are, to the nearest whole numbers, 22, 19 and 12 respectively, and so none of the observed deviations is anywhere near significance. Thus there is no evidence in the work of Mrs. Stewart that she wins any partial success on the separate components of colour, suit or value.

This, however, has not always been the case in successful experiments where material with two or more aspects is employed. An example to the contrary is the work of Brugmans,* which was discussed in Chapter II, p. 15. Here, it will be recalled, the subject sat in front of a kind of chess-board with eight columns and six rows of small squares. The columns were lettered A-H, and the rows were numbered 1-6, so that the experimenters in the room above could select any square at random by drawing a letter and a number from two shuffled packs. They then tried to influence the subject telepathically, so as to make him touch this particular square.

In 187 trials the percipient, Van Dam, obtained 60 complete hits, whereas the expectation was only $\frac{1}{48} \times 187$, or nearly 4. The subject, however, might choose the right row or the right column without hitting on the precise square. In all, he made 92 hits on the eight letters and 102 hits on the six numbers, but these include the 60 cases in which the square itself was correct. The probable number of hits on the square due to ESP works out at 57. This leaves us with 130 trials in which we should expect the letter to be right by chance about 16 times, and the number 22 times, whereas Van Dam scored 32 hits on the letters and 42 on the numbers. Thus his deviation from chance expectation on the letters was +16, and on the numbers +20. These are the equivalents of 4·2 and 4·7 standard deviations respectively, and are unquestionably significant. In this case, therefore, we have abundant evidence that, even when the guesser missed the precise square chosen by the experimenters, he was yet able to get very frequently either the row or column in which this square was situated.

* II, 6.

If, however, his ESP was never sufficiently accurate to locate the exact square, but could tell him only that the square was sometimes in a certain row or in a certain column, we should expect him to alight on the exact square by a combination of chance and telepathy $\dfrac{92 \times 102}{187}$, i.e. 50 times, but, as we have seen, he was completely successful no less than 60 times. There is some evidence, though it is not conclusive, that there was more than a chance association between the hitting on the rows and on the columns.

In Coover's* experiments with playing-cards, on the other hand, there is no evidence that, apart from the complete card hits, his subjects were scoring significantly on the separate aspects of suit or value.

## (2) *Two-Symbol and Five-Symbol Cards*

(Sittings Nos. 69–76, 78, 80, 82, 84, 86, 88)

Between 13th December 1948 and 28th February 1949, fourteen sittings were devoted to an attempt to discover whether Mrs. Stewart's intrinsic scoring rate was higher with a choice of five symbols than with a choice of only two. To make the other conditions as uniform as possible, we employed the same initial letters (C, F, H, K, T) of animal names in both types of test. In the two-symbol experiments it was essential to ensure that each of the five letters was presented to the agent the same number of times in order to eliminate the effect of differences in scoring rate among the five symbols themselves. We arranged this by dove-tailing into the four sheets of five-symbol tests ten blocks of 20 two-symbol trials, and using for each block a different pair of letters chosen from the ten possible binary selections of the five letters.

To cite an actual case, at Sitting No. 69, on December 13th, sheets 1, 3, 6, 9 were ordinary TTN(30) experiments with the usual five cards in the box, and the agent reshuffling the cards at the end of each sheet of fifty trials. Before the start of each *column* of sheets 2, 4, 5, 7, 8, Mrs. Stewart was told by (EA) the particular pair of letters the agent would use for that column. The actual pairs for the ten columns were: FC, KH, FT, HC, KT, KC, TH, KF, CT and FH, taken in this order. It will be seen that each letter occurs just four times. There were variations in the order of the ten selections on different occasions, and also in the arrangements for the sheets. For instance, on 31st January 1949, sheets 1, 3, 5, 7 were five-symbol tests and sheets 2, 4, 6, 8, 9 were two-symbol experiments.

The agent for ten of the fourteen sittings was Mrs. Hales, for two

* II, 1.

others Miss J. Edis, while Mrs. Holding and Mrs. S. A. Edis were the agents at one sitting each.

Before each experiment a random sequence of the digits 1 and 2 was chosen from Tippett's tables of random numbers. 200 digits chosen in this way were written in the first 20 cells of the A-columns of five sheets. A random sequence of the digits 1–5 chosen also from Tippett's tables was also written in the usual way in the 25 cells of the eight A-columns of the other four sheets.

The TTN(30) technique was employed in both five-symbol and two-symbol tests, and the only difference was that in the two-symbol tests, the agent shuffled his pair of cards and looked at their faces for 30 seconds at the start of each *column*.

At the first sitting of the series Mrs. Stewart told us that she did not expect to succeed at guessing only two symbols.

## THE RESULTS

On the 2,800 two-symbol trials there were 1,467 hits as compared with an expectation of 1,400. Thus we have a deviation of +67, which is the equivalent of 2·53 standard deviations and the corresponding odds against chance are about 87 to 1—a result of borderline significance.

On the 2,800 five-symbol trials there were no fewer than 702 direct hits, which gives an excess of 142 above the number chance might be expected to produce. The critical ratio is 6·71, and the odds against chance are more than $10^{10}$ to 1.

The intrinsic percentage rates for two-symbol and five-symbol tests are 4·78 per cent and 6·34 per cent respectively. But the difference between the two intrinsic rates of scoring is not in the least significant. The variance of $I_2$, the intrinsic percentage for two symbols, is very large, and works out at 713·1 per 25 trials, while that for $I_5$ the intrinsic percentage for five symbols, is only 103·6 per 25 trials. Hence the variance of the difference of the two percentage rates is $(713·1 + 103·6)/112$, i.e. 7·29. This gives a standard error for the difference of 2·7, which is greater than the observed difference (6·34 − 4·78), i.e. 1·56. Indeed, although only borderline significance is shown by the results of the 2,800 trials with two symbols, the probable number of hits due to ESP is 134, which compares favourably with 177, the probable number obtained by ESP with the five symbols. It is quite possible that a much larger number of trials would reveal that the five-symbol cards show a significant superiority over the two-symbol cards, but on the present scale of the experiment the very large variance of the two-symbol trials completely masks any real difference that may exist.

Certainly the testing of ESP with only two symbols is, from a statis-

301

tical standpoint, a wasteful and insensitive method, and Mrs. Stewart, at any rate, found it almost unbearably monotonous.

## (3) *Distraction Experiments*

(Sittings Nos. 60, 61, 63, 66, 67)

Between 11th October and 6th December 1948, experiments were done to test whether Mrs. Stewart would do better when (EP) talked to her while she wrote down her guesses than when he preserved a grim silence. During sheets 1, 3, 5, 7 (P) and (EP) were both allowed to laugh and talk as much as they pleased, and (EP) tried to sustain an amusing conversation. On some occasions (P) dispensed with calling 'Right' after each guess. For sheets 2, 4, 6, 8 on the other hand, both (P) and (EP) remained silent during the 50 trials, except that (P) called 'Right'. That is, so far as (P) and (EP) were concerned, the atmosphere was formal and rigid during the 'even' sheets, but jolly and informal for the 'odd' sheets. Needless to say, the agent in the lounge was never allowed to speak during the presentation of the cards on any occasion. The informal experiments were known as TTN(30)D, and the formal ones as TTN(30)S, where D and S stand for *distraction* and *silence* respectively.

The same method was used at two other sittings, Nos. 64 and 65, but, as agents in opposition were employed in these, we have thought it best to exclude them from the count. The persons who acted as (EP) for this series were F.B., Dr. Brendel and Miss J. Edis, all of whom are good conversationalists. At Sitting No. 63 Dr. Brendel tried the effect of reading aloud to (P) from the *Daily Telegraph*, and he also read some poems; but Mrs. Stewart declared that she hated being read to, and this practice was discontinued. The agents employed in this series were Miss J. Edis, Dr. Allen, Mr. and Mrs. J. Hazell, Dr. Brendel and Mrs. Hales, each on a single occasion.

On the TTND or 'conversation' series the total score was 279/1,000, while that on the TTNS or 'silent' series was 268/1,000. Both results were highly significant, with odds against chance which exceed 500 millions to 1 in the first case and 5 millions to 1 in the second. But the difference of 11 between the two scores is not in the least significant. Perhaps, however, we ought not to have expected much from the experiment. Because Mrs. Stewart had been distracted and amused for $2\frac{1}{2}$ minutes, it was not likely that her spiritual mercury would fall to zero during the succeeding $2\frac{1}{2}$ minutes of formal silence. She may have been still enjoying the jokes of the last period or looking forward to the next spell of badinage.

What the experiment does seem to show is that distracting conversation does not interfere with the working of her ESP faculty, but this again was only to be expected since (P) makes no effort at concentration during her guessing. Like Shackleton she writes down her letters almost automatically without waiting for any visual image to enter her mind. But if involuntary whispering by the agent in the next room was the source of her success, we should have found a considerable falling off in the score when a person nearby was bombarding her with continuous conversation and bursts of laughter. The 'silent' condition ought to have been the more favourable for the picking up of faint whispers, but the actual results show nothing of the kind. Though the score on the total of 2,000 trials, D and S, is 547, with a critical ratio of 8·2, it is not possible to conclude that the attempt to amuse Mrs. Stewart had any effect on her ESP. It will be recalled that in the 2,000 five-symbol tests that were alternated in batches of 50 with playing-cards, there was an almost identical score of 549 direct hits, and in this case there were no special efforts by (EP) to sustain an interesting conversation. However, the comparison is complicated by the fact that in the latter series we were employing, almost exclusively, one of our best agents, Mrs. Hales.

## (4) *Experiments with Lead Screens*

(Sittings Nos. 22, 23, 34, 35)

It has often been suggested[1,2] that telepathy may operate through some kind of physical radiation which emanates from the brain of the agent and impinges on the brain of the percipient. The phenomenon of precognitive telepathy, were it fully established, would, of course, render the radiation theory very improbable, since in physics an effect can never precede its cause. There is plenty of evidence that thinking is accompanied by electrical disturbances within the cerebral cortex, but so far as we are aware very little is known about the emission of electromagnetic radiation by the human brain. And even were it demonstrated that, when we form mental images, complex wave-patterns are propagated into space, it would not be easy to understand how such patterns, impinging on another brain, could generate similar images that would be intelligible to the second brain. Moreover, millions of different patterns from countless human brains would all be hitting the brain of the percipient at the same time, and it is difficult to believe that this could result in anything but a chaotic medley of confusion. At present there are no reasons for the supposition that the brain contains anything analogous to a wireless receiving set. The truth is that our total ignorance of the correlation, if such there be, between cerebral activity and specific thoughts makes any wave-theory of telepathy an unprofitable speculation today. Before any progress can be made along these lines, we shall require a vastly more detailed knowledge of the patterns of electrical impulse which are produced in the brain when we perform definite types of mental operation. But we think it is a mistake to insist, as so many prominent writers on telepathy have done, that physical radiation theories are impossible or even absurd. Dr. A. J. Robertson[1] has pointed out that many of the stock objections such as the necessity for a code by which the percipient discovers the meaning of the wave-patterns which impinge upon his cortex, or the fact that telepathy does not appear to obey the law of inverse squares, are, upon analysis, not so insuperable as at first sight appears.

For instance, Robertson observes that physical and biological systems are known where the effect produced by a given stimulus does not depend upon the size of that stimulus, provided that it is above a certain threshold value. Thus, when a single nerve fibre is stimulated, the resultant electrical disturbance transmitted along the fibre is independent of the size of the stimulus. A decline in the intensity of the radiation would not necessarily imply any loss of intelligibility. Or again, there might be in the brain a receptor mechanism having a response that is proportional to the logarithm of the stimulus magnitude, so that a large decline in intensity of radiation would produce only a small change in the magnitude of the response.

And if there were some means by which wave patterns in the brain of the agent induced similar patterns in the brain of the percipient, such patterns might be interpreted by the latter without the use of any code.

Telepathy might, in its working, resemble that of a television set. Mental pictures constitute a universal language.

There are, however, serious objections to such arguments. In his recent book *The Living Brain* (Duckworth, 1953) W. Grey Walter[4] has shown that the energy output of the cerebral cortex would be pitifully inadequate for any radiation over long distances. Again, the beam would have to be narrowly focused since it has to produce a specific geometrical pattern on the percipient's cortex. But Lashley and others have shown that the cell count on the cortex varies enormously from one person to another. It is difficult, therefore, to see how the radiation pattern of the agent could tally very exactly with the reception area of the percipient. Further, assuming that a spatial pattern is transmitted, the wave front* must possess precisely the correct curvature and the

* We are to indebted to Dr. G. D. Wassermann for the arguments in the last paragraph.

receiver's brain must be orientated very exactly in relation to this wave front. And even if the radiated pattern is not spatial, but time-modulated, there is still the energy deficiency mentioned by Grey Walter.

## X-Ray Chamber Experiments

The screening experiments which follow can have but little scientific value, and we describe them merely for the sake of completeness.

Two experiments were carried out with Mrs. Stewart sitting inside the X-ray chamber of the Royal Free Hospital. At the first of these on 6th May 1946 (Sitting No. 22), there were present Dr. E. Ulysses Williams, O.B.E., the radiologist, and his assistant, Miss McCluskey. Mrs. Y. Hales was the agent, while F.B. acted as (EP) and S.G.S. as (EA). Mrs. Stewart sat with F.B. at a small table inside the X-ray chamber which has a casing of lead, 2 mm. thick, and four lead-glass windows. The rest of the party were outside the chamber, and the sliding panel which gave access was completely closed during the experiment. (P) sat about one foot from the front wall and three feet to her right was the only lead-glass window in this wall. (A) sat on the outside directly opposite (P) and three feet from the wall, so that the line joining their heads was perpendicular to the lead wall. (A) and (EA) sat at a small table on which rested the usual plywood screen and the box containing the five cards. Dr. Williams watched S.G.S. as he presented the random numbers at the aperture, and Miss McCluskey watched Mrs. Hales as she touched the backs of the cards in response to the random numbers. The method used was TTN(30), and the experiment was labelled TTN(30)X, where X stands for *X-ray room*. Mrs. Stewart shouted 'Right' after each guess.

At the end of eight sheets (P) and (EP) emerged from the chamber, and the latter handed S.G.S. (P)'s lists of guesses. S.G.S. read aloud Mrs. Stewart's guesses, checked by Dr. Williams, and F.B. decoded and entered the numbers on the random number sheets, checked by Mrs. Hales. The recording of the code after each sheet was witnessed by Miss McCluskey.

The total score was 116/400, and the corresponding odds against chance are more than 140,000 to 1.

At the next sitting (No. 23) on 15th May 1946, Dr. Williams was absent, but Miss McCluskey was present again. On this occasion F.B. was the agent, while Mrs. Hales acted as (EP) and S.G.S. as (EA). (P) and (EP) were again inside the closed chamber with the head of the former at a distance of one foot from the front lead wall in the same position as at the previous sitting. (A) was seated outside directly opposite (P) with his back to the wall and at about three feet from it.

The usual screen rested on a small table between (A) and (EA). The five cards were in the box as usual. A rubber screen impregnated with lead was pinned to the wall inside the chamber so as to be between the heads of (P) and (A). Miss McCluskey sat on the same side of the plywood screen as S.G.S. and watched him as he showed the random numbers at the aperture. The method used was TTN(30)X. Mrs. Stewart shouted 'Right' after each guess. At the end of eight sheets (P)'s guesses were read aloud by S.G.S. checked by Miss McCluskey, while F.B. decoded and entered the figures on the random number sheets, watched by Mrs. Hales.

The score on direct hits this time was 126/400, which gives odds against chance that exceed a hundred millions to one.

It is abundantly clear that the scores on these two sittings show Mrs. Stewart at her best, and that the wall of lead between (A) and (P) had no effect whatever on the results. On the other hand, the lead casing was only 2 mm. thick, and there may have been leakage through the lead glass windows, so that the experiment was not after all of much value. It did, however, demonstrate that Mrs. Stewart was able to produce her results in a strange place and under the observation of two careful witnesses.

## Experiments With a Single Lead Screen

In January 1947, S.G.S. was able to borrow, through the kindness of Col. Langley of the Lead Sheet and Pipe Manufacturers' Federation, six sheets of lead, each measuring three feet square and ¼-inch thick. These six sheets were piled against each other and packed into a wooden frame on a stand which Dr. Brendel had kindly constructed. The stand was provided with two handles, so that with some difficulty it could be shifted by two men. Thus a mass of lead 1½ inches thick was fixed in an upright position with two edges of the square horizontal.

This screen was first used at Sitting No. 34 on 27th January 1947, and Mrs. Stewart sat in the lounge close to the fire with her head at a perpendicular distance of five feet from the centre of the screen. On the far side of the screen and close to it was placed the card-table bearing the usual plywood screen and card box. The agent, F.B., sat with his head close against the centre of the lead screen, and on the other side of the plywood screen sat S.G.S. who showed the random numbers at the aperture. There were also present Mrs. Y. Hales (TK), Dr. Brendel, Mr. D. A. Stewart, Mr. D. Makgill and Mr. A. Stewart, but these were all seated near the fire, so that none of them could see agent or card box.

Five sheets only were devoted to this experiment, and the method

306

used throughout was TTN(30). The experiment was referred to as TTN(30)L, where L stands for *lead screen*. Decoding and checking were carried out by F.B. and Dr. Brendel. The direct score was 74/250, and the corresponding odds against chance are more than 6,000 to 1. There is no doubt that the rate of scoring—7·4 hits per run of 25—is well up to Mrs. Stewart's normal level, and there is no evidence of any inhibition caused by the sheets of lead. There were, however, possibilities of reflection from objects in the room of any radiation emanating from (A)'s brain, so that the experiment cannot be regarded as conclusive in any way. Nor, of course, is there any certainty that the radiation, if there were any, would be absorbed by lead.

Sheets 6–8 on this evening were ordinary TTN(30) experiments with the lead screen removed. These tests were not, however, intended as a 'control' on the 'screened' tests, since, if such were our intention, we should have alternated the two types of experiment in batches of 50 trials in the usual way. We were curious to see whether a high score would be obtained with (A) and (P) separated by a distance of only 5–6 feet. In order that (P), sitting by the fire in her original position, should not be able to see the agent's face or the cards, (A) and (EA) changed places, so that Mrs. Stewart could, if she cared to look, see the random numbers and the agent's legs and feet under the card table.

The score 39/150 is above the chance expectation (30), but not significantly so. The most probable interpretation is that it represents a sessional decline on the previous high scoring, such as we frequently noticed with Shackleton on the last sheet or two.

At our next sitting, No. 35, on 3rd February 1947, the same lead screen was again used, but this time it was placed in the kitchen. Mrs. Stewart sat by the fire in the lounge with her head at a perpendicular distance of ten feet from the centre of the screen. Directly behind the screen was the card-table on which stood the plywood screen and card box.

Dr. Brendel, the agent, sat with the back of his head close against the centre of the lead screen while S.G.S., who acted as (EA), was on the far side of the plywood screen. Mrs. Stewart was sitting near the fire with her back to the lead screen but, as stated, ten feet away. There were also present Mr. D. A. Stewart, Mr. David Makgill and Mr. A. Stewart, all sitting in front of the fire. F.B., acting as (EP), sat by Mrs. Stewart and called 'Right' after she had recorded each guess. Sheets 1–5 were devoted to the TTN(30)L experiment. As in the previous sitting, decoding and checking were done by F.B. and Dr. Brendel. The direct score was 72/250, and the corresponding odds against chance exceed 1,700 to 1.

For sheets 6–8 the lead screen was removed, and the ordinary TTN(30) method was employed with Dr. Brendel still the agent. It should be added that throughout the evening the door between lounge and kitchen was slightly ajar. For the last three or four sheets Mrs. Stewart was doing a cross-word puzzle between columns. She said she was not feeling particularly tired. The score for sheets 6–8 was 33/150, which is a purely chance result. Thus we observe once more a curious decline after the removal of the lead screen.

However, if we combine the results of Sittings 34 and 35 and use the observed variance, we find that the difference $7 \cdot 3 - 6 \cdot 0$, i.e. $1 \cdot 3$, between the scoring rates per 25 trials for sheets 1–5 and sheets 6–8 is not nearly significant.

It would have been more satisfactory if the percipient had been enclosed completely in a thick lead chamber, but this was not possible, and the construction of such a chamber was scarcely a feasible project at the time.

## (5) *Experiments with Zener Cards*

For the last two sittings, Nos. 129, 130, with Mrs. Stewart we employed Zener cards instead of cards with names of animals. At this late period her guessing had fallen to the chance level, and in the hope that novelty would stimulate her faded powers we changed to the symbols used by Rhine, with which she had been very successful in 1936. The usual TTN(30) method was employed, and in recording her guesses Mrs. Stewart wrote O for circle, + for plus, R for rectangle, S for star, and W for wavy lines. In both experiments Mrs. Holding was the agent, and (P) sat in the kitchen with F.B. who acted as (EP) and (TK).

For 16th January 1950, the direct score was 86/400, and that for 23rd January 1950 was 78/400. These are purely chance results. Nor were any of the displacement scores significant.

# CHAPTER XVIII

# A General Survey of the Data

Between August 1945 and January 1950, 130 sittings were held with Mrs. Stewart. With the exception of the two experiments done at the Royal Free Hospital and the six sittings of the London-Antwerp* series, the work was carried out in her own home at Marchmont Road, Richmond, Surrey. Owing to the fact that both F.B. and S.G.S. were fully occupied by other professional work it was not found possible to carry out the experiments at very regular intervals. Thus in 1945 twelve sittings were held, twenty-one in 1946, in 1947 only twelve, while in the years 1948 and 1949 there were twenty-seven and fifty-six respectively; the last two experiments were done in January 1950. It will be seen that more than half the work was done in 1948 and 1949 during which period S.G.S. held the Perrott Studentship in Psychical Research at Trinity College, Cambridge. These were in fact our busiest years, and for months at a stretch two evenings a week were devoted to the experiments. Until the summer of 1947 Mrs. Stewart received no remuneration for her services, but in the autumn of that year she told us that her financial circumstances would not permit her to continue with the work without some payment for her loss of time. It was fortunate at this juncture that S.G.S. was awarded by the Central Research Committee of the University of London a small grant which was used to keep the experiments going, albeit at very irregular intervals. A larger sum, made available by the Perrott Studentship, enabled us to proceed at a quicker pace in the years 1948 and 1949.

Unfortunately, when we restarted work after the summer vacation of 1949, we found that Mrs. Stewart's scores had fallen to the chance level, and, though we continued for another thirteen sittings, she did not recover the ability to produce significant results. Only on one occasion, 31st October 1949, when Mr. Ritchie Calder, Science Editor of the *News Chronicle*† paid us a visit, did she achieve a borderline score of

* XVI, 10.
† Cf. *News Chronicle* 28th November 1949.

309

97/400 (odds about thirty to one against chance). This was a TTN(30) test in which Mrs. Holding was the agent. But this was apparently just a feeble flicker of a dying flame.

At the end of January 1950, both F.B. and S.G.S. felt that they could not afford to go on paying Mrs. Stewart with no expectation of any further positive results, and the experiments were reluctantly abandoned. Mrs. Stewart had maintained a high level of scoring for a period of four years, and neither Shackleton nor any American subject—not even the best subject of Martin* and Stribic—has kept the ball rolling so long. We have no explanation to account for this ultimate collapse of her powers. Even under the most favourable conditions, guessing at the names of five animals year in and year out must conduce to a soul-deadening monotony that can only end early or late as a 'sad mechanic exercise', bereft of all spontaneity. The marvel is not that Mrs. Stewart's ESP has for the time being disappeared, but that it lasted so long. Even if she never makes another significant score, her varied contribution to the study of telepathy remains unique and unrivalled by any other subject.

In the four years over which the experiments range there is a grand total of 50,300 calls. The term 'call' in this context means a single presentation of a random number by (EA). Thus when several agents focus at the same time on the same or different cards, only one call is counted. The above total comprises 'clairvoyance' as well as 'telepathy' tests, those done at 'rapid' as well as at 'normal' rate, and experiments with two-symbol cards and also with playing-cards and Zener cards.

## Telepathy Totals (Five-symbol Experiments)

In the grand totals which follow it has been considered advisable to leave out of the counts:

(a) all experiments in which two or three agents were in *opposition* since the scores of the different agents are not independent as explained in Chapter XIV, p. 234; (b) the TTN(30)E tests designed to eliminate the possibility of precognitive clairvoyance since the method of checking did not permit us to estimate displacement hits (Chap. XV, p. 257); (c) all experiments at the 'rapid' rate of calling (Chap. XII, p. 216); (d) all 'clairvoyance' tests (CTN) (Chap. XII, p. 209); (e) sheets 1, 3, 5, 7 of Sitting No. 56 and 2, 4, 6, 8 of 57 where several code arrangements were presented to the agent in rapid succession, i.e. TTND4(3) and TTND3(3) (Chap. XII, p. 213). All other five-symbol experiments are included, whether one or more agents took part simultaneously.

* III, 4, 5.

We are then left with a grand total of 37,100 (0) trials, and these yielded a score of 9,410 direct hits (i.e. hits on the (0) or target card) as compared with an expectation of 7,420. Thus we have a deviation of +1,990 and a critical ratio of 25·8. It is a little difficult to estimate accurately the odds against chance for such a large critical ratio, since the normal and binomial curves do not coincide very closely at the tail-end of the distribution, but, on an extremely conservative estimate, these odds must be of the order of $10^{70}$ to 1. We are indebted to Professor Evelyn Hutchinson[1] of Yale for the following useful comparison. He notes that if the *whole* of this work had been repeated *once every minute* during the entire history of the earth, which originated about three thousand million years, or $1·57 \times 10^{15}$ minutes, ago, it would still be fantastically improbable that results of the significance of those actually obtained would have been encountered by chance. If we were able to include the 'opposition' scores and the TTN(30)E experiments the significance would be even further enhanced, and the odds would then probably be in the neighbourhood of $10^{100}$ to 1. The 2,600 clairvoyance tests which gave only chance results would only slightly reduce the critical ratio.

## *The* (+1) *and* (−1) *Displacement Scores*

Corresponding to the 37,100 'target' or (0) trials considered above, there are 24/25 of this number, i.e. 35,616 (+1) trials, which yield a score of only 6,775 (+1) hits compared with 7,123·2, the chance expectation. This gives a *negative* deviation of 348·2, which is the equivalent of −4·61 standard deviations.

Thus Mrs. Stewart obtained far fewer precognitive (+1) hits than we should expect her to get by chance alone.

Similarly the 35,616 post-cognitive (−1) trials gave only 6,863 (−1) hits as compared with 7,123·2, the expected number. Here again we have a *negative* deviation of 260·2, which corresponds to a critical ratio of −3·45.

These below-chance deviations on the (+1) and (−1) cards are small in comparison with the tremendous positive deviation on the 'target' card, but they show, none the less, very significant trends and demand further investigation which will be undertaken later. (See Chap. XIX.) There is little doubt that the deficiency of (+1) hits is largely due to a strong tendency for (P) to miss the first trials of target doubles. Mrs. Stewart's average score on the 'target' or (0) card for the above 37,100 trials works out at 6·34 hits per run of 25 calls, and her 'intrinsic' scoring percentage (see Appendix B, 12) is 6·70 per cent. That is, she knows by

ESP nearly seven cards in every hundred on the average. This may seem not much to boast about, but, since the average is maintained over nearly forty thousand trials, it is, in reality, a tremendous achievement.

## The Agents

Including those who took part in the Cambridge-Richmond experiments, exactly thirty persons have worked in the capacity of agent with Mrs. Stewart. Her scores with fifteen of these, that is 50 per cent, showed positive deviations which, with each person, exceeded three standard deviations. If we assume a critical ratio of three as our criterion for a successful agent, we can say that Mrs. Stewart has been successful with 50 per cent of her agents as compared with 27 per cent observed in the case of Shackleton.

It should be pointed out, however, that of the thirty agents with whom she tried, thirteen attended only a single sitting and eleven of the thirteen acted as agent for only 200 calls. With three of the last eleven (P) reached our level of significance, and with two others she made scores of 55/200 and 53/200 (corresponding to critical ratios of 2·65 and 2·30 respectively). It is possible, therefore, that if Mrs. Stewart could have continued with a few of the people who came to only one sitting, the percentage of successful agents might well have exceeded 50 per cent.

In estimating her performances with individual agents, we have had to ignore all experiments with two or more agents in conjunction or in opposition. 'Split agent' experiments have been counted, since such experiments could not succeed unless both the agents showed ESP ability. We have also excluded (a) all tests with two or fifty-two symbols, (b) tests at 'rapid' rate, (c) experiments in which (P) wrote down her guesses in her own time,* (d) those in which several codes were presented to the agent in rapid succession, and (e) clairvoyance tests.

With the above omissions, there were eleven agents with each of whom Mrs. Stewart worked for a thousand calls or more. Their names and scores are given in the following table:

---

* In (c) we include the experiment of p. 214.

TABLE 9

| Name | Trials | Score | CR | Intrinsic percentage score |
|---|---|---|---|---|
| Hales, Mrs. Y. C. | 11,000 | 2,923 | 17·2 | 8·2 |
| Bateman, F. | 6,800 | 1,839 | 14·5 | 8·8 |
| Holding, Mrs. E. M. | 4,200 | 997 | 6·1 | 4·7 |
| Brendel, Dr. F. C. L. | 1,800 | 440 | 4·7 | 5·6 |
| Rozelaar, L. A. | 1,600 | 466 | 9·1 | 11·4 |
| Soal, Mrs. S. G. | 1,400 | 354 | 4·9 | 6·6 |
| Morgan, Dr. Louise | 1,300 | 353 | 6·4 | 8·9 |
| Kearney, R. A. M. | 1,200 | 287 | 3·4 | 4·9 |
| Whelan, R. H. | 1,200 | 290 | 3·6 | 5·2 |
| Edis, Miss J. | 1,000 | 279 | 6·2 | 9·9 |
| Molyneux, Mrs. | 1,000 | 188 | — | — |

The finest performance is undoubtedly that of Mrs. Hales with whom Mrs. Stewart maintained an intrinsic rate of 8·2 per cent over a grand total of 11,000 trials and during a period of more than four years. But the palm for the highest scoring rate must go to Mr. Rozelaar though this rate (11·4 per cent) is estimated on a total of only 1,600 trials. With Mrs. Holding (P) has done better than appears in the table, since with this agent she was highly successful in a number of opposition and conjunction experiments which are not taken into account.

Mrs. Stewart scored below chance expectation with S.G.S. as agent, though the score (66/400) with CR of −1·7 is not significant. She has frequently made high scores a few minutes after being introduced to an agent for the first time. Thus on the first occasion of her meeting Miss W. Hewson, Dr. J. H. Blaney, Dr. F. C. L. Brendel and Mrs. M. Longmate, the scores (out of 200) were 67, 63, 60 and 58 respectively, while with Dr. Louise Morgan and Dr. H. S. Allen, who were also strangers to her, she made scores (out of 400) of 109 and 113 respectively.

As a general rule, when an agent was unsuccessful after two or three attempts, we discontinued with that person. It follows that, with the exception of Mrs. Molyneux, the principal agent in the Cambridge experiments, Mrs. Stewart achieved significant scores with all persons who continued with her for at least a thousand trials.

Concerning the types of agent with whom she was most successful it is difficult to reach any satisfactory conclusion. Our general impression is that she produced exceptional scores with persons whom she obviously liked. On the other hand, she was moderately successful with one or two agents with regard to whom she had expressed faint disapproval or

313

shown even active antagonism. It will be recalled that with Shackleton the type of displacement produced varied to some extent with the agent. But, so far as we have been able to discover, not only the main features but also the minor characteristics of Mrs. Stewart's phenomena remained the same for all agents with whom she made significant scores.

## Decline Effects*

Mrs. Stewart's results show a very marked falling off in the rate of scoring for the last two segments of the run, i.e. on trials 16–25, compared with that obtained in the first three segments, i.e. on trials 1–15. This effect was absent in the work with Shackleton. On the assumption of a uniform rate of scoring, we should expect the 9,410 direct hits on the 37,100 trials to be about equally distributed among the five segments. That is, we should expect an average of 1,882 hits per segment. The observed numbers are given in the following table:

### TABLE 10

### Distribution of 9,410 direct hits

| Trials | (1–5) | (6–10) | (11–15) | (16–20) | (21–25) |
|---|---|---|---|---|---|
| Hits | 1,953 | 2,050 | 1,907 | 1,745 | 1,755 |
| Scoring rate per 25 | 6·58 | 6·91 | 6·43 | 5·88 | 5·91 |

The marked drop on the scoring rate for trials 16–25 will be obvious to the reader. In fact, the scoring rate per 25 trials for guesses 1–15 works out at 6·64, while that for guesses 16–25 is only 5·90. This is a difference of 0·74. Using the observed standard deviation, 2·32 for 25 trials, we find that the standard error of the difference is 0·1229, so that the actual difference, 0·74, is more than six times the standard error. Thus the probability that the drop in scoring rate was due to chance is very small; the odds against this exceed fifty millions to one even when we take into account the fact that two segments can be chosen out of five in ten different ways. Mrs. Stewart rapidly climbs to her peak in trials 6–10, and then begins to descend, slowly at first and then with a sudden drop after the fifteenth trial. But even at her nadir (1,745) her score is still enormously beyond the level of chance expectation.

This crowding of hits into the first three segments of the run is undoubtedly responsible for the wide divergence of the numbers of runs of 1, 2, 3, 4, or more consecutive hits from the expected values. The observed and expected numbers of such runs are given in Appendix D, p. 381. It will be seen that there is a large deficit of isolated successes or

* See also Appendix H for a more detailed analysis.

'singles' and a considerable excess of runs of three, four or more consecutive hits. For example, there are twelve unbroken runs of seven successes as compared with an expectation of only 1·4. The longest unbroken run is a 'nine' made on two occasions.

## Position Effects in ESP

Of late there has been a growing realization among parapsychologists that card-guessing involves something more than getting occasional hits on isolated targets. We are beginning to see that ESP functioning, in accordance with the law of proximity in Gestalt psychology, is related in peculiar ways to patterns and configurations in the target sequence. This was first noticed in the work of Shackleton who scored at a higher rate on (+1) and (−1) displacement when the card to be guessed was sandwiched between two cards of the same denomination. That is, on certain patterns he made higher scores than on others. Quite recently Dr. J. G. Pratt and Mrs. E. Bond Foster of Duke University have discovered some striking effects in positional scoring in a re-examination of the twelve year old work of Dorothy H. Martin and Frances Stribic done originally in the University of Colorado prior to the year 1938. It will be recalled (Chap. V, p. 58) that these experimenters conducted an extensive series of clairvoyance tests with a number of subjects. The experiments, as we have indicated, are among the best reported in American card-guessing. Up to date Pratt and Foster have been concerned only with the work of Martin and Stribic's two best subjects, Mr. C. Jencks and Miss D. W. Both these percipients, in the series studied, worked under similar conditions. A pack of 25 Zener cards was shuffled behind a screen, and the subject guessed the order of the cards from top to bottom of the pack, which remained undisturbed till the guessing was complete. The averages of correct guesses on the target or (0) card made by Mr. C. J. and Miss D. W. were almost identical, these being 7·3 and 7·5 respectively for a pack of 25. These results are extremely significant. But Pratt[2,3,4] and Foster have now disclosed an effect which lay unsuspected for twelve years. They found that both Miss D. W. and Mr. C. J. produced very significant forward (+1) displacement of a *negative* kind. That is, each tended to avoid scoring hits on the card which immediately followed the target card at which the percipient was aiming. In the case of D.W. the total (+1) negative deviation amounts to 3·36 standard deviations, but with Mr. C. J. it reaches the high figure of 9·1 standard deviations. Thus Mr. C. J.'s record constitutes the most remarkable case of displacement encountered since the experiments with Shackleton.

Now the accompanying diagram, Fig. (i), will make it obvious to the reader that if a guesser, who is scoring high on the target or (0) card, changes his guess symbol much more frequently than would occur in a random or haphazard sequence of symbols this fact will in itself create automatically the illusion of significant negative (+1) and (−1) displacements in an extended series of trials.

| Guess | Target |
|:---:|:---:|
| B | D |
| A ———→ | A |
| C | E |

Fig. (i)

In the above example the percipient scores a direct hit on target A. He has made two changes of guess in three consecutive trials. His guess B, being different from A, makes a (+1) miss on A which immediately follows target D, and the guess C makes a (−1) miss on A which immediately precedes target E. To take an extreme case: if he changes his guess symbol at every trial it is clear that he will score a (+1) miss and a (−1) miss for almost every direct hit he makes. Hence, if his score on 'direct' targets is high above chance expectation, his scores on (+1) and (−1) targets will be slightly below chance in the long run.

Provided, then, that a percipient has a very marked tendency to avoid repeating his guesses, and is scoring well above chance expectation on the target card, there is nothing unusual in the discovery that his (+1) and (−1) scores are, in a long series, significantly below the chance level. It is only to be expected.

But what is remarkable about Martin and Stribic's two subjects is that they produced very significant forward (+1) *negative* displacement even in those regions of the scoring sheet where there were no direct hits. The backward (−1) displacement for such regions was normal and what would be expected by chance.

Now the fascinating discovery made by Pratt and Foster is that the tendency to *avoid* the card one place ahead was not confined to cases like that in Fig. (i), but was a dominant feature in cases where there was no hit on the target card, as in Fig. (ii):

| Guess | Target |
|:---:|:---:|
| A | B |
| C | D |

Fig. (ii)

Here there was found a highly significant tendency for guess A, which has missed its own direct target B, to miss also the (+1) target D, always provided that D has been missed by its own direct call C. That is, in the case of a pair of direct failures in succession, the second failure was very frequently preceded by a precognitive failure on the same target card. This might suggest that when ESP is not functioning so as to produce direct hits, there is sometimes a secondary kind of ESP in operation which takes the form of an avoidance drive.

In a world adapted primarily to sense perception, ESP is a disturbing influence which must be suppressed in the interest of perceptual efficiency. Hence there arises an unconscious avoidance drive, which tends to cancel the ESP drive. In normal perception it must be assumed that the ESP drive is just balanced by the avoidance drive, so that normal perception is not influenced by ESP. On the other hand any temporary increase in the ESP drive will tend to increase the avoidance drive and thus produce prolonged negative scoring.

At the first of the two guesses in Fig. (ii) the target D is an ESP impression in the offing, as it were. The avoidance drive therefore causes a different symbol A to become conscious. At the second of the two guesses, D is now trying to consciously emerge as a direct target and this is again inhibited by the substitution of a different symbol C.

Another way in which we can describe the statistical effect mentioned above is to say that in the case of consecutive misses on the direct targets, the total $(+1)$ forward displacement score is exceeded very greatly by the total $(-1)$ backward displacement score worked out for these pairs and that this holds for both the subjects Miss D. W. and Mr. C. J.

Quite a different situation arises in the case of pairs which consist of a miss followed or preceded by a direct hit. Such cases are represented schematically by (a) and (b) respectively in Fig. (iii).

| (a) Guess | Target | |
|-----------|--------|------|
| A | B | Miss |
| C | C | Hit |

| (b) Guess | Target | |
|-----------|--------|------|
| A | A | Hit |
| B | C | Miss |

Fig. (iii)

The tendency now is for the forward $(+1)$ displacement score in case (a) to be greater than the backward $(-1)$ displacement score in case (b). This difference, however, is significant only in the case of the subject Miss D. W. but is still suggestive in the case of Mr. C. Jencks.

In fact, the general trend in case (a) is towards a forward *positive* $(+1)$ displacement, and this is the reverse of the $(+1)$ forward *negative* displacement noted with pairs of misses.

317

There is, in fact, a tendency for the subject to anticipate a direct hit precognitively one guess before he reaches it in the sequence.

Thus case (a) in Fig. (iii) becomes:

| Guess | Target |
|-------|--------|
| C     | B      |
| C     | C      |

Fig. (iv)

Quite possibly the percipient is unable to distinguish subconsciously between a correct impression that is precognitive and one that is direct. He may, for instance, in cases such as that shown in Fig. (iv), believe that he is guessing directly two consecutive cards bearing the same symbol.

As Pratt and Foster carefully emphasize, it is not at present possible to say which is the correct interpretation out of a number of possibilities that the authors suggest in order to cover these interesting findings. Our own suggestion that there are regions of the scoring sheet in which ESP is functioning so strongly that the censor allows both direct hits and (+1) hits to escape into consciousness, and other regions in which ESP is so weak that the censor can cope with both direct and precognitive hits, may of course prove to be quite unacceptable in the light of further enquiry. The work of Pratt and Foster is presented not as a complete study but as a progressive programme of tentative research in which more and more records will be examined and reported upon after they have been subjected to analysis similar to that applied to the work of Miss D. W. and Mr. C. J.

Although the experimental conditions under which D.W. and C.J. worked are very similar, the results of these two subjects exhibit some curious differences. But this is only to be expected when we consider the quality of uniqueness which is a characteristic of extra-sensory phenomena.

Physical phenomena are characterized by their uniformity and psychological phenomena in general by their greater variability. As we pass from physics to biology, thence to classical psychology, through psychotherapy to psychical research, we find an ever increasing degree of variability in the results of experiment. In parapsychology, each subject's performance represents the reaction of his own personality to the experimental situation, and this reaction is modified by the extra-personal relations of the group in which he is working. For instance, it was found with Mr. C. J. that, as the number of correct hits on the target card increased within the run, the average negative forward (+1) displacement on a pair of consecutive misses also increased numerically in a significant correlation. There was a similar though somewhat slower

318

numerical increase on the average positive backward (−1) displacement on pairs of consecutive misses which ran parallel to the increase in the number of direct hits in the run. No such relationship between direct and displacement scoring was observed in the case of the other subject, Miss D. W.

Again, the authors found that the negative score on forward (+1) displacement was, with Mr. C. J., particularly marked on pairs of consecutive misses that followed immediately after direct hits, but this was not true of Miss D. W. Pratt and Foster suggest that Mr. C. J.'s strong negative forward displacement after a direct hit, may be his own personal reaction to a successful hit on the target card at which he is consciously aiming. This would imply that Mr. C. J. was at an unconscious level aware of having succeeded by ESP and responded in a way that was peculiar to his own psychological make-up. Another subject might produce a quite different response. Indeed we often find chronological variations* in types of ESP functioning even in the same individual when his records are studied over a sufficiently long period of time. In other series by Mr. C. J., both earlier and later than the one under present consideration, forward negative displacement on pairs of consecutive misses is absent, though the subject still maintains his high scoring on the target card. This does not mean that in selecting Mr. C. J.'s (DT) series for special examination from the mass of his other work the authors have created a mere statistical artifact. For they show by means of a '$t$' test that if we work out the average difference per run of (+1) and (−1) scores obtained from pairs of consecutive misses, the corresponding '$t$' value is 7·5 instead of the expected value zero, with 299 degrees of freedom. Such a value would be expected to occur by chance only once in about $10^{11}$ such series.

The appearance of both positive and negative displacement in different regions of the scoring sheet opens up interesting possibilities. It may well prove to be the case that displacement in card-guessing is less an exception than a normal accompaniment of scoring on a sequence of targets, as indeed Carington's work seemed to suggest. Quite possibly in series which show no over-all displacement there may sometimes exist both positive and negative displacements related to certain features of the target sequence which are separately significant, but which cancel each other on the whole.

The findings of Pratt and Foster are certainly thought-provoking, if very puzzling, and until many more cases of high scoring have been analysed for such effects, we ought to be cautious in our attempts to explain them.

* But in geomagnetism we also find chronological variations of the earth's magnetic field which, though typical, are by no means very regular.

# CHAPTER XIX

# Position Effects with Mrs. Stewart[1,2]

W ith Mrs. Stewart we can ask the same fundamental question that we asked in the case of the Martin-Stribic percipients: Is the subject's rate of success in hitting an ESP target affected in any significant way by the pattern or sequence of targets in which it occurs? Though the answer is Yes, we shall see that Mrs. Stewart has her own peculiar ways of responding to variations in the target sequence.

Now we have already noted (p. 311) that on her 35,616 (+1) and (−1) trials she shows highly significant deficits in the numbers of (+1) and (−1) hits. Moreover, throughout the bulk of her work she exhibits a very marked tendency to avoid repeating the same call in a pair of consecutive guesses. If we split up the guess sequence of a single run of 25 into 12 consecutive non-overlapping pairs, we should expect on the average, if the distribution were random, 20 per cent or 2·4 pairs in which both symbols were the same. Such repeats we shall refer to as 'call-doubles'. Pairs of guesses in which the symbols are different we shall designate 'non-doubles'. Now in round numbers, instead of producing 20 per cent of 'call-doubles', Mrs. Stewart produces only 14 per cent in the whole of her guessing. It follows, then, from what we have said before (p. 316), that we have apparently a ready-to-hand explanation of the 'negative' displacement scoring. It might be simply an artificial effect due to the deficiency of 'repeats' in the guessing allied with high scoring on the target card. But both F.B. and S.G.S. suspected that there was more in the story than this. For example, as far back as 1946 we had noticed a curious position effect that was very marked in the earlier sittings. This was of the nature of a reinforcement by the second member of a 'target double'. In configurations of the type illustrated by Fig. (v) there was, over an extended period, a highly significant tendency to score a direct hit on the second member of a target double after a miss on the first member. Thus:

| Guess | Target |
|-------|--------|
| A | B |
| B ⟶ | B |

Fig. (v)

The rate of scoring on such a configuration was significantly higher than it was on the second member of a 'non-double' in the target sequence shown in Fig. (vi).

| Guess | Target |
|-------|--------|
| A | B |
| C ⟶ | C |

Fig. (vi)

When S.G.S. visited Duke University in the spring of 1951, one of his main objects was to discuss the Stewart records with Dr. J. G. Pratt, who had made such interesting discoveries in connection with the work of Martin and Stribic. With the assistance of Dr. Pratt and another enthusiastic young parapsychologist, Mr. Kenneth Bates, S.G.S. worked at our records for five weeks.

It was decided at the outset to discard the last ten sittings, Nos. 121–30, during which Mrs. Stewart's faculty was not functioning. Actually it would not have made the slightest difference to any of our conclusions had the results of these ten sittings been included in the counts.

The grand total of 37,100 direct trials on which our previous findings were based is thus reduced to 33,500, i.e. 670 sheets of 50 guesses each.

On his arrival at the Parapsychology Laboratory, S.G.S. found one of the walls almost completely covered by numerous graphs drawn by the indefatigable Dr. Pratt in order to elucidate the decline effects on the run which we have discussed only briefly on pp. 314, 395–6.

Our first task was to tabulate the 16,080 non-overlapping consecutive target pairs of which each of the 1,340 runs contained exactly twelve. Of these pairs 3,270 were found to be doubles (AA) and the remainder, 12,810, non-doubles (AB). The last target of each run of 25 was discarded in this count. The number of direct hits was counted on the first member of each 'double' and of each 'non-double'. These counts, done originally by K. Bates and S.G.S., were all re-checked by Miss M. Newton. It was found that on the first members of the target 'non-doubles' 26·8 per cent of the subject's calls made hits, but on the first members of the target 'doubles' only 17·2 per cent of the calls made hits. By chance alone we should of course expect in each case about 20 per cent of hits. We thus made our first discovery, that Mrs. Stewart had been scoring high above chance on the first trials of the 'non-

Y                                              321

doubles' but significantly below chance on the first trials of the 'doubles'. In other words, her tendency was to miss a target when that target was immediately followed by one of the *same* symbol. This implied some kind of apparent precognitive ability on her part, though she might not be actually foreseeing a future event. Obviously to miss the first member of the target double systematically she would have to be aware that the pair was in fact a 'double', and this would entail a knowledge of the second card in the double before it was actually focused by the agent.

In order to show that there was a highly significant difference between the two cases shown in Figs. (vii) and (viii)

| Guess | Target | | Guess | Target |
|:---:|:---:|---|:---:|:---:|
| B $\longrightarrow$ A | | | A $\longrightarrow$ A | |
| C or A | A | | C or B | B |
| Fig. (vii) (Double) | | | Fig. (viii) (Non-Double) | |

we made out a simple contingency table which gave $\chi^2 = 127\cdot7$ with one degree of freedom, the corresponding odds against chance being of the order of $10^{27}$ to 1. This leaves no room for doubt that the effect is a genuine one.

It is important that the reader should note that this low score on the first trials of target 'doubles' is not merely a failure to demonstrate ESP on such targets. It represents a deliberate avoidance of the target. In fact, the negative deviation amounts to nearly four standard deviations with corresponding odds against its being due to chance alone of about ten thousand to one. It certainly looks as if unconscious motivation is at work. What Mrs. Stewart's motive was can only be conjectured. If the reader will glance back at Fig. (vii), he will observe that by scoring a miss on the first of a target double Mrs. Stewart automatically, at the same time, registers a $(+1)$ precognitive miss. It may well have been that unconsciously she was anxious to avoid scoring $(+1)$ precognitive hits. When she began the new series of experiments in 1945, there is good reason to think that she was somewhat jealous of Shackleton's performance and the publicity which it received. The main feature which distinguished Shackleton's work from that of previous telepathic subjects was the fact that over a long period he was guessing correctly the card one place ahead. Now Mrs. Stewart may have been motivated unconsciously to avoid producing the $(+1)$ displacement which she obtained in 1936, perhaps by a dislike of imitating Shackleton. It would therefore be more original if she avoided the $(+1)$ card and produced a negative displacement score. It is true that by scoring high on the target (0) card and frequently changing her call, she would automatically have obtained a significant negative score on both $(+1)$ and $(-1)$ cards

322

in the long run, but possibly (from our knowledge of her we think certainly) she failed to realize this. If this conjecture is correct, it might be asked: Why then did she avoid the card one place ahead only when it was the second of a target double? Here the answer may be that it is possible that her precognitive powers have declined very much since 1936, and that in 1945 she was only able to recognize the $(+1)$ card when its image was reinforced, i.e. when it was the second of a target double. But if she scored a hit on the first trial of a non-double, she would then make an automatic miss on the $(+1)$ card. She would therefore gain her object by missing deliberately the first trials of the target doubles. All this, of course, is mere conjecture, but we think there is little doubt that our subject was a little jealous of Shackleton, at any rate subconsciously, since, whenever his name was mentioned, she would turn the conversation.

A division of the data into eight consecutive chronological samples of almost equal numbers of sheets shows that the effect described above was remarkably constant throughout the period of Mrs. Stewart's guessing.

In the above analysis the sequence of targets was broken up into consecutive non-overlapping pairs; this was done to ensure statistical independence. But it is clear that a certain proportion of the material is lost by this method of treatment. In a run of 25 trials there are actually 24 consecutive target pairs instead of twelve, if we remove the restriction that the pairs must not overlap. It was of interest to see whether the low score observed on the first of target doubles would be accentuated when we examined the first of target triples (AAA) or of quadruples (AAAA), etc. If reinforcement played any part in enabling Mrs. Stewart to recognize that a target was the first of a double, triple, or longer run of the same symbol, we might expect her to be more successful in her recognition when the run was a triple or quadruple than when it was only a double, since in the former cases several precognitive images of the same symbol might combine to produce a more forcible impression on her unconscious mind.

This indeed proved to be the case. On single or isolated targets she scored 29·4 per cent of hits, 18·8 per cent on the first members of target doubles, and 13·2 per cent on the first trials of target triples. There was, in general, no further decline on the first members of quadruples and longer sequences. In fact, the percentage of hits for the first trials of these longer sequences combined is 15·9, which is slightly higher than that for triples. In these counts we have abandoned the method of splitting up the data into non-overlapping pairs, and since we confine our attention to the hits on *first* trials of doubles, triples, etc., there can be no objection to this procedure.

323

If we consider a sequence of targets all of the same symbol, such as a target triple or a quadruple, then it is clear that the rate of scoring on the second or later members of the sequence is not independent of that on the first member. For example, if the guesser scores low on the first trial of the sequence and tends to change her call, she will score at a somewhat higher rate on the second trial.

In spite of this slight degree of interdependence of scoring on the members of a like-symbol sequence, it is interesting to note that, if we work out the scoring rates, not on the first trials only of the various types of sequence, but on all the trials of the sequence, we get a consistently regular decline as the sequence increases in length. In fact, the group scoring rates for singles, doubles, triples, quadruples, quintuples and sextuples, are, respectively, 29·4 per cent, 20·9 per cent, 16·5 per cent, 13·8 per cent, 13·3 per cent and 4·2 per cent. There are no runs of the same symbol of greater length than six in the target sequence. It would appear then that in the longer sequences there is deliberate avoidance, not only of the first card, but also of some of the following cards.

In passing, we may remark how absurd it would be to attempt to explain such phenomena on the assumption that ESP is only another name for involuntary whispering. For the experimenter (EA), showing random numbers at the aperture of the screen, would, at the beginning of a run of the same digit, have not only to whisper this digit, but also to indicate to the agent on the other side of the screen whether it was the initial member of a target double or a target triple. The agent, in his turn, having decoded the number into the corresponding animal name, would have to indicate to Mrs. Stewart in the next room whether it was the forerunner of a double or a triple. And Mrs. Stewart, having picked up this knowledge, would then have to substitute for the name picked up one of the other four symbols. And all this would have to be compressed into two and a half seconds!

It seems highly probable that the negative (+1) displacement is in part motivated, and implies some sort of precognitive ability in the subject.

But this is not the whole of the story. Our next discovery was that Mrs. Stewart's tendency to score below chance expectation was confined to those target doubles in which she did not repeat her call, that is, to those cases for which the guesses at the first and second members of the target double were different symbols as in Fig. (ix) and Fig. (x).

| Guess | Target | | Guess | Target |
|-------|--------|---|-------|--------|
| B | A | | A | A |
| C | A | | B | A |
| Fig. (ix) | | | Fig. (x) | |

324

On the other hand, in those cases where the target double was accompanied by a 'call double' she scored high *above* chance expectation on the first member of such a target double. In fact, there was no significant difference between her rate of scoring on the first members of this class of target doubles and on the first members of target non-doubles. That is, the first trials of target doubles associated with call doubles behaved just like the first trials of target non-doubles. Figs. (xi) and (xii) illustrate the cases in which a call double accompanies a target double.

| Guess | Target | Guess | Target |
|-------|--------|-------|--------|
| B | A | A | A |
| B | A | A | A |
| Fig. (xi) | | Fig. (xii) | |

The first step we had to take in order to find out whether the call sequence had anything to do with the negative scoring effect which we had noticed on the first trials of target doubles was to separate the 3,270 non-overlapping pairs of target doubles into two groups, those with, and those without, call doubles. The two groups were then arranged in a four-fold table so as to show the number of hits and the number of misses on the first targets in the case of each group. A chi-squared test applied to this simple contingency table gave $\chi^2 = 19 \cdot 22$, and with one degree of freedom, the observed difference between the scoring rates for the group with call doubles and that with no call doubles would be expected to occur by chance only once in 100,000 cases.

We have mentioned (p. 321) that the percentage of hits on the first members of *all* target doubles was 17·2. But our table shows that the percentage of hits on the first trials of the 386 pairs with call doubles is as high as 25·1 per cent. On the other hand, the percentage of hits on the first trials of the 2,884 pairs without call doubles is as low as 16·2 per cent.

We have thus clear evidence that only the first trials of those target doubles that are *without* call doubles give rise to significant below-chance scoring. To complete the study of the effect of call doubles, we made a similar comparison between the scoring rates on the first members of the target *non*-doubles (i) when these were accompanied by call doubles, and (ii) when there were no call doubles. We found that, on the first trials of the 1,321 pairs of non-overlapping target *non*-doubles which were associated with call doubles, 26·8 per cent were hits, and, curiously, the percentage of hits on the first trials of the 11,489 target *non*-doubles which were without call doubles was also 26·8. Thus, in the case of targets which are *non*-doubles, the rate of scoring on the first trial is unaffected by the repetition or change of the subject's call. Moreover, the 25·1 per cent success found when a pair contains both call doubles and target doubles is not significantly different from the 26·8 per cent found when the targets are non-doubles.

We must now ask: What interpretation is it possible to put upon the fact that Mrs. Stewart scored significantly below chance expectation on the first member of a target double only when the two calls (or guesses) of the pair were different from each other (or non-double)?

We have seen that, *as a general rule*, our subject used her ESP ability to miss the first target when she was presented with two or more identical targets in succession. But, in order to accomplish this, it was necessary for her to detect by ESP that the two targets were identical. She had, in fact, to perceive (precognitively, in some sense,) that she was not dealing with an isolated target, but with a double, triple, etc. But we may reasonably assume that her ESP faculty did not work infallibly in this sense any more than it served without fail to identify the isolated single targets on which she made significant positive scores.

When, however, the subject's ESP faculty failed to inform her that her target was the first of a double or longer sequence, this did not mean that her extra-sensory powers had no opportunity to operate. She could still use her ESP faculty on each separate target just as if it were an isolated one. Indeed, the very fact that the data which allowed her to devise a motivated 'negative' scoring were lacking left her free to respond positively to each target as though it were completely isolated.

Now if Mrs. Stewart failed to appreciate the fact that two consecutive targets formed a double, and that therefore she ought to avoid hitting the first of them, she would treat each of them as a single target, and the coming into play of her natural tendency to hit single targets would tend to result in her calling doubles. By isolating those cases in which doubles in the calls are associated with doubles in the targets, we have brought together into one group those instances in which the subject failed to recognize by ESP that the targets were double, and this gives us a special class of target doubles in which her ordinary positive scoring tendencies prevailed.

If we are correct in this interpretation, we have here an example of a particular pattern in the target sequence which generally produced negative scoring, but which did not always do so. We appear to be dealing here with one of those rare instances in which we are able to demonstrate statistically what investigators have suggested many times on the basis of clinical impressions. This is, that there is much more evidence for ESP in our results than is brought out by ordinary methods. Usually, we have to be satisfied with a net result in which positive scoring and negative scoring trends may partially cancel each other out.

Apparently in this case we have successfully separated the opposing trends and have found a special condition (call doubles) which was accompanied by a score above the chance level on the first cards of target doubles, although the percipient usually scored below the chance level on the first members of target doubles.

## Change of Call in Relation to ESP Success or Failure

In broadcasts (September and October 1951) on 'The Significance of Parapsychology', Mr. Antony Flew[3,4] of the Department of Moral Philosophy at Aberdeen University made the suggestion that ESP should be thought of, not as a form of perception or cognition, but as a kind of guesswork. The sort of question which Mr. Flew had in mind was the following: Do persons who consistently score at the chance level in card-guessing arrange their guesses in a different pattern from people who, like Shackleton or Mrs. Stewart, score high above expectation over long periods? Quite apart from any consideration of the target sequence, does the guessing behaviour of successful ESP subjects present features which distinguish it from the guessing of normal persons? Do such subjects, for instance, tend to change from one symbol to another more frequently than is the case with normal guessers? And might we not be able, by studying the guess patterns of successful ESP subjects and comparing them with those of ordinary people, to obtain some light on the extra-sensory process?

We may, of course, readily agree with Mr. Flew that ESP bears no resemblance to sense perception or to normal cognition. When, in everyday life, we claim to know something, we can usually produce reasons for this claim; we may have had ocular demonstration, or have remembered some happening, or have reached our conclusion by means of some argument, or have been told something by somebody. But the card-guesser who makes a hit can usually produce no reason for writing down one particular symbol rather than another. Until the results are checked, he possesses, as a rule, no confidence at all that his guess is correct. He cannot, therefore, be said to be cognizing anything in the ordinary sense of the term. Nor, in general, does he appear to be perceiving anything. All he seems to be doing is writing down a sequence of symbols without making any effort to control or direct his associative processes.

Nevertheless, we fail to understand how a mere study of guessing-patterns, by itself, can throw any light on ESP. We have every reason to believe that with random, or even approximately random target sequences, guess patterns *not intended for those sequences* will not, in the long run, yield extra-chance scores. This has been established by the numerous cross-checks that have been applied to successful card-guessing series. This fact alone should throw some doubt on the usefulness of Mr. Flew's suggestion.

It seems to us much more likely that a study of guessing habits made in relation to special types of target pattern will provide a clue, not to the ESP process itself, but to certain minor mysteries connected with its working.

In the hope that something may ultimately be achieved along these lines, Dr. Pratt and S.G.S. embarked upon the investigation of Mrs. Stewart's data which we shall now describe.

The question with which we are concerned in this section has to do with the extent to which the subject must break away from her habitual call sequences in order to make an ESP hit. We know that, if a person is asked to compile mentally a long list of symbols chosen from, say, five different types, this subjectively-formed sequence will not, normally, be even approximately a random distribution of the five symbols. And this will be true whether the compiler has tried consciously to make a random series or has used the method of free association. However vigilant he may be, the compiler will sooner or later fall into sequence habits which will persist over a period and then perhaps be replaced by other patterns. Sequence habits, then, will be found in any card-guessing test which does not yield a very high proportion of hits. The presence of these non-random call patterns implies a tendency for each call to be determined by preceding responses instead of by the ESP target at which the call is aimed. If the guesser is to succeed in making a call that corresponds to the target, instead of one that simply follows by habit from the preceding calls, it is logical to suppose that he must break away from his normal associative tendencies.

We are assuming here, however, that the break in the subject's sequence habits occurs precisely at the point where he scores an ESP hit. The assumption that he goes on following his usual associative habits until he gets an ESP impression which is strong enough to cause him to break through his ordinary sequence patterns is perhaps the simplest one to make. We must recognize, however, that this is not the only way in which impressions from outside could be superimposed on the subject's own peculiar patterns of calling. It is conceivable that the ESP target is capable of influencing the subject's choice of calls one, two, or even more trials in advance of the point where the actual ESP hit is scored. In fact, the guesser might know in advance that a particular target symbol is coming up, say, on the third trial ahead, and this ESP knowledge might influence him to choose at that point one of his habitual sequence patterns which will end up on the third call of the sequence with the symbol that will score a hit. If ESP should operate in this anticipatory fashion, by affecting the subject's choice among his habitual call patterns, such selections might be made most easily at points in his associative chain of responses where the links are weak. We should then have the ESP process working in such a way as to take advantage of the guesser's habitual sequences without having to break them up by coming into action only at the moment the target is presented.

In the present investigation we confine ourselves to a single feature of the call sequence, namely, the frequency of *doubles* in the guess series; so that this study is merely an introduction to the more general problem of the relation of ESP performance to the subject's personal habits of association. We wish to see whether there is any evidence in support of the first, that is, the simpler, of the two hypotheses which we have outlined above, looking at a single aspect—repeat of call. We ask the question: When Mrs. Stewart makes her guess at the second symbol of a target pair, does she complete a call double with greater frequency when this second guess scores a hit than when it makes a miss? In order to answer this question it was necessary to classify the 16,080 non-overlapping pairs of trials in two ways. First, did the second trial of the pair score a hit or a miss? Next, did the subject's second call, the one involved in the second trial, form with the first call a double or a non-double? By means of these dichotomies we constructed a four-fold contingency table for which chi-squared worked out to be 1·11. With one degree of freedom this is not in the least significant. In fact, those pairs with a hit on the second trial included 11·0 per cent of call doubles while those with a miss on the second trial contained 10·5 per cent of call doubles. The difference is not significant, and at first sight it would seem that Mrs. Stewart called as many doubles when making hits as when she made misses, in spite of the fact that her total score on these 16,080 trials was highly significant.

Since this analysis did not support our first hypothesis, we examined the results to discover whether there might be a genuine effect which was somehow obscured and cancelled out by the pooling of the subject's data over a period of four years.

The results quoted below show, on the whole, that Mrs. Stewart had a strong aversion from calling double, since the expected frequency in a random distribution is 20 per cent, instead of about 11 per cent which was her actual frequency. It seemed surprising that Mrs. Stewart was able to score at the high level at which she did without approximating more closely to theoretical expectation in her number of doubles.

We decided, therefore, to divide the data into the eight consecutive chronological samples of nearly equal numbers of sheets alluded to on p. 323. When this was done, it became obvious that there was a marked change in the subject's tendency to call doubles between the first and last of these samples.

For the greater part of her guessing, she called fewer doubles than her average number for the entire series, but in the last sample she actually called more doubles than would be expected in a random distribution. Thus, in the first sample, there are 6·9 per cent of doubles, and in the last 23·7 per cent, while the average for the entire series is 10·6 per cent.

For each of these eight samples we constructed a four-fold contingency table analogous to that which we set up for the whole series of 16,080 pairs of trials. That is to say, the separate samples were classified as call-doubles or non-doubles and again as hits or misses on the second trials of call-doubles and non-doubles. A chi-squared was computed for each of the eight samples, and in the case of three samples (Nos. 4, 5 and 8) the values of chi-squared were significant, these being 10·53, 9·47 and 8·37 respectively. The values for the other five samples did not even approach significance. In each of the samples with a high chi-squared value, the significance is due to the fact that the number of doubles formed by those pairs in which the second call made a hit came closer to the expected value of 20 per cent than was the case with the other five samples.

We can evaluate the total effect, taking into account the change in the frequency of call-doubles (which occurred during sample No. 7), by adding the chi-squared values for the eight individual samples. This gives a total value of chi-squared equal to 32·31, with eight degrees of freedom. A value as high as this would occur by chance only once in 5,000 such series.

It is interesting to observe, by an inspection of the actual table, how consistently Mrs. Stewart tended to call more doubles in making a hit during the earlier part of her work in which she was under-doubling, and fewer doubles when she was scoring a hit towards the end of the series at the time when she showed a general tendency to over-double. For every sample except the last, there is a larger ratio of doubles to non-doubles in the pairs of which the second call scored a hit than in those with the second trial giving a miss.

The chronological study therefore seems to indicate that the subject did, to some extent, succeed in modifying her current tendencies to under-double or to over-double in order to make the calls that scored her ESP hits. This breaking away from her habitual preferences, as we expected, brought the frequency of doubles in the calls closer to the random frequency that prevailed in the target series. It is surprising, however, that the difference between the numbers of call-doubles associated with hits and misses respectively is not even greater than it was found to be. Four of the eight chronological samples showed virtually no difference. It is conceivable, if not probable, that the doubling tendency is the strongest associative pattern with which the ESP process has to contend. This would make it all the more important to study other call sequences in relation to hits and misses.

The interpretation of the findings which we have suggested may seem to be the obvious one. However, before it can be offered as the correct psychological explanation of the results, it is necessary to envisage another way in which the excess of call doubles with the second member making a correct hit could have been produced. If Mrs. Stewart showed a general tendency to make positive extra-chance scores on (+1) forward displacement as well as on the direct target, this would have produced the doubles effect under consideration. This will be clear from the accompanying figure:

| Guess | Target |
|:-----:|:------:|
| A | B |
| A | A |

Fig. (xiii)

This configuration might be interpreted in either of two ways. We might suppose that our subject at her first trial made a precognitive (+1) hit on the target A, and then at her second trial scored a direct hit on the same target. Or we might suppose that, in order to score a direct hit at her second trial, she doubled her call, and that the apparent precognitive hit was due to chance.

We have seen (p. 311) that on the whole series the total (+1) displacement score is *below* expectation to a significant degree, but it is conceivable that in certain defined areas of the target sequence there might be (+1) scoring that is significantly above chance expectation, and negative (+1) scoring in other regions.

It was necessary, therefore, to examine Mrs. Stewart's data for evidence of forward positive displacement, and to do this in those regions of her records where any genuine tendency to hit the target one step ahead by ESP could be tested independently of her direct-target scoring and the secondary effects related to it. We therefore examined those pairs of trials which gave two direct target misses to see whether there was any significant tendency for the first call to hit the second target of the pair; and to make this check as free as possible from all those factors and peculiarities in her records that might affect displacement scoring, we left out of account the pairs of misses with a double in either the calls or the targets.

To our surprise this analysis did yield apparent evidence of positive (+1) displacement at a quite significant level, but we shall omit here the detailed results. As we explain in Appendix E, p. 382, we discovered a non-random element in the target distribution which, though it has not affected the expectation of direct (0) hits, may conceivably have had some effect on the expectation of (+1) and of (−1) hits, even in the miss areas of the target sequence. Until the matter has been more fully looked into we feel that it would not be safe to affirm that there is a genuine (+1) (positive) displacement in these regions of the scoring sheet. It would not follow, however, as an inescapable conclusion, that the presence of a genuine tendency for positive (+1) diplacement in the miss areas of Mrs. Stewart's columns explains the excess of call-doubles of which the second member gave a direct hit. The former effect *could* account for the latter; but whether in fact it *does* account for it, we can ascertain only by seeing how the two findings are related.

We can obtain a picture of the relation between the two findings which is adequate to show whether we are dealing with *one* effect or *two* distinct effects by seeing how the two sets of observations compare in significance throughout the eight chronological sections of the data. If they are both part of one general displacement effect, the results should vary together in significance, whereas if they do not vary together, they would clearly be different effects. The positive (+1) displacement in the miss areas was evaluated by a chi-squared test for each of the eight chronological samples, and this set of chi-squared values was compared with the set obtained for the eight samples of the call-double data. The fourth sample of data, which gave the highest chi-squared (10·53, with one degree of freedom), actually gave the lowest (1·0, with one degree of freedom) for (+1) displacement, whereas the sixth sample gave the highest chi-squared value for (+1) displacement (10·9) and the lowest (0·01) for the call-double data. A regression test of the relation between the two sets of chi-squared values gave a regression coefficient with a negative value, showing that the two sets of observations are clearly not based upon a *general* (+1) displacement effect.

This is not to say, of course, that the observed excess of call-doubles with the second call a direct hit over those with the second call a miss may not be described as a kind of positive (+1) displacement combined with a direct hit on the same target. But this interpretation would require the assumption that two high-scoring (+1) displacement tendencies were working concurrently, but independently, in different regions of the scoring sheet. We prefer what seems to us the simpler explanation, that Mrs. Stewart overcame to some extent her aversion from calling doubles in order to score some of her hits on the direct target.

## The Converse Problem

The question which we shall now discuss is, in a certain sense, the converse of the one with which we have just dealt. It is this: Does making an ESP hit have such an effect on the subject's associative tendencies that there is a difference between the number of call symbols repeated *after* hits and the number repeated *after* misses? In other words, does the guesser tend to double the call that makes a direct hit significantly more often, or less often, than he tends to double the call that makes a direct miss?

In the cases of the two subjects Mr. C. J. and Miss D. W. of the Colorado experiments, there was evidence, suggestive though not conclusive, that a hit had some real effect upon the following call. It was of importance, therefore, to look for such an effect in Mrs. Stewart's data.

For this purpose we separated the 16,080 non-overlapping pairs into two groups according to whether the subject made a hit or a miss on the *first* target of a pair. Each of these two groups was then sub-divided according to whether the second call of each pair was the same as the first or different from it. We thus constructed a four-fold contingency table. We would expect the same ratio of call doubles to non-doubles when there was a hit on the first target as when there was a miss, if the two situations were independent. The four-fold table gave a value of chi-squared equal to 2·56, with one degree of freedom. Thus there appears to be no significant difference between the two ratios, and at first sight no such effect is revealed.

As in the previous investigation, however, the question arises whether there may not have been a chronological variation in effect which is obscured when the data for the four years' work are evaluated as a whole. To test whether this may have been the case we evaluated the change of call after hits and misses for the eight separate chronological samples that we used previously. The results showed that there were remarkable variations in the strength of the doubling tendency among the different samples. The first and sixth samples produced very significant values of chi-squared, these being 11·67 and 9·48 respectively, but the values for the other six samples were all less than 4. The sum of the eight values of chi-squared is 29·42, with eight degrees of freedom, and a value as high as this would occur by chance only once in about

3,000 such series. We may safely conclude that there are some factors present in the different chronological sections of the experiment which are producing a genuine difference in the proportion of doubles after hits and misses, and we are justified in making further investigation to see how to interpret this finding.

In only four of the eight samples was there a larger proportion of repeats after hits than after misses, but the two most significant chi-squared values—those for samples Nos. 1 and 6—indicate that the subject repeated her call more frequently after a direct hit than she did after a miss.

Now this effect would arise as a statistical artifact if Mrs. Stewart made a (−1) backward, positive displacement score immediately after a direct hit on the same target, as in Fig. (xiv).

|  Guess  |  Target  |
|:-------:|:--------:|
|    A    |    A     |
|    A    |    B     |

Fig. (xiv)

It is clear that this configuration admits of two interpretations. We might suppose that her successful guessing of the target card has caused the subject to repeat her call, or that, immediately after her direct hit, she has scored a post-cognitive hit.

We know that Mrs. Stewart scored high above expectation on the direct or (0) target. If, in addition, positive backward (−1) displacement also occurred in the series, and if hits of these two sorts were made independently of one another in a statistical sense, we should occasionally expect to find both forms of ESP operating in relation to the same target. For this to happen it would be necessary for the subject to give the same call on adjacent trials, as it is possible for the direct call and the following call both to hit the same target only if they are identical.

After a miss on the direct target, however, the tendency of the subject to score a hit on backward (−1) displacement would actually reduce the number of call-doubles, as the subject would necessarily have to change her response in order to make a backward (−1) hit after a direct miss.

To discover whether a *general* (−1) positive displacement tendency was the explanation of the 'repeat of call' effect, we analysed Mrs. Stewart's data for (−1) displacement in those pairs of which neither trial gave a direct hit. We also omitted the pairs with call- or card-doubles, as we did in the preceding investigation. In this region of the target sequence there was some suggestion of positive scoring on (−1)

334

displacement, though it was not actually significant. To see whether (−1) displacement might explain the excess of call doubles after hits, we worked out the chi-squared values for (−1) displacement for each of the eight chronological samples, and compared these with the corresponding change-of-call values of chi-squared. We confined ourselves to samples Nos. 1 and 6, since these afforded the most striking evidence of ESP influence upon the doubling tendency. The results showed that, for these two most important samples, there was no significant (−1) displacement, as one sample gave a chi-squared value of 0·4 and the other a value even closer to zero, there being one degree of freedom in each case.

Consequently, the significantly higher proportion of call doubles after hits could not be explained as an artifact due to a general positive scoring on (−1) displacement.

We conclude, therefore, that there is a real difference in the sequence of calls after hits and misses in Mrs. Stewart's data, and that the earlier suggestive evidence relating to change of call in the Martin and Stribic series has been confirmed, though in our case we are concerned with a repeat of call, and not a change of call, after a hit. What possible psychological interpretation can we give to this finding?

In the earlier studies of change of call by Pratt and Foster, it was thought that such effects might provide experimental evidence that a card-guessing subject has some kind of knowledge of his ESP success, inasmuch as he appears to be reacting to it. But in the later discussion of the results it was recognized that there was an alternative interpretation which could not be completely ruled out.

This was that certain targets in the series somehow became exceptionally effective for the ESP process, and that the subject sometimes reacted to one of these singular targets, not by one call only, but by two, or even more, calls.

From the earlier evidence it appears that the characteristic reaction was to change the call immediately after a direct hit.

On this view that certain targets affect more than one call, we may suppose that in these cases the subject made a direct hit on such an 'effective' or 'singularized' target, and then responded to it again by *psi*-missing on his following call.

Mrs. Stewart, on the other hand, tended to repeat the call symbol that scored a hit. Quite possibly this is a case of a 'singularized' target which is available first as a direct target and then as a (−1) target. If this is so, perhaps we ought not to expect any general evidence for (−1) displacement in the 'miss' areas of the target sequence.

We still see no way to distinguish finally between two possible interpretations of the change- or repeat-of-call effect: (i) the subject's reaction to making a successful guess reflected, perhaps subconsciously, by a change or repeat of call, and (ii) a spread of influence around certain singularized targets which somehow become available for more than one type of ESP functioning.

It may be, however, that there is less difference between these two interpretations than at first sight appears.

When we say that a change in the subject's patterning of his calls is a reaction to success, we tend to imply that he is consciously aware of having made an ESP hit. On the other hand, we must recognize that there is no sharp division between consciousness and unconsciousness,* but that these concepts represent the two extremes of a continuum. Parapsychologists have been forced, by their failure to find experimental evidence to the contrary, to assign *psi*-processes to the unconscious end of the range of mental activities. Apart from memory, the results of *psi*-tests probably represent the best evidence available that unconscious mental processes do occur. Research workers in ESP have never ceased to be interested, however, in finding some special situation or device which will enable the *psi*-subject to show that he is sometimes influenced, be it in ever so subtle or momentary a manner, by the fact that he is employing his ESP faculty. For example, Mrs. Stewart was apparently influenced by some aspect of the situation when she scored a hit, and this influence was strong enough to cause her to repeat the call and thus score a second (−1) hit on the same target.

This is a step, albeit a small one, towards our objective in the search for some method which enables the subject to signal when he has sucessfully used his ESP ability.

The analysis of Mrs. Stewart's records which we have reported in this chapter surely reveals the *psi*-process, in her case, as a tremendously complicated network of tendencies working often at cross-purposes with one another. We note first a consistent tendency to score high above expectation on the target or (0) card. But when we examine her records more closely, we find that she scores consistently below chance expectation on the first trials of target doubles, triples, etc. A still closer inspection reveals that this happens only with those target doubles which are not associated with call-doubles, and that the first members of target doubles with call-doubles behave just like the first members of target non-doubles. Then we discover that the negative tendency is even more potent in the case of the first members of triples and longer sequences of the same symbol. We next observe what looks like consistent below-chance scoring on (+1) and (−1) displacement targets, but

* Cf. a paper by Slater in *The Physical Basis of Mind*, by P. Laslett.

when we look more closely, we find that this negative tendency is largely confined to those regions of the scoring sheet in which direct hits predominate and that in the 'miss' areas there is apparently significant above-chance scoring on the (+1) target.

# CHAPTER XX

# Science and ESP Research

In this concluding chapter we shall examine the attitude of orthodox scientists to the experimental investigation of telepathy, and consider also certain criticisms.

Many scientists would like to see telepathy discredited. They feel that their materialistic preconceptions are incompatible with the experimental findings. Preferring dogma to empiricism, they have abandoned the scientific method so far as ESP is concerned.

Indeed, as Professor Evelyn Hutchinson* has remarked in a recent article, the reason why many scientific workers do not accept these results is simply that they do not want to, and they avoid doing so by refusing to examine the full detailed reports of the experiments in question. He adds that the level of irrelevant bad taste to which some of the criticisms published in respectable journals have fallen is almost incredible.

If, as may readily be conceded, the facts of telepathy and precognition do not fit into the mechanistic framework upon which the physical sciences are based, then surely it is of the utmost importance to investigate these alleged facts with the greatest impartiality. So long as people ignore the findings of psychical research and imagine that they can dispose of inconvenient discoveries by stigmatizing them as 'occult', they are in danger of repeating the errors of the fundamentalists when confronted with the Copernican hypothesis.

That ordinary men of science are very uneasy about the experimental demonstration of extra-sensory perception is clear from the following passage taken from an article in *Mind* (October 1950) by A. M. Turing[1] on *Computing Machinery and Intelligence*. Professor Turing writes: 'These disturbing phenomena seem to deny all our usual scientific ideas; how we should like to discredit them! Unfortunately, the statistical evidence, at least for telepathy, is overwhelming. The idea that our bodies move simply according to the known laws of physics together

* XVIII, 1.

with some others not yet discovered, but somewhat similar, would be one of the first to go.' This writer has here stated very succinctly the outlook of the scientific materialist. According to this view, human beings are just material aggregates which behave according to the laws of quantum theory. The brain is, in this view, no more than an electrical switchboard of amazing complexity, but without an operator. The deadly sequel to this philosophy is that human beings have no ethical or moral responsibility for their actions since the latter are determined by the laws of physics.

But human beings at least *appear* to be acting with purpose and striving towards future goals. It must appear to any dispassionate observer that humans, far from being exquisite pieces of mechanism, set before themselves ideals which they try to realize and for which they are often prepared to die. In his article *The Faith of a Scientist* Professor A. C. Hardy[2] points out that if mankind decided to control marriages by law, it could, by allowing some and prohibiting others, gradually in the course of time alter the human race. That is, humanity would be able to guide its own evolution towards some ideal in the future. This, says Hardy, is a logical deduction from modern biological science. But if this is true it follows that mechanistic biology does not embody the whole truth about life.

The sort of outlook sketched in the paragraph we have cited from Turing's paper is indeed little more than a modernized version of the views of T. H. Huxley, who, when addressing a public meeting in 1868, told his listeners: 'The thoughts to which I am now giving utterance and your thoughts regarding them are expressions of molecular changes in the matter of life.' But as it is, even the most ardent epiphenomenalists of today have failed to give us anything like a convincing argument that there must always be an exact correspondence between mental and molecular states. In his book *The Organization of Behaviour* D. O. Hebb[8] points out some formidable difficulties which confront any isomorphic theory of the relation between mental events and cortical activity, even if ESP is left out of consideration. Let us consider a few typical obstacles.

There is first the intricate problem of the transfer of function. A person who has learned to write with his right hand can, without further training, write tolerably with his left hand or with his toes or can sign his name with a pencil held between his teeth. Yet different motor areas are involved in controlling the muscles of the hand, the toes and the neck. How does a different group of neurons automatically enact the same pattern?

Again, we recognize a tune the first time that we hear it transposed into a different key. What switches the activity of the neurons from one network to another?

And here is a fact concerning visual perception.[9] By the measurement of electrical potentials on the visual cortex it has been established that there is a one-to-one correspondence between points of the retinal image, when, say, a white square is looked at, and the retinal neurons in that area of the visual cortex which undergoes excitation. But on the cortex the square is represented by a curvilinear quadrilateral of varying shape. Despite this, the object is always identified as a square. And two squares of different sizes would cause even greater variations in the shape of the excited area of the cortex.

Experiments on the brains of animals make it difficult to suppose that memories are localized in specific regions of the brain. K. S. Lashley[10] reports that rats were taught to jump at a white triangle and to avoid a white × when both figures were on a black background, but to choose the × and avoid the triangle if the background was striped. Then their craniums were opened and the fibres connecting the visual and motor areas of the cortex were completely severed. After recovery the rats learned to execute these difficult feats of visual generalization as quickly as normal rats.

Lashley informs us that 'memory disturbances of simple sensory habits in monkeys follow only upon very extensive experimental destruction including almost the entire associative cortex. Even combined destruction of the prefrontal, parietal, occipital and temporal areas, exclusive of the primary sensory cortex, does not prevent the animal from forming such habits although pre-existing habits are lost and their reformation greatly retarded.'

Such evidence precludes the existence of a special memory region in the brain and it is exceedingly difficult in the face of it to believe that memory is preserved by such devices as the setting up of permanent circulating nervous currents in the neural network. For when the visual cortex of a rat was removed by *arbitrary cuts* till only a sixtieth of this area was left, the animal—which had been previously taught some feat such as jumping at a triangle—could still be trained to achieve the feat. Even if the memories were stored, not in a single circuit, but in multiple circuits, it is difficult to suppose that arbitrary cuts made in all directions would leave any circuit undamaged.

Moreover, as McCulloch[11] points out, we can hardly suppose that memories are represented by permanent reverberatory currents in brain circuits since all such reverberatory activity ceases in deep sleep, and is destroyed by epileptic shock-waves. Yet memory survives such dislocation. Again, Lashley tells us that 'the same cells which bear the visual memory traces are also excited and play a part in every other visual reaction of the animal.' Surely the memory currents would be interfered with by those arising from the other forms of visual activity. And no mechanical theory up to the present has been able to suggest how old memories are stored. No sooner is a network theory elaborated than it encounters some stubborn facts with which it is unable to cope and has to be discarded.

For those who refuse to admit that mental and physical functioning are equally real but absolutely distinct modes of activity though correlated, there seems to be no hope in the search for mechanical models. For the correlation between brain and mind cannot be expressed in terms of space-time equations.

Professor J. C. Eccles in a paper in *Nature* (July 1951) has made the suggestion that certain neurons in a critical state can be fired by some external influence which seems to be of the nature of psycho-kinesis. The 'influence' arranges that these critically poised neurons are fired at the correct instant and in the correct order. Now in order to be discharged a neuron has to receive signals from two or more other neurons. Thus the firing of the 'critical' neurons would release discharges from other groups of neurons and the 'influence' might thus guide the pattern of a volitional process in the motor cortex. Coming as they do from an eminent neuro-physiologist, these suggestions might well be the starting-point of a new theory of the working of the brain which might supersede the old mechanical theories.

Now if mechanical theories have failed to provide any intelligible theory of mental phenomena such as memory or learning it seems unlikely that they will prove any more successful in the case of telepathy. The fundamental fact of telepathy is the existence of a correspondence, partial or complete, between a mental pattern of A and a mental pattern of B, and, as we have seen, it has proved impossible to establish any exact isomorphism between mental and physical patterns. To seek for a *causal* explanation of telepathy may be merely a case of a question that is wrongly posed. We shall probably have to accept non-causal correspondence between mental states as an irreducible fact of nature. Perhaps all we can hope to do is to clarify the conditions, physical and mental, under which telepathy manifests. We may also expect to discover that processes akin to clairvoyance and psycho-kinesis are at work continually in the biological processes of morphogenesis and in the psychological processes of perception and memory.*

* Dr. G. D. Wassermann has given us valuable help with the arguments of the above section.

## Philosophers and ESP Research

It is perhaps significant that, with some notable exceptions, philoso
phers have taken far more interest in ESP than the academic psycholo
gists. The writings of Professor C. D. Broad of Cambridge and of Pro
fessor H. H. Price of Oxford on philosophical questions connected with
our subject are well-known. Both these distinguished men have repeatedly
expressed their conviction of the soundness of the evidence for ESP
Two enthusiastic recent recruits from among the philosophers are Mr
C. W. K. Mundle, Head of the Department of Philosophy at the Univer
sity College of Dundee, and Mr. Antony G. N. Flew, who is Lecturer in
Moral Philosophy at the University of Aberdeen.

Mr. Mundle contributed a most interesting paper to a symposium
organized by the Aristotelian Society at its meeting in July 1950 to
discuss the question: Is psychical research relevant to philosophy?

Mr. Mundle stressed that what is peculiar and common to para
normal phenomena is that such phenomena apparently involve causal
relations between 'events separated by a spatio-temporal gap and not
mediated by any continuous chain of events', and he suggested that this
is the root of the mental bewilderment which many scientists feel in the
presence of such phenomena. He also remarked that in certain types of
*psi*-phenomena, there is a temporal clustering of certain events which
must be regarded as effects about a certain event which must be re
garded as their common causal source, and that some of the effect-events
in such clusters *precede* the event which is their causal source.

Professor Broad, who was chairman of the meeting, remarked that
the peculiarities noted by Mr. Mundle were, in reality, special cases of a
more general feature which distinguishes normal from paranormal
happenings. There are certain limiting principles which we intuitively
take for granted in all the activities of normal life and in our scientific
theories. Some of these principles appear to be self-evident, and others
are deduced from ordinary experience, and seem to be so universal that
we never question them. Broad classifies these principles under four
general heads: (a) Principles of causation; (b) Limitations of the action
of mind on matter; (c) Dependence of mind on brain; and (d) Limita
tions on the ways of acquiring knowledge.

Paranormal phenomena are those which apparently conflict with one
or more of these limiting principles.

Philosophers, said Broad, have always been vitally interested in these
principles, and since in his opinion there is conclusive evidence that
there are happenings, called paranormal, which conflict with these

principles, it follows that parapsychology is highly relevant to philosophy.

Like Mr. Mundle, Mr. Antony Flew thinks that the evidence for successful card-guessing is scientifically sound. He says that the work with Shackleton and Mrs. Stewart has 'impressively confirmed in our own less exuberant intellectual climate many of the findings of Professor Rhine and his colleagues in North Carolina.' Mr. Flew is not prepared, however, to accept the interpretation which Dr. Rhine puts upon the work. He asserts that the latter is wrong in supposing that the experiments demonstrate any kind of dualism of mind and matter. Rhine, he complains, is continually talking about 'the reach of the mind in space', or the 'transcendence of the human mind over time and space', whereas the actual findings of the experiments can be expressed quite simply without the use of such misleading phraseology. Mr. Flew thinks that there are such things as mental processes, feelings, perceptions, etc., but apparently no such entities as minds. 'Mind', in fact, is, according to the school of philosophy to which Mr. Flew belongs, an unnecessary term which leads to confused thinking. It is essential, therefore, to avoid terms like Mind, Subconscious Self and so on, which imply the existence of vague entities and even vaguer hypotheses, and confine our discussions to the data which are actually observed.

In the second of his broadcasts, entitled *A New Name for Guesswork?* Mr. Flew* has much that is cogent to say about precognition. He points out, we think correctly, that there is no necessary incompatibility between the possibility of forecasting certain classes of future events and the freedom of the human will.

In ordinary life we are constantly making successful predictions about the future behaviour of other people, such as that 'Tom Jones will visit Cornwall next summer in order to collect geological specimens.' But if the prediction is fulfilled, that obviously does not imply that Tom is under compulsion to visit Cornwall; he possesses the same amount of freedom to go or not to go as human beings normally possess with regard to such exercises of choice. None of us is absolutely free.

The essential difference between a 'normal' prediction and a '*psi*-prediction' is that in the former kind of forecast we know the reasons on which it is based, but in the '*psi*-prediction' we are unable to discover any method by which the percipient arrives at his knowledge of the future event. Further, it seems clear that even a paranormal prediction can indicate only a probability and not a certainty. When Mr. Dunne dreamed of the railway accident (Chap. VI, p. 75), there was nothing to prevent him from writing a strong letter to the L.N.E.R. company urging them to take special precautions on the particular section of the

* XIX, 4.

line seen in his dream. Whether the company would have taken any notice of his letter is another matter, but in the literature of the subject there are certainly many predictions which could have been rendered false by the taking of appropriate action.

A more serious difficulty about *psi*-prediction is that it apparently implies that causation can work backwards in time. In the case of Mr. Dunne and his dream it would be most unreasonable to suppose that the dream was the cause of the accident which happened to the Flying Scotsman several months later, since dreams are not usually found to have such violent psycho-kinetic consequences. If the two events are causally linked, we should naturally assume that in some sense the dream was induced by the future accident.* But such an assumption would be inconsistent with our ordinary usage of the terms 'cause' and 'effect'. By the very definition of the terms a cause must precede its effect. But, as Mr. Flew hints, it may turn out that though the notion of causation is an indispensable one for the practical activities of normal life, it cannot be applied in the sphere of the paranormal. Or, as Mr. Mundle suggests, some modifications of the definitions of cause and effect may have to be elaborated, so as to include paranormal causation as well as normal causation.

When, in one case, an agent looks at a card symbol and the sensitive writes down the same symbol two seconds later, and, in another case, the sensitive writes down a symbol two seconds before the agent looks at the card bearing that symbol, it would certainly seem that, in either case, there is a functional relation between the two events. And in neither case does there appear to be any chain of intermediate events linking the members of the pair. It would appear probable, therefore, that the functional dependence is of essentially the same nature in the case of the $(+1)$ hit as in the case of the $(-1)$ hit.

Mr. Flew thinks that the mental distress which many scientists experience, when confronted with the now established facts of *psi*-phenomena, is not so much due to a feeling that these facts are in conflict with any particular one of the limiting principles so clearly enunciated by Professor Broad, as that they seem to challenge all the basic explanatory concepts and maxims of modern science.

Actually we suspect that the annoyance shown by the average scientist has a simpler explanation. He does not concern himself overmuch about basic principles. When he is confronted with, say, a spontaneous or experimental case of precognition, he feels that not only is he unable

---

* It might, however, be suggested that the mind of the dreamer was influenced not by the future event itself but by a pre-existing mental pattern of the event. Cf. Chap. X, p. 169.

to suggest an explanation, but that no explanation could ever be forth-coming. His irritation is due to the fact that he faces a dead end. But rather than admit this to himself, he will suggest that there was fraud or inaccurate recording, or that chance-coincidence was responsible; any hypothesis, however improbable, will serve so long as it restores him to the realm of the familiar and the everyday.

Such reactions are, however, not peculiar to the scientist, but are shared by most intelligent men when faced with facts which they cannot explain. Strange to say, however, when such a man meets with a para-normal experience of his own, his whole attitude towards that par-ticular type of experience seems to change as if by magic. He no longer expresses disbelief in similar facts related by others. One of us, S.G.S., remembers a conversation he had with the late Sir James Jeans, who said that he found precognition of the paranormal kind very hard to accept. Immediately, however, when telepathy was mentioned, the ex-pression on his face lightened, and he remarked that of course he had no doubt about telepathy, since he had had experiences of this kind himself!

It is not so much the fact that paranormal experiments are difficult to repeat successfully, as the lack of any hypothesis or body of doctrine by which these odd results can be interpreted and classified, that causes most scientific men to ignore them. Scientists, as a whole, dislike experi-menting in regions where there are no working hypotheses to guide them. Hypnotism, for example, has been accepted as a fact by psychologists for at least forty years. But the amount of experiment on hypnotic phenomena which goes on in psychological laboratories is extremely small. This is due largely to the difficulty experimenters have found in constructing any satisfactory theory of the hypnotic state. We have scarcely a better theoretical understanding of hypnotism today than in the days of Esdaile.

If this is true of hypnosis, which is a phenomenon relatively easy to obtain, how much longer may we have to wait before any working hypothesis of the *psi*-function is evolved!

But at the present stage there is a real danger that, in our impatience, we may build up doubtful theories like those of Dunne on precognition. Instead of wasting time in the construction of sterile hypotheses, it will be far better for us to carry out more experiments in an attempt to discover the pieces of the puzzle which are missing, and without which no worth-while edifice of theory can ever be built. When we have a far greater number of well-established facts than we possess at present, useful hypotheses may begin to suggest themselves, and these in turn will lead us to the discovery of new facts.

## Recent Criticisms of ESP Research

A major fallacy which underlies much of the opposition of scientific men to the facts of extra-sensory perception is the tacit, though arrogant, assumption that everything really worth knowing about the Universe has already been discovered, and that it is now merely a question of the filling in of the details.

It is assumed that nothing which does not obey the laws of physics, as we know them today, can possibly be true. But a very little reflection ought to show the absurdity of such a contention. Professor Broad* has pointed out more than once that, but for the accident that certain substances such as lodestone and amber are fairly common on the Earth's surface, mankind might have remained ignorant of the phenomena of electro-magnetism. In that case any unorthodox scientist who discovered faint traces of such phenomena would probably have been derided. It is true that very great progress has been made in the physical sciences, but we remain in the deepest ignorance concerning the probable relation between cerebral and mental phenomena.

When a physicist asserts categorically that there can be no such thing as extra-sensory perception, he is simply making an illegitimate excursion outside his own province. The question of the existence of *psi*-phenomena is to be settled on the adequacy of the evidence, and on that alone. As we have seen in the preceding pages, many eminent philosophers, psychologists, and biologists have expressed their considered judgment that the evidence for telepathy at least is now adequate, both as regards quality and quantity. Nowadays there is very little criticism of the experimental evidence that need be taken seriously. More often than not the would-be critic betrays the fact that he has not even taken the trouble to make himself conversant with the published reports which he presumes to criticize. A case in point is that of Professor Skinner, a psychologist now at Harvard University. Professor Evelyn Hutchinson* of Yale had written a long and careful account of the Shackleton experiments for the *American Scientist*. In a later issue of the same journal, Skinner wrote a letter attacking card-guessing experiments in general, and the Shackleton experiments in particular. This letter contained so many mis-statements and errors of fact that it was clear both to Evelyn Hutchinson and to S.G.S. that Skinner had not read the Shackleton report at first hand. For instance, he spoke of packs of cards shuffled by hand whereas no such packs were used in our experiments. He also hinted that recording errors might afford a possible explanation of the results, whereas separate records were kept of card

* XV, 2.                           † IV, 25.

lists prepared before the experiment and of Shackleton's own guesses recorded by himself and these independent records could be re-checked at any future time.

In a recent book *The Psychology of the Occult* (London 1952), D. H. Rawcliffe* attempts to show that successful experiments in parapsychology are, without exception, based on methodological errors. Now it is essential that a would-be critic should be meticulous in his description of detail and in matters of fact. This critic omits relevant details when these do not help his case and distorts other facts. He concentrates for the most part on inconclusive and weak experiments and fails to mention some of the crucial ones. He thus presents a highly misleading and fragmentary version of the experimental situation. In his discussion of ESP there is no mention of the very important Pearce-Pratt experiments, or of those of Martin and Stribic or of the work of Tyrrell and Whately Carington, in which all sensory cues were ruled out absolutely. In his chapters on mediums there is no mention even of Mrs. Piper who convinced men of the calibre of William James, Richard Hodgson, and Sir Oliver Lodge. And though the author stresses the importance of mechanical recording he appears to have been unaware of the electric recorder used by Tyrrell or of the experiments of David Kahn.

We have already in Chapter XI repudiated Mr. Rawcliffe's attack on the Shackleton experiments, and here we shall merely point out a serious distortion. On p. 477 he remarks: 'The door in his Shackleton experiments was purposely "left an inch or two ajar in order to facilitate hearing" the verbal signals of the assistant experimenter—an unwise precaution at best!'

But what Mr. Rawcliffe omits to mention is that in the Soal-Goldney report it is definitely stated that for the first nine sittings *both* doors between the two rooms were completely closed. Further, Shackleton, working with prepared random numbers, scored a significantly higher average of (+1) hits on the first eight occasions than on the next eight† during which one door was slightly ajar. On Rawcliffe's theory of 'double whispering' we should certainly not expect this to be the case.

Indeed, with the random number method at the 'normal' rate of calling, with Miss Elliott as agent, the scoring rate per 24 trials was 7·39 for the first eight sittings, whereas for the next eight (one door slightly ajar) it was only 6·56 hits per 24 trials. There were 64 sets of (+1) trials in the first series and 71·88 sets in the second series. Using the observed standard deviation of 2·36 for 24 trials, we find that the critical ratio of the

* XI, 13.
† Sitting No. 9 was a 'counters' experiment, and hence is omitted from consideration.

difference of the two rates of scoring exceeds 2. The odds therefore in favour of the supposition that Shackleton did better with the door shut than when it was open are about 20 to 1 and this result hardly squares with any theory of whispering

One would have thought that before attempting to criticize statistical experiments Mr. Rawcliffe would have made himself acquainted with the elementary principles of statistical evaluation. Yet this writer actually confuses the size of a sample with the significance of the result for he says that the Shackleton series would be a weak support for Soal's conclusions since their total number is only 6,690 guesses which is a small number compared with the number of guesses in the American experiments. Actually there were, in all, 11,378 (+1) trials and these gave odds far exceeding $10^{35}$ to 1 against the hypothesis that the result was due to chance. But the *number* of trials has nothing to do with the *significance* of the result.

Again, (p. 472) speaking of the telephone experiment in which Mrs. Stewart and the agent were 8 or 10 feet from their instruments, Mr. Rawcliffe expresses surprise that there should be as many as 60 hits in 200 trials. But he concludes that 200 guesses are too few to be of any significance! Yet the 'odds against chance' are of the order of 2,000 to 1.

This pathetic misunderstanding of principles is again illustrated on p. 471 of his book, where he accuses Soal of 'optional stopping' in connection with 529 (+2) and 529 (−2) trials with Shackleton which yielded critical ratios of 4·62 and 5·21 respectively. A statistician would have realized that with two critical ratios at such a level, optional stopping—if it were a fact—would be of no importance whatever. Indeed, it would be absurd to apply the principle of optional stopping to the work of subjects like Shackleton or Mrs. Stewart whose scoring rates remained at a constant high level over a period of years, with ever increasing critical ratios, and with 'odds against chance' amounting to $10^{35}$ to 1 and $10^{70}$ to 1 respectively. Wherever these series are stopped, a highly significant total score is obtained.

A successful critic has to show that the best experiments are faulty. It will not do for him to find errors in, say, the early work of Rhine and then conclude that later experiments based upon an incomparably more rigorous technique are equally invalid. On the same grounds we should have to reject most of present-day physics because the pioneers often did not refine their methods at the first approach. But what Mr. Rawcliffe demands is that all experiments should at once reach the level of perfection. Such a requirement could be made only by one who has but a nodding acquaintance with experimental progress in science. The questionable experiments of Riess, Drake, Carpenter and Phalen, which in the present book we have scarcely considered to be worthy of mention, do not in any way discredit later series. Weak papers in science do not decrease the value of strong ones and every scientific journal contains a mixture of excellent work and more dubious material.

Moreover, the later series of successful experiments in ESP provide confirmation of the findings of previous workers. We are no longer dealing with an occasional isolated success but now with a whole series of well-conducted and highly significant experiments carried out under stringent conditions.

Mr. Rawcliffe's book has its touches of comedy, as, for instance, when he seems to hint that professional psychologists who study ESP, such as Dr. Gertrude Schmeidler (and we might add Dr. R. H. Thouless, Professor Gardner Murphy, Professor C. A. Mace), are only 'amateurs' whose incompetence discredits their experiments. It is difficult to discover any contribution from Mr. Rawcliffe to the field of psychology. *The Psychology of the Occult* would, we feel, have reached a higher standard of scholarship had the author taken lessons from the psychologists whom he affects to despise. Dr. Thouless[5] has aptly stated the crux of the case against Rawcliffe in a sentence: 'The real difference between Mr. Rawcliffe and the experimental psychical researcher (or parapsychologist) is that between the Inquisition and Galileo. He knows beforehand what can and what cannot happen; the psychical researcher wants to find out by experiment.' (*Journal* of the Society for Psychical Research, May–June 1952, p. 627.)

## Is ESP a Statistical Artifact?

In the preceding chapters we have urged that the best experiments in ESP cannot be attacked on methodological grounds or dismissed as cases of the imperfect elimination of normal sensory cues. Nor can such series be reasonably attributed to simple fraud. It has been demonstrated further that the statistical methods of dealing with the data are as sound as those employed in the other branches of science.

In a recent article entitled *Statistical Significance in Psychical Research*, published in *Nature*, 25th July 1953, Mr. G. Spencer Brown has suggested that the so-called random distributions to be found in certain well-known tables of random numbers do not always behave in practice as we should expect according to accepted probability theory. Mr. Brown does not dispute the mathematical validity of the formulae which are employed in card-guessing but he attacks the fundamental concept of randomness itself, on which these formulae are based. In support of his criticism that physical randomness is in practice ill-defined and unverifiable, he claims that by pairing off two series of random digits 1–5 chosen without previous examination from, say, Fisher's tables, he has obtained significant deviations from the mean score in one or two instances, and an apparent decline effect in another case. These results have not yet been published in detail, but Mr. Brown maintains that ESP coincidences are in no sense meaningful, but are merely examples of a breakdown in accepted probability theory. That is, telepathy, for instance, is not to be regarded as implying any real causal relation between the mental processes of two persons, but is merely something in the nature of a statistical artifact. Until Mr. Brown's findings have been criticized by statisticians and confirmed by other workers, it is not possible to predict whether or not both ordinary scientists and ESP investigators will be compelled to adopt rather higher standards of significance in their experimental work.

Now the unanswerable objections to Mr. Brown's contention that ESP phenomena are merely examples of a hitherto unnoticed defect in accepted probability theory, are:

1. The persistent scoring above chance expectation, week after week, and year after year, under first-class experimental conditions, of subjects like Miss Johnson, C. Jencks, Hubert Pearce, Basil Shackleton and Gloria Stewart.

2. The fact that, in many series, changes in the experimental conditions, or in the agents, produce consistent and highly characteristic changes in the nature of the results. We need only refer the reader to the highly significant and consistent displacement shifts which regularly followed a change in the rate of calling with Shackleton and Mrs. Stewart. See pp. 151, 157, 158, 161, 210, 214–18 and pp. 60, 85, 246, 266, 389 for other examples.

Mr. Brown's main contention is that the concept of randomness applies only to an infinite series of events and that all finite series are imperfectly random. Further, since there exists no complete series of tests by which we can decide whether a given series of finite length is random, and since the applications of the ordinary probability formulae are based on the concept of physical randomness, which is a vague and ill-defined notion, we must not be surprised if the formulae occasionally break down in practice and indicate causal relations which may be illusory.

Mr. Brown disclosed that his two or three significant deviations obtained in long series of 'mock' ESP experiments in matching sets of random digits were of the order of about three standard deviations and such meagre results will not bear comparison with any of the outstanding ESP work described in this book.

Moreover, in his paper to *Nature* Mr. Brown displayed great ignorance of the experimental work in ESP by stating that in demonstrations of telepathy control series have not been used, and that such control series might give results that were as curious as the ESP results themselves. The obvious and adequate control is to check series of guesses against packs of cards for which they were not originally intended. Mr. Brown seemed unaware that in most of the major experiments extensive checks of this kind have been made, with results that were always in reasonable agreement with chance expectation. That is, the 'cross-checks' failed to produce anything even remotely resembling the high scores of the original experiments.

When this was pointed out to Mr. Brown (*Nature*, 26 September 1953) he cited *other kinds* of control experiment which gave significant deviations. But in two of the three examples quoted (Coover and Forwald) faulty experimental conditions were probably responsible, while in the case of Nigel Richmond ESP and PK were not excluded in the control.

But, more important, the extensive researches of G. Schmeidler, B. Humphrey and the most recent work of Humphrey and Nicol, with groups of persons, has revealed highly significant correlations between the ESP scores and certain personality traits of the scorers. With increasing consistency it is coming to light that the above-chance deviations are to a large extent produced by the socially adjusted, extravert types of personality, and the below-chance scores by the introvert, maladjusted types.

Thus in their paper *The Exploration of ESP and Human Personality* J. Fraser Nicol and Betty M. Humphrey (*Jour. Amer. Soc. for Psych. Res.* Vol. XLVII, October 1953) found a highly significant positive correlation ($P = 0.0015$) between the trait of self-confidence and above-chance scoring on ESP cards. In a total of 30 subjects tested for ESP, 16 were graded by means of well-known personality questionnaires as self-confident and the remaining 14 as lacking in self-confidence. It was found that 81 per cent of the confident people produced scores above the average level and 79 per cent of those classed as 'un-confident' scored at or below the average level.

Each person was made to guess through 16 packs of ESP cards, and it was noted that those lacking in self-confidence began by scoring as well as those who were confident, but whereas the latter group continued to score at a consistent above-chance level, the success of the former group was short-lived, and declined rapidly to a below-chance average.

Above-chance scoring was also found to be associated very significantly with emotional stability.

Now such results as these are meaningful, and cannot be explained away as statistical artifacts as Mr. Brown would explain them.

Throughout this book we have drawn attention in footnotes to experimental results which are entirely at variance with Mr. Spencer Brown's hypothesis but in the present section we have gathered together a few of the most important reasons why Mr. Brown's contention is erroneous. Take first the question of the persistence of high-scoring shown by the major ESP subjects.

Let us consider for example the Stewart experiments in which blocks of 50 trials in which the agent did not look at the cards were rigidly or randomly interspersed with blocks of 50 in which the cards were known to the agent. On each occasion 200 'telepathy' trials were mixed with 200 'clairvoyance' trials. For each set of 200 the expectation is 40 hits. The results are displayed below in chronological order.

*Hits in* 200 *trials*

(T = Telepathy; C = Clairvoyance)

|   | 1945 |    |    |    |    | 1947 |    |    |
|---|----|----|----|----|----|----|----|----|
| T | 67 | 58 | 62 | 58 | 60 | 54 | 55 | 65 |
| C | 51 | 42 | 29 | 47 | 38 | 35 | 36 | 31 |

|   | 1948 |    | 1949 |    |    | *Totals* |
|---|----|----|----|----|----|-------|
| T | 39 | 56 | 49 | 51 | 33 | 707 |
| C | 38 | 43 | 40 | 37 | 42 | 509 |

In the 13 sets of 200 'telepathy' trials no fewer than eight have deviations as high as 15. The extra-chance effect on as small a number of trials as 200 is more marked than in the majority of biological and psychological experiments.

In fact, the first score of 67/200 alone corresponds to odds against the result's being due to chance which amount to about half a million to one! Indeed, if Mr. Spencer Brown's assumptions were correct, such enormous discrepancies between mathematical theory and observed fact would render statistics useless as a scientific instrument. If Mr. Brown is right we shall have to dispute the conclusions of thousands of papers published every year which are based on odds of no more than a few hundred to one.

And an exactly similar argument would apply to the data of the Pearce-Pratt experiments, those of Martin and Stribic, those of Tyrrell and others.

We repeat here what we have said earlier, that the evidence for ESP does not, and cannot, depend on series which give odds of the order of a thousand or fifteen hundred to one since we do not know how many persons in England and America are engaged in card-guessing experiments. But we do know that if every person in England had repeated the 11,000 odd trials of the Shackleton series or the Pearce-Pratt series it would be fantastically improbable that a single individual should have produced results even remotely resembling the results actually observed in either of these series. And in both series the experimental conditions were very satisfactory.

So far as ordinary card-guessing is concerned there is no reason whatever to suppose that well-shuffled packs of Zener cards give results which are not in strict accordance with the orthodox probability formulae. The monumental series of half a million matchings by the statistician Greenwood of cards against guesses for which they were not intended showed conclusively that experimenters can rely on the binomial formulae. All this has to be set against any findings which Mr. Spencer Brown may publish. If indeed this critic can, by matching two ordered sequences, each of one thousand random numbers 1–5 chosen systematically and without previous study from *any* of the current tables, obtain a deviation from chance expectation with odds which exceed even $10^5$ to 1, the writers of this book will henceforth abandon the hypothesis of ESP! They would, of course, require chapter and verse which would enable them to check the series for themselves.

Moreover, before placing reliance on the results obtained by Mr. Brown from random tables, they would need to know how many such artificial experiments produce only chance deviations. If one series gives a critical ratio of, say, 3, and twenty similar sets produce nothing remarkable, the final result may be insignificant. Optional stopping is also important here.

If the reader turns again to the above list of 'telepathy' and 'clairvoyance' scores, the difference of the scores in the first and second lines will be obvious. The 'clairvoyance' scores are all reasonably close to mean chance expectation and there is a difference between the total 'telepathy' and the total 'clairvoyance' hits of 198. Indeed, whereas the first series gave 'odds against chance' of $10^{19}$ to 1, the second series gave a deviation of only $-11$ hits.

But statistical artifact is no respecter of the experimental conditions and the difference can be due only to the fact that in one case the sender looked at the cards and in the other he did not.

## Is Statistical Artifact a Respecter of Persons?

It will be recalled that S.G.S. subjected 160 persons to ESP tests with Zener cards and found the results of more than 120,000 guesses to be in good agreement with probability theory in regard to the (0) and

($\pm$1) trials. Now a statistical artifact could not distinguish between personalities. Yet two persons, each of whom had claimed paranormal powers before they were tested, produced extra-chance results high above average. And, even more inexplicable on Mr. Spencer Brown's theory, when Shackleton and Mrs. Stewart were re-tested a few years later they both continued week after week and year after year to produce high scores with ever increasing critical ratios! This is surely incomprehensible on the theory that ESP is a mere statistical artifact. Why should a supposed non-randomness be any respecter of persons?

We should surely, if there was anything in Mr. Spencer Brown's ideas, expect some of the other 158 persons to exhibit similar extra-chance scoring. The same tables of random numbers were used throughout the work. And why did the cross-checks both in the case of Shackleton and of Mrs. Stewart always produce scores which were in close agreement with those expected on the binomial theory?

Again the persistence of ESP scoring in the case of two or three subjects *only* was noticed in the Martin and Stribic work. The remainder continued to score at the chance level.

## Comparison of Mrs. Stewart with a Contemporaneous Guesser

On the dates 28th April 1947, 5th, 12th and 19th May 1947, while Mrs. Stewart sat in the kitchen making her guesses under TTN or T2SCTN conditions, Mr. D. A. Stewart, sitting near the fire in the lounge, in a position from which he could not see the cards in the box, wrote down his own guesses for these same cards.

On a total of 1,000 'telepathy' trials Mrs. Stewart scored 263 direct hits, and this corresponds to CR = 4·98 with odds against the result being due to chance of about a million to one.

The contemporaneous guesser, D. A. Stewart, obtained, however, only 194 direct hits which gives a deviation from the expected number (200) of only −6. Yet the same series of target digits 1–5 was employed for both guessers. Once again we ask: Why is statistical artifact a respecter of persons?

There are, of course, numerous other examples of this important feature throughout both the Shackleton and Stewart series. For instance, in the cases of both Mrs. Stewart and Shackleton, there were consistent and profound changes in the displacement scores which followed immediately on the doubling of the speed of calling, and a return to normal when the speed returned to its original rate.

Such features* are not statistical artifacts but evidence of real psychological differences. How does Mr. Spencer Brown reconcile these redoubtable observations with his own peculiar theories?

## The Present Outlook

At the time when we write, numerous investigations are in progress at universities and research centres. In the academic session 1951–2 London University awarded another degree (that of M.A.) to Mr. F. Claude Palmer for a piece of experimental research entitled *The Influence of Unconscious Factors as Revealed in Experiments on Telepathy and Mental Testing in the Same Group of Individuals.*

During the same session Dr. G. D. Wassermann, a mathematical physicist, was awarded a grant by Durham University in order to carry out an extensive programme of experimental work in ESP.

During the session 1952–3 post-graduate students in psychology of Birkbeck College, University of London, have through the co-operation of Professor C. A. Mace been working on ESP in collaboration with the Society for Psychical Research.

Recently Dr. W. H. C. Tenhaeff has been appointed to a Chair of Parapsychology in the University of Utrecht.

At Rhodes University in Grahamstown, South Africa, Mr. Maurice C. Marsh, Lecturer in Psychology under Professor E. H. Wild, has been carrying out an extensive long-distance ESP experiment between Grahamstown and Cape Town, a distance of about five hundred miles.

In this experiment three hundred and seventy-one subjects attempted to reproduce drawings selected by the experimenter, as in Carington's work, but by the use of a modified technique. The percipients, most of whom were students at Rhodes University, were first of all asked to make a list of fifty 'easily drawn unmistakable objects' and to send their lists to the investigator. From the 15,842 objects thus suggested Mr. Marsh chose a hundred, each of which had been mentioned only once. The names of these hundred objects were written on slips of paper and put in a sealed box with a slit in the top.

It was then arranged that on each day for twenty-five days, an agent or sender in Cape Town should shake out two slips from the box and then make outline drawings of the objects taken from the box. Thus, altogether, fifty of the hundred objects were employed as targets, and the remaining fifty served as controls. When the sender had completed his two drawings, he locked them away to ensure that no one else should

* We would also ask Mr. Spencer Brown how his theory can account for the curious Martin and Stribic experiment described in Chapter V, p. 58.

see them or divulge any information about them. Sometime during the following twenty-four hours the percipients or receivers in Grahams town were to attempt to reproduce the two target drawings. The 17,440 drawings made by the percipients or guessers were randomized and coded, and then despatched with the fifty target drawings and the fifty 'control' drawings to three independent judges for assessment. The judges were asked to match the subjects' drawings against the hundred target and 'control' drawings which were mixed together. These judges had no means of discovering whether a particular one of the hundred drawings had been used as a target or as a 'control'.

The matchings gave significantly more hits on the target drawings than on the 'control' drawings. Further, on the target drawings themselves, there were significantly more hits than would be expected on the basis of the preliminary frequencies of selection.

The most interesting feature exhibited by the results was the observation that the percipients' drawings tended to hit the fifty target drawings *as a group* rather than the two targets aimed at by the percipients on any particular day.

In other words, just as in Carington's original experiment, there was displacement of successful guesses on to the targets displayed on previous or following days.

The final report on this interesting investigation has not yet been published, but when Mr. Marsh was in London last spring, *en route* for Duke University, he assured S.G.S. that his results were highly significant. That all sensory cues were ruled out must be clear from the nature of the experiment and the precautions taken to ensure that the judges could not distinguish between targets and 'controls'.

As another example of the growing interest taken by the English universities in parapsychology, the Committee of Advanced Studies at Oxford University has quite recently made a year's grant to Mr. William G. Roll for the establishment of a small parapsychology laboratory at Oxford. Mr. Roll is a graduate student working on a thesis which deals with the philosophical implications of ESP. He intends to carry out ESP experiments with the use of hypnosis, and will work under the supervision of Professor H. H. Price, who is also an active participant in the experiments.

Even in America, where psychology is far more behaviourist and materialistic than in this country, there are signs that parapsychology is finding its way into psychological textbooks. Dr. A. A. Roback Professor of Psychology at Emerson College, in his new book the *History of American Psychology* gives, in a chapter entitled 'The Phenomenal Expansion of American Psychology', a review of the historical beginnings of parapsychology in the United States, and the psychologists who have taken part in *psi* investigations. The author also points out how Professor William McDougall helped to bring parapsychology into the American university.

In conclusion we shall quote some passages from the address which Dr. R. H. Thouless[7] delivered to the Royal Institution of Great Britain on 1st December 1950, entitled *Thought Transference and Related Phenomena*. 'In all science, an unexpected experimental result is a challenge to the basis of our expectations and so becomes a possible starting point of theoretical advance. The failure of the Michelson-Morley experiment to reveal the expected motion of the earth relative to the ether made necessary the reconstruction of the theory on which the expectation of a detectable ether drift was based. By good fortune, this situation also produced the genius of Einstein who was able to take the essential step in the reconstruction of theory which made the Michelson-Morley result explicable.

'I suggest that the discovery of the *psi* phenomena has brought us to a similar point at which we must question basic theories because they lead us to expectations contradicted by experimental results. The history of physics should encourage us to pay attention to the unexpected experimental result and to regard it as an invitation to reconsider the theory which underlies our expectations. The theory must be changed until it leads us to expect that to happen which in fact does happen. In the fact that we have experimental results that are unexpected and inexplicable, we have in parapsychology a situation favourable to a profitable advance in theory.

'I think the one lesson we can learn from the history of theoretical physics is the desirability of flexibility of mind in approaching such problems. The obstacle to new theoretical insights in the past has been rigidity in holding to old conceptions. Because the conceptions belonging to the science of the past may become embedded in the language we use, we are very much inclined to mistake them for necessary truths. It is not, of course, possible to say which of our old conceptions must be given up in order that we may begin to understand *psi*. If I knew that, I should be in a position to lay the foundation for the new science which will include *psi*. I am certainly not in such a position.

'I can only suggest that we must be ready to question all our old conceptions and to distrust all our habits of thought.

'There is one conception of current scientific thought which has a degree of prestige that makes it difficult to question, which nevertheless, I think is perhaps one of the limiting conceptions it may be necessary to discard. This is the system of ideas sometimes called the "psychosomatic theory" which regards all mental phenomena as aspects o physical events in the nervous system.

'Dr. Wiesner and I have suggested that perhaps the *psi* process is no essentially paranormal but is the normal process by which I am informe about external events by the mediation of events in the nervous system and that paranormal *psi* processes are simply cases in which this mediation is discarded and I am directly aware of an external event. Such a view necessarily implies the discarding of the psychosomatic theory since the "I" referred to must be something other than the nervous system itself or any aspect of it.'

# APPENDIX A

# Non-Mathematical Terms and Abbreviations

---

(*a*) GENERAL TERMS USED IN PARAPSYCHOLOGY.
(*b*) SPECIAL TERMS USED IN THE SHACKLETON EXPERIMENTS.
(*c*) SPECIAL TERMS USED IN THE STEWART EXPERIMENTS.
(*d*) SPECIAL TERMS USED IN THE 1934–9 EXPERIMENTS.

## (*a*) General Terms

1. PSI. A general term coined by Dr. R. H. Thouless and Dr. B. P. Wiesner to cover processes and factors in the human personality or in nature which appear to transcend or deny the accepted limiting principles of science.
2. PARAPSYCHOLOGY. The study of *psi*-processes in the human or animal mind.
3. ESP (Extra-Sensory Perception). A term coined by Dr. J. B. Rhine of Duke University, N. Carolina. It is defined as a partial or complete correspondence (*a*) between the mental patterns of two persons A and B which is not to be accounted for by normal sense-perception or by inferences drawn from sense-perception or by chance-coincidence *or* (*b*) between a mental pattern of a person A and an object or event in the physical world which is not to be accounted for by normal sense-perception or by inferences drawn from sense-perception or by chance coincidence. In neither (*a*) nor (*b*) need the correspondence be between contemporaneous patterns or between a mental pattern and a physical object which are contemporaneous.
4. TELEPATHY. An extra-sensory correspondence between a present mental pattern of A and a present, past, or future mental pattern of B. The possibility of clairvoyance must have been eliminated.
5. PRECOGNITIVE TELEPATHY. An extra-sensory correspondence between a present mental pattern of A and a future mental pattern of B.

6. POST-COGNITIVE TELEPATHY. An extra-sensory correspondence between a present mental pattern of A and a mental pattern of B of which B was conscious in the past but of which he is not contemporaneously conscious.

7. CLAIRVOYANCE. An extra-sensory correspondence between a present mental pattern of A and a past, present or future object or event in the physical world. In order to establish clairvoyance by experiment it is necessary to show that there is no mental pattern correlated to the physical event which belongs to the past, present or future experience of any person other than A. That is, the event must never at any time be the object of sense-perception.

8. PRECOGNITIVE CLAIRVOYANCE. An extra-sensory correspondence between a present mental pattern of A and a future object or event in the physical world.

9. RETROCOGNITIVE CLAIRVOYANCE. An extra-sensory correspondence between a present mental pattern of A and a physical event which happened in the past.

10. PK (PSYCHOKINESIS). An alleged direct influence exerted on a physical system by a person without the use of any known physical instruments or intermediating forms of physical energy. The term is usually employed to cover experiments in which certain persons are alleged to have influenced the fall of a die by means unknown to science.

11. GESP (General or undifferentiated ESP). Any technique for the demonstration of extra-sensory perception which permits either telepathy or clairvoyance or both to operate. An example is an experiment in which one person guesses at the figures on cards which are being looked at by a second person. In such a case it is impossible to say whether the extra-sensory stimulus is the card itself as a physical object or the image of the card which is in the second person's mind.

12. THE AGENT. In an experiment for telepathy, the person who looks at the card, drawing, or other stimulus object. This person is sometimes called the SENDER or TRANSMITTER.

13. THE PERCIPIENT. In any ESP experiment, the person who makes the guesses or 'calls' in attempts to identify the stimulus object. More generally the person who receives an ESP impression whether in an experiment or spontaneously. This person is sometimes called the SUBJECT, GUESSER or RECEIVER.

14. TARGET CARD. The symbol or picture which is intended by the experimenter to be the stimulus object which the percipient is trying to identify. More specifically it means the card focused by the

agent or experimenter at the moment when the percipient records his guess, and in this sense it is called the (0) card.

15. ZENER CARDS. Cards used in ESP experiments which bear one of the five symbols: circle, plus sign, rectangle, star, and wavy lines. The cards are made into packs of 25, and, as used by Rhine, each pack contains exactly five cards of each symbol. In his 1934-9 experiments, however, S.G.S. used packs of 25 which contained random distributions of the five Zener symbols, so that, in general, there were not equal numbers of each symbol in a pack. This method greatly simplifies the statistical evaluation of displacement phenomena.

16. FIVE-SYMBOL CARDS. Cards similar to Zener cards, in which any five distinct types of symbol are used, such as the pictures of five different animals or the initial letters of their names, or five different colours, etc.

17. DT (DOWN THROUGH). A clairvoyance technique in which a person guesses at the order of a pack of cards from top to bottom without any of the cards being touched or removed until the 25 guesses are completed.

The danger attached to this method is that, unless the pack is placed in a box or envelope, or behind a screen, the guesser may catch a glimpse of the bottom card or recognize the top card from specks on its back.

18. BT (BROKEN TECHNIQUE). A clairvoyance technique in which each card is lifted off the pack by the experimenter as the percipient makes his guess and is placed face downward on another pile. The guesses are not checked till the end of the run of 25 cards. If this method is employed, the experimenter and guesser should be on opposite sides of an opaque screen or the guesser may 'learn' the cards from irregularities on their backs.

19. TRIAL. Each single guess at a card or stimulus object.

20. RUN. A group of trials; more specifically the successive calling of a pack of 25 five-symbol cards. Thus $N$ runs comprise $25N$ (0) trials, but $24N$ (+1) or (−1) trials and $23N$ (+2) or (−2) trials.

21. SESSION. A unit of an ESP experiment which comprises all the trials done on a single occasion, e.g. the trials done in an evening's sitting.

22. SCORE. The number of correct guesses or 'hits' obtained in a given number of trials. Thus 60/200 means that 60 guesses were correct out of 200 trials. The term is also used for the number of hits in a run of 25 trials.

361

23. CALL. The symbol selected by the percipient in his attempt to identify the target card.

## (b) Special Terms Used in the Shackleton Experiments

1. (A). Agent.
2. (P). Percipient.
3. (EA). The experimenter who controlled the agent. His task was to present the random numbers or counters at the hole in the screen, to call out the serial number which was the signal for Shackleton to write down his guess, and to record the code (i.e. the order of the five cards in the box) on the scoring sheet.
4. (EP). The experimenter who controlled the percipient. He sat beside Shackleton and watched him as he made his guesses. His main tasks were to see that Shackleton kept in step with the serial numbers called aloud by (EA), to see that Shackleton did not leave his seat, and to record anything of interest connected with the guessing.
5. (O) (Observer). His function was to satisfy himself that the experiment was carried out in a scientific manner. He was allowed to take any steps he wished to ensure that no one taking part in the experiment cheated or failed to exercise proper care in carrying out his allotted task. He was asked to see that the decoding and checking were accurately done.
6. PRN (Prepared Random Numbers). Experiments in which the cards to be focused by the agent were determined by random lists of the digits 1–5 prepared from mathematical tables before the experiment began.
7. COUNTERS. Experiments in which the card to be looked at by (A) was determined by (EA)'s drawing a counter from a bag or bowl which contained equal numbers of similar discs in five different colours.
8. THE (a) COLUMN. The left-hand column of the scoring sheet with its two divisions of 25 cells—A for actual card targets and G for guesses.
9. THE (b) COLUMN. The right-hand column of the scoring sheet which also provided for 25 calls and 25 targets.
10. THE CODE. A record on each scoring sheet of the order of the five cards as they lay in the box in front of the agent. It was written thus: $\begin{smallmatrix} P & E & G & Z & L \\ 1 & 2 & 3 & 4 & 5 \end{smallmatrix}$. It gave the order of the cards as seen by (A) from left to right. The letters are the initials of the names of

the five animals, and the order was changed after every sheet of 50 trials.

11. DECODING. The translation of Shackleton's G-columns of guesses at the five initials into the corresponding numbers 1–5 by means of the code on each sheet, and the copying of these numbers into the G-column of the corresponding sheet of random numbers. This was usually done at the end of each session.

12. CHECKING. The ticking-off and counting of the (0) hits in each column and also the displacement hits. The scores for each column were recorded thus: 2/8/5/7/4, where the centre figure is the (0) score, those to the left of the centre the (+1) and (+2) scores, and those to the right the (−1) and (−2) scores.

13. DUPLICATE RECORDS. Copies of the original signed scoring sheets made at the end of the experiment and posted immediately to Professor C. D. Broad.

14. TP. *Telepathy* experiments in which the stimulus objects were *pictures* of five animals.

15. TL. *Telepathy* experiments in which the stimulus objects were the initial *letters* of the animals' names.

16. TA. *Telepathy* experiments in which the stimulus objects were five words *associated* with the five animals, i.e. TRUNK, NECK, MANE, BEAK and STRIPES.

17. TPN. *Telepathy* experiments with *pictures* looked at by the agent at *normal* speed, i.e. with an average interval of 2·60 seconds between successive presentations.

18. TPS. *Telepathy* experiments with *pictures* looked at by the agent at the *slow* rate, i.e. with exactly five seconds between successive presentations.

19. RAPID RATE. An increased rate of presentation of counters or random numbers at the aperture of the screen, which gave an average interval of 1·42 seconds between successive calls.

20. CP. *Clairvoyance* experiments in which the stimulus objects were *pictures* of animals.

21. CC. A *cross-check* obtained by the comparison of each guess in the (*a*) column, not with a target in the (*a*) column but with the corresponding target in the (*b*) column of the scoring sheet and the counting of the number of hits thus obtained. Similarly, each guess in the (*b*) column is compared with the corresponding target in the (*a*) column. In the case of Shackleton the cross-check was made only for the displacement scores, which alone were significant.

363

## (c) Special Terms Used in the Stewart Experiments

The abbreviations (A), (P), (EA), and (EP) have the same meaning as in the Shackleton experiments. In addition we have:

1. N. Normal rate of calling. (The average time for 25 calls was 58 seconds.)
2. R. Rapid rate of calling. (The average time for 25 calls was 35 seconds.)
3. (TK) (The time-keeper). His function was to note and record the number of seconds occupied by each run of 25 trials.
4. T. Telepathy.
5. C. Clairvoyance.
6. TLN. *Telepathy* experiments at *normal* rate in which the agent *lifted* the cards in the box one by one and *looked* at them.
7. CTN. *Clairvoyance* experiments at *normal* rate in which the agent *touched* the backs of the cards without knowing the letters on their faces.
8. TTN(x). *Telepathy* experiments at *normal* rate in which the agent looked at the five cards for about x seconds at the beginning of each sheet and then turned them all faces downward. As each random number was presented at the aperture in the screen the agent *touched* the back of the appropriate card without lifting it.
9. TTR(x). *Telepathy* experiments at *rapid* rate in which the agent looked at the five cards for about x seconds at the beginning of each sheet and then turned them all faces downward. As each random number was presented at the aperture in the screen the agent *touched* the back of the appropriate card without lifting it.
10. T2SCTN(x). *Telepathy* experiments at *normal* rate with *two* agents in different rooms. One of these (called the *screen* agent) was shown the random numbers but did not see the cards, while the other (called the *cards* agent) shuffled the five cards and looked at their faces for x seconds at the beginning of each sheet. He then turned them faces downward and took no further part in the experiment. At the end of each sheet (EA) recorded on his scoring sheet the cards agent's code. As the random numbers were shown by (EA) at the aperture in the screen, the screen agent touched the backs of five blank cards.
11. T2SCLN. Experiments similar to T2SCTN(x) experiments except that the *cards* agent *looked* at the row of five cards throughout the duration of the sheet of 50 trials. He then reshuffled his five cards.

12. TTN($x$)X. TTN($x$) experiments in which (P) and (EP) were inside the *X-ray chamber* of the Royal Free Hospital with (A), (EA), and (O) outside.

13. TTN($x$)T. TTN($x$) experiments in which the *telephone* was used and (A) and (P) were about 100 yards apart.

14. TN. *Telepathy* experiments at *normal* rate in which (A) imagined a code-order for the five initials but had only five blank cards in front of him in the box. This was a *pure telepathy* experiment which did not, however, exclude the possibility of precognitive clairvoyance.

15. TTN($x$)E. TTN($x$) experiments in which the possibility of clairvoyance (including precognitive and retrocognitive clairvoyance) was *excluded*. Five special cards were used, each one corresponding to one of the usual cards E, G, L, P, Z. The letters on the special cards were the first (in three cases the first two) letters of the surnames of persons known both to S.G.S. and F.B. (but not to Mrs. Stewart) who, in some particular, resembled the five animals represented by the letters E, G, L, P, Z.

16. TTN($x$)L. TTN($x$) experiments in which (A) and (P) were separated by a *lead* screen.

17. T2OTN($x$). *Telepathy* experiments at *normal* rate with *two* agents in *opposition*. One of these (called the screen agent) sat at the screen in the usual way, while the other (called the second agent) sat where he could see the random numbers shown by (EA) at the aperture in the screen. The agents, at the start of each sheet, each chose a code from a group of four, arranged their five cards to tally with the code chosen, and gazed at the five letters for $x$ seconds. They then turned their cards faces downward and *touched* the backs of the cards corresponding to the random numbers shown at the aperture in the screen. The codes had been so arranged that, whichever two were chosen, the agents would be focusing on different letters when a random number was shown at the aperture in the screen.

18. T3OTN($x$). Telepathy experiments similar to the T2OTN($x$) experiments, but with *three* agents all focusing on different cards at the same time (i.e. in opposition).

19. T2CTN($x$). TTN($x$) experiments with *two* agents in *conjunction*, one called the screen agent in the usual position at the screen and the other called the second agent, sitting where he could see the random numbers shown by (EA) at the aperture in the screen. At the start of each sheet the screen agent shuffled his five cards inside the box, and the second agent arranged his own cards in the same

order on a table. Thus at each presentation both the agents focused on the same symbol.

20. T3CTN($x$). Telepathy experiments similar to the T2CTN($x$) experiments but with *three* agents all focusing on the same symbols.

21. TLNA. TLN experiments in which (TK), (A), and (EA) were in England while (P) and (EP) were in Merksem near *Antwerp*, Belgium.

22. T2OLNA. TLNA experiment in which there were *two* agents in *opposition*.

23. TLNC. TLN experiments in which (A) and (EA) were in *Cambridge*, while (P) and (EP) were in Richmond, Surrey.

24. TTNS($x$). *Telepathy* experiments at *normal* rate, in which (A) shuffled the five cards, laid them in a row faces downward, and then rapidly lifted each card *separately*, looked at it, and let it fall face downwards into its place in the row. The whole operation took about $x$ seconds. When (EA) showed the random numbers at the aperture in the screen (A) *touched* the backs of the corresponding cards without lifting them.

25. TTND$y$($x$). TTN($x$) experiments in which (A) shuffled the cards with eyes shut and laid them faces downward in a row. He then looked at them quickly, one by one, putting each one face downwards after he had looked at it. The whole operation took about $x$ seconds. (EA) then showed to (A) in rapid succession, $y$–1 other sequences of five cards and removed them, the operation for each sequence taking about $x$ seconds. The experiment then proceeded, (A) touching the backs of the cards as the random numbers were shown at the aperture in the screen. In practice, $x$ was three and $y$ either three or four.

26. TTN($x$)OT. TTN($x$) experiments, in which (EA) called 'one' at the start of each column of 25 trials, and then remained silent until he had shown the 25 random numbers at the aperture in the screen. He then called 'right'. (P) started to write down her guesses when (EA) called 'one' and continued to write them in her *own time*. (EP) called 'right' when (P) had finished each column of 25 guesses. It follows that (A) and (P) were generally out of step during the experiment.

27. TTN($x$)D. TTN($x$) experiments during which (EP) talked amusingly or read to (P) while she wrote down her guesses in order to *distract* her attention.

28. TTN($x$)S. TTN($x$) experiments in which both (EP) and (P) were *silent* during the guessing except that (P) called 'right' after each guess.

29. TTN(30)2. TTN(30) experiments in which only *two* symbols were used instead of the usual five.
30. TLP. *Telepathy* experiments with *playing*-cards in which (A) *lifted* them and *looked* at them one by one.
31. TTN(30)Z. TTN(30) experiments in which *Zener* cards were used instead of cards bearing the initials of the names of animals.

## (d) Special Terms Used in the 1934–9 Experiments

1. PC (Pure Clairvoyance). In these experiments with packs of Zener cards contemporaneous telepathy was excluded, but not precognitive telepathy.
2. PCA. *Pure clairvoyance* experiments in which the checking was done after every five guesses with the percipient looking on.
3. PCB. *Pure clairvoyance* experiments in which the results were not checked until the end of 25 guesses and the percipient was not allowed to watch the checking.
4. PCS. *Pure clairvoyance* experiments in which the percipient (P) and the witness (W) sat at opposite ends of a table about four feet apart. Between them was an opaque wooden *screen* measuring about 3′ broad and 2′ 6″ high with no gap between the screen and the table. The experimenter (E) sat on the same side of the screen as (W), but at the side of the table and close to the screen. The pack of cards rested face downwards on the table close to the screen on the same side of it as (W) and (E). (E) lifted off the cards one by one without looking at them, and laid them faces downward in a pile on the table. As he lifted off each card, (E) called aloud 'First guess' or 'Next', as the case might be. As (E) gave this signal, (P) called aloud his guess which was recorded independently by both (E) and (W). The checking was done at the end of 25 trials, and (P) was not allowed to move from his seat on the other side of the screen during the checking by (E) and (W).
5. PCD. *Pure clairvoyance* experiments by the DT method described on p. 29 or by a variation of it.
6. UT. *Undifferentiated telepathy*. Another name for GESP or general extra-sensory perception, in which successful results might be attributed to either telepathy or clairvoyance or to both.

   More specifically S.G.S. used the letters UT to denote a certain technique by which a large number of percipients was tested. For a full description the reader is referred to Chapter VII, p. 114.
7. UTM. Undifferentiated ESP by a screened matching method. See Chapter VII, p. 117.

# APPENDIX B

# Mathematical Terms and Explanations

---

*Note.* In what follows no attempt is made to provide rigorous definitions of such terms as *probability, equal likelihood, mean value,* etc., and the reader is referred to such text-books as H. Cramer's *Mathematical Methods of Statistics* for a satisfactory theoretical discussion. The object of this section is to furnish a useful account of the practical application of probability to elementary problems in card-guessing.

1. RANDOM NUMBERS. Suppose we have a machine which, by means of an electrical or mechanical device, prints in a row some one of the five letters A, B, C, D, E at every trial, repeats of the same letter being possible. Suppose further that we print sequences of 100 trials. Then the total number of *different* sequences we could obtain is clearly $5^{100}$. If in the long run we find that each of these $5^{100}$ different arrangements turns up approximately an equal number of times we say that the machine is a random selector. To decide whether the machine is working randomly we should have to do a large multiple of $5^{100}$ trials.

If however we consider a single batch of 100 trials there is no very clear meaning to be attached to the statement: This batch constitutes a random sequence of 100 trials. The probability that the batch would consist of 100 A's is very small indeed but this bizarre arrangement is just as possible as any one of the other $5^{100}-1$ arrangements.

We could, however, show that the mean expectation of A's in 100 trials is 20 with the same expectation for each of the other four letters. We could also prove that the mean expectation of isolated *doubles* (e.g. EB*AA*CEE D) is 12·736, of isolated *triples* e.g. (D*AAA*CEB*BBB*E) 2·52 and so on for other patterns such as *ABBA*, etc.

Most writers would say that a random batch of 100 would be a batch in which each of the numerous patterns had a frequency which approximated to its mean expectation, always making allowance for the fact that, on the average, in every 20 patterns selected about one would deviate from its mean by more than two standard deviations one by more than three standard deviations in every 370, etc. To test each one of the billions of possible patterns in this way would be a practical impossibility and compilers of tables of random digits usually apply a few tests such as a check on the frequency of the different symbols, the 'runs' test, the 'gap' test, etc. and assume, with reasonable justification, that if these tests give satisfactory results the sequence is approximately random.

## Practical Application

Suppose that we wish to obtain a random sequence of the five animal initials E, G, L, P, Z. We first peruse a standard table of random numbers such as *Tables of Random Sampling Numbers* by M. G. Kendall and Babington Smith (Cambridge University Press 1939). We next agree that *either* of the digits 0, 1 shall stand for E; *either* of the digits 2, 3 for G; *either* of 4, 5 for L; *either* of 6, 7 for P; and *either* of 8, 9 for Z.

We next prepare two packs of cards. The first pack we number 1 to $N$, where $N$ is the number of pages in the tables, and the second pack 1 to $X$, where $X$ is the number of columns on a page. Having shuffled the two packs we draw a card from each. This decides the page at which to open the table and the column of digits to use. We take the digits in the order in which they occur in the column, and translate them into the corresponding letters by means of our pre-arranged code.

Thus the sequence 1 5 5 6 9 8 3 3 2 0 1 . . . becomes E L L P Z Z G G E E . . . By compiling a long list of such symbols, we could make up packs of 25 cards for use in ESP experiments.

The advantage of such 'random' packs over those which contain exactly five cards of each symbol is that, with the 'random' packs, the probability of there being a 'hit' at any trial is always 1/5, and this is true whether we consider (0) hits or, say, (+1) or (−2) hits.

2. PROBABILITY. A *practical* method of estimating probability in the case of such material as playing-cards, etc., is given by the following rule. If there are $N$ events and of these $n$ possess a certain characteristic $C$, then the ratio $n/N$ gives the probability $P$ that when an event happens it will possess the character $C$.

*Example*: There are 52 cards which can be drawn from a pack of ordinary playing-cards. Of these 52 cards 12 will be picture-cards. Hence the probability that a card drawn at random will be a picture-card is given by $P = 12/52$, i.e. $3/13$, i.e. $1/4 \cdot 3$.

If the probability $P$ that a certain event will happen is $1/N$, this is equivalent to the statement that the odds *against* the happening of the event are $N—1$ to 1. Thus the odds against a picture-card being drawn from a pack of playing-cards are $3 \cdot 3$ to 1.

Similarly, such a statement as $P < 0 \cdot 001$ means that the odds against a certain event's happening by chance alone are more than 999 to 1.

In problems connected with such material as playing-cards, dice, etc., the estimation of $P$ depends essentially on an enumeration of (i) the total number of cases, and (ii) the number of cases favourable to the particular event in which we are interested. Such problems are essentially questions of permutations and combinations, i.e. of pure mathematics.

But if we require to know the probability that a slate-dresser in Britain will contract silicosis in twenty years at his job, it is clear that the problem is much more complicated. We cannot question every slate-dresser in the country. We can form only an estimate of $P$ by examining a large sample of the population of slate-dressers. And it is important that we should choose our sample in a random fashion. It would not do, for instance, to select most of our dressers from slate quarries that are equipped with up-to-date machinery for sucking up dust, or from those which are almost destitute of such facilities.

We should have to spend considerable thought in getting a sample that was truly representative of the slate-dressers of Britain.

3. MEAN VALUE (or EXPECTATION). If in a card-guessing experiment the probability of a success at each trial is constant we find the 'mean' or 'expected' number of successes (or 'hits') by multiplying the probability of success at each trial by the total number of trials. Thus with ESP (five-symbol) cards the 'mean' or 'expected' number correct in $N$ trials is $N/5$. With playing-cards the expected number that will be completely correct is $N/52$; with *colour* correct $N/2$; with *suit* correct $N/4$; and with *value* correct $N/13$.

In an actual experiment, the number of hits obtained—even though only chance is at work—is generally either below or above the 'mean' value. But if the experiment were repeated a very large number of times, the average (or arithmetic mean) of the various numbers of correct guesses obtained would approximate closely to the mean value, always provided that only chance is operating.

It is important to notice that, if we use 'random' packs, a high degree of success on, say, the (0) category (direct hits) does not affect the mean chance expectation on the other categories such as (+1) (precognitive).

4. DEVIATION. This is the amount by which the actual number of hits obtained differs from the mean chance expectation. When the number of hits is greater than the expected number, we attach a plus sign (+) to the deviation, and speak of a *positive* deviation; when it is less, we attach a minus sign (−), and speak of a *negative* deviation.

5. MEAN SCORE. The *average* of a number of experimental scores each obtained on the same number of trials. Thus, if in guessing at 10 packs of 25 Zener cards a person gets the scores: 5, 1, 2, 7, 8, 6, 4, 3, 3, 6, his mean score is

$\frac{1}{10} \times (5 + 1 + 2 + 7 + 8 + 6 + 4 + 3 + 3 + 6)$,

i.e. $\frac{1}{10} \times 45$, i.e. 4·5.

That is, we add the separate scores and divide the sum by the number of scores.

6. VARIANCE. This is a mathematical measure of the amount of dispersion of a number of scores about their mean or average score. Consider the two sets of eight scores:

(a) 5, 4, 6, 6, 4, 7, 5, 3.
(b) 1, 10, 0, 12, 5, 2, 1, 9.

In both cases the average or mean score is exactly 5. But there is a difference between the two sets which meets the eye. In the first set (a) no score deviates very much from 5, the average, whereas in the second set (b) three scores are very much below 5 and another three high above the average. We should say that in the (b) series there is a far greater dispersion or 'scatter' than in the (a) series although the average is the same in each case.

In order to obtain an average measure of this dispersion about the mean score, we should first work out the individual *deviations* of the different scores from the mean score, and tabulate them thus:

(a) 0, −1, +1, +1, −1, +2, 0, −2.
(b) −4, +5, −5, +7, 0, −3, −4, +4.

It is clear that some deviations are positive and some negative, but it is only the numerical size of the deviations that counts here. To get a measure of the total dispersion for each series, we might ignore the negative signs and merely add the sets of numerical values, but this, unfortunately, for many reasons, would make

371

statistical theory rather difficult. What we actually do, therefore, is to *square* each deviation and add together the squares to obtain a measure for the total dispersion. We have

(a) Squares: 0, 1, 1, 1, 1, 4, 0, 4. Total: 12.
(b) Squares: 16, 25, 25, 49, 0, 9, 16, 16. Total: 156.

Hence in (a) the 'average dispersion' per run is 12/8, i.e. 1·5, whereas in (b) it is 156/8, i.e. 19·5.

However, in working out this 'average dispersion' or *variance* as it is called, we have based our estimates in each case on only eight samples or scores. If the series (a) and (b) were produced by two card-guessing percipients A and B respectively, who were guessing packs of 25 Zener symbols, we should have to allow them to go on guessing for hundreds of runs instead of only eight runs in order to get a more trustworthy estimate of their average dispersion, i.e. their mean variance per run.

Now it can be shown by statistical theory that, when we have only a limited number of scores at our disposal, we can get a much closer approximation to the *true* variance by dividing the sum of the squares of the separate deviations, not by the number of scores but by *one less than this number*.

In other words, if the deviations of the $N$ scores available are $d_1, d_2, \ldots d_N$, a good estimate of the mean variance of the population to which the $N$ scores belong is given by

$$(d_1{}^2 + d_2{}^2 + \ldots + d_N{}^2)/(N-1).$$

Thus in our two examples, we should take 12/7, i.e. 1·71 and 156/7, i.e. 22·3 as our estimates instead of 12/8 and 156/8.

When $N$, the number of scores, is large (say 100) there is not much difference whether we divide by $N$ or by $N-1$.

In practice, the average or mean of a number of scores seldom works out to a whole number, and the computation of $d_1{}^2, d_2{}^2,$ $\ldots d_N{}^2$ is therefore rather tedious, especially when $N$, the number of scores, is large. It can readily be shown, by very simple algebra, that the expression $(d_1{}^2 + d_2{}^2 + \ldots + d_N{}^2)/(N-1)$ for the estimate of variance, can be obtained by the following rule.

Square each of the $N$ *scores*. Divide the *sum* of the squares by $N$. From this result subtract the *square* of the average, or mean score. Multiply the remainder by the fraction $N/(N-1)$.

Thus in our example (b) above, the sum of the squares of the eight scores is 356. Dividing this by 8 we obtain 44·5. The mean score is 5. Subtracting the square of this we obtain 44·5 − 25, i.e.

372

19·5. The fraction $N/(N-1)$ is 8/7, so that the estimate of variance is 19·5 × 8/7 or 156/7, i.e. 22·3 as by the first method.

7. STANDARD DEVIATION. The square root of the variance of a number of scores is called the standard deviation of a score. Thus, for case (a) above, the standard deviation is $\sqrt{1\cdot71}$, i.e. 1·31, and for case (b) it is $\sqrt{22\cdot3}$, i.e. 4·72. These are, however, the *observed* standard deviations for a set of 25 trials by the two percipients $A$ and $B$ respectively.

If nothing but chance is at work, and 'random' packs of 25 cards are employed, it is easy to calculate by the theory of probability the expected proportions of cases in which no hits, 1 hit, 2, 3, . . . up to 25 hits, will occur, when a person guesses through a number of packs of 25 cards.

Thus with $N$ packs of cards the numbers of packs with no hits has the expectation 0·003778 × $N$, with 1 hit 0·023612 × $N$, with 5 hits 0·196015 × $N$, with 12 hits 0·001171 × $N$, with 16 hits 0·000002 × $N$, and so on.

By the use of these frequencies it is possible to calculate what is called the *theoretical variance* of the score for a pack of 25 five-symbol cards. This works out to be exactly 4, i.e. 25 × 1/5 × 4/5.

There is no difference in essential principle between observed and theoretical variance. In the first case we base our computation on the *actual* scores obtained in an experiment, but in the second case we substitute 'expected scores' for 'actual scores'.

The theoretical variance for the score on a pack containing $N$ five-symbol cards randomly mixed is given by the compact formula

$$V = N \times \tfrac{1}{5} \times \tfrac{4}{5}, \text{ i.e. } 0\cdot16 \times N.$$

Hence the theoretical standard deviation is $\sqrt{V}$, i.e. $0\cdot4\sqrt{N}$, where $N$ is the total number of trials in the group. More generally, if the probability at each trial of there being a hit is $p$, then the probability of there being a miss is $1-p$, say $q$, and the expected proportions for 0, 1, 2 . . . up to $n$ hits in a group of $n$ trials are given by the successive terms in the expansion of $(q + p)^n$ by the binomial theorem, where $q + p = 1$. From these frequencies it can be deduced, by a method identical with that described above, that the theoretical variance for the score on a group of $n$ trials is given by $V = np(1-p)$. Hence the theoretical standard deviation is, by definition, $\sqrt{np(1-p)}$, and this is known as the binomial formula for standard deviation. The underlying assumption is that the probability $p$ of there being a hit at any trial remains constant throughout the group of trials. This will be strictly true for work with cards only if the distribution of symbols to be guessed is a random distribution.

But, in actual practice, moderate deviations from randomness have only a slight effect on the value of the theoretical standard deviation.

When there is any doubt about the use of the binomial formula for the standard deviation in a card-guessing experiment, the observed variance about the theoretical mean 5 should be found for 25 trials, and then the observed variance for $n$ trials can be found by multiplying the first value by $n/25$.

The observed standard deviation can be employed in place of that given by the formula $0.4\sqrt{n}$. If the percipient is scoring very significantly above mean chance expectation, the observed standard deviation from $n/5$ (the theoretical mean) will as a rule exceed $0.4\sqrt{n}$.

8. CR (CRITICAL RATIO). The binomial distribution, for which $p$, the probability of there being a hit, is constant for each trial, and other distributions which differ only slightly from the binomial, tend to approximate to a particular distribution called the 'normal distribution' provided that $p$ is not too small and $n$, the number of trials, is moderately large. The normal distribution is represented by a certain kind of bell-shaped curve and many physical characters, such as height, weight, acuity of hearing, etc., are distributed according to this law. The precise shape of the normal curve is dependent upon the standard deviation of the given distribution, but, in any case, it is possible to calculate from the curve what fraction of the total population will deviate from the mean by amounts which exceed $x$ standard deviations where $x$ is any number we like to choose. Since the normal curve is perfectly symmetrical on each side of the mean ordinate, it follows that positive and negative deviations from the mean which exceed $x$ standard deviations will constitute equal fractions of the total population. Now the actual deviation (positive or negative) of a card-guessing score divided by the theoretical standard deviation is known as the critical ratio (CR). The critical ratio is preceded by a plus or minus sign according as the score is greater than or less than the mean chance expectation. In fact, the CR is the $x$ mentioned above. Tables, based on the normal curve, have been compiled which give the odds against the occurrence by chance in any experiment of a critical ratio (either positive or negative) as large as that actually observed. With $p = 1/5$ and $n$, the number of trials, not less than 200, the error due to the use of the normal distribution in place of the binomial will be fairly small. Actual

tables for the use of those who wish to carry out card-guessing experiments are given in Appendix C.

9. SIGNIFICANCE OF THE DIFFERENCE OF TWO MEANS. In card-guessing experiments we often wish to know whether a change in one of the conditions of a test has any significant effect on the percipient's rate of scoring. When we carry out such an investigation, we must try as far as we can to keep all conditions other than the one whose effect we wish to estimate constant.

Moreover, since a subject's scoring may tend to fall off towards the end of the experimental session, we shall do well to alternate the two conditions in blocks of say 50 trials.

Having performed the experiment, we first work out the mean score for 25 trials under each condition. Suppose these mean scores to be $x_1$ and $x_2$. What we require to know is whether $x_1 - x_2$, the difference between the two scores, is so large that it is unlikely to have been the result of chance coincidence. We must therefore find the theoretical standard deviation of this difference.

By the method described in Appendix B, 6, p. 372, we estimate the *observed* variance for 25 trials about the mean score under each condition. If we denote these two variances by $V_1$ and $V_2$, and if $N_1$ and $N_2$ are the numbers of sets of 25 trials done under each condition, then it can be shown that the variance of the difference $x_1 - x_2$ is given by $V = V_1 / N_1 + V_2 / N_2$, and the standard deviation of $x_1 - x_2$ is $\sqrt{V}$. We then find the critical ratio $(x_1 - x_2) / \sqrt{V}$, and look up Table 11, Appendix C, p. 379, to read off the odds against the occurrence by chance of such a critical ratio. This method will generally give fairly accurate results if the numbers $N_1$ and $N_2$ are not smaller than 30.

For values of $N_1$ and $N_2$ less than 30, Fisher's method for small samples should be used instead.

If the percipient who is being tested under the two conditions is scoring very significantly above chance expectation, the observed variances for 25 trials may be considerably in excess of 4, the theoretical variance. If the value 4 is used for $V_1$ and $V_2$, the significance of the difference $x_1 - x_2$ may be greatly overestimated. As a rule, no serious error will arise if we substitute for both $V_1$ and $V_2$ the observed mean variance per 25 trials for the total $N_1 + N_2$ sets.

*Example.* We ask the question: When working with the agent Miss Elliott at the normal speed of calling, did Shackleton score at a higher rate with prepared random numbers (PRN) than when 'counters' were employed? As we are concerned here with only

(+1) trials and there are only 24 (+1) trials in a column, we shall naturally work out our mean scores and mean variances on 24 and not on 25 trials. $N_1$ and $N_2$ will now be the numbers of sets of 24 trials for PRN and counters respectively, so that $N_1$ is 157·875 and $N_2$ is 65·75.

Now we have

$x_1$ = the mean score on 24 (+1) trials with PRN $\quad\quad = 6·974$
$x_2$ = the mean score on 24 (+1) trials with counters $\quad = 6·677$
Difference $x_1 - x_2 = \quad\quad\quad\quad\quad\quad\quad\quad\quad + 0·297$
$V_1$ = the variance for a set of 24 (+1) trials with PRN $\quad = 5·5689$
$V_2$ = the variance for a set of 24 (+1) trials with counters = 8·0278
Hence $V_1/N_1 = 5·5689/157·875 \quad\quad\quad\quad\quad\quad\quad = 0·0353$
and $V_2/N_2 = 8·028/65·75 \quad\quad\quad\quad\quad\quad\quad\quad\quad = 0·1221$.
And the variance of the difference of the means

$$= 0·0353 + 0·1221 = 0·1574.$$

The standard deviation of the difference = $\sqrt{0·1574}$ = 0·396. Hence the critical ratio = 0·297/0·396 = 0·75. Since the critical ratio is less than 1, there is clearly no significant difference between the scoring rates in the experiments with prepared random numbers and those with counters.

10. DIFFERENCE OF MEANS OF SMALL SAMPLES. When the numbers of scores available for the comparison of two means are small (say when $N_1$ or $N_2$ is less than 30) the above method is not very accurate. We then employ the following technique due to R. A. Fisher. Suppose that the two sets of scores are $x_1, x_2, \ldots x_m$ and $y_1, y_2, \ldots y_n$. Find the two mean scores $\bar{x}$ and $\bar{y}$. Find the deviation of each $x$ from $\bar{x}$ and of each $y$ from $\bar{y}$. Square each of the $m + n$ deviations, and divide the sum of the squares by $m + n - 2$. Extract the square root of the quotient and so obtain a quantity $s$. Compute now a statistic $t$, given by

$$t = \frac{\bar{x} - \bar{y}}{s} \sqrt{\frac{nm}{m + n}}.$$

We must next look up Student's table of $t$-values and read off the value of $P$ which corresponds to the computed $t$-value with $N$ degrees of freedom where $N = m + n - 2$. The value of $P$ found from the table gives the probability that a value of $t$ as large as that computed would arise through chance coincidence alone.

*Example.* Twelve sheets of guesses under TLN conditions were alternated with twelve sheets of guesses made with TTN(30) conditions. Is Mrs. Stewart's rate of scoring higher under TLN conditions than under TTN(30) conditions?

The TLN scores on each set of 50 trials were 9, 13, 15, 8, 15, 11, 15, 15, 12, 13, 18, 13.

The TTN(30) scores were 13, 15, 11, 12, 10, 15, 13, 9, 12, 17, 15, 12.

Hence for TLN the mean score $\bar{x}$ is 157/12, and for TTN(30) the mean score $\bar{y}$ is 154/12. The sum of the squares of the deviations of the TLN scores from $\bar{x}$ is given by sum of squares of the scores minus $12\bar{x}^2$, i.e. $2141 - 157^2/12$, i.e. 86·917.

Similarly the sum of the squares of the deviations from $\bar{y}$ of the TTN(30) scores is given by $2036 - 154^2/12$, i.e. 59·667.

Hence the sum of the squares of the 24 deviations is $86·917 + 59·667$, i.e. 146·584.

And $s^2$ is 146·584/22, i.e. 6·663.

Hence $s$ is $\sqrt{6·663}$, i.e. 2·581.

And $\bar{x} - \bar{y}$ is 3/12, i.e. 0·25.

Hence $t$ is $\dfrac{0·25}{2·581}\sqrt{\dfrac{12 \times 12}{24}}$, i.e. 0·237.

Looking up the table of $t$ opposite $N = 12 + 12 - 2$, i.e. 22, we find that $P$ lies between 0·8 and 0·9. This means a value of $t$ as high or higher than 0·237 would occur by chance about 8 or 9 times out of 10. Thus there is no reason for our attributing any significance to the difference between the rates of scoring in the TLN and TTN(30) experiments.

11. DISPLACEMENT. Responses to targets other than those for which the calls were intended. Responses to targets *preceding* those for which the calls are intended are described as 'post-cognitive' and are designated (−1), (−2), (−3), etc. Similarly, responses to targets *following* the assigned targets are described as 'precognitive' and labelled (+1), (+2), (+3), etc.

When five-symbol cards in packs of 25 are employed, it should be borne in mind that for (+1) or (−1) trials there are 24 and not 25 calls, and for (+2) or (−2) trials there are only 23 calls to be considered.

Thus the mean chance expectation of hits for (+1) or (−1) trials is 4·8 for 24 trials and that for (+2) or (−2) trials is 4·6 for 23 trials.

In the investigation of displacement it is highly desirable to use a random sequence of five symbols, and not packs of 25 which contain equal numbers of cards inscribed with each of the five symbols. Otherwise the statistical procedures for the estimation of chance expectation and standard deviation are rather complicated.

12. INTRINSIC RATE OF SCORING. According to one theory of the

working of ESP, the guesser knows completely a certain number of cards by ESP, and the correct hits which he obtains on the remainder are the result of chance. As we have mentioned in Chapter XVII, p. 297, this is not the only theory that is possible though it may seem the most probable.

To apply the theory to five-symbol cards, suppose that the total number of guesses is $n$, and the total number of hits is $s$. Now if $x$ cards are known completely by ESP, the chance expectation of hits on the remaining $n-x$ cards will be $(n-x)/5$.

Hence we have the simple relation

$$x + \tfrac{1}{5}(n - x) = s,$$

and from this we obtain $x = (5s - n)/4$ for the probable number of cards known by ESP.

The scoring rate is then $x/n$, and the '*intrinsic*' *percentage rate of scoring* is $100x/n$, which is equal to $125s/n - 25$.

Thus Mrs. Stewart obtained 9,410 (0) or 'direct' hits in 37,100 trials. Here $n = 37,100$; $s = 9,410$; $s/n = 0.25364$. And $125s/n - 25 = 6.7$.

This means that, on the average, she knew by ESP nearly seven cards in a hundred.

13. CORRECTION FOR OPTIONAL STOPPING. Dr. J. A. Greenwood suggests the following correction to allow for the effect of stopping an experiment at a favourable point. The experimenter agrees to carry out his test in blocks of guesses of suitable size, the blocks to contain pre-assigned numbers of trials. He fixes beforehand an upper limit $N$ to the number of blocks and plans to stop at the *end* of a block. Then, if $+x$ is the CR attained at the actual stopping-point, and $P$ is the corresponding probability read from the normal tables, the *true* probability of getting $x$, or a higher CR, at any of the $N$ block terminals, cannot exceed $NP$.

# APPENDIX C

TABLE 11

This table gives, for a normal distribution, corresponding values of $x$ and $n$, where $x$ is the critical ratio (i.e. the ratio of the observed deviation to the standard deviation) and $n$ to 1 are the odds against the occurrence by chance of a critical ratio as large as $x$, either positive or negative.

| $x$ | $n$ | $x$ | $n$ |
|---|---|---|---|
| 0·674 | 1·00 | 3·2 | 727 |
| 1·000 | 2·15 | 3·3 | 1,033 |
| 1·5 | 6·48 | 3·4 | 1,483 |
| 1·8 | 12·92 | 3·5 | 2,149 |
| 2·0 | 20·98 | 3·6 | 3,142 |
| 2·1 | 27 | 3·7 | 4,637 |
| 2·2 | 35 | 3·8 | 6,915 |
| 2·3 | 46 | 3·9 | 10,390 |
| 2·4 | 60 | 4·0 | 15,770 |
| 2·5 | 80 | 4·5 | 147,190 |
| 2·6 | 106 | 5·0 | 1,744,000 |
| 2·7 | 143 | 5·5 | 26,000,000 |
| 2·8 | 195 | 6·0 | 500,000,000 |
| 2·9 | 267 | 7·0 | $4·0 \times 10^{11}$ |
| 3·0 | 369 | 8·0 | $8·3 \times 10^{14}$ |
| 3·1 | 516 | | |

# Runs of Successes and Success Groups for 37,100 Trials with Mrs. Stewart

We have noted in Chapter XVIII, p. 314, that Mrs. Stewart tended to pack her hits into the first three segments of the run of 25 trials. It is of interest, therefore, to compare the numbers of isolated hits (or 'singletons'), 'doubles' (i.e. pairs of consecutive hits), 'triples' (runs of three successes), etc., with the numbers that might be expected by chance.

The expectations of 'singletons', 'doubles', 'triples', etc., are computed from the following formulae:

$$E_1 = np(1-p)^2 + 2p^2(1-p)$$
$$E_2 = np^2(1-p)^2 - p^2(1-p)(1-3p)$$
$$E_3 = np^3(1-p)^2 - 2p^3(1-p)(1-2p)$$
$$E_4 = np^4(1-p)^2 \text{ approx.}$$
$$E_5 = np^5(1-p)^2 \text{ approx.}$$

etc.,

where $p$ is the 'observed' probability of a successful guess, and $n$ is the number of trials. Since the 37,100 trials yielded 9,410 (0) hits, the value of $p$ is 9,410/37,100, i.e. 0·2536388; $n = 37,100$.

We thus obtain Table 12.

The counts have been carried out from the end of one column of 25 to the beginning of the next without any breaks in the sequence.

An inspection of the following table shows a marked deficiency of isolated hits or 'singletons' and more runs of 3, 4, 5, etc., than chance would predict. The effect would appear to be due, largely, to the crowding of hits into the first three-fifths of the run.

## TABLE 12

Expected and observed numbers of unbroken runs of 1, 2, 3, . . . hits in a series of 37,100 (0) trials by Mrs. Stewart.

| Number of hits in the run | Expected numbers of runs | Observed numbers of runs |
|:---:|:---:|:---:|
| 1 | 5,241·984 | 4,932 |
| 2 | 1,329·535 | 1,220 |
| 3 | 337·213 | 394 |
| 4 | 85·533 | 127 |
| 5 | 21·695 | 38 |
| 6 | 5·503 | 8 |
| 7 | 1·396 | 12 |
| 8 | 0·354 | 1 |
| 9 | 0·090 | 2 |
| 10 | 0·023 | 0 |
| 11 | 0·006 | 0 |
| 12 | 0·001 | 0 |

## *The Method of 'Success' Groups*

In a run such as *fsffsssffssssfsffssfsffff* in which *s* denotes a success, and
$$1 \quad 2 \quad\; 3\; 4\; 5\; 6$$
*f* a failure, there are six 'success' or '*s*' groups separated by seven '*f*' or 'failure' groups. Now if the 9,410 hits were randomly distributed among the 37,100 trials, it is possible to calculate the theoretical expectation of the number of 'success' or '*s*' groups by a formula due to Mr. W. L. Stevens. If *a* denotes the actual total of hits and *b* the actual total of misses, then the expected number of 'success' groups is given by $E = a(b+1)/(a+b)$, and the theoretical variance of this expression has been shown to be given by
$$V = Eb(a - 1)/(a + b)(a + b - 1).$$
Writing $a = 9,410$ and $b = 27,690$, we find for the expected number of success groups $E = 7,023·51$.

The number actually counted is only 6,734, and so there is a deficit of 289·51. The variance works out to 1,329·49. Hence the standard deviation is $\sqrt{1,329·49}$, i.e. 36·46.

Thus we have a deficit amounting to 7·94 standard deviations, with odds against chance of the order $10^{14}$ to 1. This result confirms the crowding of hits, an effect which was absent in the Shackleton experiments.

# APPENDIX E

# Concerning the Target Lists

In connection with the five-symbol experiments with Mrs. Stewart, certain tests for randomness were applied to the target distribution. It was found that the numbers of the five animal initials E, G, L, P, Z employed in the first 42 sessions were nearly equal. Further, the numbers of the initials C, F, H, K, T, which were used in all but three of the remaining sessions, approximated closely to equality.

For the 33,500 trials considered in Chapter XIX, p. 321, the number of doubles was counted (three identical target symbols in success being estimated as two doubles, four alike in a group as three doubles, etc.) and was found to be in satisfactory agreement with the expected number. Similarly, the number of triples was counted (a quadruple being estimated as two triples, etc.) and was found to differ from the expected number by an amount within the limits of random sampling.

We found, however, a very significant deficiency in patterns of the type ABA in which two like symbols are separated by a different symbol. The assistant who prepared the stock of thirty thousand digits, which determined the sequence of animal targets, did this work about the year 1943 before the experiments with Mrs. Stewart began. It seems very possible that this gentleman failed to carry out his instructions carefully since the target lists of the 1934-9 series, which were selected personally by S.G.S. from seven-figure logarithmic tables by the method described in Chapter VII, p. 106, did not show the deficit of ABA patterns. Possibly the digits may have been selected at too close intervals. But the compiler had never met Mrs. Stewart or seen any of her records, and he had no other connection with the experiments. It is now impossible to discover precisely what he did, since news reached S.G.S. some time ago that he is dead.

It was important, therefore, for us to make reasonably sure that our statistical treatment of the data was valid, and that we were not misled into wrong conclusions.

Fortunately, it is easy to demonstrate from the actual records that

382

the deficiency in the pattern ABA had no effect on the expectation of direct hits on the target card. It will be recalled that each record sheet contains two columns of 25 trials each, known as the (a) and the (b) columns. For the 670 sheets considered we have made a complete cross-check by scoring for direct hits the targets of the first column on the page, the (a) column, against the calls of the second, or (b) column, and the calls of column (a) against the targets of column (b). We have thus, in all, 33,500 trials, and the cross-check registers 6,711 correct guesses, as compared with a binomial expectation of 6,700. This gives a positive deviation of only 11. The standard deviation, with $p = 1/5$, is 73·2. Moreover, the observed standard deviation for 25 trials in the cross-check is found to be 1·962, which is in close agreement with 2, the binomial standard deviation.

Now Mrs. Stewart actually scored 8,694 hits on the 670 sheets, which gives an excess equivalent to 27 standard deviations. Had her guessing habits been correlated in any way with any non-random aspects of the target distribution, the cross-check would assuredly have revealed a significant excess or deficit of direct hits; and this is not the case.

Further, the totals for the cross-check were made after every ten sittings, and at no stage in the count did the accumulated deviation of the observed total from binomial expectation reach 1·5 standard deviations.

We went further than this and fitted the distribution of scores produced by the cross-check to a binomial distribution with $p = 1/5$. That is, we compared the expected numbers of scores of (0, 1,) 2, 3, 4, . . . 9, (10, 11, . . . 25,) with the numbers obtained in the cross-check, and found a chi-squared value of 14·23 with 9 degrees of freedom. This gives a probability value $P$ which lies between 0·1 and 0·2, and this is not abnormal. In fact, the distribution of the cross-check made a satisfactory fit with the theoretical binomial distribution.

Though the above analysis provided ample justification for the use of binomial formulae in the estimation of the expectation and significance of direct hits, we carried out an additional test.

We checked the distribution of the 670 *first targets* on each page for randomness in the following manner. The target digits for these trials were decoded into the animal initials by means of the code at the top of the sheet. In the total series of 120 sessions there were three sets of animal initials: E, G, L, P, Z, for sessions 1–42; C, F, H, R, T, for session 43; and C, F, H, K, T, for sessions 44–120. In order to reduce these to a uniform set of targets for the purpose of the present study, the letters A, B, C, D, E were taken to represent each of the three sets of animal initials, in alphabetical order as shown. To this uniform set of 670 'targets', the following tests of randomness were then applied. The observed frequencies of A, B, C, D, E, were 140, 128, 142, 124, 136, respectively, and 134, i.e. $\frac{1}{5}$ of 670, is the expected number in each case. This distribution gives a chi-squared value of 1·8, with 4 degrees of freedom, and $P$ the probability value lies between 0·7 and 0·8, which is quite normal.

There were 426 single targets (429·12 were expected), 85 isolated doubles (85·70 expected), 22 isolated triples (17·11 expected), 2 isolated quadruples (3·42 expected), and no longer sequences of the same symbol (0·85 expected).

Further, there were 110 instances of the ABA type of pattern, compared with the expected number of 106·88. Thus, all the observed figures are in excellent agreement with those expected on the assumption of a random distribution. Indeed, since the five cards in the box were shuffled after each sheet of 50 trials, we should naturally expect the decoded first digits of each page to constitute a random series.

Now on these 670 trials Mrs. Stewart scored 172 direct (0) hits, whereas the expected number is $\frac{1}{5} \times 670$, i.e. 134. We have, then, a positive deviation of 38, which is the equivalent of 3·67 standard deviations. Thus, even for this group of 670 random trials, the odds against the results' being due to chance are about 4,000 to 1.

There are also additional considerations which may be mentioned. For instance, in the 2,600 'clairvoyance' trials, in which the agent did not look at the cards, there were 509 direct hits, a negative deviation of 11, whereas the 2,600 'telepathy' trials, in which an agent looked at the cards and which were rigidly alternated or randomly mixed with the 'clairvoyance' trials, gave no fewer than 707 direct hits, i.e. a positive deviation of 187. This very remarkable difference cannot be explained in terms of any statistical artifact; it is clearly a psychological effect.

Again, in the London-Antwerp experiments, the random numbers were compiled by S.G.S., by F.B., or by members of the mathematical staff of Queen Mary College working under direct supervision. These six sittings show the same high rate of scoring as the remainder of the work with Mrs. Stewart.

Further, in the 2,000 playing-card experiments, the random numbers were selected by S.G.S. himself from Fisher's tables. These 2,000 trials gave 78 guesses that were completely correct, with odds against chance of more than $10^9$ to 1.

But while it is abundantly clear that the deficit of ABA patterns in the target sequence can have had no effect on the theoretical expectation and variance of direct hits, we have still to examine whether it might possibly account for the low-scoring on the first trial of a target double which was discussed in Chapter XIX, p. 322. To investigate this question we selected the first *target pairs* on each of the 670 sheets. Of these pairs 151 were doubles and 519 non-doubles. To ascertain whether the doubles were randomly distributed among the non-doubles we applied a method identical with that described in Appendix D, p. 381, for 'success groups' and 'non-success' groups. In the present application a 'double' played the part of a 'success' and a 'non-double' stood for a 'failure' or 'miss'. We found 111 groups of 'doubles' separated by 'non-doubles' whereas 118·2 groups were expected according to Stevens's formula. This gave a critical ratio of −1·6, which is without significance. Hence there is no evidence of any undue crowding or dispersal of the doubles. Now the 151 doubles gave only 22 hits on the first trials, while the 519 non-doubles gave 150 hits on their first trials. A simple contingency table gave a chi-squared value of 12·59 with one degree of freedom.

The corresponding odds against the occurrence by chance of such a difference between the proportions of hits on the first trials of doubles and non-doubles are about 2,000 to 1.

We see then that the 'doubles' effect, which is so marked throughout the data as a whole, is equally apparent in the 670 first pairs, which undoubtedly form a random series.

Another ingenious test due to Mrs. Esther Bond Foster confirms our conclusion that the effect is a genuine one and not a statistical artifact, but for the details we must refer the reader to the *Journal of Parapsychology* (September 1951, pp. 200, 201).

Though we have found a non-random feature in the *vertical* target sequence, there is good reason to believe that the 25 horizontal sequences, each of 670 initials, which were obtained by taking the $n$th target *letter* in every ($a$) column, $n$ being any number from 1 to 25, will satisfy all the ordinary tests for a random distribution. And similarly for the 25 horizontal sequences each consisting of a letter in the same position in all ($b$) columns. A few such horizontal series have been tested by S.G.S., and, so far, the results have been as satisfactory as they were for the first targets of the ($a$) columns.

Most of what we have written of Mrs. Stewart's work is concerned with direct hits on the (0) or target card and the significance of the results is beyond dispute. The decline effect and the 'doubles' effect are also indubitably genuine. But the non-random element in the 'vertical' target series would render risky any pronouncements about displacement effects more especially those in connection with (+2) or (−2) displacement. The high score obtained on the (0) card would produce automatically a significant deficit of $(+2)$ and $(-2)$ hits owing to there being too few target patterns of the type ABA. To be on the safe side therefore we have refrained from giving any detailed discussion of either $(+1)$ or $(+2)$ displacements.

# A Partial Confirmation of Certain Shackleton Effects

In the year 1950 Mr. G. W. Fisk, a member of the Society for Psychical Research, initiated a large-scale card-guessing project, the primary object of which was to discover high-scoring subjects. A leaflet was issued to a number of experimenters in various localities which gave instructions how to carry out experiments in GESP with packs of Zener cards made up according to Dr. Rhine's prescription. The agent who looked at the cards was to sit behind a screen 3 feet square and the packs of cards provided by the Society were to be thoroughly shuffled by the experimenters. The scoring sheets, also provided by the Society, were, when completed and signed, to be returned to Mr. Fisk. In all, 236 persons took part as guessers and of these one produced very high scores over a short period. We are concerned here with the work of the remaining 235 subjects.

Of these, 17 completed 48 or more runs of 25 trials each, 28 did 17 to 47 runs each, another 51 persons completed 16 runs each, and the remaining 139 did less than 16 runs apiece. The scores of the good subject were excluded.

In all, a grand total of 3,859 runs or 96,475 trials was obtained from the 235 subjects. So far as direct hits on the target card are concerned there were 19,447 successes, which is not significantly different from 19,295, the expected number. In fact the deviation (+152) amounts to only 1·23 standard deviations and is of no importance whatever.

On the 92,616 (+1) trials however there were only 17,980 hits, i.e. a *deficit* of 543·2 from the expected number (18,523·2). This deficit corresponds to a critical ratio of −4·45 with odds of more than 100,000 to 1 against the chance hypothesis.

Further, on the 92,616 (−1) (post-cognitive) trials there were only 17,866 hits, i.e. a deficit of 657·2 from chance expectation. This deficit is the equivalent of —5·40 standard deviations with corresponding odds of more than ten millions to one against the chance hypothesis.

The negative deviations of both the (+1) and the (—1) scores were found to be widely distributed throughout the whole of the data and not to be due to the scores of a few individuals.

The first idea to suggest itself to Mr. Fisk and Dr. West, the research officer of the Society, was that the deficit was possibly due to some non-random feature of the card-distribution. On the advice of S.G.S., therefore, a cross-check was carried out on a total of 15,175 trials (607 runs) by comparing the subjects' calls with the target cards of the following run. The results of this check were remarkably close to chance expectation. For the (—1), (0) and (+1) cards the deviations were only —12, +2, and —6 respectively. This makes the assumption of a statistical artifact very improbable indeed. Again the fact that the effect is not confined to the work of one or two experimenters seems to render the hypothesis of deliberate cheating out of the question. Moreover, if sensory cues had not been guarded against, the result would surely have been a significant excess of *direct* hits and not a deficiency in the displacement hits, and there is no such success on the (0) card.

It is satisfactory to note that when the calls of these 607 cross-check runs were compared with the targets for which they were intended, the critical ratios for (—1) and (+1) hits were —4·20 and —4·12 respectively, while on the (0) card there was an excess of only 6 above expectation. Thus, the batch used in the cross-check confirms the general findings for the whole of the data.

One goes on to ask, naturally, how it came about that such a large number of persons in different localities and working with different experimenters contributed to the same type of effect in such remarkable unison.

The clue, perhaps, is that the tests were all organized by the one person, Mr. Fisk. In fact Mr. Fisk constitutes the only link with the 235 persons who took part in the experiments and it is interesting to speculate whether it was his sub-conscious which determined the kind of phenomena that were to happen. As the person in supreme control of the assistant experimenters and the multitudinous details of the tests, he may not only have organized the experiments but in addition have been a deciding factor in dictating unconsciously the general trend of their outcome. Subconsciously, Mr. Fisk may have desired to reproduce some features of the Shackleton results. If this is so it opens up a fascinating field of exploration. For instance, may it not have been the subconscious of S.G.S. which determined that neither Basil Shackleton nor Mrs. Stewart should succeed in clairvoyance tests? Further, in tests where large numbers of percipients participate it may be the mind of the principal experimenter which largely decides whether or not there will be significant results of any description. It would seem that Mr. Fisk succeeds brilliantly when in control of a group experiment, as did Whately Carington, whereas Mr. Denys Parsons and Dr. West are completely unsuccessful. S.G.S. himself has had no success with mass experiments but only with subjects like Mrs. Cooper, Basil Shackleton and Mrs. Stewart, who were highly endowed with paranormal gifts.

What seems to be emerging is that the personality of the chief investigator whether he be actually present at the tests or not has a vital influence on their outcome.*

* In this connection it is of interest to refer once again to the Hutchinson-Mac-Farland experiment mentioned in the footnote on p. 246, Chap. XIV. The remarkable difference in the results of the GESP experiments obtained by the two investigators when working simultaneously with the same guessers might, at first sight, be attributed to the fact that one experimenter was a good telepathic agent and the other a poor agent. But the problem is not so simple as this. For in a second series of DT (clairvoyance) experiments in which ordinary telepathy was apparently ruled out, MacFarland, in 7,650 trials, again obtained from his subjects a deviation of + 173 (CR = 4·84), while the same subjects obtained with Dale Hutchinson as experimenter an insignificant deviation of only −15. In other respects the experimental conditions were the same as those mentioned on p. 246. It would seem that the personality of the experimenter is an important factor even when telepathy is excluded.

# The Experiments of Kahn and Neisser

A very carefully controlled series of experiments in general ESP was recently carried out by Messrs. David Kahn and Ulric Neisser of Harvard University in which 177 college students acted as guessers. In these tests the percipient recorded his choice by blacking in with a special pencil one out of a horizontal row of five blank rectangles printed on a scoring sheet, and in so doing attempted to locate the position of a shaded rectangle on a 'target' sheet which had been placed in a locked cabinet or in a sealed envelope. Both the 'target' sheets and those on which the subjects made their guesses were identical forms adapted for use in connection with the International Business Machine (IBM). The sheets were (except in the case of one series) impressed on each side with 150 rows of five blank rectangles and thus each sheet provided space for 300 calls. Tables of random numbers were used to decide which rectangle on each row of five was to be blacked out as the target. There were five series of experiments (Nos. 1–5) and, in general, different batches of percipients took part in each series; in addition, the experimental conditions varied somewhat from series to series. As a rule the same 'target' sheet of 300 trials was guessed at by all the subjects of a given series. Each subject was given an answer sheet and was informed of or shown the general location of the target sheet. The numbers of subjects in the five groups varied from nineteen to sixty-three.

In Series 1, 2, and 5 the distance between target sheet and guessers ranged from under a mile to over 500 miles while in Series 3 and 4 the target sheets were in the same room as the subjects, being placed between two heavy sheets of cardboard enclosed in heavy manilla envelopes and under the constant surveillance of two experimenters.

At the end of each series, the sheets were collected by the experimenters and deposited with either the Harvard Bureau of Tests or the Educational Records Bureau in New York City. The number of correct hits for each subject was counted automatically by the IBM machine which operates by recording the closures of electrical circuits which are made when the percipient's pencilling has been placed on the correct rectangle. In addition to the machine count a hand-count was carried out as a check by Mrs. L. A. Dale of the American Society for Psychical Research.

Since a large number of subjects were guessing at the same targets the binomial formula for the standard deviation was not strictly applicable. In fact if the subjects showed mass preferences for certain positions in the row the binomial method would lead to an over-estimation of the significance of the results. It was actually the case that the percipients tended to avoid the first and last rectangles in the row. The appropriate method of evaluation was that of Greville. It seems a pity, therefore, that only in the first two series comprising 15,677 out of a grand total of 43,278 trials was Greville's method applied. Series 1 and 2 gave odds against chance of 300 to 1 by the ordinary binomial formula but odds of only 160 to 1 when scored by Greville's method.

On the grand total (43,278 trials) for Series 1–5 the binomial formula gave a critical ratio of $+3.26$ with corresponding odds against the result being due to chance of about 2,000 to 1. It seems likely that the true odds may be considerably less than this figure though still of ample significance.

Since the experimenters who supervised and collected the percipients' records were kept in ignorance of the compilation of the target sheets, and the actual counting of hits was carried out by persons with no interest in the results, it would appear that fraud or bias on the part of the experimenters was eliminated.

## Secondary Findings

### (a) DECLINE EFFECT

In every series except No. 2 the guesser after completing the 150 trials printed on the front of his scoring sheet was asked to turn over and fill in the 150 trials on the other side. The decline in rate of scoring for the last 150 guesses is quite extraordinary.

On a grand total of 26,427 trials for calls 1–150 there is a positive deviation of $273.6$ which corresponds to a (binomial) critical ratio of $4.21$, whereas on the 16,851 trials for calls 151–300 there is a *negative* deviation of only $2.2$ which is purely a chance result.

The critical ratio of the difference between the scores for the two sides of the page is $2.66$ and the odds against such a difference being due to chance are 250 to 1.

It would seem that significant scoring took place only on the first 150 trials and that thereafter there were only chance results.

In Series 2, however, the 63 subjects concerned were asked to guess only the first 150 trials, the reverse side of the sheet being blank. In this case there was no decline from the first 75 trials to the last 75. In fact there was a slight increase in the scoring rate during the last half page but this was not significant.

## (b) EFFECT OF DISTANCE

In Series 1, 2 and 5, for which the 103 guessers were at a substantial distance from the concealed target (ranging from less than a mile up to more than 500 miles), a total of 21,364 trials gave a positive deviation of 217·2 (binomial method) with corresponding odds of 10,000 to 1 against the result being due to chance. It seems reasonably certain that had Greville's method been used the distance experiments would still have been fairly significant.

## (c) COMPARISON OF FREE AND RIGID CONDITIONS

Several experimenters in telepathy have claimed that the results are most successful when the subject is allowed to make his guesses when he feels in the mood, and least successful when he attempts to guess cards at the bidding of an experimenter. Scherer showed that subjects made extraordinary scores when permitted to perform tests in their own time and at their own pleasure but obtained only chance results when they worked at the order of another person. Kahn and Neisser allowed the subjects of Series 1, 2 and 5 to make their guesses under 'free' conditions laid down as follows: The experimenter explained the nature of the test to the subject and gave him an answer sheet. He was then told to try to duplicate the distant 'target' sheet at any time during the next few days, and to pick a time when he felt relaxed and free from disturbance. He did not have to fill in the whole sheet at one sitting but could do a few guesses whenever he felt like it.

Series 4 on the other hand was done under extremely rigid conditions. The subjects volunteered in answer to an advertisement. The testing was done on two different days with a fresh target sheet for each day. The percipients were herded together in a classroom, they were given minute printed instructions, they had to fill in a lengthy personality inventory, and the whole business was extremely formal and very tiring. No joking was permitted.

The 103 subjects who worked in the 'free' situation scored a positive deviation of 217·2 on a total of 21,364 trials which gave a critical ratio of 3·71. The 52 subjects who worked under the 'rigid' conditions obtained a deviation of only +10·0 on a total of 15,360 trials—a purely chance score. The critical ratio of the difference of the two scores was 2·24 with odds of about 80 to 1 against the difference being due to chance.

The experiment is far from conclusive since the same subjects were not employed in the two tests. The method is admitted by the authors to be unsatisfactory on several counts.

### (*d*) NEGATIVE FINDINGS

(i) On the other hand the experimenters found no significant dichotomy in an attempt to repeat the 'sheep' and 'goats' experiment of Dr. Schmeidler. In fact neither 'sheep' nor 'goats' showed the slightest sign of any ESP ability in the Kahn-Neisser test. Since the subjects were volunteers there were in this case only 12 'goats' compared with 62 'sheep'. The authors consider that Schmeidler's work, though valuable, is difficult to repeat rigorously owing to the wide connotation that can be given to the terms 'sheep' and 'goats'.

(ii) The authors find no evidence in support of the hypothesis that the greater the degree of acceptance of the actual occurrence of ESP the higher the scoring level will be.

(iii) They find no correlation between the subjects' confidence in ESP ability and their actual scoring level. This is quite contrary to the findings of Humphrey and Nicol (Chap. XX, p. 351).

(iv) A comparison of the ESP performance of 50 'expansive' subjects with that of 23 'compressives' showed no significant difference. The authors admit, however, that their experiment was not altogether comparable with those of Dr. Humphrey since in the present case the compressive-expansive ratings were based upon the use of a single picture in a sealed envelope which the subjects of Series 3 and 4 were asked to reproduce. Moreover, the material of transmission (mere identification of spatial positions of five objects in a row) may have been unfavourable for a demonstration of Dr. Humphrey's findings.

(v) *Personal and Social Adjustment and ESP Scores.* It will be remembered that Humphrey found suggestive correlations between a subject's personality adjustment and his ESP scores, and that Schmeidler discovered highly significant correlations between ESP and Rorschach scores by the use of Munroe's 'inspection' technique. In the present experiments Kahn and Neisser employed a more recent scale known as the Heston Personal Adjustment Inventory. This consists of 270 questions designed to test the six characteristics: (1) Analytic thinking; (2) Sociability; (3) Emotional stability; (4) Confidence; (5) Good personal relations with other people; and (6) Home satisfaction. Low scores on these areas of the scale indicate poor adjustment.

The inventory was administered to 47 subjects of Series 4 and, of these, 27 obtained a 'below the average' score on the Heston scale and the remainder an 'above the average' score.

A simple contingency table showed that there were odds of about 25 to 1 in favour of a positive correlation between good personal adjustment and above-chance ESP scores. The result of course is merely suggestive. Actually, out of the 27 poorly-adjusted subjects 19 scored *below* mean chance expectation and only 7 above, whereas of the 20 well-adjusted persons 13 scored above the chance level and 7 below it.

# A Further Analysis of Decline Effects in Stewart Data

In the spring of 1951 Dr. J. G. Pratt of Duke University carried out an independent examination of the Stewart data for decline effects within the run. For the purpose of this survey, however, Dr. Pratt omitted from consideration all data from the last ten sittings (Nos. 121–30) during which period Mrs. Stewart's scores had declined to the chance level. Dr. Pratt's analysis, therefore, is based upon a chronological series of 32,500 (0) trials as compared with the total of 37,100 considered by ourselves in Chapter XVIII, p. 314. But whereas in our own work no distinction was made between (*a*) and (*b*) columns of each sheet, Dr. Pratt carried out separate analyses for the two columns and this led to the discovery that there were interesting differences in the patterns of decline followed by the (*a*) and the (*b*) columns. The observed numbers of hits in the five segments of the (*a*) column are shown in Table 13 and it appears that there is a regular decline in the scoring rate from the first five trials to the last segment of the run.

TABLE 13

*Distribution of* 4,234 (0) *hits in col.* (*a*)

| Trials | (1–5) | (6–10) | (11–15) | (16–20) | (21–25) |
|---|---|---|---|---|---|
| Hits | 996 | 983 | 806 | 743 | 706 |
| Scoring rate per 25 | 7·66 | 7·56 | 6·20 | 5·71 | 5·43 |

In the (*b*) column, on the other hand, the scoring rate shows a rapid rise during the second segment followed by a very slight rise to a peak in the third segment. After this there is a steep decline during the fourth segment followed by a slight recovery during the last five trials. This is shown by Table 14.

## TABLE 14

*Distribution of* 4,130 (0) *hits in col.* (b)

| Trials | (1–5) | (6–10) | (11–15) | (16–20) | (21–25) |
|---|---|---|---|---|---|
| Hits | 747 | 879 | 890 | 788 | 826 |
| Scoring rate per 25 | 5·75 | 6·76 | 6·85 | 6·06 | 6·35 |

It is clear that in the second or (b) column Mrs. Stewart is slower in reaching her maximum scoring rate than in the first or (a) column. Moreover, in the (a) column the decline sets in earlier. This is apparent from the two graphs below.

Table 15 shows the distribution for the (a) and (b) columns taken together. The pattern agrees with that given in Table 10, Chapter XVIII, p. 314.

## TABLE 15

*Distribution of* 8,364 (0) *hits in cols.* (a) *and* (b)

| Trials | (1–5) | (6–10) | (11–15) | (16–20) | (21–25) |
|---|---|---|---|---|---|
| Hits | 1,743 | 1,862 | 1,696 | 1,531 | 1,532 |
| Scoring rate per 25 | 6·70 | 7·16 | 6·25 | 5·89 | 5·89 |

There is in fact a marked drop in the scoring rate for trials 16–25.

The difference in pattern in the two columns is remarkable and is possibly due to some psychological factor arising out of the few seconds' break at the end of the first column.

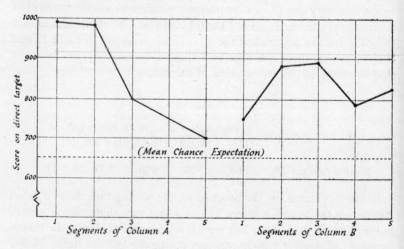

Distribution of hits on the direct target in relation to the order of trials on the record page—1,300 runs of Stewart data collected over a four-year period.

# W. L. Stevens's Method of Evaluation

Suppose that a pack of $N$ cards contains $k$ different sorts of symbol which we shall refer to as $1, 2, 3, \ldots k$. Let there be $a_1$ cards of the first symbol, $a_2$ of the second, etc. up to $a_k$ cards of the last or $k^{\text{th}}$ symbol. Suppose also that the $k$ symbols are guessed $g_1, g_2$, etc. up to $g_k$ times, so that, clearly,

$$N = a_1 + a_2 + \ldots + a_k = g_1 + g_2 + \ldots + g_k.$$

Then, provided that the $N$ cards are adequately shuffled, the expected number of successes or 'hits' on the $N$ guesses will, if chance only is operating, be given by

$$E = \frac{1}{N} \sum_{r=1}^{k} a_r g_r .$$

Now if $E_1 = \sum_{r=1}^{k} a_r g_r,$

and $E_2 = \sum_{r=1}^{k} a_r g_r (a_r + g_r),$

W. L. Stevens has shown that the theoretical variance is given by

$$V = \frac{1}{N^2 (N-1)} [E_1^2 - N.E_2 + N^2.E_1].$$

The values of $E$ and $V$ are computed for each pack of $N$ cards that is worked through, and added together to find the total expectation and the total variance. The standard deviation is then the square root of the total variance.

*Example*: With Rhine's packs of cards, $k = 5$ and $N = 25$.

Also $a_1 = a_2 = a_3 = a_4 = a_5 = 5$.

Hence the expected number of hits $E$ is 5 and the variance $V$ reduces to

$\frac{1}{120} [625 - g_1^2 - g_2^2 - g_3^2 - g_4^2 - g_5^2]$.

This is a maximum when $g_1 = g_2 = g_3 = g_4 = g_5$, so that the maximum variance for a single pack is $25/6$. Hence for $n$ trials, i.e. $n/25$ packs, the standard deviation cannot exceed $\sqrt{(n/6)}$, i.e. $0.408 \sqrt{n}$.

# References

CHAPTER I

1. 'Telepathy and Clairvoyance in Classical Antiquity' by Professor E. R. Dodds. An essay from *Greek Poetry and Life*, Oxford University Press. Reprinted in *J. of Parapsychol.*, Vol. 10 (December 1946), pp. 290–309.
2. *Phantasms of the Living* by E. Gurney, F. W. H. Myers and F. Podmore. 2 vols. London 1886. (Abridged edition 1918.)
3. *The New York Times Magazine.* See issues for 11th June 1950 and 2nd July 1950.
4. 'Record of experiments in thought-transference at Liverpool' by Malcolm Guthrie and James Birchall. *Proc. S.P.R.*, Vol. I (1883), pp. 263–83.
5. 'Further report on experiments in thought-transference at Liverpool' by Malcolm Guthrie. *Proc. S.P.R.*, Vol. III (1885), pp. 424–52.
6. 'An account of some experiments in thought-transference' by Oliver J. Lodge. *Proc. S.P.R.*, Vol. II (1884), pp. 189–216.
7. 'Note on thought-reading' by A. M. Creery. *Proc. S.P.R.*, Vol. I (1882), pp. 43–6.

CHAPTER II

1. *Experiments in Psychical Research* by John E. Coover. Palo Alto: Stanford University Press, 1917.
2. 'Dr. Rhine's recent experiments in telepathy and clairvoyance and a reconsideration of J. E. Coover's conclusions on telepathy' by R. H. Thouless. *Proc. S.P.R.*, Vol 48 (1935), pp. 24–37.
3. 'Rhine or Reason: A critique of ESP' by John McLeish. *The Modern Quarterly*, Vol. 5, No. 4, Autumn 1950. Lawrence and Wishart.
4. 'New Evidence (?) for "Extra-sensory perception"' by Chester E. Kellogg. *The Scientific Monthly*. October 1937. Vol. XLV, pp. 331–41.

5. 'A technique for the experimental study of telepathy and other alleged clairvoyant processes' by Professor L. T. Troland. (Albany; no date).

6. 'A report on telepathic experiments done in the psychology laboratory at Groningen' by H. J. F. W. Brugmans. *Compte-Rendu du Premier Congrès International des Recherches Psychiques.* Copenhagen 1921.

7. *Preliminary studies of a vaudeville telepathist* by S. G. Soal. Bulletin 3 of the University of London Council for Psychical Investigation, London, 1937.

8. 'A method of scoring coincidences in tests with playing-cards' by R. A. Fisher, Sc.D., F.R.S. *Proc. S.P.R.*, Vol. 34, pp. 181–5 (1924).

9. 'Evidence for clairvoyance in card-guessing' by Ina Jephson. *Proc. S.P.R.*, Vol. 38, pp. 223–68 (1929).

10. 'A behaviourist experiment in clairvoyance' by Ina Jephson. *Proc. S.P.R.*, Part 128, pp. 99–114.

11. 'Report of a series of experiments in clairvoyance conducted at a distance under approximately fraud-proof conditions' by Th. Besterman, S. G. Soal and Ina Jephson. *Proc. S.P.R.*, Vol. 39, pp. 375–414 (1931).

12. *A contribution to experimental telepathy* by G. H. Estabrooks. Boston S.P.R., Bulletin 5 (1927).

13. 'Thought Transference' by F. L. Usher and F. P. Burt. *Annals of Psychical Science* (London), Vol. VIII, pp. 561–600 (1909).

14. 'Quelques expériences de transmission de la pensée à grande distance' by F. L. Usher and F. P. Burt. *Annales de Science Psychique*, Vol. XX, pp. 14–21 and pp. 40–54 (1910).

15. 'Some early experiments providing apparently positive evidence for extra-sensory perception' by W. Whately Carington. *Jour. S.P.R.*, Vol. 29 (1935), pp. 295–305.

16. 'The broadcasting experiment in mass-telepathy' by V. J. Woolley, M.D. *Proc. S.P.R.*, Vol. 38 (1928), pp. 1–9.

17. 'Experiments in supernormal perception at a distance' by S. G. Soal. *Proc. S.P.R.*, Part 123 (1932), pp. 165–362.

CHAPTER III

1. 'Extra-Sensory Perception' by Joseph Banks Rhine. Boston. Bruce Humphries (1934).

2. 'Some selected experiments in extra-sensory perception' by J. B. Rhine. *Jour. of Abnormal and Social Psychology*, September 1936, Vol. XXXI, pp. 216–28. (See also *J. of Parapsychol.*, Vol. 1 (1937), pp. 70–80.)

REFERENCES

3. 'The visual cues from the backs of the ESP cards' by J. L. Kennedy. *J. of Psychol.*, Vol. VI (1938), pp. 149–53.
4. 'Studies in extra-sensory perception I.' An analysis of 25,000 trials by Dorothy R. Martin and Frances P. Stribic. *J. of Parapsychol.*, Vol. 2, No. 1, (March 1938), pp. 23–30.
5. 'Studies in extra-sensory perception II.' A review of all University of Colorado experiments by D. R. Martin and F. P. Stribic. *J. of Parapsychol.*, Vol. 4 (December 1940), pp. 159–248.

CHAPTER IV

1. 'Variance of the ESP Call Series' by J. A. Greenwood. *J. of Parapsychol.*, Vol. 2 (1938), pp. 60–4.
2. 'Variance of a general matching problem' by J. A. Greenwood. *Annals of Math. Statistics*, Vol. IX (1938), pp. 56–59.
3. 'Exact probabilities for the matching hypothesis' by T. N. E. Greville. *J. of Parapsychol.*, Vol. 2 (1938), pp. 55–9.
4. 'The solution of a problem in probability' by T. E. Sterne. *Science*, Vol. 86 (1937), pp. 500–1.
5. 'Statistical aspects of ESP' by Willy K. Feller of Brown University. *J. of Parapsychol.*, Vol. 4 (1940), pp. 271–98.
6. 'A review of Dr. Feller's Critique' by J. A. Greenwood and C. E. Stuart. *J. of Parapsychol.*, Vol. 4 (1940), pp. 299–319.
7. 'Analysis of a large chance control series of ESP data' by J. A. Greenwood. *J. of Parapsychol.*, Vol. 2 (1938), pp. 138–46.
8. 'An experiment to test the rôle of chance in ESP research' by Clarence Leuba. *J. of Parapsychol.*, Vol. 2 (1938), pp. 217–21.
9. 'A summary of mathematical advances bearing on ESP research' by T. N. E. Greville. *J. of Parapsychol.*, Vol. 3 (1939), pp. 86–92.
10. 'Über Unwillkürliches Flüstern' by F. C. C. Hansen and A. Lehmann. *Phil. Stud.*, Vol. XVII (1895), pp. 471–530.
11. 'Involuntary whispering considered in relation to experiments in thought-transference' by Henry Sidgwick. *Proc. S.P.R.*, Vol. 12 (1897), pp. 298–316.
12. 'Experiments in "unconscious whispering"' by J. L. Kennedy. *Psychol. Bull.*, Vol. XXXV (1938), p. 526.
13. 'Wissen um Fremdes Wissen' by F. von Neureiter. Gotha: Leopold Klotz (1935).
14. 'The case of Ilga K: Report of a phenomenon of unusual perception' by Hans Bender. *J. of Parapsychol.*, Vol. 2 (March 1938), pp. 5–22.

15. 'On limits of recording errors' by Gardner Murphy. *J. of Parapsychol.*, Vol. 2 (1938), pp. 262–6.

16. 'The rôle of selection in ESP data' by V. W. Lemmon. *J. of Parapsychol.*, Vol. 2 (1939), pp. 104–6.

17. 'A Critique of Rhine's "Extra-sensory Perception"' by Raymond R. Willoughby. *Jour. of Abn. and Soc. Psychol.*, Vol. XXX (1935), pp. 199–207.

18. 'Size of stimulus symbols in extra-sensory perception' by J. G. Pratt and J. L. Woodruff. *J. of Parapsychol.*, Vol. 3 (1939), pp. 121–58.

19. 'A case of high scores in card-guessing at a distance' by Bernard F. Riess. *J. of Parapsychol.*, Vol. 1 (1937), pp. 260–3.

20. 'Further data from a case of high scores in card-guessing' by B. F. Riess. *J. of Parapsychol.*, Vol. 3 (1939), pp. 79–84.

21. 'A Summary of some negative experiments' by E. T. Adams. *J. of Parapsychol.*, Vol. 2 (1938), pp. 232–6.

22. 'An experimental study of extra-sensory perception' by James C. Crumbaugh, M.A. Thesis (1938). Southern Methodist University Library.

23. 'Critique of the premises and statistical methodology of parapsychology' by C. P. Heinlein and J. H. Heinlein. *Jour. of Psychology* Vol. V (1938), pp. 135–48.

24. 'Further card-guessing experiments' by Raymond R. Willoughby. *Jour. of General Psychol.*, Vol. XVII (1937), pp. 3–13.

25. 'Marginalia' by G. Evelyn Hutchinson (Yale University). *American Scientist*, Vol. 36, No. 2 (1948).

26. 'Theoretical Implications of Telepathy' by Margaret Knight. *Science News*, No. 18, Penguin Books.

27. 'An Evaluation of Extra-sensory Perception' by H. Rogosin. *Jour. of General Psychol.* (1939), 21, pp. 200–17.

28. 'Telepathy in the Psychophysical Laboratory' by Lucien Warner and Mildred Raible. *J. of Parapsychol.*, Vol. 1 (March 1937), pp. 44–51.

CHAPTER V

1. 'Clairvoyant blind matching' by J. G. Pratt. *J. of Parapsychol.*, Vol. 1 (1937), pp. 10–17.

2. 'ESP tests with American Indian children' by A. A. Foster. *J. of Parapsychol.*, Vol. 7 (June 1943), pp. 94–103.

3. 'A study of card-guessing in psychotic subjects' by Robert Shulman. *J. of Parapsychol.*, Vol. 2 (1938), pp. 96–107.

4. 'ESP and Intelligence' by Betty M. Humphrey. *J. of Parapsychol.*, Vol. 9 (March 1945), pp. 7–16.

5. 'General extra-sensory perception with a group of fourth grade retarded children' by Esther May Bond. *J. of Parapsychol.*, Vol. 1 (1937), pp. 114–22.

6. 'An unusual case of extra-sensory perception' by Raleigh M. Drake. *J. of Parapsychol.*, Vol. 2 (1938), pp. 184–98.

7. 'Telepathy and Medical Psychology' by Jan Ehrenwald, M.D. W. W. Norton & Co., New York, 1948.

8. 'Children's Drawings in a Projective Technique' by Paula Elkisch. *Psychological Monographs*, Vol. 58 (1945), pp. 1–31.

9. 'An ESP Test with Drawings' by C. E. Stuart. *J. of Parapsychol.*, Vol. 6 (1942), pp. 20–43.

10. 'An ESP Experiment with Enclosed Drawings' by C. E. Stuart. *J. of Parapsychol.*, Vol. 9 (1945), pp. 278–95; showing backward displacement.

11. 'GESP Experiments with the Free Response Method' by C. E. Stuart. *J. of Parapsychol.*, Vol. 10 (March 1946), pp. 21–35.

12. 'A Second Classroom ESP Experiment with the Free Response Method' by C. E. Stuart. *J. of Parapsychol.*, Vol. 11 (March 1947), pp. 14–25; showing forward displacement.

13. 'Success in ESP as Related to Form of Response Drawings I. Clairvoyance Experiments' by Betty M. Humphrey. *J. of Parapsychol.*, Vol. 10 (June 1946), pp. 78–106.

14. 'GESP Experiments II' by B. M. Humphrey. *J. of Parapsychol.*, Vol. 10 (September 1946), pp. 181–96.

15. 'Some Personality Characteristics Related to ESP Performance' by Burke M. Smith and B. M. Humphrey. *J. of Parapsychol.*, Vol. 10 (December 1946), pp. 269–89.

16. 'Personality Measurements and ESP Tests with Cards and Drawings' by C. E. Stuart, B. M. Humphrey, Burke M. Smith and Elizabeth McMahan. *J. of Parapsychol.*, Vol. 11 (June 1947), pp. 118–46.

17. 'An interest inventory in relation to ESP scores' by C. E. Stuart. *J. of Parapsychol.*, Vol. 10 (1946), pp. 154–61.

18. 'ESP Performance and the Expansion-Compression Rating' by D. J. West. *Jour. S.P.R.*, September-October 1950, Vol. XXXV, No. 660, pp. 295–308.

19. 'A New Scale for Separating High- and Low-Scoring Subjects in ESP Tests' by B. M. Humphrey. *J. of Parapsychol.*, Vol. 14 (1950), pp. 9–23.

20. 'ESP Subjects Rated by Two Measures of Personality' by B. M. Humphrey. *J. of Parapsychol.*, Vol. 13 (1949), pp. 274–91.

21. 'Separating the Sheep from the Goats' by G. R. Schmeidler. *J. Amer. Soc. Psychic. Res.*, (1945) Vol. 39, pp. 47–50.

22. 'Progress Report on Further Sheep-Goat Studies' by G. R. Schmeidler. *J. Amer. Soc. Psychic. Res.*, (1946) Vol. 40, pp. 34–6.
23. 'Personality Correlates of ESP as shown by Rorschach Studies' by G. R. Smeidler. *J. of Parapsychol.*, Vol. 13 (1949), pp. 23–31.
24. 'ESP Performance and the Rorschach Test' by Gertrude R. Schmeidler. *Jour. S.P.R.*, Vol. XXXV, November-December 1950.
25. 'Rorschach Variables in relation to ESP Scores' by G. R. Schmeidler. *J. Amer. Soc. Psychic. Res.* (1947) Vol. 41, pp. 35–65.
26. 'The Relation of ESP to Mode of Drawing' by Betty M. Humphrey. *J. of Parapsychol.*, Vol. 13 (1949), pp. 31–46.

CHAPTER VI

1. 'Report on Cases of Apparent Precognition' by H. F. Saltmarsh. *Proc. S.P.R.*, Vol. 42, Part 134.
2. 'Supernormal Faculties in Man' by E. Osty, London, 1923.
3. 'An Experiment with Time' by J. W. Dunne, London, 1927.
4. 'A Report of Some Communications Received Through Mrs. Blanche Cooper' by S. G. Soal. *Proc. S.P.R.*, Vol. XXXV, Part 96, December 1925, pp. 471–594. Section 4 (pp. 560–589) contains the case of 'Gordon Davis'.
5. 'Experiments Bearing on the Precognition Hypothesis: I. Pre-Shuffling Card-Calling' by J. B. Rhine. *J. of Parapsychol.*, Vol. 2, No. 1 (March 1938), pp. 38–54.
6. 'The Rôle of ESP in the Shuffling of Cards: II' by J. B. Rhine, Burke M. Smith and J. L. Woodruff. *J. of Parapsychol.*, Vol. 2 (June 1938), pp. 119–31.
7. 'Mechanically Selected Cards: III' by J. B. Rhine. *J. of Parapsychol.*, Vol. 5 (1941), pp. 1–57.
8. 'Precognition Reconsidered' by J. B. Rhine. *J. of Parapsychol.*, Vol. 9, No. 4 (December 1945), pp. 264–77.
9. 'Variation of Time Intervals in Pre-Shuffle Card-Calling Tests' by Lois Hutchinson. *J. of Parapsychol.*, Vol. 4 (December 1940), pp. 249–70.
10. 'Evidence of Precognition in the Covariation of Salience Ratios' by J. B. Rhine. *J. of Parapsychol.*, Vol. 6, No. 2 (June 1942).
11. 'The Personality of Man' by G. N. M. Tyrrell (Pelican Books). (Penguin Books, England, 1946.)
12. 'Some Experiments in Undifferentiated Extra-Sensory Perception' by G. N. M. Tyrrell. *Jour. S.P.R.* (April 1935), pp. 52–71.
13. 'Further Research in Extra-Sensory Perception' by G. N. M. Tyrrell. *Proc. S.P.R.*, Vol. 44 (1936), pp. 99–168.

REFERENCES

14. 'A Preliminary Communication Concerning the "Electronic Reactions" of Abrams with special reference to the "Emanometer" Technique of Boyd' by Sir Thomas Horder *et al.* London: John Bale and Danielsson Ltd., 1925.

15. 'The Measurement of Emotion' by W. Whately Carington. New York, Harcourt, Brace and Co., 1922.

16. 'A quantitative study of trance personalities' by W. Whately Carington (Part I). *Proc. S.P.R.* (1934), Vol. 42, pp. 173–240.

17. 'Ditto Part II' by W. Whately Carington. *Proc. S.P.R.* (1935), Vol. 43, pp. 319–61.

18. 'Preliminary experiments in precognitive guessing: I' by W. Whately Carington. *Jour. S.P.R.* (1935), Vol. 29, pp. 86–104.

19. 'Precognitive guessing: II.' Revised and extended analyses by W. Whately Carington. *Jour. S.P.R.* (1936), Vol. 29, pp. 158–67.

20. 'The quantitative study of trance personalities (Part III)' by W. Whately Carington. *Proc. S.P.R.*, Vol. 44 (1936–7), pp. 189–222.

21. 'The quantitative study of trance personalities (New Series I)' by W. Whately Carington. *Proc. S.P.R.* (1938–9), Vol. 45, pp. 223–51.

22. 'Experiments on the paranormal cognition of drawings (Part I)' by W. Whately Carington. *Proc. S.P.R.* (1940), Vol. 46, pp. 34–151.

23. 'Ditto (Part II)' by W. Whately Carington. *Proc. S.P.R.* (1940), Vol. 46, pp. 277–334.

24. 'Experiments on the paranormal cognition of drawings' by W. Whately Carington. *J. of Parapsychol.*, Vol. 4 (1940), pp. 1–129.

25. 'Some observations on the experiments with drawings' by W. Whately Carington. *J. of Parapsychol.*, Vol. 4 (1940), pp. 130–4.

26. 'Experiments on the paranormal cognition of drawings (Part III).' Steps in the development of a repeatable technique by W. Whately Carington. *Proc. Amer. Soc. Psychic. Res.* (1944), Vol. 24, pp. 3–107.

27. 'Experiments on the paranormal cognition of drawings (Part IV)' by W. Whately Carington. *Proc. S.P.R.* (1944), Vol. 47, pp. 155–228.

28. 'American Experiments on the Paranormal Cognition of Drawings' by Ernest Taves, Gardner Murphy and L. A. Dale. *Jour. Amer. Soc. Psychic. Res.*, Vol. 39, July 1945, pp. 144–50.

29. 'A Repetition of Carington's Experiments with Free Drawings' by Gertrude R. Schmeidler and Lydia W. Allison. *Jour. Amer. Soc. Psychic. Res.*, Vol. 42, No. 3, July 1948, pp. 97–107.

30. 'The Carington Free-Drawing Approach to the ESP Problem' by C. E. Stuart. *J. of Parapsychol.*, Vol. 8 (June 1944), pp. 127–38.

404

REFERENCES

## CHAPTER VII

1. 'Fresh light on card-guessing—some new effects' by S. G. Soal.
   *Proc. S.P.R.*, Vol. 46 (1940), pp. 152–98.
2. 'Telepathy and clairvoyance in the normal and trance states of a
   "medium" ' by J. B. Rhine. *Character and Personality* (1934), Vol.
   3, pp. 91–111.
3. 'Report on a series of experiments with Mrs. Eileen Garrett' by
   K. M. Goldney and S. G. Soal. *Proc. S.P.R.* (1938), Vol. 45, pp.
   43–87.

## CHAPTER VIII

1. 'The Statistical Significance of Dispersed Hits in Card-Guessing
   Experiments' by Professor M. S. Bartlett. *Proc. S.P.R.*, Vol. 48,
   Part 176, April 1949.
2. 'Reply to Professor Bartlett' by S. G. Soal. *Proc. S.P.R.*, Vol. 48,
   Part 176, April 1949.
3. 'A Scientist Tests His Own ESP Ability' by C. G. Abbott. *J. of Parapsychol.*, Vol. 2 (1938), pp. 65–70.
4. 'Further Evidence of Displacement in ESP Tests' by C. G. Abbott.
   *J. of Parapsychol.*, Vol. 13 (June 1949), pp. 101–6.

## CHAPTER IX

1. 'Experiments in Precognitive Telepathy' by S. G. Soal and K. M.
   Goldney. *Proc. S.P.R.*, Vol. 47 (1943), pp. 21–150.
2. 'Distribution of Entries in a Contingency Table' by W. L. Stevens.
   *Annals of Eugenics*, Vol. VIII (1938), pp. 238–44.

## CHAPTER X

1. 'An Introduction to the Theory of Statistics' by G. Udney Yule and
   M. G. Kendall.
2. 'The Experimental Evidence for PK and Precognition' by C. W. K.
   Mundle. *Proc. S.P.R.*, Vol. 49, July 1950, pp. 61–78.
3. 'Essai d'interprétation des Expériences de Soal et Goldney' by
   Raphael Kherumian. *La Revue Métapsychique*, No. 8, d'Octobre-
   Novembre-Décembre 1949.
4. 'The Time Machine' by H. G. Wells. Thomas Nelson and Sons.
5. 'The Fourth Dimension' by C. H. Hinton. George Allen and Unwin
   (1904).

6. 'The Philosophical Implications of Foreknowledge' by C. D. Broad. *Proc. Aristotelian Society*, Supplement XVI (1937), pp. 177–209.
7. 'Time as Minkowski's "Fourth Dimension"' by C. T. K. Chari, M.A. (Department of Philosophy and Psychology, Madras Christian College). *The Astrological Magazine*, Vol. 41, No. 1 (January 1952), pp. 1–10.
8. 'Is Time Metrizable?' by C. T. K. Chari. *The Indian Philosophical Congress* 1951, pp. 129–41.
9. 'Time' by M. F. Cleugh. Methuen 1937. (Contains criticism of Dunne's theory.)
10. 'Mr. Dunne's Theory of Time' by C. D. Broad. *Philosophy*, Vol. X No. 38.

CHAPTER XI

1. 'A Method of Evaluating the Reinforcement Effect' by T. N. E. Greville. *J. of Parapsychol.*, Vol. 15 (June 1951), pp. 118–21.
2. 'The Reinforcement Effect in ESP Displacement' by J. G. Pratt. *J. of Parapsychol.*, Vol. 15 (June 1951), pp. 103–17.
3. 'Examination of ESP Records for Displacement Effects' by William Russell. *J. of Parapsychol.*, Vol. 7 (June 1943), pp. 104–17.
4. 'Position Effects in the Soal and Goldney Experiment' by Betty M. Humphrey and J. B. Rhine. *J. of Parapsychol.*, Vol. 8 (September 1944), pp. 187–213.
5. 'Soal and Goldney's precognitive telepathy experiments' by Betty M. Humphrey. *J. Amer. Soc. Psych. Res.*, Vol. 38 (1944), pp. 139–59.
6. 'Correspondence on the Shackleton Experiments' by J. M. Harrison and S. G. Soal. *Jour. S.P.R.* (May-June 1944).
7. 'A Note on Negative Deviation' by S. G. Soal. *J. of Parapsychol.*, Vol. 8 (1944), pp. 311–15.
8. 'A New Displacement Effect in ESP' by Edward Bindrim. *J. of Parapsychol.*, Vol. 11 (September 1947), pp. 208–21.
9. 'Experiment on paranormal guessing' by R. H. Thouless. *Brit. J. Psychol.* (1942), Vol. 33, pp. 15–27.
10. 'The Problem of Psi-Missing' by J. B. Rhine. *J. of Parapsychol.*, Vol. 16 (June 1952), pp. 90–129.
11. 'The Shackleton Experiments: A Comment by S. G. Soal on an Investigation by R. C. Read' by S. G. Soal. *Jour. S.P.R.*, Vol. XXXV (September-October 1950).
12. 'Paranormal cognition: Some observed results in Mr. Soal's further experiments' by Kenneth Richmond. *Jour. S.P.R.*, Vol. XXXII (June-July 1941).

13. 'The Psychology of the Occult' by D. H. Rawcliffe, London, Derricke Ridgway, 1952.

1. 'Discussion: The Experimental Establishment of Telepathic Precognition' by Professor C. D. Broad. *Philosophy*, Vol. XIX (November 1944), pp. 261–75.

1. 'Telepathy. An Outline of its Facts, Theory and Implication' by Whately Carington. Methuen and Co. Ltd., London (1945).
2. 'Agents in Opposition and Conjunction' by S. G. Soal and F. Bateman. *J. of Parapsychol.*, Vol. 14 (September 1950), pp. 168–92.

1. 'Matter and Memory' by Henri Bergson. Authorized translation by Nancy Margaret Paul and W. Scott Palmer. London, George Allen and Unwin Ltd. Fourth Edition.
2. 'The Relevance of Psychical Research to Philosophy' by Professor C. D. Broad. *Philosophy*, Vol. XXIV, No. 91, October 1949, pp. 291–309.
3. 'The isolation of the percipient in tests for extra-sensory perception' by G. Redmayne. *Proc. S.P.R.*, Vol. 46 (1941), pp. 245–55.
4. 'A Comparison of Five ESP Test Procedures' by Betty M. Humphrey and J. G. Pratt. *J. of Parapsychol.*, Vol. 5 (December 1941), pp. 267–93.
5. 'Telepathy and Clairvoyance Reconsidered' by J. B. Rhine. *J. of Parapsychol.*, Vol. 9 (September 1945), pp. 176–93.
6. 'A Digest and Discussion of Some Comments on "Telepathy and Clairvoyance Reconsidered" ' by J. B. Rhine. *J. of Parapsychol.*, Vol. 10 (March 1946), pp. 36–50.
7. 'A Digest of Comments on Dr. Rhine's "Telepathy and Clairvoyance Reconsidered" ' by W. Whately Carington, Dr. Hettinger, Dr. R. H. Thouless, G. N. M. Tyrrell, Prof. C. D. Broad and Denys Parsons. *Proc. S.P.R.*, Vol. XLVIII (1946), pp 8–27.
8. 'An Experiment in Pure Telepathy' by Elizabeth A. McMahan. *J. of Parapsychol.*, Vol. 10 (December 1946), pp. 224–42.
9. 'A new method and an experiment in pure telepathy' by William R. Birge. *J. of Parapsychol.*, Vol. 12 (1948), pp. 273–88.

10. 'The Experimental Situation in Psychical Research' by S. G. Soal. (Society for Psychical Research 1947). Ninth Myers Memorial Lecture.

11. 'On the nature of psi phenomena' by Robert H. Thouless and B. P. Wiesner. *J. of Parapsychol.*, Vol. 10 (1946), pp. 107–19.

12. 'Telepathy and Human Personality' by J. B. Rhine with Introduction by S. G. Soal. The Society for Psychical Research. The Tenth Myers Memorial Lecture (1950).

13. 'Human Personality and its Survival of Bodily Death' by Frederick W. H. Myers. London, Longmans, Green, 1903.

CHAPTER XVI

1. 'Extra-Sensory Perception after Sixty Years' by J. G. Pratt, J. B. Rhine, Burke M. Smith, Charles E. Stuart and Joseph A. Greenwood. (1940). New York. Henry Holt and Company.

2. 'A Further Report on the Midas Touch' by Professor Gardner Murphy. *Jour. Amer. Soc. Psychic. Res.*, Vol. 37 (1943), pp. 111–18.

3. 'Psychical Research and Personality' by Professor Gardner Murphy. *Proc. S.P.R.*, Vol. XLIX, Part 177 (November 1949). Presidential Address delivered at a General Meeting of the Society on 8th June, 1949.

4. 'A Trans-oceanic ESP Experiment' by J. B. Rhine and Betty M. Humphrey. *J. of Parapsychol.*, Vol. 6 (March 1942), pp. 52–74.

5. 'The Statistics of Salience Ratios' by J. A. Greenwood. *J. of Parapsychol.*, Vol. 5 (1941), pp. 245–9.

6. 'Terminal Salience in ESP Performance' by J. B. Rhine. *J. of Parapsychol.*, Vol. 5 (1941), pp. 183–242.

7. 'A Check on Salience Relations in ESP Data' by J. G. Pratt, Betty M. Humphrey and J. B. Rhine. *J. of Parapsychol.*, Vol. 6 (March 1942).

8. 'A Second Zagreb-Durham ESP Experiment' by Elizabeth A. McMahan and J. B. Rhine. *J. of Parapsychol.*, Vol. 11 (December 1947), pp. 244–53.

9. 'A Reciprocal Distance GESP Test with Drawings' by J. H. Rush and Ann Jensen. *J. of Parapsychol.*, Vol. 13 (June 1949), pp. 122–34.

10. 'Long-Distance Experiments in Telepathy' by F. Bateman and S. G. Soal. *Jour. S.P.R.*, Vol. XXXV (July-August 1950), pp. 257–72.

11. 'Extra-Sensory Perception of Cards in an Unknown Location' by Elizabeth A. McMahan and Joan Lauer. *J. of Parapsychol.*, Vol. 12

(March 1948), pp. 47–57. [The results of this experiment were quite inconclusive and there was no satisfactory evidence of ESP in any of the tests.]

CHAPTER XVII

1. 'Telepathy and Electromagnetic Waves' by A. J. B. Robertson, D.Sc. *Jour. S.P.R.*, Vol. XXXIV (January-February 1947), pp. 7–10.
2. 'Some Considerations as to a Physical Basis of ESP' by J. H. Rush, Department of Physics, Denison University. *J. of Parapsychol.*, Vol. 7 (March 1943), pp. 44–9.
3. 'Multiple Aspect Targets in Tests of ESP' by Esther Bond Foster. *J. of Parapsychol.*, Vol. 16 (March 1952), pp. 11–22.
4. 'The Living Brain' by W. Grey Walter. Duckworth 1953.

CHAPTER XVIII

1. 'Methodology and Value in the Natural Sciences in Relation to Certain Religious Concepts' by G. E. Hutchinson, Professor of Biology at Yale University. *The Journal of Religion*, Vol. XXXII (July 1952), pp. 175–87.
2. 'Change of Call in ESP Tests' by J. G. Pratt. *J. of Parapsychol.*, Vol. 13 (December 1949), pp. 225–36.
3. 'Displacement in ESP Card Tests in Relation to Hits and Misses' by J. G. Pratt and Esther Bond Foster. *J. of Parapsychol.*, Vol. 14 (March 1950), pp. 37–52.
4. 'A Further Study of ESP Displacement in Relation to Hits and Misses' by J. G. Pratt and Esther Bond Foster. *J. of Parapsychol.*, Vol. 14 (June 1950), pp. 95–115.

CHAPTER XIX

1. 'ESP Performance and Target Sequence' by S. G. Soal and J. G. Pratt. *J. of Parapsychol.*, Vol. 15 (September 1951), pp. 192–215.
2. 'Some Relations Between Call Sequence and ESP Performance' by J. G. Pratt and S. G. Soal. *J. of Parapsychol.*, Vol. 16 (September 1952), pp. 165–86.
3. 'Minds and Mystifications' by Antony G. N. Flew. The first of two talks on the significance of parapsychology. *The Listener*, 27th September 1951, p. 501.
4. 'A New Name for Guesswork?' by Antony G. N. Flew. The second of two talks on the significance of parapsychology. *The Listener*, 4th October 1951, p. 549.

CHAPTER XX AND APPENDICES

1. 'Computing Machinery and Intelligence' by A. M. Turing. *Mind* (October 1950).
2. 'The Faith of a Scientist' by A. C. Hardy, M.A., D.Sc., F.R.S., Fellow of Merton College, Linacre Professor of Zoology and Comparative Anatomy, Oxford. The Lindsey Press, 14 Gordon Square, London, W.C.1. Reprinted from *Faith and Freedom*, Vol. 2, Part 2 (1949).
3. 'On multiple matching with one variable deck' by T. N. E. Greville. *Annals of Math. Statist.*, 1944, Vol. 15, pp. 432–4.
4. 'The Heston Manual and Personal Adjustment Inventory' by J. C. Heston. World Book Co., Yonkers-on-Hudson, 1949.
5. 'Review of The Psychology of the Occult' (D. H. Rawcliffe) by R. H. Thouless. *Jour. S.P.R.*, May-June (1952).
6. 'Studies in Extra-Sensory Perception. Experiments utilizing an electronic scoring device' by S. David Kahn. *Proc. Amer. Soc. for Psych. Res.*, Vol. XXV, October 1952.
7. 'Thought Transference and Related Phenomena' by R. H. Thouless. Address to the Royal Institution (1950).
8. 'The Organization of Behaviour' by D. O. Hebb. London, Chapman & Hall (1949).
9. 'The Retina' by S. L. Polyack, Chicago. Univ. Chic. Press (1941).
10. 'In Search of the Engram' by K. S. Lashley. Symposia of the Society for Experimental Biology, Number IV. Physiological Mechanisms in Animal Behaviour. Cambridge Univ. Press (1950).
11. 'Cerebral Mechanisms in Behaviour' by L. Jeffres. Hixon Symposium. Wiley, New York (1951).
12. 'The Exploration of ESP and Human Personality' by J. Fraser Nicol and Betty M. Humphrey. *Jour. Amer. Soc. for Psych. Res.* Vol. XLVII, October 1953.
13. 'Statistical Significance in Psychical Research' by G. Spencer Brown. *Nature.* 25 July 1953.
14. Reply to No. 13 by S. G. Soal, F. J. M. Stratton and R. H. Thouless. Also letter by G. Spencer Brown. *Nature.* 26 September 1953.
15. 'New World of the Mind' by J. B. Rhine. William Sloane Associates Inc. New York (1953).

# Index

Abbott, Dr. C. G., 130 (*see* Displacement)
Aberdeen, University of, 342 (*see* Flew)
Abram's magic box, 88 (*see* Carington)
Adams, Prof. E. T., negative results of, 48
Agent, defined, 360
Agents, in BBC expt., 20
  in 1927-9 expts., 21-2
  in 1934-9 expts., 107, 115, 116
  in 1936 Shackleton expts., 120-1, 127
  in 1936 Stewart expts., 122-3
  in 1941-3 Shackleton expts., 148, 158, 167
  in 1945-9 Stewart expts., 313
  (*See* Conjunction; Imagery; Instructions; Opposition; Split-agent)
Albert, Mrs. G., Agent for Shackleton, 166-7
  Agent in opposition expt., 185-7
Albicerius (Carthaginian diviner), 1
Alcohol, effects of on ESP, 33 (*see* Drugs; Warcollier)
Aldred, Mr. J. (Agent for Shackleton):
  In 1936 expts., 120-1, 127
  In 1941-3 expts., 158-60, 167-8, 177-8, 216
  Decline effect noted with, 187-8
  Negative scoring with, 188-9
  Change in type of displacement with, 197, 266
  Results refute whispering theory, 197
Allen, Dr. H. S. (Queen Mary College), 204
  Agent in Stewart expts., 204
  Agent in opposition expt., 233-4
  Compiled random numbers, 288
  Agent in playing-cards expt., 296
  Agent in distraction expt., 302
  Initial score with Mrs. Stewart, 313
Allison, Mrs. Lydia, 91
American Psychological Association (symposium of), 49
American Scientist, 346
American Society for Psy. Res., 91, 268, 351, 391

Amytal, 33-5 (*see* Sodium Amytal)
Animals, Pictures of, 135
  Initials of names of:
    In Shackleton expts., 159
    In Stewart expts., 200
  Change to new set of, 224
Antwerp, 284, 286, 292-3 (*see* London-Antwerp expts.)
Aristotelian Society (Symposium on Psy. Res.), 342
Aristotle, 53
Associated words expt., 176-7 (*see* Price, Prof. H. H.)
Association theory of telepathy, 281-2
  Experiment to test theory, 282-3
Associative tendencies in guessing, 328-9
Austin-Dallas expts. with drawings, 274-6 (*see* Rush, J. H., and Jensen, Mrs. A.)

Bard College, 91
Barrett, Sir W., 5
Bartlett, Prof. M. S.:
  Evaluation of Variance, 126-7
  On Multiple Determination, 129
Bateman, Frederick (F.B.):
  Introduced, 199
  First meeting with Mrs. Stewart, 209
  Agent in TLN expt., 209
  Agent in TTN expt., 213
  Agent in TTND4(3) expt., 213
  Agent in rapid rate expt., 217
  Agent in split-agent expt., 220-2
  Agent in opposition expt., 230-1
  Agent in pure telepathy expt., 255-8
  Agent in lead screen expt., 306
  Checked London-Antwerp expt., 288-9, 291
  Compiled random numbers, 288
  (EP) in telephone expt., 276-8
  (EP) in distraction expt., 302
  (EP) in X-ray chamber expt., 305-6
  Intrinsic scoring rate with, 313
Bateman-Brendel expts., 222-3
Bates, Kenneth, 321
BBC expt. of 1927, 20, 26
Bedford College, 220 (*see* Jacobs)

411

Regress, infinite (in Dunne's theory), 173
Reinforcement, 320 (see Multiple determination)
Repeatability of ESP expts., 52
Repetition of expansive-compressive expts., 67, 69
Repetition of Miss Jephson's expts., 17-18
Repetition of personality effects, 393
Repetition of Rhine's expts., 104-19, 131
Reynolds, Mr. J. C. (agent in Cambridge-London expts.), 283-4
Rhine, Dr. Joseph Banks (Duke University), 15
  Early career of, 25
  Early expts. at Duke U., 25-36
  Expts. with H. Pearce, 28-34
  Expts. with drugs, 33-6
  Expts. in pure telepathy, 35-6
  Criticisms of early work and replies to:
  Inept criticisms, 44-5, 49, 53
  On defective cards, 37
  On use of binomial formulae, 37-8
  On inadequate shuffling, 39-40
  On optional stopping, 40-2
  On involuntary whispering, 43-4
  On recording and checking errors, 44-5
  On improper selection of data, 46
  On discussion by American Psychological Assocn., 49
  Expts. in prediction by, 77-82
  Expts. with Mrs. Garrett, 107-8, 185
  Views on negative scoring, 188-9
  Views on telepathy and clairvoyance, 252
  Views on Shackleton expts., 265-6
  Long-distance expts. by, 267-8, 270-3, 273-4
  Rhine justified in use of 5-symbol cards, 298
  Interpretation of ESP findings by, 343
Rhine, Dr. Louisa E., 25
Rhodes University (Grahamstown), 365 (see Marsh, Maurice)
Richet, Prof. Charles (cases of prediction), 74
Richmond, Kenneth:
  Rechecked Shackleton records, 145
  Visited Shackleton expt., 156
  Testimony of, on visual cues, 195
Richmond (Surrey), 122, 123, 278-9, 285, 288
Riess, Prof. Bernard F., 348
Roback, Dr. A. A. (see History of American Psychology), 356
Robbins, Prof. H. (evaluation of multiple determination), 180
Robertson, Dr. Andrew J. (on radiation theory of telepathy), 304
Robot box (used in Marion expts.), 101-2

Rochford (Essex), 75-6 (see Davis, Gordon)
Rockefeller foundation (sponsors parapsychology), 23
Rogosin, H. (inept attack on Rhine), 53 (Psychical expts. anti-social), 53
Roland Gardens, 13d, 106, 114, 120
Roll, Mr. W. G. (Oxford expts. in ESP), 356
Rorschach test, description of, 71
  Use in Schmeidler's expts., 71-2
Royal Free Hospital, X-ray chamber expts. at, 305-6, 309
Royal Institution (Dr. Thouless lectures to) 23
Rozelaar, Mr. L. A. (rechecked Shackleton records), 145
  Visited Shackleton expt., 161
  Testimony of, 161
  (EP) in Stewart expts., 202, 204
  Agent in 'split-agent' expts., 221-2, 226
  Agent in 'opposition' expt., 231
  (EP) in 'opposition' expt., 234
  Agent in pure telepathy expt., 252-3
  Agent in telephone expts., 277
  Intrinsic scoring rate with, 313
Runs of hits (see Success runs)
Rush, Mr. J. H., on long-distance expts. with drawings, 274-5 (see Jensen; Austin-Dallas expts.)
Russell, Bertrand (atomic theory of mind), 281

Saffery, Mr. (visited Stewart expt.), 242
St. Augustine, 1
Salience ratio (for run and segment), 81-2, 271-2, 274 (see Middle salience; Terminal salience)
Saltmarsh, Mr. H. F., cases of prediction, 74
  On prediction and the specious present 169
Schmeidler, Dr. Gertrude:
  'Sheep and goats' expt., 70
  Expts. with Rorschach test, 71-2
  Stresses importance of right mental environment, 72
  Effect of intellectual attitude on scoring, 192
  Kahn finds expts. hard to repeat, 393
Scientific Monthly, The, 49 (see Kellogg)
Scientists and ESP:
  Attitude of scientists in early twenties, 23
  ESP can be no longer ignored by, 23-4
  Scientists disturbed by ESP, 338-9
  Prof. Turing's views, 338-9
  Prof. Eccles on ESP and working of brain, 341
  Lack of working hypotheses in ESP, 345
Score, defined, 361 (see Mean score)

Runs of successes with, 380-1
Totals for TTN(x) expts., 216
Fall of scores to chance level, 309-10
Position effects with, 320-37
Stewart, Mrs. J. O.:
  (Assisted in Stewart expts.), 206, 208, 209, 233
  Checked decoding, 206
Stribic, Miss Frances P., 47, 58-60 (see Martin, Miss D.)
Stuart, Dr. Charles:
  Expts. on ESP and personality, 68
  College interests inventory by, 68
Success groups, method of, 381
Success runs, expectation of, 380
  Applied to Stewart results, 381
  In expt. with Miss Levine, 269
  (See Success groups)
Suggestion (effect on Shackleton's scoring), 148-9

Target doubles (effects with Mrs. Stewart):
  Negative scoring on first member of, 321-2
  Exception to this rule, 326
  Change of call related to success or failure, 328-32
Telepathy (defined), 7-8, 359-60
  Views of Myers on, 258
  Views of Rhine on, 252
  Views of Thouless on, 255
  Association theory of, 281-3
  Radiation theory of, 303-4
  (See Pure telepathy; Precognitive telepathy; Extra-sensory perception; Clairvoyance)
Temperature readings (used in prediction expts.), 81-2
Tenhaeff, Dr. W. H. C., 355 (see Utrecht)
Terminal salience, 271 (see Salience; Middle salience)
Testimony (see Witnesses)
Thouless, Robert H. (English psychologist):
  Comments on Coover's results, 13
  Lecture on ESP to Royal Institution, 23
  Extract from lecture, 357-8
  Further expts. to test truth of ESP unnecessary, 50, 203
  Glasgow repetition of Rhine's expts., 131
  Suggestions for a pure telepathy expt., 253-4
  Comments on telepathy and clairvoyance, 255
  Clairvoyance and sense-perception, 259
  On D. H. Rawcliffe, 349
  Definition of psi, 359

(See also Wiesner, B. P., and footnote on p. 55 of which substance is due to Thouless)
Timing expts. (with Mrs. Stewart), 212-3, 216-8
  (With Shackleton) (see Calling: rates of)
Tippett's random tables (used in Shackleton expts.), 137
Transfer of function, 339-40
Troland, Prof. L. T. (expts. in ESP), 14-5
True cognitions, 313, 377-8 (see Intrinsic scoring rate)
TTN expts. (totals for), 216
Turing, Prof. A. M. (on ESP a disturbing phenomenon), 338-9
Turner, Miss May (percipient in long-distance test), 267, 269 (see Ownbey)
Two-symbol expts., 300-1
  Comparison with 5-symbol expts., 301
Tyrrell, Mr. G. N. M., expts. with machine, 49
  Personality of Man (book by), 82
  Theory of apparitions, 82
  ESP expts. with Miss Johnson, 82-7, 250-1
  Expts. with pointer apparatus, 83
  Electrical machine described, 83-4
  Resistance of subject to use of commutator, 85
  Results at variance with S. Brown's theory, 85, 352
  No resistance to delay-action mechanism, 85
  Resistance to mechanical selector, 85
  Brilliant success with random numbers, 85-6
  No evidence that Fisk method was used, 86
  Expts. in precognitive clairvoyance, 87
  Results of p.c. expt. cited by Rhine, 79
  Work ignored by Rawcliffe, 347
  (See Fisk; Johnson, Miss G. M.)

University College London, (1936-9 expts. at), 106-7, 116, 118, 131
University College of Dundee (see Dundee)
University of Aberdeen (see Aberdeen)
University of Colorado (see Colorado)
University of Durham, 355 (see Wassermann)
University of London (awards for P.R.), 309, 355
University of London Council for Psychical Investigation, 98, 116
University of Utrecht, 355 (see Tenhaeff)
Unsuccessful agents, 167
Upton-on-Severn (Mrs. Stewart evacuated to), 199